P·s·y·c·h·o·t·h·e·r·a·p·y f·o·r t·h·e 1·9·9·0·s

P·s·y·c·h·o·t·h·e·r·a·p·y
f·o·r t·h·e 1·9·9·0·s

Edited by

J. Scott Rutan, Ph.D.

THE GUILFORD PRESS
New York   London

© 1992 The Guilford Press
A Division of Guilford Publications, Inc.
72 Spring Street, New York, NY 10012

Printed in the United States of America

This book is printed on acid-free paper.

Last digit is print number: 9   8   7   6   5   4   3   2   1

Library of Congress Cataloging-in-Publication Data

Psychotherapy for the 1990s / J. Scott Rutan, editor.
    p.   cm.
    Includes bibliographical references and index.
    ISBN 0-89862-798-2
    1. Psychotherapy.   2. Psychotherapy—Social aspects.   I. Rutan,
J. Scott.
    [DNLM: 1. Psychotherapy—trends.   WM 420 P97547]
    RC480.P8254   1992
    616.89′14—dc20
    DNLC/DLC
    for Library of Congress   91-35424
                                                                    CIP

Preface

Those of us who practice psychotherapy in this day and age face a time of exceptional opportunity and unusual restriction.

Psychotherapy has finally gained legitimacy in scientific circles and with the public-at-large. (In more liberal areas, being in therapy is now a badge of honor, whereas in the not-so-distant past it would have been a source of shame.) There is ample research evidence to suggest that at least some forms of psychotherapy are effective (though of course much less evidence as to how or why). We are at least able to state categorically that some forms of psychotherapy are better than no psychotherapy at all. Pressed by economic demand, we have become more thoughtful about evaluating our work, descending somewhat from our protected posture of the analyst who deems it inappropriate to consider "efficiency" or "measured outcome studies" in the art of psychotherapy.

Furthermore, we are in a time of enormous ferment in theory-building about personality, psychopathology, and technique. Classic theory has undergone metamorphosis from the old drive and instinct foundation to a reliance on interpersonal aspects of personality formation. This is true of all the modern modifications of psychodynamic theory (ego psychology, self psychology, and object relations theory). In addition, systems theorists are considering the multidimensional aspects of personality formation that extend beyond the margins of pure biology, pure learning theory, or pure parental influence. Behavioral theory has added considerable depth and subtlety, and most behaviorists now speak of the importance of the therapeutic relationship, including transference. There are also advances in examining the mind–body interface, advances in understanding the relationship between biological and psychologic etiologies of both psychopathology and physical illness. Feminist theorists are continuing the work of Horney, Thompson, and others, by examining the impact of culture on sexual development.

We have the added advantage of practicing in an era when there is much higher quality teaching and training available than ever before. In addition, there are ever-increasing advances in technique — group therapy, family therapy, child and adolescent therapy, short-term therapy, cognitive therapy, etc. — with advanced training available in each speciality.

Though we still have far to go, there have been substantive gains in the certification and regulation procedures for all disciplines. It is less and less possible for untrained individuals simply to hang out a sign.

On the other hand, there are also problems in the present culture that seriously restrict and at times threaten to compromise the traditions of our professional practice. Although psychotherapy has always rested upon the sacrosanct private and confidential relationship between therapist and patient, we now find ourselves fighting off intrusions into that relationship from economic factors, governmental regulations, and third-party payers. Much needed and long-awaited patient protections, such as informed consent, present novel problems to the therapist. Many eyes today have access to our diagnoses of patients, and there is increasingly a demand that we diagnose in medical, pathological systems that do not fit comfortably with the more humanistic, "educational" tenets of psychodynamic theory. Our treatment plans are increasingly influenced by insurance companies that may have conflicting views on what is best for the patient.

The regulators who "evaluate" our work to judge whether to continue payment are usually focused on symptom relief. DSM-III-R is a classic example of what is happening — our patients are considered collections of symptoms or illnesses that can be treated individually. Our patient presumably "has a depression," rather than "is depressed." The practice of long-term, character-changing psychodynamic psychotherapy is becoming difficult to manage except on a private basis with patients who can afford the treatment without third-party assistance.

The sanctity of the therapeutic relationship is also being breached by legal incursions into the structure of practice. In an attempt to protect society, we are increasingly placed in difficult positions by agents of social control. By law we are supposed to report our patients if they threaten to kill themselves or others, abuse their children, any children, or elders. On the other hand, we wonder how we can help such troubled individuals if we immediately "turn them in" when they finally begin to talk of their most troubled thoughts and acts.

As the number of psychotherapists increases and the funds for supporting psychotherapy diminish, there is in-fighting among the various professions that provide mental health services. Physicians try to keep psychologists from gaining access to third-party payment; psychologists fight physicians for the "privilege" of prescribing medications; social workers in turn fight nurses. We need as colleagues to find a more harmonious cooperation that will benefit our patients and ourselves.

This book is about how the practice of psychotherapy has been altered—for good and ill—in the modern age. It is an integrative view of the plurality observed in a teaching hospital and will provide, it is hoped, another step toward creative integration.

Contributors

ROB ABERNETHY, M.D. Director, General Psychiatry Practice, Massachusetts General Hospital, Boston, Massachusetts; Instructor, Department of Psychiatry, Harvard Medical School, Boston, Massachusetts.

ANNE ALONSO, Ph.D. Psychologist, General Psychiatry Practice, Massachusetts General Hospital, Boston, Massachusetts; Associate Clinical Professor of Psychology, Department of Psychiatry, Harvard Medical School, Boston, Massachusetts.

THEODORE I. ANDERSON, M.D. Psychiatrist, General Psychiatry Practice, Massachusetts General Hospital, Boston, Massachusetts; Associate in Psychiatry, Harvard Medical School, Boston, Massachusetts.

MAX DAY, M.D. Assistant Clinical Professor of Psychiatry, Department of Psychiatry, Harvard Medical School, Boston, Massachusetts; Massachusetts Mental Health Center, Boston, Massachusetts; Extension Service of the Boston Psychoanalytic Society, Boston, Massachusetts.

STEPHEN DURANT, Ph.D. Clinical Fellow in Psychology, General Psychiatry Practice, Massachusetts General Hospital, Boston, Massachusetts; Clinical Fellow in Psychology, Department of Psychiatry, Harvard Medical School, Boston, Massachusetts.

SHERMAN EISENTHAL, Ph.D. Associate Professor of Psychology, Department of Psychiatry, Harvard Medical School, Boston, Massachusetts; General Psychiatry Practice, Massachusetts General Hospital, Boston, Massachusetts.

TIMOTHY C. ENGELMANN, M.D. Associate Director, The Adolescent Program at Winthrop Hospital, Winthrop, Massachusetts; The Somers Trust Psychological Associates, Andover, Massachusetts.

MAURIZIO FAVA, M.D. Director of Depression Research, Clinical Psychopharmacology Unit, Massachusetts General Hospital, Boston, Massachusetts.

JAMES L. GRIFFITH, M.D. Associate Professor of Psychology, Department of Psychiatry, University of Mississippi School of Medicine, Jackson, Mississippi; Co-director, Family Therapy Program, University of Mississippi Medical Center, Jackson, Mississippi.

JAMES E. GROVES, M.D. Psychiatrist, General Psychiatry Practice, and Medical Director, Short-Term Therapies Unit, Massachusetts General Hospital, Boston, Massachusetts; Assistant Clinical Professor of Psychiatry, Department of Psychiatry, Harvard Medical School, Boston, Massachusetts.

PAUL HAMBURG, M.D. Eating Disorders Unit/General Psychiatry Practice, Massachusetts General Hospital, Boston, Massachusetts.

SAMUEL R. JAMES, Ed.D. Clinical Fellow, Harvard Medical School, Boston, Massachusetts; Clinical Instructor in Psychology, Department of Psychiatry, Massachusetts General Hospital, Boston, Massachusetts.

MICHAEL JELLINEK, M.D. Psychiatrist, General Psychiatry Practice, Massachusetts General Hospital, Boston, Massachusetts; Associate Professor of Psychology, Department of Psychiatry, Harvard Medical School, Boston, Massachusetts.

MARY McCARTHY, M.D. Psychiatrist, Department of Psychiatry, Massachusetts General Hospital, Boston, Massachusetts.

STEPHEN P. McDERMOTT, M.D. Director, Cognitive Therapy and Research Program, General Psychiatry Practice, Massachusetts General Hospital, Boston, Massachusetts; Assistant Medical Director, Cognitive Therapy Unit, Westwood Lodge Hospital, Westwood, Massachusetts; Clinical Instructor in Psychiatry, Department of Psychiatry, Harvard Medical School, Boston, Massachusetts.

A. EUGENE NEWMAN, Ph.D. Clinical Associate in Psychology, Massachusetts General Hospital, Boston, Massachusetts; Clinical Instructor in Psychology, Department of Psychiatry, Harvard Medical School, Boston, Massachusetts.

HELEN RIESS, M.D. Psychiatrist, Center for Group Therapy, and Eating Disorders Unit, Massachusetts General Hospital, Boston, Massachusetts; Instructor, Department of Psychiatry, Harvard Medical School, Boston, Massachusetts.

J. SCOTT RUTAN, Ph.D. Associate Clinical Professor of Psychology, Department of Psychiatry, Harvard Medical School, Boston, Massachusetts; Director, Center for Group Psychotherapy, Massachusetts General Hospital, Boston, Massachusetts.

JOSEPH E. SCHWARTZ, M.D. Psychiatrist, Department of Psychiatry, Massachusetts General Hospital, Boston, Massachusetts; Assistant Clinical Professor of Psychiatry, Department of Psychiatry, Harvard Medical School, Boston, Massachusetts; Member, Boston Psychoanalytic Society and Institute, Boston, Massachusetts.

LINDA SHAFER, M.D. Associate Psychiatrist, Department of Psychiatry, and Director, Sexual Dysfunction Section of General Psychiatry Practice, Massachusetts General Hospital, Boston, Massachusetts; Instructor, Department of Psychiatry, Harvard Medical School, Boston, Massachusetts.

ELIZABETH L. SHAPIRO, Ph.D. Clinical Instructor, Department of Psychiatry, Harvard Medical School, Boston, Massachusetts; Assistant

Director, Post-graduate Fellowship in Psychodynamic Psychotherapy, General Psychiatry Practice, Massachusetts General Hospital, Boston, Massachusetts.

LOIS SIMS SLOVIK, M.D. Assistant Professor of Psychology, Department of Psychiatry, Harvard Medical School, Boston, Massachusetts; Director, Family Therapy Program, Massachusetts General Hospital, Boston, Massachusetts.

SAUL TUTTMAN, M.D., Ph.D. Clinical Professor of Psychiatry, Department of Psychiatry, Albert Einstein School of Medicine, New York, New York; Training and Supervising Psychoanalyst, New York Medical College Psychoanalytic Institute, Valhalla, New York.

FRED D. WRIGHT, Ed.D. Assistant Professor of Counseling Psychology in Psychiatry, University of Pennsylvania School of Medicine, Philadelphia, Pennsylvania; Director of Education and Training, Center for Cognitive Therapy, University of Pennsylvania, Philadelphia, Pennsylvania.

Contents

PART V. THE PRACTICE OF PSYCHOTHERAPY

I

THEORETICAL PERSPECTIVES

瑞

The Value System
of the Psychotherapist

J. SCOTT RUTAN

JAMES E. GROVES

Everyone sits in a prison of his own ideas.
— ALBERT EINSTEIN

O ne of the intriguing aspects of the current psychotherapy scene is the multitude of competing philosophies and theories about how psychotherapy is supposed to work. Each theory has some accumulated research and much subjective data to support the hypothesis that it is a viable theory that yields effective therapeutic technique. Perhaps it is important to recognize that no "correct" answer is yet available to explain the human condition fully. Indeed, it is important to recognize that theories are, at least in part, value systems more than scientific statements.

The classic value system of the psychodynamic psychotherapist maintained that the therapist should be "value free." That is, the values the therapist held, however good and noble, should in no way be communicated to the patient. Rather, the role of the therapist was to examine and enhance the patient's own values. Somehow the "therapeutic neutrality" of Freud's position came to be mistaken for "value freedom." In recent years this position has been questioned from several points of view. For one thing, it is doubtful whether it is possible to be value free. Further, as the relationship in psychotherapy takes on more and more importance, it has been questioned whether the therapist *should* attempt to keep values hidden. In this chapter we will explore the place of therapist's values in the psychotherapeutic relationship.

From the beginning of recorded history, human beings have concerned themselves with describing the "good" life, the "right" way to live, the codification of worthy and unworthy behaviors (Nussbaum, 1986). Centuries of scholarship contributed to this ethical inquiry, yet those of us involved in the practice of psychotherapy are rarely exposed to this body of literature, even though our efforts to help people live the "good" life efforts are present from the outset. Evaluations produce diagnostic formulations, and by their nature formulations imply an ideal (Perry, Cooper, & Michels, 1987, pp. 545-550).

The thought that psychotherapists are involved in ethical inquiry is anathema to some who prefer to believe that we are value free professionals simply (and objectively) assisting our patients in living happier lives. Yet, without exception, all psychotherapists have ethical belief systems embedded with articles of faith.

ETHICS: A VIGNETTE

Suppose for a moment that you are the male therapist for a 37-year-old woman dealing with the following situation after 2 years of excellent work in psychotherapy.

> The patient had been sexually abused as a child, and with therapy had been making painful and courageous strides in her goal to become a fully functioning adult. In recent weeks she has developed a strong sexual attraction to a person at work, the first man with whom she felt safe enough to allow such feelings. He is a married man who remains in his unhappy marriage solely to provide a two-parent family for his children, which was something he had not had himself.

> At different times, she has held quite different points of view about whether this man represents a good choice for her first sexual relationship. Sometimes she feels that because of his clear compassion and tenderness, as well as his unavailable status, he is an ideal choice of partner with whom to experiment. He has been forthright and honest from the beginning and has never led her to believe he might leave his wife for her.

> At other times she feels this man represents a terrible choice because she, even more than most, needs an honest and complete relationship in which to begin her sexual explorations. In this mode she argues

that, when all is said and done, this is just another illicit relationship about which she will feel ashamed. Her instincts seem to warn her that she is repeating a painful part of her history.

Her best friend, a divorcee whose faithless husband left her, takes the position that she would be doing an awful disservice to the wife of this man. The friend argues that it is immoral to have sexual relations with a married man. The friend wonders what it means that the patient has no feeling about the pain she might inflict on a stranger just to meet her own needs.

What would *your* position be? What interpretations would you make? If she sleeps with this man, would you consider her behavior acting out or a sign of growth? Should she concern herself with the wife of the man, a woman she has never met? For that matter, should she consider the possible impact on the life of the man himself? Should she fulfill her own needs, even if they conflict with the needs of others? How are the needs of self and others balanced?

And what of the transference? As her therapist, you know that a part of the attraction to the "unavailable" man at work resides in a wish to avoid sexual feelings for you. The displacement of her affections resolves negative aspects of the transference. Do you interpret this? She is thirty-seven. The two to five years it usually takes to work this through may place her beyond child-bearing and foreclose that option.

And what of the countertransference? Are you collaborating with the displacement in order to avoid your reciprocal feelings? Are you avoiding interpretation to avoid her sexual or negative feelings? Are you tending *toward* interpretation to satisfy your own half-sublimated maternal and phallic drives?

These are not questions you can avoid. Any interpretation, clarification, comment, confrontation—or even a decision to remain mute!—represents an ethical and moral decision, as well as a technical one.

Ethics is defined as the system or code of morality of a particular person, religion, group, or profession (where morality is the ability to deal with or be capable of making distinctions between right and wrong). Science (which psychotherapy often presumes to be) is defined as a branch of study or knowledge concerned with establishing or systematizing facts. Historically, ethics and science have been viewed as at least separate, if not antithetical: Science is descriptive, ethics is prescriptive; science rests upon facts, ethics upon judgment (Whitley, 1984; Kuhn, 1977). Science is concerned with "what is," whereas ethics is concerned with "what ought to be." Thus, the psychotherapist must pursue two separate but crucial paths.

Across such a spectrum begin to emerge the ethical problems that confront us each day in our private offices. For example, are patients free to change or not change? Should we exert coercion? Do we help or shape? Do we look for "cure" or "positive growth?"

Perhaps most fundamentally, do we encourage our patients to rebel against a repressive environment or adjust to it? (Most definitions of pathology are essentially measures taken from a norm; we tend to define pathology by eccentricity, which reduces the "healthy" options of humanity for radical and creative adaptations to life's ills.)

Another ethical dilemma that we face each day involves expectations. Are the personal goals of our patients realistic? Do we encourage unrealistic goals out of our own hope, greed, or naivete? Hadley and Strupp (1976) found that "undertaking unrealistic goals or expectations" constituted a major cause of failure in psychotherapy (pp. 1291–1302).

What are the goals of treatment? Are they the patient's goals? We all know that patients may not know enough of themselves upon entering treatment to set realistic goals. But do we have any better capacity to set goals? This question comes up most pointedly at times of termination — especially for the newer professional who feels the termination of a patient quite directly at bill-paying time! Financial considerations often cloud judgment of when it is in the best interest of patients to stop therapy.

FAITH: A SPECULATION

So far we have primarily discussed matters of ethics — how should individuals live? We maintain that it is impossible not to take some ethical position, since even not to do so is itself a decision with moral consequences.

But let us move deeper, to the question of faith. Codes of ethics are extensions of faith systems. We all have our basic assumptions upon which we base our views of life. It is impossible to live without *some* schema or system.

Most of us embed our basic faith in a more "scientific" concept, *theory*. We attend the various theoretical "churches" before we decide which one to join. Do we tithe to the church of psychoanalysis, behaviorism, biology, cognitive therapy, or psychopharmacology, to mention just a few? Within those churches, do we belong to the conservative or the liberal wing? We have before us proponents of a screaming cure, a reasoning cure, a realism cure, a decision cure, an orgasm cure, a meaning cure, even a profound rest cure (Jurjevich, 1973).

Theories of personality are based more upon faith than upon testable (that is, empirical) bases, though there have been some recent attempts to change this. It is devilishly difficult to study ourselves empirically. The problem with all study of human behavior is, how to find Archimedes's place of detached observation necessary to step back and observe the self.

A further problem is that the empirical study of the human condition also represents a leap of faith—a conviction about the preference of hard data over soft data as accurate representations of reality. So, we have to accept as fact that we are involved in a leap of faith when we join one theoretical church or another. (If you require any further proof simply present the same clinical material to three or four different "experts" and compare their assessments. Even if they belong to the same church, their responses will differ considerably. More importantly, so will their suggestions about technique.)

Under the vaulted arches of psychodynamic theory, for example, there are clear differences in the initial assumptions (Alonso, 1989; Miller, 1984, pp. 615–628). In classical structural theory, pathology is the result of unresolved conflict, specifically sexual in origin. The curative process involves using a dyadic relationship to make the unconscious conscious through interpretation.

Interpretation, in turn, is based upon close inspection of the interaction between patient and therapist, looking for signs of transference distortions. In ego psychology, pathology stems from irreconcilable tension between the demands of the id and the social demands of the society. Healing occurs by providing more effective defenses through an analysis of the defenses used by the patient. In object relations theory, pathology results from damaging early relationships, resulting in an impaired capacity for authentic object relatedness and formation of a whole self. The curative process rests upon the establishment of a successful holding environment and the interpretation of the nature of object longings, specifically seen in the projective identifications used by the patients. The neo-analysts understand pathology to be the result of culture impinging on a benign blank slate. Healing in this tradition comes through a real relationship with the therapist, a corrective emotional experience, that leads to the recovery of an overly accommodated self and finally to a state of psychological autonomy. Table 1.1, adapted from Alonso (1989), summarizes some of the sub-churches of psychoanalysis:

TABLE 1.1. Psychoanalysis: Models of Mental Functioning

1. *Classical*. (S. Freud) Dual instinct theory; topographical model (conscious, preconscious, unconscious); structural model (id, ego, superego); development through stages of infantile sexuality (oral, anal, phallic) epigenetically, each stage building on the previous one, pathology resulting from fixations at various stages; mourning versus melancholia; Oedipus complex; sibling rivalry. (Spinoffs, Jungian school [archetypes, collective unconscious] and Neoanalytic [A. Adler, K. Horney, H.S. Sullivan, etc.], see culture and its values as working through the Classical framework.)

2. *Object Relations*. (M. Klein, Winnicott, Fairbairn, Guntrip, Mahler, Bowlby, Jacobson, and partly, Kernberg; this school arose around and within Ego Psychology.) "Precipitates" occur within the ego depicting the libidinized object—S. Freud. Hallmark of the Object Relations School is internal representations of the self and the other, especially positive and negative representations (Klein: The world of the infant is comprised of the good breast and the bad breast). Epigenesis is replaced with the progression from the Paranoid-schizoid position to the Depressive position (in which the infant develops appropriate guilt about the infantile attack on the good breast; syn: "the development of the capacity for concern," D. W. Winnicott.) Especially important is attachment bonding theory, layers of the True and False Self, and the developmental task of reconciling contradictory positive and negative images. This school is especially useful for formulating the conflicts of borderline and psychotic patients. Spinoffs: Modern-day Kleinians, who still hold with some of the more outrageous Kleinian credos, e.g., *early* Oedipus complex, in the first year of life.

3. *Ego Psychology*. (A. Freud, Hartmann, Reik, E. Kris, Erikson, etc.; this school is sometimes taken to include the Object Relations group.) Focus is on "autonomous spheres of functioning" of the ego and ego defense mechanisms that impair and facilitate adaptation; also on identification; and the vicissitudes of guilt and shame; there is little modification of basic Classical credos otherwise. This framework is especially useful in formulating the fixed and repetitive (neurotic) symptoms in relatively healthy patients.

4. *Self Psychology*. (Kohut and company) Mental structures of id, ego, and superego are replaced by the cohesive self, developing toward ambitions and ideals in parallel developmental lines of object development and narcissistic development. Development runs from the fragmented self (in narcissistic personality this is glued together by the grandiose self) to the cohesive self, the energy source being the idealized selfobject. Pathology is the fragmentation of the self through parents' empathic failures; transferences are idealizing and mirroring, and therapy is empathic mirroring plus transmuting internalizations.

5. *Lacanian (Postmodern) School*. (Lacan) The unconscious is structured like a language; pathology of the psyche is analyzed by deconstructionist methods; distortions in the self are corrected by re-stating distorted syntactical elements in the patient's speech and thought patterns.

Differences in theoretical schemata should not unduly disturb us. By suggesting that we operate on leaps of faith, we are not implying that psychotherapists are quacks. Ultimately in practice, all the experts will probably be "right," to the extent that each describes a part of the human condition that in its totality is too complex for any one of us to comprehend. Like the blind observers of the elephant, we each describe accurately one or another aspect but not all.

Nonetheless, it is important to acknowledge that all theories take a moral position. All presume to know something about what the good life is. All have implications about the ideal person. It is on the basis of these fundamental assumptions that theories rest. For example, some presume it is "better" to feel than to think, while others begin with the opposite premise. Some take the position that individuals must assume all responsibility for the ills that beset them; others focus their attention on helping individuals accept and live with the awful burdens that fate (or parents) has inflicted upon them. All too many place the individual at the center of the universe, diminishing the role of social responsibility and concern for the welfare of others. All theories have their values about what constitutes "better" ways of coping or behaving.

VALUES: NORMALCY

Schools of diagnosis function even more clearly as faith systems when they explain their notions of normalcy — an endeavor few systems attempt with much success. Opinions about who are the mentally ill and who are the sane have changed over time.

The aberrant of society have been always been regarded with ambivalence. Over the course of history they have been revered as prophets and slaughtered as witches; they have been sources of terror, awe, and disgust. Society's responses to them have been as varied as its understanding. Depending upon the era, the mentally ill have been considered possessed by demons to be shunned, or children of God to be followed — the worst and best of society.

Modern mental health professionals have done little better in this regard. As recently as the 1940s and 1950s mildly depressed patients were lobotomized; in the 1950s and 1960s homosexuals were given extensive courses of electroshock therapy; and even today political deviants are often "diagnosed" as crazy. These are powerful examples of values passing under the guise of science.

Hippocrates (c. 460–355 B.C.) viewed mental illness as an understandable medical phenomenon. His early hypotheses included attribution of insanity to increased humidity in the brain, understanding depression as an excess of black bile, and tracing hysteria to the womb moving about within a woman's body (Jones, 1922). Although the specific suggestions are humorous by modern standards, it is clear that Hippocrates did not view mental illness as evil or deserving of punishment. His stance was not always the predominant one.

In 2000 B.C., the Sumerians had attributed the unusual behaviors of the mentally ill to possession by evil spirits. This led naturally to dramatic societal responses. Often, "possessed" individuals were beaten, exiled, or killed. Since these behaviors were religious phenomena, the therapists were usually religious figures. In some cases there was an attempt to "heal" the possessed individual, and this typically involved some magical powers of the healer. In American history, the mentally ill were often deemed sinners, possessed by Satan. Still others were judged to be witches and killed.

Thus, from the beginning of our curiosity about mental illness and normalcy, spiritual values have been central in that distinction.

VALUES: CULTURE

Our faith about what is and is not normal is highly dependent upon the age in which we happen to live. In the Age of Enlightenment, for instance, reason became elevated to a position of supremacy, considered to be a "permanent universal entity, which was the same for all men of all ages and all countries" (Ellenberger, 1970, p. 195). Man was also viewed as a social being for whom society was created. The life of ideal person was directed by the requirements of reason and society. Authority lost its power and was replaced by science which used analysis as a way to understand and manage the world. Emotions were viewed as disturbances of the rational mind, passions were considered tyrannous, and fantasies were suspect. Science promised a great new world and was to be used for the benefit of all. Humankind was on the march and with the use of science and reason progress was sure to follow. Conversely, progress was confirmation of the value of reason. It was a period of optimism, intellectual and religious tolerance, and social concern.

Romanticism, which arose as a reaction to the Age of Enlightenment, elevated feelings and the irrational to positions of supremacy. The individual was also elevated and the eccentricities, particularly the emotional ones, of the individual were enlarged and accepted. Rather than view the individual as being guided by society, the Romantics viewed society as something which the individual needed to escape. Nevertheless, they also placed a great deal of importance on the value of friendship and other close relationships. The ideal person was someone of extreme sensitivity enabling him or her "to 'feel into' Nature and 'feel with' other men," having "a rich inner life, belief in the power of inspiration, intuition and spontaneity" (Ellenberger, 1970, p. 202) and in the importance of the emotional life. It was an era of great passion, of the power of love over status, and of the value of nature over every day commerce and business. Progress was not a process determined by reason. Rather, human life was a process of spontaneous unfolding, "a series of metamorphoses" (p. 200).

Within the field of mental health, it was also an era that gave rise to the exploration of the irrational and the unconscious, to the study of dreams and fantasy, to the development of psychotherapy and psychodrama. It was an era that highlighted the importance of psychology in the creation and cure of illness. The leaders in this field included Reil (Harms, 1957, pp. 804–809), Iderer (1835), and Neumann (1959). As Ellenberger ably illustrates, the work of these men is strikingly similar to that of Freud and Jung and later dynamic psychologists.

Both the definition and treatment of the mentally ill have been closely linked to faith since the beginning of mankind's interest in the "unusual" and "different" among us. Freud certainly understood this, and much of his writing concerned the metaphysical aspects of life (1913–17/1957, 1914/1955, 1919/1955, 1920/1955, 1923/1961, 1930/1961, 1937–39/1964).

VALUES: TECHNIQUE

As we select one of the various "churches" within which to practice and become learned in the mystical writings and secret languages of our chosen faith, we then become schooled in the particular rituals of that system. In our field we refer to these as the *techniques* of psychotherapy. Technique always follows and is rooted in theory. This is our only salvation from the sin of pure intuition — unless one belongs to a faith system that elevates pure intuition to a grand scale. We develop our technique, including our fundamental therapeutic stance, the focus of our observation, the manner of our words and actions, based upon our theoretical assumptions about what most helps our patients.

We run another very important risk: We promulgate ourselves. Some of us, for example, believe that it does a patient more good in the long run to explore the potential "deeper" meanings before prematurely offering mere information. We cannot prove the benefit, but we believe it, and the clergy from whom we learned it (our supervisors and therapists) believed it too. We probably believe it because those important individuals believed it and taught it to us with conviction. And typically, if we are trained in a particular tradition, we are required to be treated in that tradition as well. Thus, analysts-in-training are themselves psychoanalyzed. We often develop the same mentality as religious sects, distrusting those from different camps, especially the unsaved who begin from very different assumptions than ours. From our novitiate, we run the risk of perpetuating an unexamined faith system generation unto generation, accepting as truth that which is really faith.

We present our morality to our patients in a variety of ways every day. How the therapist in the vignette above responds will communicate a great deal of the therapist's faith system. Verbal conditioning is a powerful stimulus, reinforcer, and therefore an evoker of behavior (Greenspoon, 1955, pp. 409–416; Krasner, 1958, pp. 148–170; Shapiro & Birk, 1967, pp. 153–162). When we lift an eyebrow, frown, attend to some material and not to others, we are powerfully reinforcing certain behavior. Even Freud suggested that sometimes "the pure gold of analysis will have to be diluted by the copper of suggestion" (1919b, p. 168).

What if a patient comes to us full of guilt over not having been with a parent at the moment of death? The response of the therapist illustrates the faith system. One therapist might try to soothe the patient by teaching that guilt is a natural human response in the loss of any loved one, telling the patient that it cannot be assumed that there was any real deficiency in the behavior demonstrated around the death. Another might agree with the patient that the behavior was most unloving and selfish and begin the arduous task of helping the patient suffer through recognition that came too late. Still another might suggest some techniques that might be learned that could reduce the guilt. Yet another therapist might prescribe medication to reduce the suffering. All these therapists are compassionate and deeply concerned about their patients. They are competent and able. But they have different belief systems. Therefore they have different views of the ideal person. If they are descendants of the Age of Enlightenment, they view this guilt as irrational and therefore bad. If they are *somatikers* they worry that the biological system is out of balance. And so it goes.

These things are self-evident. Yet, every day we hear colleagues present their positions with the certainty that only a fundamental religious sect can equal. Not only is it impossible to be "value free" in our work, since that in itself is an ethical position, it is not even desirable to be free of values. How could we ever engage in true empathy and relationship with our patients if we had no moral position about the events in their lives? Kierkegaard (1945), reflecting on Socrates, suggested how difficult that position would be. "How rare the magnanimity of the helper who can be sufficiently concerned with the other person's self-realization and sufficiently free of his own need to dominate that he is willing to be merely an 'occasion' for the other's achievement of his own 'values.'" (p. 25).

VALUES: ONE POSITION

We confess: Our own church is psychoanalytic theory. Membership in this sect implies a great deal. For one thing, it implies that one is involved in an educational venture as well as a medical one. Freud began as a physician trying to cure physical maladies, but one of his earlier interests was how physical ailments could be relieved by *talking*. At this point the healer's role became that of listener more than talker. Freud was clear from the beginning that he did not consider psychoanalysis a practice that should be exclusively the domain of physicians. He called his technique psycho*analysis*, indicating his faith in the healing process of education and understanding. Freud wrote (1937/1964), "One must not forget that the relationship between analyst and patient is based on a love of truth, that is, on the acknowledgment of reality, and that it precludes any kind of sham or deceit." (p. 243). In that regard he belongs to a philosophical tradition that holds that "the truth shall make you free" (John 8:32). Freud's genius was in realizing that the truth must include unconscious truth, the world of feelings and memories and impulses. Not to imply that we are involved in a didactic exercise — far from it. Ours is a highly emotional art, but the immediate goal of the enterprise is greater self-knowledge. The ultimate goal is maturation.

This not only informs how we treat patients, it informs how we understand them. In psychodynamic practice we believe that human behavior is not random, but rather that human beings behave as they do for human reasons. Therefore, it is unfortunate (if not pathetic) to consider that the DSM-III-R settles all meaningful issues about distinctions among people. In the psychoanalytic model, we are as interested in understanding our patients as in curing them. They come to see us because they are unhappy, unfulfilled, lonely, or just curious.

Psychotherapy, in our church, is a type of postgraduate education about oneself.

Of course, our view is a leap of faith, just as all are. And within psychoanalytic theory, there coexist with various degrees of harmony many differing sects. We argue about how many neuroses will fit on the head of a pin just like the people of faith before us.

The object relations theorists suggested a different beginning point for the formation of personality. No longer were human beings understood as purely need-reducing, drive-oriented beings, but rather beings inherently designed to be in relationship with others. Fairbairn felt that the drive was a signpost to the object, indicating that drives, while important, are subordinate to relationships. Winnicott is supposed to have made the seemingly absurd statement, "There is no such thing as a baby," by which he meant that a baby does not exist in isolation but only in relation to the mother. Sullivan often said that it takes people to make people sick, and it takes people to make people well again.

To be an object relations theorist has its own implications. Freud approached the task of therapy from an expert–object point of view. The healing occurred via the skill of the analyst. His patients came to "be analyzed," not to be "in analysis." In Freud's view, the therapist had the skill and "did therapy" to his patient.

Object relations theory postulates that the fundamental element in the formation of personality is the need to be object-related. Put more simply, all of us yearn to love and be loved. This, in turn, dramatically affects how psychotherapy is understood and practiced. For one thing, the relationship between therapist and patient is no longer so much expert–object as it is Buber's I/Thou (1878/1958). For another, the relationship between therapist and patient becomes central, since that represents the most current and available data to use in the analysis of the patient's object relatedness. Thus, when we find ourselves filled with feelings of abhorrence for our patients, we are in the midst of a primary defense against the fundamental reality that this patient yearns to be in relationship with us and is trying his or her best to do so. This position certainly requires a leap of faith on occasion! Nonetheless, many have taken the position of Stone (1961): "purely technical or intellectual errors can, in most instances, be corrected, but a failure in a critical juncture to show reasonable human response which any person inevitably expects from another on whom he deeply depends can invalidate years of patient and largely skillful work" (p. 111). Annie Reich (1951) said, "Countertransference is a necessary prerequisite of analysis, if it does not exist, the necessary talent and interest is lacking" (p. 38).

CONCLUSION

All that has gone before has been a prolegomenon for discussing the special faith of the psychotherapist. In our sect, the healing (or soothing, or education) that occurs happens through and by virtue of relationships. This is not to imply that all relationships are healing. There are quite destructive relationships as well. But certain relationships represent the most powerful healing and maturing agent that we know for psychological pain.

Ferenczi, who had been one of the inner circle, broke with Freud over his conviction that it was the relationship that was central in therapeutic change: He believed the indispensable healing power in the therapeutic gift to be love, and that psychoanalytic cure is in direct proportion to the cherishing love given by the psychoanalyst to the patient (1931).

Etienne Esquirol (1772–1840), the early French psychiatrist who was Pinel's favorite pupil and who is generally credited with having taught the first course in psychiatry in 1817, wrote, "Il faut aimer les aliénés pour être digne et capable de les servir." (1838, p. 465) ("One must love the crazy ones to be worthy to serve them.")

Our conclusion, then, we hope, is obvious: It is neither good nor bad to have a faith upon which you base your practice — it is inevitable. There is not one right faith, though there are wrong ones. Finding out which is which is a difficult and perhaps impossible task. Indeed, we have intentionally polarized the issue. We would not support the thesis that psychotherapy is only a belief system, a leap of faith. There is science and fact and empirical substance in our quest. Just because we operate upon basic assumptions does not make those assumptions nonfactual or false. We could take the same arguments we have used and conclude that physics is also a faith system, but that does not deny its capacity to verify and repeat its findings. Perhaps psychotherapy is at the moment primitive and as we learn more will become less a faith system and more a science. For now it is only possible to be clear about the faith system within which we operate. Without the willingness to examine our morality, we run the risk of unconsciously and cavalierly imposing it upon our patients.

In closing, perhaps it is well to return to our ethical vignette: What should the therapist do or not do in the case of the 37-year-old woman with the married man? Our own faith holds that there *is* one perfect solution — but imperfect man cannot ever know it for certain. Human beings have, by their nature, to struggle with doubt. Our position is that it is not — nor should be — easy to decide what to do. It is only possible to struggle and strive to do the right thing. And if it at some point becomes less effortful or easy, then the *absence* of doubt should itself serve as a dire warning.

REFERENCES

Alonso, A. (1989). Psychodynamic psychotherapy. In A. Lazare (Ed.), *Outpatient psychiatry: Diagnosis and treatment* (2nd ed.). Baltimore: Williams & Wilkins.

Buber, M. (1958). *I and Thou* (2nd ed.) (R.G. Smith, Trans.). New York: Charles Scribner's Sons. (Original work published 1878)

Ellenberger, H. F. (1970). *The discovery of the unconscious: The history and evolution of dynamic psychiatry.* New York: Basic Books.

Esquirol, E. (1838). *Maladies mentales* (Vol 1). Paris: J.B. Bailliere.

Ferenczi, S. (1931). Child-analysis in the analysis of adults. *International Journal of Psycho-analysis, 12,* 468–482.

Harms, E. (1957). Modern psychotherapy — 150 years ago. *Journal of Mental Science, 103,* 804–809.

Freud, S. (1955). The Moses of Michelangelo. In J. Strachey (Ed. and Trans.), *The standard edition of the complete psychological works of Sigmund Freud* (Vol. 13). London: Hogarth Press. (Original work published 1914)

Freud, S. (1955). The uncanny. In J. Strachey (Ed. and Trans.), *The standard edition of the complete psychological works of Sigmund Freud* (Vol. 17). London: Hogarth Press. (Original work published 1919)

Freud, S. (1955). Lines of advance in psycho-analytic therapy. In J. Strachey (Ed. and Trans.), *The standard edition of the complete psychological works of Sigmund Freud* (Vol. 17). London: Hogarth Press. (Original work published 1919)

Freud, S. (1955). Beyond the pleasure principle. In J. Strachey (Ed. and Trans.), *The standard edition of the complete psychological works of Sigmund Freud* (Vol. 18). London: Hogarth Press. (Original work published 1920)

Freud, S. (1957). Papers on metapsychology. In J. Strachey (Ed. and Trans.), *The standard edition of the complete psychological works of Sigmund Freud* (Vol. 14). London: Hogarth Press. (Original work published 1913–1917)

Freud, S. (1961). The ego and the id. In J. Strachey (Ed. and Trans.), *The standard edition of the complete psychological works of Sigmund Freud* (Vol. 21). London: Hogarth Press. (Original work published 1923)

Freud, S. (1961). Civilization and its discontents. In J. Strachey (Ed. and Trans.), *The standard edition of the complete psychological works of Sigmund Freud* (Vol. 21). London: Hogarth Press. (Original work published 1930)

Freud, S. (1964). Analysis terminable and interminable. In J. Strachey (Ed. and Trans.), *The standard edition of the complete psychological works of Sigmund Freud* (Vol. 23). London: Hogarth Press. (Original work published 1937)

Freud, S. (1964). Moses and monotheism. In J. Strachey (Ed. and Trans.), *The standard edition of the complete psychological works of Sigmund Freud* (Vol. 23). London: Hogarth Press. (Original work published 1937–1939)

Greenspoon, J. (1955). The reinforcing effect of two spoken words on the frequency of two responses. *American Journal of Psychology, 68,* 409–416.

Hadley, S. W., Strupp, H. H. (1976). Contemporary view of negative effects in psychotherapy. *Archives of General Psychiatry, 33,* 1291–1302.

Iderer, C. A. (1922). *Grundriss der seelenheilkunde.* Berlin: Verlag von T.C.F. Enslin.

Jones, W. H. S. (1922). *Hippocrates.* Cambridge, MA: Harvard University Press.

Jurjevich, R-R. M. (Ed.). (1973). *Direct psychotherapy: Twenty- eight American originals.* Coral Gables, FL: University of Miami Press.

Kierkegaard, S. (1945). *Fear and trembling: Sickness unto death.* Princeton, NJ: Princeton University Press.

Krasner, L. (1958). Studies of the conditioning of verbal behavior. *Psychological Bulletin, 55,* 148–170.

Kuhn, T. S. (1977). *The essential tension: Selected studies in scientific tension and change.* Chicago: University of Chicago Press.

Miller, J-L. (1984). Jacques Lacan: 1901–1981. *Psychoanalysis and Contemporary Thought, 7,* 615–628.

Neumann H. (1959). *Lehrbuch der psychiatrie.* Erlangen: F. Enke.

Nussbaum, M. C. (1986). *The fragility of goodness: Luck and ethics in Greek tragedy and philosophy.* Cambridge: Harvard University Press.

Perry, S., Cooper, A. M., & Michels, R. (1987). The psychodynamic formulation: Its purpose, structure, and clinical application. *American Journal of Psychiatry, 144,* 543–550.

Reich, A. (1951). On countertransference. *International Journal of Psychoanalysis, 32,* 27–41.

Shapiro, D., & Birk, L. (1967). Group therapy in experimental perspective. *International Journal of Group Psychotherapy, 20,* 153–162.

Stone, L. (1961). *The psychoanalytic situation.* New York: International Universities Press.

Whitley, R. (1984). *The intellectual and social organization of the sciences.* London: Clarendon Press.

The Integration of Therapies

ROB ABERNETHY

The psychotherapy industry is under siege. Third parties and managed medicine have already shortened the time of outpatient therapy in many contexts and continue to press for enhanced efficiency and effectiveness. In addition, many consumers are demanding briefer, more cost-effective methods that bring faster symptom relief.

In this pressured atmosphere, a movement has emerged to integrate some of the pure forms of psychotherapy, heretofore practiced separately. Outside of inpatient work, eclecticism has had a pejorative ring. The term has suggested superficial dabbling, atheoretical lack of focus, symptom relief without lasting change, and an inability on the part of the therapist to stick to one approach because of inadequate training or limited self-awareness. The implied mediocrity of eclecticism has discouraged clinicians who have experienced its effectiveness from writing about it. Scholarly journals on psychotherapy issues have eschewed reconciliation of these various clinical orientations. Research methodology in the psychotherapies has also called for pure forms in measuring outcome or comparing effectiveness. Consequently, there are few if any eclectic "all stars" in psychiatric or psychological training programs nationwide.

Two theoretical schools that have long been competitors are behaviorism and psychodynamic theory. The tradition of training in each of the separate therapies has preserved the lack of collaboration or integration. Only in its pure form, each discipline asserts, is its therapy optimally effective. Behaviorists complain that an in-depth examination of the therapeutic alliance is unnecessary and wastes time and that insights into transference phenomena are irrelevant. Psychodynamic therapists view behavioral change as superficial and short-lived if unconscious motivations are not examined and worked through. The assignment of homework and other directive techniques of the behaviorist are seen as undermining the emergence of important transference phenomena. To the dynamic therapist, improvement in the hands of a behavior therapist probably represents a "transference cure" or "simple symptom substitution." Trainees in either discipline consequently develop deep skepticism about any other approach.

In most training programs the clinical techniques of outpatient behaviorism or dynamic psychotherapy or psychopharmacology are taught in different clinical settings by experts trained in a single orientation. Only in the inpatient setting is the trainee exposed to an integrative approach with a single patient.

In this chapter I will not attempt to formulate a master theory that would include each of the available approaches to the psychotherapy patient. This is the goal of theoretical integration. Instead, I will describe an approach to technical eclecticism, which is an attempt to provide the individual patient with what the clinician deems best at the time for the patient's problem.

It is quite possible that most psychotherapy now practiced in the U.S. is technical eclecticism. Unfortunately, until recently there was no academic forum or literature to encourage eclectics to "come out of the closet." The teaching of most psychotherapy in residency programs and in postgraduate fellowships, institutes, or courses focuses on a pure form of psychotherapy. Eclecticism has not been considered academically or theoretically sound or exciting. Research comparing the psychotherapies has also focused on pure forms. The effectiveness of an eclectic or multimodal approach has received limited testing by systematic research (Wolfe & Goldfried, 1988).

It is quite possible that, after completion of training, clinicians in practice become more eclectic in response to patient need. In a sense, our patients retrain us to respond in a multimodal fashion to the multifaceted problems they present to us.

Maslow (1966) presented a warning to the proponents of separate, pure therapies: "If the only tool you have is a hammer, then you will tend to treat everything as though it's a nail!" Wachtel (1977) and Fensterheim (1983) have presented two quite different attempts to integrate dynamic and behavioral approaches. Wachtel starts with a fundamentally dynamic therapy but injects behavioral strategies when indicated. Fensterheim, on the other hand, proposes a behavior therapy that is alert to problems in the alliance or resistance and approaches these with an examination of transference phenomena and the origins of these phenomena in the patient's history.

London and Palmer (1988) have recently reviewed the history of therapy integration. At the 1932 meeting of the American Psychiatric

Association, Thomas French presented a paper that attempted to reconcile Freud and Pavlov. Prior to the 1960s, most conflicting schools of psychotherapy were psychodynamic. In 1958, Wolpe's publication of *Psychotherapy by Reciprocal Inhibition* began the era of behavior therapy. Psychodynamic and behavior therapy quickly polarized and comparative research followed. With the exception of simple phobias best treated by behavior therapy, other conditions seemed effectively treated by either behavior or dynamic therapies. As Luborsky et al. stated in 1975, quoting *Alice in Wonderland,* "Everybody has won and all must have prizes."

There is a disturbing split in the teaching and practice of psychotherapy. Certainly the thrust of training is toward pure forms. Within most training programs, separate clinics teach and treat with behavior and dynamic methods respectively. However, the prevailing nonacademic practice is probably more integrated than the training centers or literature would suggest.

The purpose of advocating integration is to enhance the effectiveness of psychotherapy and to provide the patient with a more flexible approach. At issue, of course, is whether intruding on the purity of any one method will significantly weaken it. The argument could be made that two methods mixed are weaker than one alone. Can the benefits achieved from transference analysis be unraveled by assigning behavioral homework (for example, instructing the patient to expose him or herself to a feared situation)? The experience of many brief psychotherapies as well as crisis intervention models would suggest that amalgams of therapeutic approaches are both effective and efficient.

The formal methodology of integrative psychotherapy is in its infancy. The literature contains an increasing number of reports of integrative techniques. In this chapter, I will examine the following integrative strategies:

1. Behavioral techniques to enhance psychodynamic psychotherapy.
2. Cognitive techniques to enhance psychodynamic psychotherapy.
3. Encounters with family members or significant others to enhance psychodynamic psychotherapy.
4. Grief work, genetic reconstruction, and transference consideration to enhance behavior therapy.

Two well-established integrative approaches — psychotropic medication in psychodynamic psychotherapy and the combined use of group and individual therapies—will not be included in this chapter, since they have received considerable attention elsewhere (see Rutan & Stone, 1984; Karasu, 1982; Greenhill & Gralnick, 1983).

BEHAVIORAL TECHNIQUES TO ENHANCE PSYCHODYNAMIC PSYCHOTHERAPY

A number of behavioral techniques can be used to enhance psychodynamic psychotherapy. The following techniques will be examined: assertiveness training, graduated exposure to feared stimuli, guided imagery, relaxation techniques, and token economies. It would be unlikely that psychotherapy with a single patient would include all these behavioral interventions. Specific techniques can be used to catalyze the progress of therapy depending upon the nature of the stalemate, resistance, etc.

Assertiveness Training

Patients in psychotherapy often have difficulty speaking up in interpersonal encounters with authority figures, certain family members, or peers. Insight into the origins of such fear of speaking up may be accomplished with psychodynamic therapy, but the patient may still resist the risk of expressing a certain opinion or feeling. Assertiveness training provides the patient with a framework to examine the distinction between assertiveness and aggression, as well as common ways people avoid speaking up. Most importantly, even the briefest discussion of assertiveness allows the therapist to support the patient in taking the risk. Often patients eagerly report back on their successes, expecting to share in the positive reinforcement of the experience with the therapist.

Providing assignments designed to improve assertiveness is considered unwise in traditional psychodynamic therapy. Such a tactic would reveal a value judgment of the therapist toward the patient (i.e., "you are too timid!") as well as a value held by the therapist that it is better to speak up. These disadvantages, I would maintain, are usually far outweighed by the increased self-esteem experienced by the patient who has successfully spoken up.

More elaborate attention to assertiveness might be accomplished by suggesting to the psychotherapy patient that he or she sign up for an assertiveness training course, which is often available in an adult education center at a low cost.

A 40-year-old divorced mother of three had been in twice-weekly psychodynamic psychotherapy for 4 years to deal with a mild depression and low self-esteem following her divorce. She had inherited a large fortune from her parents, who had been financially indulgent with her during her childhood and adolescence. When her oldest child entered college, the patient resolved to enforce a reasonable budget in order to help teach her daughter the discipline and self-reliance she herself had painfully learned in her late 30s. When the daughter would fail to accommodate to the budget, the patient would get angry and bail the daughter out rather than enforce the limits. In spite of insight into and working through the issues of separation from her daughter and from her parents, she still could not assert herself successfully with her daughter. Because the outbursts with the daughter persisted, the therapist decided to describe the concept of assertiveness to the patient. The patient learned the difference between assertiveness and aggression, and practiced with the therapist statements to the daughter that calmly but firmly enforced the limits of spending. The therapist addressed openly the transference implications of his encouraging the patient to assert herself, such as rekindling her longing for a strong, wise father. The patient subsequently was able to enforce the budget with her daughter and began to feel anew issues of separation from daughter, parents, and exhusband, which then became the grist for continued psychodynamic therapy. Her self-confidence improved notably as a result of her successful interventions with her daughter, and the quality of their relationship also improved.

Graduated Exposure to Fear Stimuli

Commonly the patient in psychodynamic psychotherapy will describe a place or activity that is avoided because of anxiety, fear, shame, etc. Traditionally, the psychodynamic therapist's role is to listen for connections between the patient's current fear and past traumatic experiences or previous destructive relationships with important others. Interpretations are made in order to help the patient gain insight and to work through feelings. However, the traditional approach cautions against encouraging the patient to expose him- or herself to the feared situation lest the defenses be overwhelmed. Such advice, encouragement, or direction is also considered contrary to the abstinent posture of the psychodynamic psychotherapist. Further, it could be argued by the traditional therapist that directing the patient could adversely influence the transference phenomena emerging from him or her. For example, direct encouragement to face a feared stimuli gives the patient concrete information about the therapist's wishes, and might suggest to the patient that the therapist is impatient or views the patient as defective.

However, in my opinion, the advantages of encouraging some patients to act in these situations outweigh the risks. Furthermore, the opportunity to use transference in the treatment is not lost since the therapist can pay attention to the transference reactions to behavioral interventions. Ideally, the patient and therapist can gain insight by examining untoward reactions to behavioral suggestions.

> A 25-year-old single woman living with her parents came to psychotherapy because of lack of confidence and depression. She had been socially withdrawn most of her life. Through her elementary school years, an older mentally retarded sister had lived at home and was behaviorally disruptive. The patient was unable to bring friends home or go over to their homes. During junior and senior high years the patient was teased sadistically by classmates, who called her a "loser." In her 20s, her mother chided her for not having friends and constantly badgered her to go out and socialize. Coworkers often asked her to join them for a drink after work but she always refused. Although she gained insight into the rage, shame, and guilt that stemmed from her interactions with her sister, as well as into her struggle with her mother and her anxiety at separating from the family, she was still unable to accept social invitations.
>
> To assist the patient through this resistance, the therapist introduced the behavioral concept of graduated exposure and encouraged her to spend time with her colleagues after work. At first the patient was instructed to spend only 30 minutes socializing. The patient understood the concept and agreed to try 1 half-hour encounter. Fortunately, her coworkers were delighted to see her. Gradually the patient spent more time socializing with her coworkers. The patient chose not to tell her mother about these encounters, convinced she would have said, "It's about time. What took you so long?" This conviction by the patient provided fertile ground for exploring transference generated by the behavioral intervention.

Guided Imagery

Yager (1989) has recently published a review of guided imagery as an adjunct to psychodynamic psychotherapy. The patient is encouraged to develop a fantasy from a given situation that is suggested by the therapist. The content of the patient's fantasy and the feelings it promotes facilitate catharsis and understanding of the patient's problem.

In the case example of graduated exposure presented above, the patient had previously been encouraged to imagine herself accepting the invitation to join her coworkers after work and then to develop the scene in her mind. What did she imagine happening? What would her coworkers say? What could she say in response? What would she feel? What would her mother say when she got home late?

As she began to imagine this scene, she vividly recalled encounters with classmates during junior high school. These classmates would call her a "loser, fat, and ugly." She also recalled her mother's harsh admonition to come straight home after school and to keep to herself.

Guided imagery helped the patient recall painful experiences from her past that she could relate to current conflicts. In other words, guided imagery directly facilitated the psychodynamic quest.

Relaxation Techniques

These techniques, in general, are exercises that help the patient get immediate relief from stress and anxiety. Wolpe's (1958) desensitization by reciprocal inhibition helped the patient master an imagined exposure to stress by superimposing a pleasant image. Benson (1976) has designed a brief exercise called "The Relaxation Response," which he has used in treating stress and physiologic conditions such as hypertension.

The traditional psychodynamic psychotherapist may be reluctant to compromise the abstinent posture by teaching the patient to relax. Traditional thinking encourages high affect and use of free association to gain access to affect and memories. It is presumed that the short-term exposure to anxiety will ultimately lead to long-term lessening of anxiety. However, patients with significant anxiety resist change. Relaxation techniques can teach the patient some mastery over his or her distress so he or she can risk new exposures and gain new insight and confidence. Integration of this behavioral technique with more traditional psychotherapy can often overcome resistance caused by anxiety.

A 26-year-old single male was the youngest member of a team of financial analysts who advised the director of a mutual fund specializing in foreign investments. The only member without an M.B.A., he was assigned the task of arriving at work at 5:00 A.M. to review the overnight stock market averages from foreign exchanges. He would present a 10-minute summary at the beginning of a daily strategy meeting with the director and his fellow analysts at 9:00 A.M.. He came to therapy because of severe anxiety before and during these daily presentations.

The patient's maternal grandfather was a successful, wealthy, and powerful figure in the local financial community. He had helped the patient get the job at the mutual fund. The patient's father was a modestly successful, chronically anxious man with coronary artery disease who was intimidated by his father-in-law.

The patient quickly gained insight into his fear he would fail and be like his father, his guilt about being more successful than his father with his grandfather's help, and his fear of asking his fellow analysts questions and appearing "dumb," replicating scenes he had observed between father and grandfather.

The patient enjoyed a positive transference and reported increased feelings of confidence following each therapy session. However, in spite of this work, the paralyzing anxiety concerning his morning presentations persisted and threatened his career. The therapist, therefore, introduced a relaxation procedure and provided the patient a reprint from the *Harvard Business Review* by Benson describing the procedure. The patient was encouraged to use the brief relaxation procedure upon arriving at work and again just prior to the 9:00 A.M. meeting. The patient reported almost immediate lessening of anxiety.

The efficacy of this behavioral intervention was certainly multidetermined. The patient's positive transference was itself reinforcing and calming. Nonetheless, it seems an inescapable conclusion that the behavioral intervention itself was also important. The patient concluded that his job had been saved by his ability to conduct his primary responsibility without paralyzing anxiety.

Token Economies

Token economies are behavioral reward systems commonly used in inpatient settings. Good behaviors may be rewarded with poker chips that can be used to purchase privileges such as TV time or snacks. The system is designed to maximize the patient's awareness of the consequences of his or her behavior and to minimize unhelpful emotional struggles between staff and patient about behavior.

In long-term psychodynamic psychotherapy one use of this technique is to help a single parent deal with an out-of-control child. The emotional upheaval that accompanies raising a behaviorally dysfunctional child is so powerful that techniques that help bring that child back under control are worth whatever theoretical compromises from the more classical position are implied.

A 43-year-old widow and mother of three school-age children came to therapy 1 year after her husband had died of a brain tumor. She was lonely, depressed, anxious, overwhelmed with the frustrations of parenting, and in constant struggles with her parents about the way she treated her children. The patient was started on antidepressant medication and began psychodynamic psychotherapy. Her depression improved but her parenting role continued to frustrate and sadden her. Although she gained insight into issues between her and her deceased husband about parenting and into her role vis à vis her divorced parents and her siblings, she remained unable to set limits with her children. Evenings were tense, resulting in shouting admonitions at her children and then feeling guilty and tearful. The limits she did set were vague and inconsistent.

The therapist, concerned about his patient's self-esteem and the well-being of her children, suggested a token economy approach to the children. The patient accepted the idea and implemented it. Immediately everyone began having fun with the token economy. The patient felt less anxious and guilty for the first time since her husband's death, and she attributed this buoyancy to a new sense of mastery she felt at home. The children were eager to earn chips and shared in the sense of mastery over their privileges. They also responded to the clear set of expectations that came with the token economy. Now the children could trust that their good behaviors would result in consistent privileges, whereas before they felt privileges occurred randomly, depending upon their mother's moods.

The patient's new-found confidence allowed her to communicate more appropriately with her parents and her siblings, which in turn led to more insights about herself and her history.

COGNITIVE TECHNIQUES TO ENHANCE PSYCHODYNAMIC PSYCHOTHERAPY

In the early 1970s, Aaron Beck (1976) designed a new therapy to address and challenge cognitions in the here-and-now that exacerbated and perpetrated depression. This approach seemed contradictory to the psychodynamic approach of genetic reconstruction, transference analysis, and working through. However, cognitive techniques can enhance the effectiveness of more traditional dynamic therapy. Two such techniques will be described with examples: (1) Encouraging the patient to write statements about him- or herself that are confidence-building as a challenge to the reflexive self-derogatory or dependent statements the patient will make when anxious or depressed; (2) challenging the use of imperative verbs that reinforce dependency and undermine autonomy and self-confidence. Examples of imperative verbs are: "have to, ought to, should, can't." The patient is encouraged to use the words "want to" or "don't want to" in place of the imperatives.

A 40-year-old married graduate student, mother of two college-age girls, came to therapy because of severe marital conflicts. She had moved out of the house as a result of the severe anxiety and depression she felt while living at home with her husband. Although she was lonely, she was less anxious and depressed and could study more efficiently living apart. She wanted the marriage to survive but felt she lost her confidence when she was with her husband or even when she spoke to him on the telephone.

Six months into psychodynamic psychotherapy she generally felt better. She had made a network of friends and had improved her relationship with her daughters. She had learned a great deal about her conflicted relationships with her father and husband, with whom she felt intimidated and unable to say no to any of their demands. The patient lost her sense of self when she talked to either of these two men. She experienced them as highly critical, and she experienced herself in their presence as a complete failure. Apart from those two relationships she was able to recognize that she was an honors student in a competitive doctoral program, was well regarded by her faculty, and was held in high esteem by her peers. Except for her relationships with father and husband, she felt self-confident and happy.

The therapist suggested that the patient write a short essay about her successes as a person. The patient documented her successes as a student, an artist, an employee, a friend, and a mother. She was even able to write positively about her role as wife. After reviewing the essay, the therapist instructed the patient to read it aloud to herself before each contact with her father and/or husband. This cognitive antidote gave her more confidence and allowed her to be less defensive in her conversations with these important men. She found she could spend more time with her husband constructively discussing their relationship, their parenting, and their separation. She also discovered that by being less defensive her husband seemed to respond differently to her as well. These conversations allowed her to learn how threatening her graduate studies and new professional friends were to her husband, who had never completed college himself.

A 58-year-old wealthy widow came for psychotherapy 2 years after the death of her husband. Her complaints were depression, secondary to her loss and conflicts between her and her five adult children. Her husband had been a powerful and confident man, respected by everyone. He had sheltered the patient from financial concerns, including his financial dealings with their children. He made periodic gifts of money to the children, but they never asked him for money because he expected them to be self-sufficient.

After his death, the children began to ask the patient for financial assistance. When she responded to one, the others would be hurt, angry, and jealous. When she anticipated selling one of the family's three large homes, the children began fighting over the heirlooms.

When the patient talked about her children, she used imperatives: "I should," "I ought," "I have to," etc. She never said, "I want to" or "I don't want to." Her husband had always told her what she should do when there was an issue between her and the children. He had been somewhat older than she and had allowed her to live a sheltered existence. She had no professional career, although she was sought after for her fine volunteer efforts for many charitable enterprises. She had cooks and housekeepers. Her self-esteem was assaulted without her husband's support and direction.

The therapist pointed out her repetitive use of imperative verbs and suggested that, during the sessions, she substitute "want to" or "don't want to." She described feeling very alone and self-conscious saying "want to" in the office. In part this was because it made her think more about her husband. (The therapist, unlike her husband, was not giving her helpful instructions on how to live life.) Nonetheless, she subsequently reported using the new verbs with her children and with the family lawyer and financial adviser. She also reported that she was beginning to take charge of her life. At the same time she felt more like weeping over her husband's death and over being alone. The shift in verbs had reminded her that she was both alone and in charge. Conflict with the children lessened and her working relationship with the family lawyer and financial adviser improved.

ENCOUNTERS WITH FAMILY MEMBERS

In traditional psychotherapy any contact with family members is to be avoided. The concern is that such contact distorts transference and threatens confidentiality. Contact with a family member might also suggest to the patient a lack of confidence in his or her perspective. Finally, in dynamic therapy, it is considered a compromise of the therapeutic frame to go outside the patient's *perception,* since the focus of the inquiry is on the patient's internal conflicts.

In spite of these prohibitions, there may be problems in therapy that can be rather quickly removed by contact with a family member or significant other. For example, a spouse or other family member may be resisting the patient's therapy. Contact between therapist and family member can often resolve this conflict about therapy, making it easier for the patient to change. Sometimes therapy can become stalemated because of the patient's hesitation to confront an important person in the family. Willingness to support such a confrontation in a therapy session can greatly facilitate the patient's treatment. Finally, a family member can provide a source of data that can help the therapy progress.

Certainly contact with a family member should never happen without the patient's permission, or without a thorough examination of the feelings about and ramifications of such a meeting. The patient should understand the purpose of the contact and should agree with the intent. Only in the case of suicidal or homicidal patients should such contact be made without the patient's permission.

It is doubtless true that contact with a family member influences the transference. However, when contact with a significant other facilitates therapy, any compromise to the transference work is greatly outweighed by the advantages to the patient. A corrective emotional experience with the significant family member encouraged by the therapist can be profoundly growth-producing.

A 35-year-old married woman came to therapy because of marital conflicts. Her mother, an independently wealthy and forceful woman, had died 5 years before. Her father was aloof and withdrawn. His modest income had been ridiculed by the patient's mother, who had encouraged the daughters to ignore him. After the mother's death, the daughters learned that they had inherited the mother's wealth, which further alienated the patient from her father.

In therapy the patient became aware of perpetuating her mother's behavior in her own marriage. The patient's husband was an artist with a modest income that the patient felt compelled to ridicule. As the patient examined the relationship with her parents she developed a wish to have a rapprochement with her father, who lived some 200 miles away. The thought of contacting her father made her so anxious that she could not follow through. After some time the patient asked the therapist if she could invite her father to a therapy session and begin her rapprochement in that manner.

Wishing to support the patient in building a relationship with her father, the therapist agreed, and the meeting occurred. The patient and her father subsequently developed a close and loving relationship. They shared their mutual guilt and their ambivalent love/hate feelings for the mother. The patient's marital life improved markedly.

A 35-year-old, twice-married career business woman came to therapy because of frustration and despair about infertility. Her current husband seemed initially supportive of her seeking therapy. The patient struggled with her guilt over an abortion during a brief marriage in her early 20s and with her ambivalence about her husband's wish to pursue adoption. Six months into the therapy the patient began to sense her husband's unhappiness about the therapy continuing. He gradually became openly hostile about the visits, making the work of therapy virtually impossible for her.

The therapist suggested to the patient that she allow the husband to join them in a session so that he could discuss his complaints about the therapy. The therapist said he could use this visit to explain to her husband the process and goals of therapy and to answer any questions about the process that the husband might have. The patient enthusiastically agreed, but she suggested that the husband meet alone with the therapist so that he could speak more freely.

The therapist learned from the husband that he was afraid that therapy would persuade his wife not to adopt a child but rather to pursue her successful career. He was also threatened by a stranger developing such an emotional closeness to his wife. Clarifying the goals and the process of therapy greatly relieved his anxiety, as did having the opportunity to meet the person who had become so important to his wife. At the conclusion of the session, he described feeling confident now that the therapy supported the marriage and any decision he and his wife might reach about having children.

Subsequent to this session the therapy thrived. The patient improved and the couple commenced adoption proceedings.

GRIEF WORK, GENETIC RECONSTRUCTION, AND TRANSFERENCE INTERPRETATION IN TRADITIONAL BEHAVIOR TREATMENT

During the course of behavior therapy, resistance or noncompliance can create obstacles to a successful outcome. A departure from the usual behavioral approach to address the alliance and other therapeutic problems from a dynamic perspective can often accomplish a breakthrough.

Three psychodynamic strategies that can be used to enhance behavior therapy are: grief work, genetic reconstruction, and transference interpretation.

Grief Work: A 26-year-old single male graduate student came to a behaviorist with the complaint of mild anxiety regarding his oral comprehensive exam 6 weeks in the future. He was studying European history and had excelled with honors in his class work. However, the thought of facing a panel of examiners had interfered significantly with his ability to study and prepare for the oral exam. Whenever he would sit down to read, he would become restless and distracted.

The therapist demonstrated relaxation techniques with reciprocal inhibition to relieve anxiety. However, the patient reported increased anxiety and an inability to complete the behavioral exercises.

The therapist reexamined the patient's history and discovered the patient's father had died 5 years before. The father had been a European history professor who had urged the patient to study history and become a teacher. He and his father were struggling over his choice of a major at the time of the father's death. When asked how he felt about his father, the patient began to weep, revealing his disappointment and guilt that his father would not share in his becoming an historian. He felt he would be facing his father in the oral exam. The patient returned for his third visit somewhat improved, this time having completed the behavioral tasks. He used the third visit to talk more about his father and continued to improve on subsequent visits.

Genetic Reconstruction: A 30-year-old single woman came to therapy because of a fear of phlebotomy. She had never had venipuncture in the antecubital fossa. As a child, during an annual check-up with her pediatrician, she had been terrified and hysterical before and during the finger prick blood tests. Fortunately, since childhood, no medical condition required blood tests.

Relaxation and reciprocal inhibition were begun, but the patient found it difficult even to close her eyes and think about a needle. Hypnosis was attempted unsuccessfully. After 3 visits and with little progress, the therapist reviewed the patient's history more carefully. The patient related that her mother, a severe and brittle diabetic, had given herself insulin injections twice daily in the family kitchen as far back as the patient could remember. On a few occasions, insulin reactions had required an ambulance call and hospital admission. The patient tearfully described an intense terror of having diabetes herself.

On subsequent visits the patient was able to cooperate with the reciprocal inhibition, hypnosis, and graduated exposure to a needle and syringe. Her anxiety lessened enough to allow her to have her first phlebotomy for routine blood tests.

Transference Interpretation: An 18-year-old male freshman presented at the college counseling service for help with mild symptoms of panic prior to tests. The psychiatrist who evaluated him recommended a low dose of alprazolam and brief behavior therapy that would include relaxation techniques and cognitive therapy. On the second visit the patient announced to the psychiatrist that he had not taken the medication nor had he done the cognitive assessments or relaxation exercises. He felt no better. Careful examination of the patient's history revealed that his father, a driven physician, had moved out of the house the year before the patient entered college. His parents had subsequently divorced, and his father was now living with a girlfriend he had secretly been seeing the year before the separation. The patient was profoundly bitter toward his father, whom he now saw rarely. The patient described his father as about the psychiatrist's age, and with the same kind of beard.

The psychiatrist clarified the patient's bitterness at his father and pointed out the similarity between himself and the father in age, appearance, and profession. He wondered if this might help explain the patient's refusal to take his advice. The patient talked more about the hurt and rage at his father's betrayal of the family. At the next session the patient reported improvement as well as compliance with the treatment program.

CONCLUSION

The psychotherapy industry is under siege from both the third-party payers and the unhappy consumer. Integration of theory and practice may provide a compelling amalgam that will enhance the effectiveness of therapy and make therapists more responsive to the wide array of ills that patients present.

Integration will also broaden the repertoire of strategies that the therapist can use to establish a strong alliance and to help the patient get beyond the resistance to examine and to change.

Integration in the clinical setting will pose a challenge to the training of future psychotherapists. Can we develop a unified integrated theory that allows for integrated clinical strategies to be taught in the early stages of training? At this time, most training programs begin with either dynamic theory and practice, or behavior theory and practice. Other modalities are "added on" in separate and subsequent training experiences. The current wisdom states that learning one method first is less confusing to the trainee. Is the confusion not that of the established trainers, who hesitate to address the challenge of teaching behavior and dynamic theory simultaneously? Psychopathology is always multidetermined. Early childhood experience in a genetically vulnerable individual leads to maladaptive behavior that reinforces cognitive and affective symptoms. Multidetermined pathology deserves multifaceted theory and multimodal therapies. Herein lies the challenge of integrative therapy.

REFERENCES

Beck, A.T. (1976). *Cognitive therapy and emotional disorders.* New York: Meridian.

Benson, H. (1976). *The relaxation response.* New York: Avon.

Fensterheim, H. (1983). An introduction to behavioral psychotherapy. In H. Fensterheim & H.I. Glazer (Eds.), *Behavioral psychotherapy: Basic principles and care studies in an integrative model.* New York: Brunner/Mazel.

Greenhill, M.H., & Gralnick, A. (Eds.). (1983). *Psychopharmacology and psychotherapy.* New York: MacMillan.

Karasu, T.B. (1982), Psychotherapy and pharmacotherapy: Toward an integrated model. *American Journal of Psychiatry, 139,* 1102–1113.

London, P., & Palmer, H. (1988, May). The integrative trend in psychotherapy in historical context. *Psychiatric Annals, 18,* 273–279.

Luborsky, L., Singer, B., & Luborsky, L. (1975). Is it true that everyone has won and all must have prizes? *Archives of General Psychiatry, 32,* 995–1008.

Maslow, A.H. (1966). *The psychology of science: A reconnaissance.* New York: Harper & Row.

Rutan, J.S., & Stone, W.N. (1984). *Psychodynamic group psychotherapy.* New York: MacMillan.

Wachtel, P.L. (1977). *Psychoanalysis and behavior therapy: Toward an integration.* New York: Basic Books.

Wolfe, B.E., & Goldfried, M.R. (1988). Research on psychotherapy integration: Reconsiderations and conclusions from an NIMH Workshop. *Journal of Consulting and Clinical Psychology, 56*(3), 448–151.

Wolpe, J. (1958). *Psychotherapy by reciprocal inhibition.* Stanford, CA: Stanford University Press.

Yager, J. (1989, Spring). Teaching guided imagery. *Academic Psychiatry, 13*(1), 31–38.

T·H·R·E·E

※

The Short-Term Dynamic Psychotherapies: An Overview

JAMES E. GROVES

Many papers and recent books on short-term therapy begin with a somewhat defensive comparison of short-term therapy with long-term therapy. The usual thrust is that patients in long-term therapy could be treated much more cheaply short-term. Occasionally, the assertion will be made that short-term psychotherapy is better as well—Davanloo (1980), for instance, in discussing the therapy of characterologically passive patients and masochistic personality disorders. Such assertions come with evidence but generally leave one not entirely convinced. (Those who hold that longer is always better, for instance, Schafer [1973] similarly leave one with the Scottish verdict, "not proved.")

Whether short-term psychotherapy is old wine in smaller, cheaper bottles or a whole new vintage is a question for elsewhere. The purpose here is not to continue this debate but to avoid it. Short-term psychotherapy, like psychoanalysis, is several things: a method of treatment, a body of theory, or an ideology. The present focus is short-term therapy as treatment.

Toward the end of the last century, when Breuer and Freud were inventing psychoanalysis, hysterical symptoms defined the focus of therapeutic work. When free association and dream analysis replaced hypnosis as the method of treatment, the duration of psychoanalysis increased. Over time, the trauma theory of the neuroses was replaced by the Oedipus complex, and a more broadcast, free-ranging exploration replaced the symptom as focus. Later, as exploration of the transference replaced direct suggestion, the interaction of the therapist with the patient necessarily diminished. Soon, only the rare therapist, most notably Ferenczi (1925), practiced psychoanalysis still using the more directive techniques. Freud and his followers, refining their technique in order to foster transference, found analyses growing longer as activity with the patient, confined mainly to interpretations of resistance, declined. In this way, psychoanalysis became more and more unfocused.

The history of psychoanalysis mirrors differences between short- and long-term psychotherapy. Analyses grew longer and more unfocused as the therapist grew less and less interactive. As short-term therapies became briefer, they became more focused and interactive. But *brevity, focus,* and *therapist activity* are parameters in which short-term therapies differ, not only from long-term therapy and psychoanalysis but also from one another. Patient *selection* makes up a fourth criterion in the taxonomy of the short-term psychotherapies.

Table 3.1 shows brevity, focus, activity, and selection on one axis and a quasi-historical, quasi-ideological grouping on the other. From top to bottom, it shows the five main divisions of short-term dynamic therapies currently in use. They are the interpretive short-term therapies (Sifneos, 1972; Malan, 1976; Davanloo, 1979), the existential psychotherapy of Mann (1973), the cognitive short-term therapies (Beck & Greenberg, 1979), usually grouped with the behavioral therapies, interpersonal psychotherapy (Klerman et al, 1984), a group of practitioners and theorists subsumed under "eclectic," Horowitz and colleagues (1984), Budman and Gurman (1988), and Leibovich (1981, 1983). The sixth "school" of short-term therapy belongs to Winnicott (1977), showing how arbitrary, in some sense, it is to group disparate methods at all. Winnicott could be classified with the interpretive group or with Mann but is placed at the end to suggest something trans-eclectic.

THE INTERPRETIVE METHODS: SIFNEOS, MALAN, AND DAVANLOO

Foremost in modern short-term therapy is, of course, Franz Alexander's (1971) manipulation of the interval and spacing of sessions. He formulated "flexibility" in such a way that even his critics had to take a fresh look at the nature of the therapeutic frame. Decreased frequency, irregular spacing, and therapist-dictated scheduling (rather than patient- or symptom-dictated scheduling) all decreased irrational transference elements and enhanced the reality orientation of therapy (although it increased preconscious conflicts and affect, which Alexander also called *transference*). Alexander's discoveries in manipulating the interval and scheduling of sessions suddenly caused the frame of dynamic therapy to become as interesting as the picture it surrounded. Freud, of course (1893–1895/1955), had been willing to adapt the therapeutic frame to the temporal situation of the patient, but his willingness waned over time.

With the Second World War came a glut of patients suffering from shell-shock and battle fatigue. New concepts and new theories emerged as a result of treating so many rapidly. In 1944, Grinker and Spiegel, working with soldiers, and Lindemann, working with survivors of the Coconut Grove fire, rediscovered the active short-term therapies Ferenczi and Rank (1925) had advocated and even Freud had practiced earlier. Alexander and French now popularized their method, which modified the length and spacing of sessions ("flexibility") and enabled the psychotherapist to provide the patient with a "corrective emotional experience" by playing a role that countered the patient's past experience.

Working in Boston and in London, Sifneos (1970, 1971) and Malan (1976) can be credited with independently fashioning various psychoanalytic techniques and deviations into the first whole, coherent short-term methodologies still widely in use today. The increased activity of Ferenczi and Rank, Lindemann's (1944) crisis work, Grinker and Spiegel's (1944) push for brevity, Alexander and French's flexible framework and Balint et al.'s (1972) finding and holding of the focus were all technical innovations, but none constituted a whole new method. Malan and Sifneos, however, invented ways of working that were not just arrays of techniques but whole new therapies born in the outpatient clinic.

The first category of short-term therapies features brevity, narrow focus, and high patient selectivity, but the unifying feature is therapist activity. Psychoanalytic interpretation of defenses and appearance of unconscious oedipal conflicts in the transference appear in other short-term therapies (and are often down-played), but only in these methods do interpretation and insight constitute the apex of the method, and, as in psychoanalysis, the "cure."

Sifneos (1971) contrasts anxiety-suppressive and anxiety-provoking psychotherapies. Anxiety-suppressive therapy is used for less healthy patients who are able to work and recognize the psychological nature of their illness but unable to tolerate the anxiety of deeper levels of psychotherapy. Anxiety-provoking psychotherapy is longer, less crisis-oriented, and aimed at the production of anxiety—which is then used to elicit transference material. (Whereas in psychoanalysis transference emerges, in short-term therapy it is often forced out.)

Anxiety-provoking therapy runs 12 to 20 sessions but may extend

TABLE 3.1. The Major Short-Term Psychotherapies

School	Short-term dynamic therapies	Brief (# sessions)	Focused (Therapy themes and concerns)	Active (Role of clinician)	Selective (Type of patient)
Analytic	Sifneos: Anxiety suppressive	4–10	Narrow: on crisis, coping, at conscious level	Therapist: teacher — Clarifies, supports, decreases transference	Less healthy patients but able to work and recognize psychological nature of illness
	Sifneos: Anxiety provoking	12–20	Very narrow: Oedipal conflict, grief; unconscious level; transference	Teacher — Interprets transference, resistance; Idealizing becomes ambivalent transference	Very rigid standards: "top 2–10%" of clinical population;* oedipal conflict or grief; motivation essential; psychological-mindedness tested by trial interpretation
	Malan	20–30 Fixed date*	Narrow, implicit (therapist finds it), unconscious, similar to Sifneos A–P	Doctor — Similar to Sifneos—"insight" held to be curative	Similar to Sifneos; healthy but some character pathology; able to work analytically (responds to trial interpretation)
	Davanloo	1–40 25 ca.	Broader but similar to Malan and Sifneos, plus: resistance and retroflexed anger	Critic* — Confrontive of resistance, especially around anger, D/A/I (conflict), and C/T/P (persons) triangles	Less healthy than Sifneos group: "top 30–35%"—some long-standing phobic obsessional, or masochistic personalities but must respond to "trial therapy" first session
Existential	Mann	12 Exactly*	Broader focus: (Time Itself*) & "central issue" Termination, affective state	Empathic helper — Therapist, by being with patient through separation helps in mastering developmental stage when parents failed patient	Broader patient selection but usually not borderline; some ego strengths, especially passive-dependent patients and delayed adolescents

			Focus	Role	Intervention	Patient selection
Behavioral	Cognitive	1–14 acutely; additional 24 if chronic	Conscious: "automatic thoughts"*	Coach or director*	Therapist helps define governing slogans, refutes them, assigns homework, mandates practice of new cognitions and behaviors	Not psychotic: in crisis; coped previously; not cognitively imparied; not borderline
	Interpersonal	12–16	Interpersonal field	Coach or doctor	Defines interpersonal deficits, role problems and helps reshape interpersonal behaviors*	Depressed patients at any level of health, with losses or interpersonal deficits, causing maladaptation or depression
	Eclectic	Horowitz: 12	Interpersonal + cognitive precipitating event	Counselor	Combines all of the above, especially interventions aimed at shoring up defenses, repairing stress response damage	Any level of health (except organic and psychotic conditions), but progress relates to level of health
		Budman: 20–40; variable spacing,* re-up option	Interpersonal + developmental + existential	Doctor		
		Leibovich: 36–52	One problematic borderline trait,* e.g., low frustration tolerance	Real person		
Analytic	Winnicott	1–14 On demand*	Broader focus; unconscious, transference, termination, separation, aggression	Empathic helper/ playmate	Maintains holding environment, actively interprets transference, unconscious conflicts; supplies missing developmental capabilities*	Broad, individualized; looks for response to trial interpretation

*Unique feature

to 40 or more. The focus is narrow: failure to grieve a death; inability to finish a project owing to a fear of success; triangular, futile love relationships. These neurotic high level conflicts—the standard grist of the analytic mill—are the province of anxiety-provoking therapy. The therapist serves as a detached, didactic figure who keeps the focus in view, and challenges the patient in a firm, dry fashion that discourages dependency and appeals to the intellect. This method represents a classical oedipal level defense analysis with all the lull periods removed and the anxious periods (castration anxiety, not separation anxiety) strung together. One important feature is that it serves only the 2 to 10% of the population that is able to tolerate unremitting anxiety (Flegenheimer, 1982).

In Malan's method, the therapist discerns and holds the focus without explicitly defining it for the patient. A unique feature is that Malan sets a date to stop treatment once the goal is in sight and the patient demonstrates capacity to work on his or her own; the *date,* rather than a set number of sessions, avoids the chore of keeping track if acting out causes missed sessions or scheduling errors.

Malan's method resembles that of the British object-relations school. Like Sifneos, he sees interpretation as curative but aims less at the patient's defenses than the objects they relate to. In other words, the therapist will call attention to behavior toward the therapist but rather than asking what affect is being warded off, Malan wants to know more about the original object in the nuclear conflict who set up the transference in the first place.

Davanloo's method is similar, although it might appear to be dramatically different in the famous videotapes made and shown in Montreal. By using relentless, graduated, calculated clarification, pressure, and challenge, the therapist elicits anger that is used to dig out the transference from behind "superego resistance." (In Sifneos, anxiety is the lever, in Malan, typically, it is dependency and depression.)

Davanloo starts therapy in the first session. He begins by pointing out the body language and facial expressions that demonstrate the patient's passivity, withdrawal, or vagueness. Patients who do not decompensate or withdraw are then offered a trial interpretation: The patient's need to fail and clumsiness in the interview disguise aggression toward the therapist; the patient's need to become "a cripple," to be "amputated" and "doomed," disguises rage. The therapist works with this "triangle of conflict" (which goes from *defense* to *affect* to *impulse* in relation to the "triangle of persons").

The "triangle of persons" begins with a problematic *current object,* one mentioned in the first half of the initial interview. The investigation then moves from the *therapist* whom the patient has just been

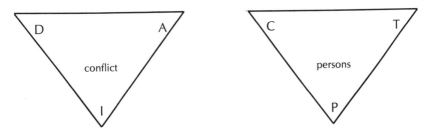

FIGURE 3.1. Davanloo's "trial therapy."

protecting from his or her anger to the *parent* who taught such patterns of responses in the first place. One or two circuits around the "D/A/I" (conflict) triangle in relation to three points of the "C/T/P" (persons) triangle constitute the "trial therapy" (see *Figure 3.1*). The "trial therapy" is a more elaborate version of trial interpretations Malan and Sifneos use to test motivation and psychological-mindedness. Davanloo's patients lack the ability to distinguish between points in the "conflict (defense/affect/impulse) triangle" or to experience negative affects directly. By trolling the D/A/I triangle around the "persons" (current object/therapist/parent) triangle," Davanloo forces the frigid patient to feel and thus creates a mastery experience for the patient. These are nonpsychotic, nonaddicted, nonorganic individuals who have a combination of retroflexed aggression and harsh superegos but, at the same time, enough observing ego to discount the apparent harshness. Davanloo's patients seem to find his method supportive; up to 35% of an average clinic's population can tolerate it—a range broader than either Sifneos or Malan claim (Flegenheimer, 1982). Failures of the Davanloo "trial therapy" typically are referred to cognitive therapy.

THE EXISTENTIAL METHOD OF JAMES MANN

Mann's insistence on a strict limit of exactly 12 sessions is unique in the field of short-term psychotherapy. Twelve sessions, which Mann chose somewhat arbitrarily and then empirically tested to his satisfaction, is sufficient time to do important work but short enough to put the patient under pressure. This set number with no reprieve thrusts the patient and the therapist right up against the existential reality they both tend to deny: Time is running out.

No other short-term therapy seems to require so much of the therapist. And Mann's treatment is open to patients further down the continuum of psychological health than patients acceptable to Sifneos and Malan. In theory, at least, even the occasional borderline patient with some well-developed strengths, some mastery of adolescent issues, and some capacity to make and break relationships with a modicum of skill is a candidate. And even if this method does not appeal to all short-term therapists, almost every subsequent theorist in the field has been influenced by Mann to some degree.

Mann has a dual focus: the "Central Issue" the patient brings in relation to the all-important issue of Time Itself. The therapist is presented as a helper who existentially *stays with* the patient through separations, helping master the developmental stages in which parents failed the patient. Mann's theoretical point of departure (which he probably derived from the empirical finding that 12 sessions was about right) is Winnicott's notion that time sense is intimately connected to reality testing, which underlies the depressive position; the attainment of the depressive position is a prerequisite for the development of the "capacity for concern" and, later, the attainment of object relatedness.

The most succinct way to view Mann's treatment is that, in some sense, both unconscious mental processes and neurotic and character-disordered structures are timeless. Thus Mann's therapy starts out timeless and rapidly becomes time-constrained. By unburying the issue of unconscious timelessness, the therapy examines childish wishfulness versus actual grown-up time. In other words, the steady ticking of the clock is used as a chisel to resculpt magical, timeless thinking.

After an initial evaluation determining that the patient is not psychotic, borderline, or organically impaired, the therapist begins to think about the "central issue" (such as problems with separation, unresolved grief, failure to move from one developmental stage to another — delayed adolescence especially). Then the therapist solicits the patient's agreement to work for a total of 12 sessions of standard psychotherapeutic length. The patient will at this point express some disbelief that 12 sessions is enough, and Mann says that if the evaluation has been accurate and the method is suited to this patient, the therapist should look the patient in the eye and say that 12 sessions will be just enough. The therapist should not compromise the time limit by suggesting at any point that further sessions will be permitted.

The early sessions are marked by an outpouring of data and the formation of a positive or idealizing transference. During this phase the therapist's job is to hold the focus on the central issue and allow the development of a sense of perfection. At about the fourth session the patient often becomes disillusioned and refocuses on symptoms. At this point the therapist makes the first interpretation that the patient is trying to avoid seeing that time is limited and that he or she may have feelings around separation. This sequence is repeated and deepens through the middle of therapy.

After the midpoint, overt resistance often occurs, perhaps in the form of lateness, absence on the part of the patient, and negative transference. The therapist examines this in an empathic and welcoming way while inwardly examining countertransference issues that may impede the work. And finally in the latter sessions comes a working through of the patient's pessimism and recollection of unconscious memories and previous bad separation events, along with an expectation of a repetition of the past. Supported by the therapist's genuine acceptance of the patient's anger and ambivalence over termination, the patient moves from a state of neurotic fear of separation and its attendant depression to a point where the patient is ambivalent, sad, autonomous, and realistically optimistic.

This short-term method is probably one of the hardest for the therapist because so much happens in such a short period of time, and the impact of emotions upon the therapist is so condensed. Although it appears to be a method that many therapists shy away from, it can if properly selected and skillfully applied, be powerfully effective and quite beautiful in its theoretical simplicity.

THE COGNITIVE APPROACH

Because the cognitive approach is often associated with behavioral therapy, it is hard to recall that its roots are in psychoanalysis and the dynamic therapies. The intellectual parents of cognitive therapy are Freud and Melanie Klein, not Pavlov and Thorndike. To see why this is so, think of mental life as consisting of an abecedarian triangle of *a*ffect (or feeling), *b*ehavior (the outcome of affect and thought), and *c*ognition (or thinking). Figure 3.2 depicts the relation among these three elements of mental life, each affecting the other reciprocally (as

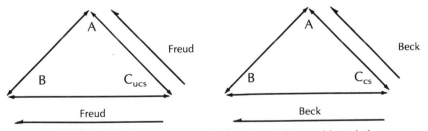

FIGURE 3.2. The mind of psychoanalysis and the cognitive mind.

well as showing the relation among limbic system, neocortex, and motor strip); they also depict the relation between psychoanalysis and cognitive therapy. Freud's focus is mainly on the relation of unconscious processes to affect and behavior as mediated through cognition. Aaron Beck's focus is the relation of *conscious* thought processes to mental life. Thus the focus of behavior therapy is behavior, treating affects and conscious cognitions only secondarily. The focus of psychoanalysis is affect and unconscious cognition (C_{ucs}). Cognitive therapy, however, focuses on affect and conscious cognition, C_{cs}, (or "automatic thoughts" as Beck calls them). It seeks to alter syllogisms that impinge on both affect and behavior.

The two cognitive therapies dealt with here are that of Aaron Beck, which one day may be used to treat more psychiatric patients than any other method in the U.S., and the all but forgotten Fixed Role Therapy (1973) of George A. Kelly. The dry, practical aspect of Beck's serves as a contrast to the strangeness of Kelly's (but they are both cognitive therapies). Beck sees cognition as encompassing a broad spectrum ranging from discreet thoughts and self-verbalizations to fantasy, imagery, and abstract beliefs and values. He posits that an individual's interpretation of events in the world is encapsulated in fleeting "automatic thoughts" that are often cognitions at the fringes of consciousness. These "automatic thoughts" mediate between an event and the affective and behavioral response. In other words, the patient labors under a set of slogans that, by their labeling function, influence his or her *Weltanschauung* and humble experimental forays into new behaviors that could change the representation of the world and the individual in it.

The basic thrust of cognitive therapy, according to Beck, is to bring the automatic thoughts completely into consciousness, to challenge them consciously, and to practice new behaviors that change the picture of the world and the self in it. The patient is exhorted to challenge these automatic thoughts and use any positive change as a wedge against the monolithic power of the "negative cognitive assumption."

The therapist schedules the patient's day-to-day activity, and the patient is asked to list in some detail actual daily activities and rate the degree of "mastery" and "pleasure" that each affords. These allow the therapist to review the week with the patient and sculpt behaviors. Cognitive rehearsals are also used to forecast the upcoming week to help the patient foresee obstacles.

To the patient the therapist explains the major premise of the cognitive model—that an intermediating slogan lies between an event and the emotional reaction. This slogan may take a verbal or pictorial form. Using a Socratic method of questioning, the therapist then elicits from the patient statements of fact that lead to a more accurate conceptualization of the problem, while at the same time interfering with the patient's obsessive reiteration of the negative cognitive set. The patient's participation in the reasoning process gives him or her a chance to experience the therapy before actually putting its principles into practice. Most of the work, however, is not done in therapy sessions but in the assigned therapeutic homework.

Kelly's "Fixed Role Therapy" (1973) is based in personal construct theory. The personal construct is neither a representation of an event nor a concept. Rather, it is a referent — a mental template — upon which events are projected by the person in order to cope with them. Under personal construct theory every individual tries to achieve maximal differentiation of events in the world with a minimum of constructs. (In other words, people seem to need to keep it simple.) Cognitive processes are channeled by individual expectations; one anticipates events by constructing referents based on past ones.

One way to look at the cluster of behavioral expectations placed on individuals is through the notion of role. A simple-minded way to think of role is just the way it is used in drama, a part that one plays and that other characters expect one to play and throw cues for the purpose of advancing the play along the lines of the script. One of the problems with personal constructs and roles is that roles may be aberrant and the constructs may be erroneous. For Kelly, however badly one chooses to act, it is in role relationships that people have their best chance of reframing constructs, introducing novelty into routines, and changing their patterns in the world.

The patient is asked to write a character sketch of him- or herself from a particular point of view. The therapist then studies this sketch and writes an "enactment sketch" that might have been written by a hypothetical other self or the character in another role. In the next session the therapist shows the patient this sketch. If the patient's response is satisfactory the therapist asks the patient to pretend that the old self has "gone to the mountains" and that the new self has materialized. The client is then to enact, as much as possible, 24 hours a day, 7 days a week, all that this new self might do, say, think, or even dream in the new role — not unlike method acting. At least 3 sessions a week are scheduled in which patient and therapist rehearse the enactment, test its effectiveness, and examine outcomes. At the end the old self "comes back" and evaluates the experience. It is not that the therapist designs a new self that is better, it is that the patient sees there is a universe of selves that can fit into the roles of life. The experiment convinces the patient of the relativity of personal constructs and provides the motivation for change into new roles.

The self-characterization is elicited in such a way as to imply that neither diagnosis nor therapy is based on hidden facts. Rather, it can be based on superficial aspects of the individual. The patient may begin to see that there is a sense in which we are what we represent ourselves to be. The therapist tells the patient to write a character sketch just as if the patient were the character in a play, to write it as though it might be written by a friend who knows the patient very intimately and very sympathetically, perhaps better than anyone could really know anyone, and write it in the third person, to start out with "John Doe is. . . ."

The therapist's role in writing the enactment sketch is quite difficult. The therapist needs to discern in the patient's sketch at least one testable hypothesis about roles and personal constructs that can be incorporated into the therapist's sketch for the new self. The hypothesis may be one that the patient has already set up in the self-characterization. For example, if the self-characterization describes the patient as "meticulous," the therapist may want to cast the patient in the role of an individual who is "casual" or relaxed. By structuring the new self's behavior the psychotherapist tries to make the patient's daily living take shape in a new world that the patient never suspected is actually there. Examples often involve asking patients to enact the opposite of character traits that are central to the personality structure of the individual. For instance, a selfish, rigid, intolerant patient may be asked to play a role that is similar but differs in that the new self is constructed as "tolerant." Pivotal in the enactment sketch is not only its construction but also its presentation to the patient. "Is this the kind of individual you would like to know?" If the answer is yes, the enactment can proceed.

Kelly describes a 2-week course of an every-other-day regimen of 7 sessions. In each session the therapist becomes a director mediating the living-through of the enactment sketch. Therapy sessions rehearse five kinds of situations: (1) interaction with a teacher or supervisor on the job; (2) interaction with peers; (3) interaction with a spouse or intimate; (4) interaction with parents; and (5) interaction in a situation involving a religious experience. Only a day or two should elapse between the assignment and the time the patient comes in to announce that it cannot be done. At this point the therapist must be prepared to support the endeavor vigorously, starting with the more superficial areas of daily living, for instance, the job situation. Rehearsing such a situation is an early treatment goal and a strenuous experience for both therapist and patient. It is constructed so that the patient can withdraw before becoming overwhelmed. Job supervision or student–teacher relationships usually lend themselves to this goal. It is better to hold off a role enactment with a spouse or intimate because the patient is likely to be reproached for "behaving strangely" and needs time to get used to the idea.

Kelly's value-free mode of operating protects the integrity of the original self of the patient and is receptive to the unfolding of the truth whether the therapist likes it or not. "At this point neither of us knows what kind of person you *should* be. That is something that will have to be developed as we go along." The essential point of this complex endeavor is to let the patient *be* the new self and observe others reacting to the new self at the same time the old self is forgotten. The new self may not be the person that the patient is to become. The object of being the new self for two weeks is not to find oneself but is primarily to see that the innermost personality is something one can create as one goes along rather than dictated from inside or imposed from without.

THE INTERPERSONAL APPROACH

Interpersonal psychotherapy is brief and active. Like the cognitive therapies, it de-emphasizes the transference—not even investigating unconscious distortions of the interpersonal field. Unique among the short-term therapies, interpersonal psychotherapy focuses not on mental content but on the process of the patient's interaction with others. In interpersonal psychotherapy, behavior and communications are taken at face value. Consequently, psychologically-minded therapists find it mechanical and dull. The strength of the method is that it poses little risk of iatrogenic harm, even to the decompensating patient, even in the hands of the inexperienced therapist.

Both the work of Klerman (1984) and Strupp and their colleagues (1984), along with Beck's cognitive model, are increasingly important in research and politics as the U.S. searches for cheaper psychotherapy. (And to provide the historical perspective, transactional analysis was also influential in its day and was popular to a degree almost unimaginable several decades later.)

Klerman and colleagues' interpersonal therapy, IPT, acknowledges its debt to other therapies in its stance and technique but claims distinction at the level of "strategies," meaning an orderly series of steps in evaluation and treatment. For patients whose depression is related to *grief*, they first review depressive symptoms, relate them to the death of the significant other, reconstruct the lost relationship, construct a narrative of the relationship, explore negative and positive feelings, and consider the patient's options for becoming involved with others.

For patients with *interpersonal disputes* causing depression, they conduct a symptom review, relate symptom onset to the dispute, take a history of the relationship, dissect out role expectations, and focus on correcting nonreciprocal expectations. For patients with *role transitions,* they review the symptoms, relate symptoms to life change, review positive and negative aspects of new and old roles, review losses, ventilate feelings, and find new role options. And, finally, with patients with *interpersonal deficits* leading to depression, they review symptoms and relate them to social isolation or unfulfillment; review past relationships, exploring repetitive patterns; and (unlike the behavioral therapies) discuss the patient's conscious positive and negative feelings about the therapist and use them to explore the maladaptive patterns elicited earlier.

While the claim of a distinctive approach at the level of strategies appears unsupportable (and "strategies" is not even indexed), they are strongly faithful to *method* (*à la* the St. Louis School of Psychiatry, the RDC and DSM-III and heirs); this fidelity provides a remarkably clear algorithm for decisions at every stage of evolution of the therapy. Thus, interpersonal therapy should "do no harm" and is so straightforward that it appears within the technical reach of the intelligent lay person, making it ideal for psychotherapy outcome research and low-cost managed health care.

As one example of method, here is the algorithm for communication analysis: Therapists should identify (1) ambiguous or nonverbal communication; (2) incorrect assumptions that the other has indeed communicated; (3) incorrect assumptions that one has understood; (4) unnecessarily indirect verbal communication; and (5) inappropriate silence — closing off communication. If the therapist identifies one or more of these, this list is run through another list of therapeutic investigations of the therapeutic relationship itself to give the patient concrete examples. Then decision-analysis, the major action-oriented technique of IPT, is used to help the patient diagnose and treat depressing interpersonal problems by finding other options.

Strupp and colleagues (Schacht et al., 1984) also specifically claim the interpersonal model. In their method, the patient's focus helps the therapist to generate, recognize, and organize therapeutic data. The "focus" is commonly stated in terms of a cardinal symptom, a specific intrapsychic conflict or impasse, a maladaptive picture of the self, or a persistent interpersonal dilemma. This "focus" is not an end but an "heuristic guide to inquiry" that helps the therapist organize the therapeutic experience. It is supposed to model a central pattern of interpersonal role behavior in which the patient unconsciously casts him- or herself. (By "unconscious" they appear to mean Freud's "preconscious" or Beck's concept of "automatic thoughts.") The arena for the investigation is interpersonal, the method for such investigations is narrative: "the telling of a story to oneself and others. Hence, the focus is organized in the form of a schematic story outline" combining to provide a structure for "narrating the central interpersonal stories of a patient's life." (p. 68)

This narrative or story contains four structural elements that are the keystone of the therapy: (1) acts of self; (2) expectations of others' reactions; (3) acts of others toward the self; and (4) acts of self toward the self. While learning this narrative, the therapist is supposed at the same time to bear in mind it is a map, not the territory itself. Nonetheless, human actions, embedded in interpersonal transactions originating in cyclic psychodynamic patterns, cause recurrent maladaptation and pain — and these features summarize the basis of the Strupp method.

Transactional analysis (Berne et al., 1973), or TA, Eric Berne's brainchild, uses the same structure as that of IPT and Strupp and colleagues. There is a systematic analysis of communication and interpersonal interaction working from presenting complaint back to previous patterns and forward to interaction with the therapist. But its characteristic construct is that interpersonal transactions come from three "ego states" — child, parent, and adult — that correspond to id, ego, and superego. Alternation among ego states is a function of the permeability of the boundaries of each. Too much or too little permeability leads to pathology: Excluding the "child" prohibits play and creativity from other states; conversely, extreme permeability keeps the patient from staying in the "adult" mode long enough to complete an undistorted interpersonal transaction.

Two principal forms of interaction give rise to interpersonal distortions. In the crossed transaction, one individual speaks from the adult state but the other actor speaks from, say, his or her own parent to the other's child. In the complementary communication the problem involves two parallel communications — one overt, one covert for a hidden agenda. This transaction is a "game," whose "payoff" — usually gratification of the "child's" goal — is its aim.

Historically, TA evolved as group treatment but can be adapted by bringing the patient's interpersonal set into the therapy room and examining this "group." The therapist who recognizes, for instance, that a game is going on in therapy can expose the game, go along with the game, ignore some games and not others, or propose alternative games.

THE ECLECTICS

The "eclectic" brief therapies are characterized by integration of other theories and techniques. Three important exemplars are considered here. Horowitz and colleagues (1984) combine theories of the stress response syndrome with the psychology of adaptation and coping in various personality types to yield an interpersonal and cognitive mixture that takes into account the dynamic unconscious as well. Budman and Gurman (1988) explore three dimensions of mental life — the interpersonal, the developmental, and the existential — to assemble a methodology that leaves no other school of short-term therapy unexploited, with the stated exception of James Mann's. And Leibovich (1981, 1984) sails into uncharted waters, by applying reality-based, supportive techniques to his brief therapy constituency, healthier borderline patients.

Horowitz and colleagues owe a debt to the literature on stress, coping, and adaptation that stretches through the behavioral, phenomenological, and ego psychology realms. The point of departure is the normal stress response: The individual perceives the event, a loss or death. The mind then reacts with *outcry* ("No, no!") then denial ("It's not true!") and these two states, denial and outcry, alternate so that the subjective experience is of unwanted intrusion of the image of the lost. Over time "grief work" proceeds so that "working through" goes to completion. The pathological side of this normal response to stress is that in the stage of perception of the event, the individual is overwhelmed. In the outcry stage there is panic, confusion, or exhaustion. In the denial stage there is maladaptive avoidance or withdrawal by suicide, drug and alcohol abuse, or counterphobic frenzy. In the more complex stage of intrusion the individual experiences alternation of flooded states of sadness and fear, rage and guilt, which alternate with numbness. If working through is blocked, there ensue hibernative or frozen states, constriction, or psychosomatic responses. If completion is not reached there is an inability to work or to love.

Horowitz's therapy basically proceeds along the older models of Grinker and Spiegel (1944) or Erich Lindemann (1944) but with modern ego psychology woven in. The therapist identifies the focus — usually a traumatic event or a loss — and tries to determine whether the patient is in denial or the in intrusion phase of maladaptation. In the denial phase perception and attention are marred by a dazed state and selective inattention. There is partial amnesia or emotional isolation. Ideational processing is crippled by disavowal of meanings. There is loss of a realistic sense of connection with the world. There is emotional numbness. In the type of maladaptation marked by the patient's being stuck in the intrusion phase of the trauma response, perception and attention are marked by hypervigilance, overactive consciousness, and inability to concentrate. Emotional attacks or pangs of anxiety, depression, rage, or guilt intrude. Psychosomatic symptoms are common here as the sequelae of the chronic flight or fight response.

Twelve sessions are used to focus on the recent stress event and work it through. In the early sessions the initial positive feelings for the therapist develop as the patient tells the story of the event and the preliminary focus on the loss is discussed. There ensues a sense of decreased pressure as trust is established. The traumatic event is related to the life of the patient as a psychiatric history is taken. In the middle phase of therapy the patient tests the therapist and the therapist elicits associations to this stage of the relationship. There is a realignment of focus with interpretations of resistances. The patient is asked to understand why these resistances are currently reasonable based on past relationships. The therapeutic alliance deepens as this phase continues and the patient works on what has been avoided. There is further interpretation of defenses and warded off contents and linkage of these contents to the stress event. In the late middle phases, transference reactions are interpreted as they occur. There is continued working through of central conflicts that emerge as termination relates them to the life of the patient. In termination there is acknowledgment of problems as well as real gains and an adumbration of future work, for instance, anniversary mourning.

A major feature of Horowitz's work is defensive styles. The "hysterical" personality is unable to focus on detail and tends to be overwhelmed by the global; the "compulsive" style is the converse, with the patient too consumed by details to experience affect. The therapist acts in either event to supplement the missing component and to damp out the component flooding the patient. In the borderline patient the well-known tendency to split is damped out by the therapist anticipating that with shame and rage the patient's world will distort into its good and bad polarities. For the patient with a narcissistic personality style the tendency to exaggerate or minimize personal actions is gently but firmly confronted. The schizoid patient is allowed interpersonal space. One of the most attractive features of Horowitz's eclectic style is that it is not competing with other schools of short-term psychotherapy but can be integrated or added in parallel with other styles.

The work of Budman and Gurman rests on the "IDE focus" — interpersonal, developmental, and existential. None of these ideas is novel, but the way they are combined systematically is nicely realized with reference to eliciting the precipitating event, its relation to the focus, the relation to development, and working through with a balance of techniques. The major focus in the IDE perspective includes (1) losses; (2) developmental dysynchronies; (3) interpersonal conflicts; (4) symptomatic presentations; and (5) personality disorders.

In the IDE method, Budman and Gurman pursue a systematic approach that begins with the individual's reason for seeking therapy at *this* time. The patient's age, date of birth, and any appropriate developmental stage-related events or anniversaries are brought in. Major changes in the patient's social support are reviewed. Especially important in the Budman–Gurman system is substance abuse and its contribution to the presentation at this time.

A major feature in the Budman–Gurman system here is the belief that maximal benefit from therapy occurs early. Given that the optimal time for change is early in treatment, the law of diminishing returns sets in as therapy becomes prolonged. Budman and Gurman are not snobbish about the capacity of any one course of treatment to cure the patient completely and they welcome back the patient who is in crisis in any successive developmental stage. A particular value of this treatment is its nonjudgmental approach, both in stopping a particular phase of therapy and its willingness to resume treatment at a later point. One can view this approach in terms of clusters of therapies ranged along important nodal points in the individual's development.

The short-term psychotherapy of Leibovich for borderline personality disorders has much in common with several other short-term therapies. The main difference is that he accepts the diagnosed borderline patient. Although he does seem to exclude the schizotypal, acting-out, and sickest types of "core" borderline patients, he does accept the borderlines who are on the border with the neuroses, the anaclitic type (and by implication the as-if borderlines). Leibovich's goal is to find borderline patients who have a greater than average potential for growth.

Leibovich's method is the longest of the short-term psychotherapies, usually running a year. Its focus is unique: Leibovich asks the patient to consider a single recurrent (borderline personality) behavioral trait such as low frustration tolerance, tendency to explode in rages, or tendency to throw oneself into overvaluing and devaluing relationships—the standard DSM-III list—and choose only one of these as a focus. The patient will complain that the problem is too large to approach in short-term therapy and Leibovich will say, "Well, let's try to do what we can with the time available."

The patient should show sufficient reality testing, good motivation, and a degree of intrapsychic and emotional separateness or personality distinctiveness (e.g., lack of tendency to fuse suddenly), although some connection with the therapist must be present. The patient should not be in a major depression and must have a capacity to do some verbalization. There should also be some stable and intact ego functions that assisted the patient at least one point during previous developmental stages. Finally, the patient must be able to recognize the existence of a focal troublesome issue or a central problematic pattern around which many difficulties revolve, and be able to harbor at least some realistic expectations. Exclusion criteria for Leibovich are individuals who are in crisis and dyscontrol; fixed psychotic projection and denial; schizoid defenses; absence of any current relationships; acute psychotic episodes; inability to accept the appropriate boundaries of the therapeutic setting (e.g., lack of any observing ego); and other more severe borderline traits.

The therapist's activity in the short-term therapy of the borderline patient is to focus and to remain as a real person without overly empathizing or fusing, and particularly to ride herd on the patient's tendency to become diffuse. The therapist here is more like a coach than in some other therapies, acting as a fiduciary at times when the patient's ego functions and defenses fail during treatment.

THE TIMELESS GENIUS OF DONALD WINNICOTT

The idea of being a short-term therapist probably would have made Winnicott laugh. He no doubt would have described himself as providing therapy of whatever duration the *patient* needed. Even a cursory understanding of the "holding environment" or the "maturational process" shows Winnicott's commitment to an equitable framework for life and psychotherapy and an implicit hostility to unfair infringements on the right to time of the child—the child of any age. So given his presumed preference for long-term therapy, how does his work shed its remarkable light on short-term therapy?

The themes of brevity, focus, therapist activity, and patient selection differentiate the various short-term therapies, and there is no reason to abandon them in a discussion of Winnicott. In terms of brevity, he could apparently remove important blocks to development in only one session. *Therapeutic Consultations in Child Psychiatry* (1971) provides examples where one, two, or three sessions are sufficient to help the individual push through a block and resume normal development. He was willing to analyze "the Piggle" in 14 sessions. (He tended to call a treatment "analysis" if it proceeded at deeper levels of the psyche and to consider the length and frequency of therapy less important.) But he agreed to intermittent therapy of the Piggle *only if* it were "on demand," only if the child could request the next session when needed. He explicitly stated that therapy that cannot be daily analysis will become superficial if it is not "on demand."

Winnicott's focus involved a broad-ranging interest in impediments to normal development, especially as pathological manifestations of aggression. His cases suggest he worked from the first communication that disclosed the nature of the patient's developmental block. When in doubt, he tended to inform the patient or go back to the patient's original communication about the focal developmental block.

In terms of therapist activity, he always kept firm the holding environment. Not that he catered to the patient or was unnecessarily gratifying; he was ever aware of the demands of the real world in terms of time and money. On the other hand, he tried not to remove from the patient anything that had originally been taken away. His activity was based on first framing the treatment and then interpreting. By the time the Piggle wandered over to him in the consulting room, he had "already made friends with" the toys; he had established the frame and entered the work and awaited her there. (And he was not just being cute; he *meant* he had made friends with the toys.) His capacity to provide a secure frame or holding environment and, alternatively, to plunge without further ado into the therapeutic work is one of Winnicott's most characteristic features. Of the therapists considered here, James Mann seems closest to using this balance of frame first, then — work.

In the realm of patient selectivity Winnicott also resembled Mann. Winnicott was open to patients who were at any level of pathology and accepted their need to regress in order to remove developmental blocks. On the other hand, both Winnicott and Mann protected the patient's welfare. Winnicott unsentimentally and without apology stated some patients are too sick and too damaged to grow, and for these, he worked toward containment and management.

It is in the area of brevity that Mann and Winnicott appear most at odds. Mann with his insistence on exactly 12 sessions; Winnicott with his insistence on either daily or several times weekly analysis or therapy on demand? How to explain this paradox: Both Mann and Winnicott are realists — time is running out, reality in the end will prevail — yet they are optimistic about the power of human loving to defeat developmental stagnation. Perhaps Mann's 12 sessions and Winnicott's "on-demand" is the therapeutic lifetime — they actually take place in the same world, the child's world, by the child's clock. The time-world of 12 sessions of Mann may be viewed in one dimension, say "from above," and Winnicott's on-demand is "cross-sectional," perhaps from the vantage point of those moments in life or therapy when the clock stops, when we are dissociated from clock time — for good or ill — for survival and for growth. Perhaps the "on-demand" schedule reproduces the stopped clock of mother love and the strict 12 sessions of Mann reproduces its sheltering but realistic framework. There are moments in the *Piggle* that support this notion, when the little girl and the dying old man discuss his death and her survival. Although it is not explicit, for Winnicott, the termination of life clearly gives love its ultimate force.

A final stylistic marker of Winnicott's therapy, one even more mysterious, is his empathy concerning communication — its nature, level, and its timing. In almost every recorded case, there is the special moment when he says, "And then I knew I must say. . . ." or "At this point I knew I must call her Gabrielle. . . ." or the like, an uncanny moment of pure intuition, one representing the summit of the therapist's art.

PATIENT SELECTION

Certain patients should be excluded from short-term treatment — patients with severe, chronic Axis I disorders, badly acting-out personality disorders, patients specifically rejecting brief treatment, patients for whom it is impossible to find a focus or for whom there are multiple, diffuse foci. The list is long (Burke et al., 1979).

And there are patients who will do well in almost any form of short-term treatment, for instance, the highly-functioning graduate student who cannot complete a dissertation. But between these ranges fall a majority of patients who present to the outpatient clinic or private practice. How does one decide which patient will do well in which therapy? And what of teaching, how can trainees be exposed to several types of short-term therapy and learn which best suit the individual therapist–patient pair before settling into the fairly narrow range experienced clinicians tend to get into.

Table 3.1 summarizes patient selection criteria in the last column, and it is possible to run down the list and narrow the range to three or four therapies likely to be best. This list can be read by working leftward along the rows summarizing each therapy. Under therapist activity and focus are criteria that may help narrow the list of most-likely-to-succeed short-term therapies even further. And the duration of treatment of various therapies may be useful from the standpoint of a patient's financial means or insurance coverage.

Another way of depicting the differential diagnosis and triage of patients to various therapies is shown in Figure 3.3. Down the left streams Axis I flowing into the pharmacologic, behavioral, group, family, and long-term therapies, and many Axis II patients as well (not shown) — although the flow of passive–dependent and high-functioning personality disorders, for instance, can be partly diverted into a number of types of short-term therapy (for instance, Mann's, Davanloo's).

The relation of focus to the type of therapy is depicted as an axis about which either the less-focused therapies or the more crisis-oriented therapies are rotated clockwise and the more internally located and discretely focused are rotated counterclockwise, Sifneos's anxiety-provoking treatment is on the extreme right, for the optimal psychoanalysand.

And what of patients wanting therapy who have no clear (or relevant) Axis I or Axis II diagnosis, for example, the "V Codes," or conditions not attributable to a mental disorder but which nonetheless constitute a focus of treatment? And what of their relation to psychological health versus "psychological-mindedness"? The capacity for insight and psychological health are related but not exactly parallel. The lower right corner of the figure is an attempt to represent this relation. The therapies are arrayed in a continuum of psychological health from left to right — Winnicott, for instance, spanning the widest range, IPT the narrowest (and one of the left most, or least "healthy"). And from bottom to top they are arrayed by the patient's capacity for insight. For instance, a fairly healthy patient with little interest in looking inward would be suitable for cognitive therapy or the method of Horowitz and colleagues. Less healthy patients, but ones with more insight (or at least more introspective bent) would be considered for Davanloo's, Mann's, or Winnicott's methods. (This figure is best considered as an abstraction to bounce ideas off, not a photograph of life.)

TEACHING SHORT-TERM THERAPY

At present, each geographic, economic, or political center of short-term treatment is dominated by the method of the reigning academic, researcher, or manager. Montreal, for instance, specializes in the Davanloo method, the Harvard Community Health Plan (an Health Maintenance Organization or H.M.O.), the method of Budman and Gurman. Trainees may have little exposure to the range of various available methods.

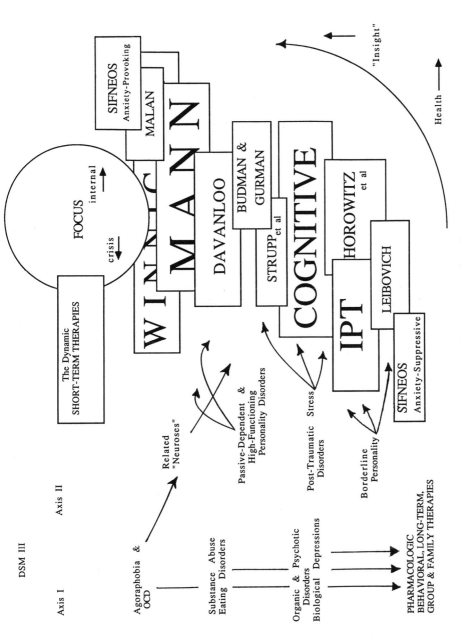

FIGURE 3.3. The short-term therapies.

57

Another problem involves didactic teaching and supervision—how does one *show* short-term methods when the trainee is still in the stage of techniques encountered around long-term therapy? And what of the issue of the great training aid offered by audio and video taping measured against patient's sense of privacy, without which some methods are seriously compromised, for instance, Winnicott's. (And, is it not true that when therapists choose treatment for themselves or for their families, they *never* elect a setting that has observers?)

A possible solution, and only a partial solution, is didactic teaching organized around the format of Table 3.1 and Figure 3.3, in combination with *blind role plays*. Blind role plays are used at Harvard to teach first-year medical students in the "New Pathways" curriculum how to interview respectfully and skillfully patients who are difficult. In brief, after a reading assignment is completed, a student in seminar receives a written paragraph describing the patient to be role-played, the disease, the problem, and some instructions on how to enact these. Another student is given a description of the doctor, the doctor's goals, prejudices, fears, and so on. After a brief role play, the instructor, who is not blind to any component of the play, guides the class over what was observed and what conclusions might be drawn. The results are usually good—sometimes very good.

To imagine teaching short-term therapy this way, picture a blind role play between a not insightful "patient" who wants and needs the 12-session crisis-oriented method of Horowitz but is blindly confronted with a "therapist" bent on the Malan approach. (Of course, all role plays need not be disjunctive.) Imaginative use of the table and figure should enable one to design a curriculum that begins to capture the variety of patient presentations in the net of the several short-term dynamic therapies.

REFERENCES

Alexander, F. (1971). The principle of flexibility. In H.H. Barton (Ed.), *Brief therapies* (pp. 28–41). New York: Behavioral Publications.

Balint, M., Ornstein, P.H., & Balint, E. (1972). *Focal psychotherapy*. Philadelphia: J.B. Lippincott.

Beck, A.T., & Greenberg, R.L. (1979). Brief cognitive therapies. *Psychiatric Clinics of North America, 2*, 23–37.

Berne, E., Steiner, C.M., & Dusay, J.M. (1973). Transactional analysis. In R-RM Jurjevich (Ed.), *Direct psychotherapy* (pp. 370–393).

Budman, S.H., & Gurman, A.S. (1988). *Theory and practice of brief therapy*. New York: Guilford Press.

Burke, Jr., J.D., White, H.S., & Havens, L.L. (1979). Which short-term therapy? Matching patient and method. *Archives of General Psychiatry, 36,* 177–186.

Davanloo, H. (1980). *Short-term dynamic psychotherapy.* New York: Jason Aronson.

Davanloo, H. (1979). Techniques of short-term dynamic psychotherapy. *Psychiatric Clinics of North America, 2,* 11–22.

Ferenczi, S., & Rank, O. (1925). The development of psychoanalysis (C. Newton, Trans.). New York: Nervous & Mental Disease Publishing.

Flegenheimer, W.V. (1982). *Techniques of brief psychotherapy.* New York: Jason Aronson.

Freud, S. (1955). Studies on hysteria. In J. Strachey (Ed. and Trans.), *The standard edition of the complete psychological works of Sigmund Freud* (Vol. 2, pp. 125–134). (Original work published 1893–95)

Grinker, R.R., & Spiegel, J.P. (1944). Brief psychotherapy in war neuroses. *Psychosomatic Medicine, 6,* 123–131.

Horowitz, M., Marmar, C., Krupnick, J., Wilner, N., Kaltreider, N., & Wallerstein, R. (1984). *Personality styles and brief psychotherapy.* New York: Basic Books.

Kelly, G.A. (1973). Fixed role therapy. In R-RM Jurjevich (Ed.), *Direct psychotherapy* (pp. 394–422). Coral Gables, FL: University of Miami Press.

Klerman, G.L., Weissman, M.M., Rounsaville, B.J., & Chevron, E.S. (1984). *Interpersonal therapy of depression.* New York: Basic Books.

Leibovich, M.A. (1981). Short-term psychotherapy for the borderline personality disorder. *Psychotherapy and Psychosomatics, 35,* 257–264.

Leibovich, M.A. (1983). Why short-term psychotherapy for borderlines? *Psychotherapy and Psychosomatics, 39,* 1–9.

Lindemann, E. (1944). Symptomatology and management of acute grief. *American Journal of Psychiatry, 101,* 141–148.

Malan, D.M. (1976). *The frontier of brief psychotherapy.* New York: Plenum.

Mann, J. (1973). *Time-limited psychotherapy.* Cambridge, MA: Harvard University Press.

Schacht, T.E., Binder, J.L., & Strupp, H.H. (1984). The dynamic focus. In H.H. Strupp & J.L. Binder (Eds.), *Psychotherapy in a new key* (pp. 65–109). New York: Basic Books.

Schafer, R. (1973). Termination of brief psychoanalytic psychotherapy. *International Journal of Psychoanalytic Psychotherapy, 2,* 135–148.

Sifneos, P.E. (1971). Two different kinds of psychotherapy of short duration. In H.H. Barton (Ed.), *Brief therapies* (pp. 82–90). New York: Behavioral Publications.

Sifneos, P.E. (1972). *Short-term psychotherapy and emotional crisis.* Cambridge, MA: Harvard University Press.

Winnicott, D.W. (1977). *The Piggle: An account of the psychoanalytic treatment of a little girl.* Madison, CT: International Universities Press.

Winnicott, D.W. (1971). *Therapeutic consultations in child psychiatry.* New York: Basic Books.

F·O·U·R

※

Cognitive Therapy: Long-Term Outlook for a Short-Term Psychotherapy

STEPHEN P. McDERMOTT

FRED D. WRIGHT

Over the past two decades, therapists have become increasingly interested in the cognitive therapies—brief psychotherapies that focus more on an individual's conscious thoughts than on his unconscious processes as the primary mechanism for understanding the individual's world and as the primary area for intervention. Of the many cognitive (and closely related "behavioral–cognitive") therapies, Beck's cognitive therapy is perhaps the best known. Beginning with his first book, *Cognitive Therapy and the Emotional Disorders* (1976), Beck and his associates have published treatment manuals including *Cognitive Therapy of Depression* (Beck, Rush, Shaw, & Emery, 1979), *Anxiety Disorders and Phobias* (Beck & Emery, with Greenberg, 1985), *Love Is Never Enough* (couples therapy) (Beck, 1988), and *Cognitive Therapy of Personality Disorders* (Beck, Freeman, & Associates, 1990). Their book *Cognitive Therapy of Depression* has served as the cognitive therapy protocol for over 10 outcome studies examining the effectiveness of cognitive therapy in the treatment of depression, both alone and with antidepressants (Hollon & Najavits, 1988). The studies (taken as a group) generally show that cognitive therapy is as effective as antidepressants in the short-term, with some studies showing increased effectiveness when cognitive therapy and antidepressants are combined. Cognitive therapy, however, seems to provide a greater long-term protection against relapse than antidepressants.

The success of these standardized outcome studies of depression has led to an increasing awareness that cognitive therapy can treat other psychiatric disorders. Outcome studies are currently underway on the cognitive therapy of anxiety disorders (including panic disorder). Treatment manuals are also being developed for the cognitive therapy of substance abuse and personality disorders.

The same economic factors that have been spurring clinicians to learn short-term adaptations of the long-term psychotherapies are having what may first appear to be a paradoxical effect — the promotion of *longer* forms of cognitive therapy. As competition increases among various mental health and medical providers for the mental-health dollars, cognitive therapists have wanted to adapt the theory and techniques originally developed for depression to more diverse disorders and ultimately more disturbed patients. They are finding that in treating these more complex disorders additional strategies are needed.

This chapter will examine some of the forces that are pushing this short-term psychotherapy into adopting longer treatment strategies. It will also show how Beck's cognitive therapy is moving beyond its behavioral roots toward its more psychodynamic perspective as cognitive therapists grapple with the problem of dealing with the personality disorder patient. But first, to understand the interaction between Beck's cognitive therapy and socioeconomic forces, the theoretical underpinnings of Beck's cognitive therapy need elaboration.

COGNITIVE THERAPY:
HISTORICAL BACKGROUND

Aaron Beck was originally trained as a classical psychoanalyst with a strong research background. It was during his research on the dreams of depressed patients that he began to question some basic psychoanalytic principals. He noticed that the main themes of these dreams seemed to be related less to "retroflected hostility" or the "need to suffer" than to the belief that the individual was somehow defective in dealing with an excessively harsh world. He saw these themes recurring in transcripts of therapy sessions, and later discovered that patients in therapy benefited most from corrections of their distorted beliefs. This led him to reformulate his thinking on the psychological basis of depression.

Beck's cognitive therapy draws upon a diverse theoretical background, including cognitive psychology, information processing theory, social psychology, behavioral therapy, and psychodynamic psychotherapy (Beck & Rush, 1989). Beck traces the earliest philosophical assumptions underlying the cognitive position to philosophers such as Emmanuel Kant, and even to some of the Greek Stoic philosophers. He traces contemporary elaborations of these early philosophical assumptions in the writings of Alfred Adler, Otto Rank, and Karen Horney. From Freud, Beck borrowed the concept of preconscious cognition and much of the structural theory and depth psychology relating to the concept of hierarchical structuring of automatic thoughts, underlying assumptions, and basic beliefs (which will be discussed further). As Beck began to elaborate further his theoretical model, he was influenced by the social psychologists and several of the early cognitive theorists. He incorporated many behavioral techniques into his evolving therapy, as he began to apply his method to depressed patients. This use of behavioral techniques for eliciting and testing distorted thoughts and beliefs led some to refer to his therapy as a "cognitive–behavioral therapy." But what distinguishes Beck's therapy from other more behaviorally-based psychotherapies is its strong reliance on discovering the common threads in the patient's emotional reactions, behaviors, and memories — underlying assumptions and basic beliefs.

This emphasis on the underlying belief systems becomes increasingly important when Beck's cognitive therapy is applied to a number of situations — to treating the personality disorders, to integrating cognitive and psychodynamic psychotherapies, such as on inpatients units that receive patients from psychodynamic outpatient treaters, and to teaching therapists who have been primarily psychodynamically based.

COGNITIVE THERAPY: AN OVERVIEW

Cognitive therapy is an active, short-term, highly structured psychotherapy. The rationale behind cognitive therapy is that affect and behavior are largely determined by the way the patient structures his or her world, and we can see the way in which patients structure their world by examining their cognitions. *The cognitive therapist does not say that cognitions "cause" or even "control" affect and behavior, but rather that affect, behavior, and cognition are intimately tied together and influence each other* (see Figure 4.1). It is by understanding, conceptualizing, and intervening primarily in the cognitive realm that the cognitive therapist helps the patient to understand and control the affective and behavioral aspects of his experience, which in turn will influence his cognitive realm.

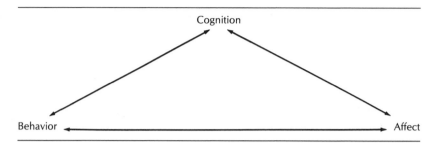

FIGURE 4.1. The interrelationships among cognition, behavior, and affect in Beck's cognitive therapy.

Cognitions are verbal or pictorial events in the stream of consciousness. They can be self-statements, such as "If this doesn't work out, I'll be ruined," "I can't believe I did that," or they can be images, such as seeing oneself alone, destitute, and dressed in rags on a darkened and foreboding street corner. Dreams, daydreams, or other forms of fantasy are cognitions, and can be used in a cognitive therapy just as in other types of therapy (Freeman, 1981).

The cognitive therapist distinguishes between two types of cognitions. The first, under the active control of the patient, is "deliberate thinking." This type would occur when an individual gives a talk before a group. In a controlled manner, the speaker considers what he is saying in front of the audience, what he will say in the immediate future, and the general direction of the talk. While he is deliberately thinking about his speech and its delivery, at the same time, he may also notice other thoughts in the back of his mind such as "They seem angry," "I wonder if they agree with me," "The guy in the third row is paying attention — he must like me," and "Someone's asleep, I must be boring." This second form of thinking, the thoughts in the back of his mind, are called "automatic thinking," a different type of cognition. It consists of more vague, often ill-formed thoughts that usually relate to the individual's assessment of his current situation. These thoughts are often expressed in shorthand (at times even just one word). Although on later reflection they may seem irrational, they always seem at least plausible. They may be readily apparent to the individual or may flit about the periphery of his consciousness. They are not, however, considered to be "unconscious" because they are always accessible to the individual who can learn to recognize them, although sometimes only after some training (Beck et al., 1979).

Essentially, the therapeutic technique is to identify, reality test, and correct distorted perceptions one has about the problems in one's life, and then to solve the now more realistic, better defined problem.

At the same time, by examining the distorted automatic thoughts, the therapist and patient together can understand some of the underlying assumptions and dysfunctional beliefs that give rise to the distortion. They can then examine the effects of these beliefs on the patient's life, while generating alternative beliefs, and together testing out which sets of beliefs are more adaptive for the individual's future.

Cognitive therapy is not merely a collection of techniques. It is an integrated form of psychotherapy in which the theoretical model guides both the assessment of the patient and the use of the individual techniques. It differs from some other forms of psychotherapy in that this model is explicitly taught to patients as a "new way of viewing their world" — in essence, it teaches them to become their own therapists. It is only when the patients learn this model that they can learn to incorporate various ways of testing distorted perceptions and beliefs once the therapy is over. This is what produces long-term change in the individual, and helps prevent relapse in the future.

To understand how cognitive therapy works, the cognitive therapy of depression will be examined in greater detail below. Following this will be a discussion of how this model has been modified to treat other psychiatric disorders.

THE COGNITIVE MODEL OF DEPRESSION

The cognitive therapist uses three concepts to explain the psychological substrate of depression: the cognitive triad, schemas, and cognitive errors (e.g., faulty information processing).

The cognitive triad is comprised of three major cognitive patterns that can be activated in the depressed patient. The first is a negative view of the present world. The patient sees the world as making exorbitant demands and/or erecting impossible hurdles that hinder his attempt to get what he believes will make him happy. The second is a negative view of the self. The individual tends to see himself as defective, inadequate, diseased, deprived, undesirable, or worthless. The individual believes he lacks the necessary attributes to go out and find in the world what he needs to be happy. The third is a negative view of the future — that the current hardships will last forever, and that he will always fail.

The cognitive therapist sees the other signs and symptoms of depression as secondary to this cognitive triad. For example, an individual who has a negative view of the world might perceive an enormous number of real or potential obstacles to achieving happiness.

His negative view of himself might lead him to believe that he cannot overcome these challenges because of his deficiencies. This results in a sense of personal helplessness and leads the individual to look for someone else on whom he can depend. He might begin to focus increasingly on his perceived deficits and shortcomings, increasing his sense of worthlessness, and interfering with his getting the needed support from interpersonal relationships. The individual will often grow more apathetic as he feels helpless, unable to tackle problems directly or with the assistance of others. His negative view of the future leads him to believe that none of this will change, and he withdraws into himself, compounding his initial discomfort, and resulting in further withdrawal, apathy, and a greater sense of helplessness.

Thus, the link is established among belief, affect, and behavior. This is an important but somewhat subtle distinction. The cognitive triad isn't made up of feelings of helplessness, hopelessness, and worthlessness, but of a negative set of beliefs about oneself, the world, and the future that can lead to these negative feelings.

The cognitive therapist uses the concept of *"schemas"* to explain how the occurrence of cognitive errors maintain these negative views. In any situation, there are a plethora of stimuli. An individual pays attention to some and disregards the rest. Think, for example, of the process you went through in deciding whether to read this book. You obviously could not assimilate all of its information in one glance, nor did you need to. Your initial goal was merely to seek out the information you needed to decide whether you wanted to invest in reading it. Hence, you sought out certain information such as the title, the book's editor, the list of contributing authors, and perhaps titles of individual chapters.

You ignored, for the time being, other information (including the body of the text) because this wasn't necessarily germane to your initial decision of whether to read the book. If you decided affirmatively, you would have other opportunities to absorb the text's meaning. Later on, information such as the title, editor, and contributing authors became less important (because you had already decided to read it), and you focused on the previously ignored text.

In any situation, an individual discriminates between relevant and superfluous information. While the process is constant, different patterns of rules dictate different situations. For example, in the situation already mentioned, you may have disregarded the "Library of Congress cataloguing and publication data" block at the very beginning of the book. But if you were the librarian responsible for cataloguing the book, this might have been the only important information you needed from the entire text.

These situation-specific patterns of information-processing rules are called schemas. The concept of the schema is important in the cognitive model because it explains the mechanism of distorted perceptions or "cognitive errors" and the resulting psychopathology.

Attention is the mechanism that produces and maintains the distortion(s). Schemas tell the individual what information in a given situation will be important and the individual then looks for this data. If it is found, he focuses his attention on it to the exclusion of other "less relevant" data. Because the depressed individual searches out data that corroborate his negative beliefs about these situations, he often overlooks the "irrelevant" positive material. This negative data then reinforces the negative belief, by serving as "evidence" that the belief is "accurate," just as the schema has also screened out any positive data that might contradict the belief. Thus, in depression, schemas are often "self-reinforcing."

The negative perceptions also determine the individual's affect — producing depressed mood and feelings of helplessness, hopelessness, and worthlessness — and influence his behavior, resulting in withdrawal, isolation, and difficulties with motivation. This negative affect and behavior in turn reinforce the idea that the negative belief is accurate. This becomes a self-perpetuating cycle. As these rules become generalized across more situations, the individual develops an overall negative view of himself, his world, and his future — the cognitive triad. The self-perpetuating negative beliefs serve as the "cognitive core" that maintains the depression.

Certain schemas are called "depressive schemas." These collections of rules give rise to depressed affect in certain situations. Because schemas are situation-specific, their information processing rules only become "activated" when the individual perceives that particular situations are relevant to that schema. Once the schema are activated, the individual begins to distort, by paying more attention to certain (negative) aspects of the situation than to other (more positive) ones. This means that depressed patients do not distort in every situation — only ones for which they have related "depressive schemas."

Unless they are psychotic, depressed patients generally do not distort situations by perceiving things that are not actually there. But by ignoring or discounting the positive aspects, the distortion can become quite extreme.

It is instructive to apply the cognitive model to an example here. Suppose an individual walks into a situation where he has a particular vulnerability, perhaps believing that he is socially awkward. One of his rules may be, "If I go into social situations, I am going to be hurt because I am going to embarrass myself." Consequently, he may be exquisitely sensitive to signs that suggest another person with whom he is interacting is rejecting him, or that his own behavior is socially awkward.

In a situation that is as ambiguous and complex as social interactions, one is likely to find some data that could confirm almost any particular belief. Our patient will look for every possible sign that he is awkward, that others are obviously picking up on this, and that they are automatically rejecting him. He will routinely ignore indications that other people are responding to him positively, that he is acting socially appropriate, or that others around him are even picking up on any possible "transgressions." His automatic thoughts might be, "See, I did it again. I said something I should not have. I did not say what I could have. I am a social klutz." His selective attention to the negative aspects of his interactions reinforces the schema that dictates rules such as "If I go into social interactions, I am going to act inappropriately and be rejected." The more repeatedly these distortions are activated, the more likely he is to look for, and even anticipate, future evidence of his schema. And the more his outlook is repeatedly distorted, the more sensitized it becomes, so that in the next interaction, he is even more likely to seek negative confirmation.

The "Causes" of Depression

As discussed above, the cognitive therapist sees the "cognitive core" of dysfunctional beliefs as the mechanism that maintains the depression. However, this does not suggest that the cognitive core is the initial etiology of the depression. The cognitive therapist does *not* believe that cognitions cause depression (Beck et al., 1979). Instead, the therapist believes that the interactions among cognitions, affect, and behavior can maintain a depression. By intervening at the level of cognitions, the therapist (and ultimately, the patient on his own), can alleviate a depression and control the likelihood that it will recur.

The cognitive therapist treats the phenomenon of depression and the cognitive structures that maintain it, and not necessarily the initial etiology. This is important to understand because the "cause" of any particular depression may not be known. Generally, most cognitive therapists believe that the causes of depression are multifactorial, including early life experiences, biochemical abnormalities, other genetic difficulties, and current life stressors. Once a depression is started, it can be maintained by this "cognitive core" of activated dysfunctional beliefs, cognitive errors, and the resulting depression triad.

These beliefs can be learned at any time, but often the more important ones are learned fairly early in life. One question that is frequently asked is whether the initial situations in which the beliefs were learned need to be ascertained before long-term change can be accomplished. The answer depends on whether one is dealing with a primarily Axis I or primarily Axis II pathology, which will be discussed in greater detail below.

THE THERAPEUTIC RELATIONSHIP

In contrast to other psychotherapies, cognitive therapy is highly collaborative. The patient and therapist work together to define the goals of the therapy, to prioritize these goals, and ultimately, when sufficient progress has been made, to terminate the treatment. Beck refers to this as a process of "collaborative empiricism." It is "a guided discovery" in which the therapist uses his or her expertise to help the patient to discover beliefs that the patient may not even realize are there, and to show how these beliefs may be affecting the patient's life. They frame each thought and belief, not as a fact to be accepted or rejected, but as a hypothesis to be tested in a scientific way. Then, the patient and therapist together test out these hypotheses, generate alternative hypotheses, and test these out as well, to determine the beliefs most functional for the patient's life. Functional beliefs facilitate the achievement of our goals and enhance our ability to define and solve day-to-day problems clearly.

This collaboration accomplishes two important goals. First, it diminishes struggles around power and authority. If a patient has an inaccurate belief, the therapist does not "argue the patient out of the belief." Instead, he tests its accuracy and adaptivity for the patient. If the therapist has a hypothesis that a particular alternative belief may be more adaptive for the patient, the patient need not blindly accept this belief, but rather accepts it as another hypothesis that needs to be tested. They use data from the past or present, or even future possibilities. If further information is needed, they devise "experiments" to test the beliefs. The experiments are not "set up" to reach "the right conclusion," because this prevents the therapist from learning if his alternate hypotheses may indeed be less adaptive for the patient than he thought.

Second, this collaboration allows the therapist to discover that although a patient's belief may be truly accurate, an aspect to his belief system, such as how the belief is put into effect, may be causing much of the problem. For example, a man may believe he cannot be assertive with his colleagues at work because he will get fired. Examination of the evidence (e.g., others who were assertive did get fired) might validate his conclusion. The patient and therapist might then focus on whether he needs to stay at this job, instead of trying to teach him to be more assertive there.

If a patient resists testing his beliefs, the consequences of not testing (or just accepting) the beliefs are examined, while further data is gathered as to the advantages and disadvantages of retaining the belief. Thus, "resistance" is dealt with on a collaborative basis, by examining the beliefs behind it, instead of attempting to infer motivation. Although the collaboration avoids setting up conflicts over power and authority in the therapy, it does not preclude the examination of such issues, in the therapy or outside of it, should they occur.

This collaborative approach also provides another advantage. It facilitates the cognitive therapy's overriding goal to teach the patient how to "be his own therapist." Through therapy, the patient learns a new way to view his world. The cognitive model is taught to the patient, enabling him to continue the work outside of the therapy.

The model is best taught to patients by providing a rationale for each stage of therapy. Without the patient's understanding of the cognitive model, the cognitive therapy may appear to be merely a collection of techniques. The patient may then have difficulty deciding which "technique" to use for which type of problem, preventing him from adequately dealing with new problems as they arise once he has left therapy. A cognitive therapy is no more a collection of techniques than a psychodynamic therapy is merely dream analysis and interpreting slips of the tongue. As with any well-developed school of psychotherapy, it is the paradigm that determines which interventions are selected and at which time.

Another feature of cognitive therapy is the therapist and patient's selection of specific target problems. Many patients resist dealing with their problems because they see them as too overwhelming, too anxiety-provoking, too depressing, etc. This not only prevents the individual from solving his problems, but may also inhibit his even examining them adequately. As a result, the problem becomes ill-defined, vague, and not very well understood. Several small or similar problems may get lumped under one related heading. For example, "problems with organization," "problems with time scheduling," and "problems with anxiety" may be lumped under "I am lazy." Frequently these subheadings will get lumped into even larger categories such as "I am depressed," "I am anxious," or "I am incompetent" because the problems are so large, vague, and ill-defined that it is not immediately apparent to the individual how he should begin to solve them.

The cognitive therapist helps the patient to begin to "operationalize" his problems. That is, the vague, poorly defined issues are broken down into concrete, discrete subunits that are more easily tackled. These subunits are prioritized and then used by the therapist to teach the patient the cognitive model of problem solving. As the patient begins to go through the prioritized list of problems, he begins to feel more hopeful and less helpless about his ability to handle them. The cognitive therapy ends when the patient has learned how to switch to a problem-solving mode by himself, not when he has finished his "list of problems."

The structure and collaborative aspects of a cognitive therapy cannot be maintained without continual feedback to and from the patient and the therapist. The cognitive therapist asks the patient to express any negative reactions to the therapist, and needs to be sensitive to any negative covert reactions (both verbal and nonverbal). Such reactions are dealt with when they arise in the same manner as any other problem in a cognitive therapy — that is, the patient is asked for his automatic thoughts, which are then discussed and tested, as with any other cognitions. This may also include the therapist giving explanations as to any of his actions that may have been misinterpreted by the patient.

The therapist also gets feedback from the patient on how well he understands each step or intervention in the therapy. This is usually done by having the patient explain in his own words what has just happened in the therapy and why. The therapist may give feedback on what he understands the patient to be saying, and then ask for feedback from the patient about the accuracy of the therapist's understanding. In a related manner, "capsule summaries" about particular interventions as well as for each session are provided as further reinforcement and to check whether both understood what happened in the intervention or session. Initially, the therapist may provide these capsule summaries, but eventually the patient assumes the responsibility (Young & Beck, 1982).

The cognitive therapist must possess those qualities needed to maintain any psychotherapeutic alliance, including empathy, warmth, the ability to set limits, flexibility, appropriateness, etc. To quote Beck, Rush, Shaw, and Emery (1979):

> to the degree that the therapist is able to demonstrate these qualities, he is helping to develop a milieu in which the specific cognitive change techniques can be applied most efficiently.

> A word of caution is in order. Cognitive and behavioral techniques often *seem* deceptively simple. Consequently, the neophyte therapist

may become "gimmick-oriented" to the point of ignoring the human aspects of the therapist–patient interaction. He may relate to the patient as one computer to another rather than as one person to another. Some of the younger therapists who are most skilled in applying the specific techniques have been perceived by their patients as mechanical, manipulative, and more interested in the techniques than in the patient. It is important to keep in mind that the techniques detailed in this book are intended to be applied in a tactful, therapeutic, and human manner by a fallible person — the therapist. (p. 46)

THE THERAPEUTIC TECHNIQUES

The techniques in a cognitive therapy are often rather arbitrarily divided into two types: "cognitive" techniques and "behavioral" techniques. They will be discussed below.

Cognitive Techniques

Young and Beck break down the cognitive techniques into four major processes, including eliciting automatic thoughts, testing automatic thoughts, identifying maladaptive underlying assumptions, and finally, analyzing the validity of maladaptive assumptions (Young & Beck, 1982).

An important first step in a cognitive therapy is teaching the patient to identify and record his automatic thoughts. He is asked to keep daily records of his negative automatic thoughts, along with the emotions they trigger. The patient and therapist then explore rational responses to these thoughts in the therapy session — a technique that the patient learns to do outside the sessions, using the therapy for fine-tuning the process. Thus, the therapeutic work in a cognitive therapy quickly extends outside the therapy hour, as the patient takes on more responsibility for "becoming his own therapist."

Some patients identify automatic thoughts with the briefest of explanations. Other patients may have some difficulty and require further training. The cognitive therapist can use several techniques for helping the patient to identify and understand his automatic thoughts, in and out of sessions.

One powerful method is to look for shifts in mood during the therapy session. The therapist then asks the patient what is going through his mind (both thoughts and images) at that particular moment. This is an especially important technique, as it can demonstrate, at the time it happens, how the patient's automatic thoughts can affect or change his moods.

The cognitive therapist often uses imagery to help the patient elicit memories of automatic thoughts. The therapist helps the patient "reconstruct" an image of the situation that occurred (or may yet occur) by asking many open-ended questions about details of the situation and his feelings in it. By placing the patient back into the situation through the use of detailed images, the therapist can often help the patient to reexperience, and thus recall, the automatic thoughts that otherwise he may not have been able to remember.

Role playing can be used in a similar way. That is, the patient and the therapist can role play certain situations in which the patient may have been involved (or in which he may anticipate becoming involved), and examine the automatic thoughts that occur. This process can also be used to help a patient understand the perspective of another person in an interaction by having the therapist role play the part of the patient, while the patient role plays the part of the other person.

A patient may be able to recognize an automatic thought but need to "tease out" its many levels of significance before it can be further tested. One helpful technique is "inductive questioning"—the use of open-ended questions to hone in on the underlying meanings of the thought. (This differs from the more commonly used "deductive questioning" that "works backward" from a thought or event to determine its original meaning or motivation). Such questions might include: "Presuming for the moment this thought is accurate (which we will test out later), what about it bothers you? What about it is important—and what does that mean to you?"

For example, a patient reported he had become very sad when he went through a grocery store line, paid for his groceries, and left. By looking back at the situation through imagery techniques, he was able to remember having the thought, "He did not give me enough change," right before he suddenly felt sad. On the face of it, it may not be apparent as to exactly why such a thought would make the man feel so sad. Using the inductive questioning techniques described above, he and the therapist were able to ferret out the following levels of significance to this thought:

He did not give me enough change;
↓
If I tell him he was wrong, he might get angry;
↓
If he gets angry we might have a scene;
↓
If we have a scene, I might lose control and yell back at him;
↓

If I yell at him, all my friends and neighbors will see me lose
control, and no one will want to be my friend;
↓
No one will be able to help me with my problems;
↓
My problems will overwhelm me;
↓
I will lose my job and family;
↓
I will become "a street person."

The patient was able to recall walking out of the store, with an
image of himself as destitute and dressed in rags. It is through this
inductive questioning (also known as "the downward arrow technique")
that the patient and therapist are able to understand the *idiosyncratic*
meaning to the automatic thoughts.

Once the patient and the therapist have identified key automatic
thoughts, the therapist teaches the patient how to test their validity and
adaptiveness. As Young and Beck (1982) state, "The therapist demonstrates to the patient that the *perception* of reality is not the same as
reality itself." (p. 196) An important first step is for the therapist to help
the patient view the thought not as a "fact" but instead as a hypothesis
(until the thought can be tested later).

Several techniques can be used to determine the validity and
adaptiveness of the automatic thought. The patient and therapist look
for facts that either confirm or contradict the automatic thought. It is
important to note that one does not just collect evidence against the
automatic thought (as in "arguing the patient out of" his automatic
thoughts). One also examines the potentially distorted data that the
patient has "collected" that help maintain the automatic thoughts. The
patient and therapist then may look for alternative explanations for the
evidence they have obtained. For example, observe the following brief
interaction:

THERAPIST: Let us take a look at the last time you felt really down.

PATIENT: Well, yesterday, I was trying to put together a charcoal grill
and it just wasn't working out. I started getting increasingly
frustrated and angry, and remembered having the thought "I'm
stupid," and just feeling very down.

THERAPIST: Let us take a look at that automatic thought. What evidence
do you have that you are "stupid?"

PATIENT: Well, anyone with a 5th-grade education should be able to put together a charcoal grill, and I couldn't.

THERAPIST: Were you able to put the grill together?

PATIENT: Well, I did eventually, but it still took too much time.

THERAPIST: So you did have the ability to put the grill together. You just did not do it as quickly as you thought you should?

PATIENT: I guess so. But I kept thinking I wasn't going to be able to do it, and I still felt pretty dumb about taking so much time.

THERAPIST: So one piece of evidence for this thought, "I am stupid," is that you were unable to put the grill together as quickly as you thought you should. Are there any other possible reasons why someone might have a hard time putting together a grill?

PATIENT: Well, I suppose they might have a hard time if they weren't mechanically inclined.

THERAPIST: Are you mechanically inclined?

PATIENT: No.

THERAPIST: Okay. Are there any other reasons why someone might have a hard time putting together a grill?

PATIENT: I suppose if they started getting really angry and frustrated, it wouldn't help.

THERAPIST: So if someone gets angry and frustrated, it can get in the way of doing something like putting together a grill, especially if someone is not already mechanically inclined?

PATIENT: That's right. I've seen that happen before.

THERAPIST: What about if a person is feeling depressed?

PATIENT: Well, I suppose that would also slow him down. I know it slows me down in other things that I do.

THERAPIST: Were you feeling either angry, frustrated, or depressed while putting the grill together?

PATIENT: All three.

THERAPIST: All right, let us look at the other side of it. What evidence do you have that you are not stupid?

PATIENT: Well, I have a master's in business administration; I've done pretty well on my job.

THERAPIST: Anything else?

PATIENT: I always did well in school and I have friends who will ask me for advice when they need help.

THERAPIST: So, if we look at the evidence for and against the thought, "I am stupid," we see that you have done well in school, got a master's in business administration, and are doing well at work. You also have friends who ask for your advice. You were, however, having a difficult time putting together a charcoal grill as quickly as you thought you should when you were feeling angry, frustrated, and depressed. Which of these possible explanations do you think best explains why you were having trouble putting the grill together at that time?

PATIENT: Well, I suppose it's more because I was frustrated and angry and starting to become depressed about not putting it together fast enough.

THERAPIST: So what effect did it have on you to keep saying to yourself, "I am stupid," as you were trying to put the grill together?

PATIENT: I guess it was making me more angry, more frustrated, and more depressed, and making it harder for me to put it together, which made me feel even more stupid.

THERAPIST: And how accurate do you think it was?

PATIENT: Well, looking back on it now, it's not too accurate.

Notice the high percentage of the therapist's statements that are open-ended questions, again avoiding the posture of arguing with the patient. This example also illustrates another important technique for testing automatic thoughts. The patient and therapist together explore what *effects* the automatic thoughts have on the patient, in addition to examining their *accuracy*. Once again, it is important to explore both the positive and negative effects of the automatic thought (or its underlying beliefs) *as perceived by the patient*. For example, a patient may have an underlying assumption, "I need to do things perfectly," which might interfere with his ability to get things done on time. He may be able to see the negative effects that this assumption (and the automatic thoughts it gives rise to) has on his ability to get things done by a deadline. What may not be so apparent to him is the underlying belief, "Unless I do things perfectly, I'll be a failure." When seen from this perspective, thoughts such as, "I need to do this over and over again until I get it perfect" seem perfectly adaptive, accurate, and advantageous. So, until one addresses the validity and adaptiveness of the underlying belief that gives rise to the automatic thought, the advantages of these assumptions will continue to appear to outweigh the disadvantages, even if these advantages and disadvantages are not readily apparent.

Identifying Maladaptive Assumptions

Many of the techniques of cognitive therapy can help an individual control and alleviate the depression he is experiencing when he is in therapy. But the cognitive therapist believes that long-term change, prevention, and control of future depressions is obtained only by identifying the underlying assumptions and beliefs that give rise to the automatic thoughts. As Young and Beck (1982) state,

> In order to identify these maladaptive assumptions, the therapist can listen closely for themes that seem to cut across several different situations or problem areas. The therapist can then list several related automatic thoughts that the patient has already expressed on different occasions, and ask the patient to "abstract the general rule" that connects the automatic thoughts. If the patient cannot do this, the therapist can suggest a plausible assumption, list the thoughts that seem to follow from it, and then ask the patient whether the assumption "rings true." The therapist should be open to the possibility that the assumption does not fit that patient, and should then work with him to pinpoint a more accurate statement of the underlying rule. (p. 200)

Analyzing the Validity of Maladaptive Assumptions

Once the underlying assumptions and beliefs have been determined, the patient and therapist use many of the same strategies for analyzing the validity and adaptiveness of these assumptions and beliefs. One may generate alternative beliefs, and look at the relative advantages and disadvantages (or costs and benefits) of each. The therapist and patient may set up certain "behavioral experiments" to test out some of these beliefs. For example, if a patient believes "I should always do things perfectly," the patient and therapist could look for the patient's predictions as to what might happen if he did not do things perfectly, and then set up specific situations in which the patient deliberately does not do something perfectly to assess whether his predictions were indeed accurate.

They might also look at the patient's predictions about alternative beliefs, including how plausible the patient believes these alternative beliefs are, and what he expects might happen if he started accepting one of them. A patient may decide that a particular alternative belief was more adaptive for his life but impossible to achieve, such as "I will be happier if I spend more time developing close relationships and less time at work." In addition to examining the patient's predictions about the consequences of spending less time at work, the patient and therapist may need to work on the impediments the patient may have to developing intimate relationships. Only by making changes in the underlying assumptions and beliefs that cut across many different situations can the patient learn how to avoid future depressions.

Behavioral Techniques

The cognitive therapist uses a variety of behavioral techniques. Though they are similar to techniques used by behaviorists, the cognitive therapist uses them in a different way and for a different purpose. Both the cognitive therapist and the behavioral therapist use these techniques to provide a depressed person with more structure, to increase the amount of pleasure the patient obtains in his life, and to overcome some of the decreased motivation, lethargy, and anhedonia he feels. One difference, however, is that the "strict" behaviorist tends to see the performance of the behavior as the exclusive goal of the intervention, and may use cognitive techniques (in a "cognitive–behavioral therapy") only to "get the patient to do the behavior." Other differences will be discussed below.

The cognitive therapist sees the behavior in a much different way. The behavior is a means of eliciting and testing the automatic thoughts, underlying assumptions, and beliefs about a situation. Much of the benefit of the behavioral technique in a cognitive therapy can occur before the behavior even occurs. When the patient and therapist discuss the behavioral assignment, they will first look quite extensively into the patient's beliefs about the feasibility of the assignment, the purpose of the assignment, the chance for successful completion, and the perceived ultimate benefits and hurdles to completing the assignment. Some behavioral assignments may be preceded by more than one session for discussion of these factors.

The ultimate goal is not just the completion of the assignment. Rather, the assignment is also used to examine the patient's beliefs about his internal and external resources for dealing with problems, the effects of his predictions of probability of success both in terms of his ability to do the assignment and what he will get from it, and the thoughts that caused successful experiences to become perceived as unsuccessful.

Thus, although the therapist uses behavioral techniques in ways similar to the behavioral therapist, the rationale for the use of the techniques, the preparation of the assignment, and the evaluation of the results by the patient and therapist are framed by the cognitive conceptualization of the patient's problems. This problem-solving method is then explicitly taught to the patient.

One important aspect of all homework assignments, "behavioral" and/or "cognitive," is the "win-win concept." The patient's ability to perform the homework assignment is seen as a success. However, if the patient is unable to do it, then the assignment still is a success, provided that the patient is aware of and can record the automatic thoughts he has when he is unable to do it. This is seen as a valuable source of data about the automatic thoughts that impede the performance of the task, which is the purpose (at least in part) of making the assignment. Thus, as long as the patient can observe his automatic thoughts, the assignment is a success, regardless of whether it is completed. The patient and therapist can then work on how to respond to the automatic thoughts and set up new strategies that will allow him to perform the assigned tasks — a goal that stands in great contrast to the behavioral therapist's objectives.

Some of the more commonly used behavioral techniques used in cognitive therapy are discussed below (from Young & Beck, 1982).

Activities Scheduling

Depressed patients often have trouble structuring their time, and simply scheduling their activities out of the session can both provide them with sources of positive experiences, and at the same time prevent the negative rumination that often occurs in unstructured time. Scheduling can often diminish the patients' sense of anhedonia and increase their motivation, which in turn can counteract their hopelessness and helplessness.

Mastery and Pleasure

Often an important source of a patient's lack of motivation and anhedonia is his belief that he will be unable to experience pleasure if he tries to do anything correctly and effectively. One way to help counteract these beliefs is through the use of mastery and pleasure recording. To do this, the patient keeps track of his activities hour by hour throughout the day. He then rates these activities on a scale of, for example, 0 to 100, on how much pleasure and sense of mastery the activity provided for him. Patients who state they can do nothing right and do not derive pleasure from anything are often surprised at how much pleasure and mastery they feel throughout their days. The mastery and pleasure ratings can also serve to provide more directed activity scheduling by providing data on which activities the patient enjoys, but has difficulty doing. Eventually, the patient handles the activity on his own.

Graded Task Assignment

An important part of activity scheduling, or any behavioral assignment, is to provide an assignment that is within the patient's reach. Giving an assignment that is too difficult and overwhelming may in fact serve to reinforce the patient's negative predictions and beliefs about himself. To help patients start tackling some of the larger and more overwhelming tasks, the therapists break down the task into smaller parts, each of which will move him toward completion of the task as a whole. The tasks are graded according to increasing difficulty, with each step not only working toward the completion of the entire task, but also allowing the patient to gain confidence and any skills that are necessary to complete the task. A graded task assignment can provide a powerful tool for eliminating a patient's hopeless and helpless beliefs.

Cognitive Rehearsal

Sometimes patients have difficulty starting even small steps toward completing major tasks. This is often because of overwhelming negative thoughts about their ability to begin or complete the task. One technique that can help the patient deal with these thoughts is "cognitive rehearsal," in which the patient is asked to imagine each step required toward beginning and completing the proposed task. This allows the patient to see more concretely the requisite steps before the task is attempted and allows the patient and therapist to work out any anticipated problems beforehand, giving the patient a greater sense of confidence in tackling—and completing—the task. In addition, it can serve as a valuable source of data for both the patient and therapist, in that dysfunctional automatic thoughts may be brought into open discussion and resolved before interfering with the completion of a task.

Distraction Techniques

Some patients have difficulty with overwhelming affect (including depressed mood, anxiety, or anger) that interferes with their ability to concentrate on the tasks at hand, and sidetracks them while they are performing the tasks. Patients can be taught forms of attention diversion to help reduce temporarily these painful affects, through cognitive techniques (such as thought blocking or performing mental calculations), imagery techniques, use of social supports, or physical activity. Generally, the therapist stresses that these techniques are useful in the short-term. For long-term improvement the patient needs to address the negative cognitions and deal with them.

COGNITIVE THERAPY: OTHER DISORDERS

The theoretical model and techniques of the cognitive therapy of disorders other than depression derive from those of the cognitive therapy of depression—and vary only in their areas of emphasis. Because of this, the experienced cognitive therapist can seamlessly integrate the treatment of the various syndromes that are frequently seen in the same patient. Brief descriptions of the cognitive therapy of these other disorders are described below.

Cognitive Therapy of Anxiety

In the treatment of anxiety disorders, the basic model of cognitive therapy is not the cognitive triad of the negative view of oneself, one's world, and one's future, but instead, an overemphasis by the patient on the danger within any one situation with an accompanying underestimation of his resources for handling it. Many of the same methods are used to test patients' perception of danger in a given situation and the distortions of their ability to deal with it. Often many of the same behavioral techniques are useful, such as breaking big, overwhelming, and frightening tasks into smaller, more manageable subunits.

One major difference between dealing with anxious and depressed patients is that patients who are depressed will usually "carry their depression around with them." That is, they are generally always depressed to some extent, and therefore the dysfunctional cognitions are readily apparent in the session. With anxiety disorders, patients are often anxious in specific situations, and thus may not be aware of the dysfunctional automatic thoughts in other situations, such as the relative safety and comfort of their therapist's office. When they are in anxiety-provoking situations, the anxious affect may distract them from being aware of and therefore remembering their automatic thoughts.

The therapist may be able to help the patient remember some automatic thoughts that precede and are concurrent with their anxious episodes by helping them to recall in detail the events preceding the episode. Frequently, though, the therapist and patient need to create anxious situations to get at the anxiety-provoking automatic thoughts (and eventually their underlying beliefs).

For example, a socially anxious patient may need behavioral assignments that put him in anxiety-provoking social situations to understand the specific automatic thoughts that arise in these situations. Sometimes it is sufficient just to have the individual imagine the anxiety-provoking situation. For some patients, however, the imagery techniques are not enough, and the anxiety-provoking situation needs to be reproduced either in the session or outside of it.

Again, as in the discussion of behavioral techniques in depression, the goal is not to put the patient merely into anxiety-provoking situations for "desensitization," that is, the diminution of an anxiety from repeated exposure. Rather, it is by exposing the individual to the situation, examining the subsequent automatic thoughts, teaching him how to respond to his automatic thoughts, and finally testing out his underlying beliefs that change can occur in this anxious situation and in others.

Cognitive Therapy of Panic Disorder

In the cognitive conceptualization of panic disorder, a panic attack is the result of the patient's "catastrophic misinterpretation" of physical and mental sensations of anxiety or conditions such as caffeine intoxication, alcohol withdrawal, fatigue, etc. For example, the panic patient may initially feel anxious, and begin to notice the physical and mental symptoms that often accompany this anxiety — a fast heartbeat, a sensation of a shortness of breath, or light-headedness. The patient prone to panic disorder will begin to misinterpret these sensations as signs of imminent danger He may see his fast heartbeat as a sign that he is having a heart attack, or his shortness of breath that he is choking or about to stop breathing; he may see light-headedness as a signal of imminent fainting, seizures, or "going crazy."

These concerns increase anxiety, which in turn increases the sensation (and his vigilance of them), which then amplifies the concern about the sensations and strengthens the belief in the misinterpretations. This situation escalates to the point where a chain reaction occurs as the cycle repeats itself. The belief, which may have been "I feel like I am going to have a heart attack," becomes "I am having a heart attack, I am going to die." Consequently, the panic-stricken patient misinterprets normal nonspecific autonomic arousal as an impending catastrophe such as death, loss of control, danger to self or others, or severe humiliation.

The cognitive therapy techniques for panic disorder focus on teaching the patient to experience these sensations without the catastrophic misinterpretations by reality-testing the automatic thoughts they arouse. The therapist also teaches the patient to induce these sensations by using hyperventilation, physical exertion, imagery techniques, spinning in a chair, etc. As the patient learns to self-induce these symptoms, he gains a greater sense of control over the experience, and learns to disqualify his beliefs in the catastrophic misinterpretation.

The cognitive therapy of panic and other anxiety disorders also strongly emphasizes the role of avoidance in the anxious patient. While initially the cognitive therapist focuses on symptom cessation, later, he, with the patient, searches out subtle ways in which the patient has incorporated avoidance of anxiety-prone situations into his life. The patient is taught to recognize and respond to the behaviors and the cognitions that form the basis of both the anxiety and the avoidance. He reality-tests continually the cognitions related to his active avoidance, which eliminates this source of diminished pleasure and mastery. He then confronts further his underlying beliefs that overemphasize danger, and underemphasize his resources for handling it.

Cognitive Therapy of Substance Abuse

The cognitive therapy of substance abuse focuses on the patient's beliefs about the positive effects of the substance he abuses, his underestimation of its negative effects, and his overestimation of the power of the cravings or urge to use the substance. It also considers the patient's underestimation of his resources for dealing with these cravings.

In a cognitive therapy, the patient initially learns to understand the disadvantages of the substance in his life, while at the same time questioning objectively the usually misperceived advantages of using the substance. He learns to understand that there are certain "high-risk circumstances" in which he is more likely to experience urges. In some cases, he can learn to minimize these situations, such as avoiding former places where he abused the substance, or people with whom he abused it. But many he cannot and should not avoid, such as those involving where he lives, his work situation, and such mood states as anger, anxiety, or boredom. These he learns to tolerate and deal with in a more functional manner. For example, a cocaine addict is at home the day after payday, feeling bored. He remembers similar times in the past when he's relieved the boredom with cocaine, and begins to experience a craving for it. He has the automatic thought, "I can't stand this," which in turn begins and then facilitates his drug-seeking behavior.

Intervention can take place in many different points in the above scenario. He can use distraction to diminish the urge. He can use predetermined coping statements to deal with his automatic thought "I can't stand this." He can learn to schedule his time better to help prevent boredom. In some cases, for patients for whom the substance abuse seems particularly situationally-related and time-limited, the patients may learn new techniques for controlling their substance abuse without necessarily eliminating the use entirely (for example, for patients who have limited problems with alcohol abuse, overeating, etc). Other patients not only learn how to abstain from the use of the substance, but also to deal with relapses if and when they occur. They learn not to presume catastrophically that a relapse implies that they can *never* give up the substance, nor that it relegates them to a life of unending abuse.

Once the patient's use of the substance is under better control, the patient and therapist can begin to work directly on the cravings for the substance, and the patient's often catastrophic thoughts about his addiction such as, "If I don't get a drink now, I'll just die," or "If I don't get some cocaine now, I'll go crazy." The patient learns to confront and control his craving sensation in much the same way that the panic patient learns to confront and control his fears about his anxiety symptoms.

Cognitive Therapy of Relationship Problems

Communication is an integral part of any relationship. An individual needs to communicate what he wants from his partner, and what he is willing to give. Communication within a couple is often reduced over time to a type of "shorthand." This type of communication may be beneficial for the couple because they are able to communicate a vast amount of information in a very short period of time. However, it can also have profound disadvantages for the couple undergoing interpersonal problems. The vague, poorly described messages may become a set-up for misinterpretation.

In addition, couples may imbue certain actions with special idiosyncratic meanings, making them "symbols" of issues about which the recipient partner is particularly vulnerable. For example, an individual who has concerns about his ability to be loved and cared for in a relationship might be particularly concerned about a partner's dependability. He might attribute special unintended meanings to his partner's actions. If his partner is repeatedly a few minutes late for certain meetings, the individual may think, "See, I can't depend on her for little things like showing up for meetings on time, how am I ever going to count on her for something important?"

This example highlights an important difference between cognitive therapy for couples and other types of psychotherapy, in that it does not exclusively emphasize communication skills but stresses the importance of each person's examining his own beliefs about himself and his partner. In every relationship, there are parts that individuals like or dislike, to varying degrees. In order for a relationship to flourish, or even survive, each partner must feel that at least a minimum number of his needs is being met. Each must also meet a certain number of his partner's needs.

There are two ways for an individual to fulfill a need within a relationship — to have the partner meet the need, or to have the individual fulfill it on his own. Each choice involves certain basic beliefs that affect which option the individual uses. Some include beliefs about one's own needs: "I don't have a right to ask for that." "I don't deserve to be treated that way (positively or negatively)." "He *must* meet this need; I can't do this for myself." Others include beliefs about one's partners needs: "If I give in to this demand, she'll just keep demanding more until I'm just a servant for her." "I've already given more than my fifty percent in this relationship — now it's her turn (to meet my needs)." Thus, before one can consider communicating about one's own needs or one's partner's needs, one must deal with the various strategies one develops to get needs fulfilled based on these various beliefs.

The patient and cognitive therapist will examine some of the cognitive errors inherent in the beliefs mentioned above, such as "should" statements, mind-reading, jumping to conclusions, etc. They will also test out the beliefs each individual has about himself, such as what he deserves in a relationship, and what he can provide for himself (as opposed to "needing" from his partner). This is done within the context of the relationship — that is, how the individual's beliefs affects himself and his partner. Much of this work is done within the couples therapy session, although sometimes it's more advantageous to meet for a few sessions with one or both members individually.

At the same time, the therapist and couple examine the process of communication between the members of the couple, and their beliefs about it. Communication is crucial to getting one's needs met by one's partner, and discovering what one's partner's needs are. But before effective communication can occur, one must deal with certain basic beliefs about the process of communication. For example, "She should have known it would bother me when she did it (without my having to tell her)." "If he loved me, he'd do that without my needing to ask." "She shouldn't need to have me tell her I love her—she should already know that."

Thus although communication is an important part of maintaining a relationship, the cognitive therapist sees its role as secondary to the beliefs one has about oneself, one's partner, and the process of communication. In our illustration above, for example, part of the intervention of the cognitive therapist might be helping the individual *express* his concerns that his partner's lateness may mean she is undependable, but a much more important intervention would be helping the individual to reality test his belief, "If I can't trust my partner on the little things, how can I trust her on the important things?"

Obviously, an important early part of the work revolves around helping the individuals to examine the automatic thoughts that occur in situations in which the dysphoric affect arises, to allow for response to the automatic thoughts, and to tease out the underlying assumptions and beliefs. This is particularly important in angry interactions with couples because an immediate precursor to the anger-provoking automatic thoughts may be automatic thoughts that bring about a sense of fear or hurt. The individual learns to address these "hidden fears" and "hidden hurts" directly, while at the same time learning techniques to control his angry responses.

Other Areas of Investigation

Cognitive therapists are investigating the applicability of this form of psychotherapy for other disorders including, among other conditions, chronic depression, generalized anxiety disorder, obsessive–compulsive disorder, learning disabilities, and attention deficit disorder. In addition, cognitive therapists are examining the applicability of cognitive therapy for other treatment modalities, such as group psychotherapy and inpatient treatment (which will be discussed in greater detail later).

Cognitive Therapy of Personality Disorders

One of the most exciting areas of current research in cognitive therapy is the application of cognitive therapy to the personality disorders. This has major implications with respect to how cognitive therapy is defined, as distinct from both psychodynamic and behavioral psychotherapies, and with respect to how the cognitive therapy model will evolve. The application of cognitive therapy to the personality disorders will also affect how the model of cognitive therapy will be taught in the future. These will be discussed in more detail below.

The personality disorder patient is defined as an individual with a strong Axis II diagnosis. However, an Axis II diagnosis does not rule out concurrent Axis I diagnoses. In the cognitive therapy of personality disorders, the cognitive therapist will focus the initial treatment on controlling and containing the negative affects and behaviors associated with the Axis I disorders (such as panic attacks, episodes of major depression, suicidality) and the Axis II disorders (such as anger outbursts, self-destructive behavior, and relationship problems). As with any psychotherapy of personality disorders, issues of safety and containment are primary and determine the priority of the initial interventions. The patient who uses self-destructive methods, such as cutting or head-banging as a way of alleviating dysphoric affects, is taught other more adaptive ways of dealing with this affect, usually before getting at some of the underlying beliefs that may give rise to it.

In the initial phase of the cognitive therapy of a personality disorder, the therapist needs to build an empathic and trusting relationship with the patient. At the same time, the therapist begins to teach the patient techniques for dealing with their dysphoric affect and maladaptive behaviors. This does several things. It helps them to start eliminating some of the problems that these affects and behaviors create. It further enhances the therapeutic relationship, by building trust in the therapist and hopefulness about the therapy. And it begins to teach the patient the methods he needs to deal with the dysfunctional affect and impulses toward maladaptive behavior that will increase as he begins to deal more directly with his underlying beliefs and assumptions.

This provides a more graduated transition from dealing with simpler, more discrete issues, to tackling more complex and generalized problems. As the patient learns to understand the impact of faulty thinking such as, "If I don't get this paper in on time, I'll never make it in my profession," or "If it isn't perfect, I'll be a failure," he will eventually be able to recognize and deal with catastrophic thinking in terms of beliefs such as "If my partner isn't perfect, then he or she is terrible and dangerous" and "If this relationship doesn't work out, I'll be alone forever."

The speed with which a cognitive therapy in a personality disordered patient can progress obviously greatly depends on the severity of the illness. Personality disordered individuals often have enormous problems with trust of any form. Many will find it difficult even to express their automatic thoughts in the therapy until they have developed enough trust and confidence in their therapists. Obviously, when working with personality disordered patients, the cognitive therapist needs the same relationship-building skills such as empathy, understanding, and compassion that are required in any form of psychotherapy, particularly with severely disordered patients. The therapy can progress only at the rate at which the patient can deal with some of these very basic issues. There is a Yiddish saying, "Sleep faster, we need the pillows," that ironically addresses the idea that certain processes, by definition, take a certain amount of time to evolve. The same applies to the cognitive therapy of personality disorders.

One issue not yet addressed in the research literature is whether the cognitive therapy of personality disorders may progress faster because the therapy is more directed and structured, or because it is less regressive than less structured forms of psychotherapy. Research is currently underway at The Center for Cognitive Therapy in Philadelphia and at other centers to develop structured protocols for specific personality disorders to answer some of these questions.

One thing that ties together the cognitive therapy of all of the disorders is the basic model of cognitive therapy. In the personality disorders, the problem is still seen as underlying beliefs that give rise to automatic thoughts in certain vulnerable situations, and that these thoughts bring about and interact with dysphoric affect and dysfunctional behavior. What varies in each of the different personality disorders is the conceptualization of the probable underlying vulnerabilities and beliefs. It is important to note though that these conceptualizations of each of the personality disorders are seen merely as a set of hypotheses. The therapist needs to work with the patient to determine what are the individual's particular idiosyncratic beliefs.

Another difference between the cognitive therapy of personality disorders and cognitive therapy of Axis I disorders involves understanding and reality testing the initial events that bring about dysfunctional beliefs. This different emphasis results from the way in which the cognitive therapist views Axis I versus Axis II disorders.

Beck describes competing schemas, or sets of beliefs (Beck et al., 1990). These are usually seen in Axis I disorders. An individual can maintain two fairly distinct sets of beliefs about a given subject, and vacillate between them. Many variables can influence the patient's point of view, including his current life situation, recent stressors and other events, and possibly more physiological functions such as underlying illnesses, biochemical effects, etc.

When a person is suffering from an Axis I disorder, he may invest heavily in a more dysfunctional paradigm. But the other more functional, "competing" paradigm still can be present. It is just less "activated" (i.e., less in control of the perception of the environment and in the processing of information). Thus, a major part of the task in the cognitive therapy of an Axis I disorder is shifting the patient's focus toward the data in his environment that confirms and "reactivates" the latent, more functional paradigm, while helping the patient reality test and refute the distorted evidence that keeps alive the activated dysfunctional paradigm.

The cognitive therapist is less likely to see Axis I and Axis II disorders as a dichotomy. Rather, they are viewed as more of a continuum of investment in dysfunctional beliefs. In the Axis II disorders, the patient is invested more in the dysfunctional paradigm, often to the point that he ignores competing evidence or discounts it entirely. Often, because of the chronic nature of Axis II disorders, the patient cannot draw upon evidence from the past that can assist in refuting his current negative beliefs. This is because the patient discounts and discards any evidence in the past that did not fit the dysfunctional paradigm, instead of considering the information as part of a competing, more functional paradigm. As a result, the patient may find it difficult, if not impossible, to recall the more functional data and interpretations. Thus, an important difference in treating a severe Axis I and Axis II disorder is that the cognitive therapist cannot move the Axis II disordered patient as readily to a competing (more functional) paradigm.

This, in part, explains why the cognitive therapy of personality disorders is slower and can be more tedious than the cognitive therapy of Axis I disorders. In addition to helping the patient reality test and divest from his dysfunctional paradigms, the cognitive therapist has to help him begin the sometimes slow and laborious process of developing a whole new belief system around very vulnerable topics.

Because of the chronicity of the beliefs in Axis II disorders, many of these dysfunctional beliefs may have been formed at a much earlier period in the individual's life, such as in childhood or early adolescence, and may be imbued with memories of distorted evidence so powerful that any newer evidence to the contrary pales in comparison (e.g., "If my parents think I'm bad, I must be bad," versus "My friends like me, so I must be good"). Therefore, the cognitive therapist may have to deal with the patient's former belief system and how it evolved, before he can work effectively with the patient on developing a more adaptive set of beliefs. Thus, with a patient with a stronger Axis II component, the cognitive therapist will have to spend more time dealing with older memories than with a patient with a more powerful Axis I component.

The Axis II patient may be deficient in the skills needed to reality test dysfunctional thinking, or those needed to deal with overwhelming and labile affect, because of the chronicity and power of the dysfunctional beliefs and their earlier developmental origin. For example, if an individual believes, "No one will ever like me because I'm bad," he may spend an inordinant amount of time and energy while growing up learning to develop ways in which to avoid intimacy, while ignoring any skills necessary to encourage intimacy, because intimacy seems impossible, harmful, or both.

The Axis I patient, in comparison, may have a similar set of dysfunctional beliefs but because at some point this type of patient has had a competing set of beliefs, such as "People can get close to me because I am basically likeable," he has had reason to develop at least some social skills.

As a result, the cognitive therapist may need to help the Axis II patient develop certain skills that have seemed unnecessary in the past before the patient can begin to develop, test, and live by a more functional paradigm.

The importance of this newer addendum to the cognitive model will be discussed further below.

COGNITIVE THERAPY, BEHAVIORAL THERAPY, AND PSYCHODYNAMIC THERAPY: WHAT'S THE DIFFERENCE?

It is illustrative to note the differences as well as the similarities between these three major schools of psychiatry. But Arkowitz and Hannah (1989) discuss the difficulty in comparing schools of psychotherapy comprised of different orientations within each school. "Each orientation represents an approach that differs considerably from the others. Thus, when using the broad labels of cognitive, behavioral, or psychodynamic, we may be assuming a degree of homogeneity that does not exist" (p. 145). In addition to this warning, we must add the caveat that we will be comparing a specific cognitive therapy, Beck's cognitive therapy, with an amalgam of various orientations within the other two major schools of psychotherapies. Any more specific comparisons are beyond the scope of this chapter.

The description of how cognitive therapy is applied to personality disorders may sound strikingly similar to psychodynamic explanations of psychopathology and the methods it uses for treating them. Although the understanding and treatment methods may appear similar, the cognitive approach differs conceptually from the psychodynamic approach in two important ways—the emphasis on discovering and dealing with the "precipitating cause" of the psychopathology, and the belief in the unconscious.

In psychodynamic psychotherapy, the discovery of the early precipitants to current psychopathology is called "insight." Once discovered, this insight is used to explain current patterns of dysfunctional thinking, behavior, and affect in the individual's present world as recapitulations (or as reexperiencing and reliving patterns of interactions from the past that are similar to current events).

In contrast, from the cognitive perspective, the patient's memories of the past are seen as evidence that support certain current dysfunctional beliefs giving rise to dysfunctional thoughts, behavior, and affect in the present. The dysfunctional thoughts, behaviors, and affect arise directly from the dysfunctional *belief* not from the events in the past that may have precipitated the formation of these beliefs, as is the case with a psychodynamic approach.

This is an important distinction because it emphasizes that the beliefs that sustain these dysfunctional manifestations exist (and can be dealt with) in the present, as opposed to "chaining" present problems to past events over which the patient has little control. It also views differently how events from the past are seen as "evidence" for the current belief. Although their emotional importance to the patient is acknowledged, they are not necessarily considered by the therapist to be more important than other (more current) pieces of evidence.

Additionally, beliefs based on evidence from the past are tested in the same way as any other belief. It is the patient who determines the relative value of evidence, which is then tested with the help of the therapist. So, for example, a cognitive therapist would be unlikely to say, "The patient constantly seeks reassurance in his relationships because he never got acceptance from his cold and distant mother." Rather, he might say, "The patient excessively seeks reassureance in his relationships because of his core belief that the he is basically unloveable. This belief probably started in childhood, when he interpreted his mother's lack of affection as evidence of his unloveability, and has been reinforced by each 'unsuccessful' relationship, even though there have been many more 'successful' relationships he overlooks."

Thus the patient's interpretation or memory of past events is seen as (usually distorted) evidence that maintains the current dysfunctional beliefs. The current beliefs are tested against other evidence from the past and the present, and by "experimental" situations set up by the patient and therapist.

Another important distinction between psychodynamic and cognitive conceptualizations of the formation of current dysfunctional beliefs is that, whereas the cognitive therapist believes that early life events may have profound influence on current belief systems, he also feels that current belief systems may be affected by more recent events with little or no basis in the distant past. In classical psychodynamic thinking, current dysfunctions are always related to events from early childhood.

Thus, a cognitive therapist might not see the need to "look beyond" recent traumatic events (such as severe financial downturns, physical or emotional trauma, etc.) to explain the formation of dysfunctional beliefs. As one deals with current events, one may find beliefs linked more strongly with the past, but this is not presumed to be the case.

Furthermore, the cognitive therapist neither presumes to know all the factors in the formation of the belief, nor believes such knowledge is necessary or sufficient for dealing with the belief. The cognitive therapist believes that for any belief, there may be multifactorial precipitants to the formation of that belief (as was explained above in the cognitive view of the depression). Therefore, the cognitive therapist does not necessarily need to pursue the "precipitant" of the belief in order to eliminate its dysfunctional manifestations. Particularly for the less disturbed patient, treatment can proceed more quickly and more directly. This explains the importance of the cognitive conceptualization of Axis I and Axis II disorders as being on a continuum instead of as strict dichotomies.

The second major distinction between cognitive therapy and psychodynamic therapy concerns the concept of "the unconscious." In classical psychodynamic thinking, much of the core conflict is repressed by various defense mechanisms into the individual's unconscious, where the conflict, expressed in the form of transference reactions, slips of the tongue, and dreams, is inaccessible to the patient's conscious mind.

Cognitive therapy has no construct of "the unconscious." In cognitive therapy, consciousness is seen as a continuum from more conscious (or readily accessible) information to less conscious (or less readily available) material. Some beliefs may not be readily apparent to the individual, but this does not mean that the individual does not have access to them.

An analogy may be illustrative. One is not always "conscious" or aware that one is breathing, but one can become readily aware of this fact once attention is shifted to it. In a similar manner, an individual may not be aware of some of the thoughts that precede his affect or behavior. But by focusing his attention on these automatic thoughts, he can readily become aware of them, and understand the basic beliefs underlying similar patterns of automatic thinking.

This distinction between the "conscious–unconscious" dichotomy of the psychodynamic psychotherapist, and the "consciousness continuum" of the cognitive therapist has important implications for the patient–therapist relationship. In a psychodynamic psychotherapy, the belief that "no means yes" can put the therapist in the position of disbelieving what the patient says while the patient vehemently believes what he is saying is an accurate representation of what he feels. This represents a possible set-up for conflicts over power and control within the relationship.

The cognitive therapist can form a more collaborative relationship with the patient because he does not presume that the individual is "defending against" an understanding or knowledge of conflict. Beliefs are not presumed to be adaptive or maladaptive until examined, by the therapist and patient together. If they disagree, they search for more evidence to confirm or update their beliefs. They neither presume that the patient does not understand the problem, nor that the therapist "knows" the ultimate solution.

In the same manner, if the individual has difficulty with giving up a maladaptive belief, or with accepting a more adaptive belief (as determined by the therapist and patient), or even with examining a particular belief, he isn't labeled as being "resistant" to the therapist. Instead, the therapist and patient search for other competing beliefs. These might include: "I don't deserve to act this way," or "I don't have the ability to act that way," or "I'm afraid to act this way." They do not label the patient as being "resistant" to the therapist.

Cognitive therapy has extensively borrowed techniques from the behavioral psychotherapies. At times, parts of a cognitive therapy may appear very similar to parts of behavioral therapy, as was discussed in the section on behavioral techniques. However, the behavioral therapist chooses his techniques based on his model of classical conditioning or operant conditioning. The model is not described in terms of the interactions among cognition, affect, and behavior (as in Figure 4.1), but instead in terms of a behavior, its antecedent stimuli, and its consequences. Thus, the role of cognitions and beliefs is of secondary importance in a behavioral therapy. As Arkowitz and Hannah (1989) note, cognitive therapy and behavioral therapy take

> differing views about the important causal factors and most appropriate targets for change in psychotherapy. Behavioral therapy places a very strong emphasis on environmental determinants of behavior and the importance of behavior–environment interactions . . . Although behavioral therapy has acquired a somewhat more cognitive emphasis, it still places considerably greater emphasis on overt behavior and their interaction with environmental factors than (cognitive therapy). (p. 147)

Although the modern behavior therapist does take cognitions and beliefs into account, this is done only secondarily. The primary thrust is in dealing with (and teaching) the patient to recognize the roles of antecedents and consequences to behaviors.

In contrast, in the cognitive model, no single component (cognition, behavior, or affect) is given supremacy, as can be seen in the cognitive triangle shown in Figure 4.1. Cognitions are not considered more important than affect or behavior. The cognitive therapist merely sees these as the route to intervening in the patient's belief system. This gives the cognitive therapist greater flexibility in dealing with each of these variables, particularly in those patients with more severe psychopathology, whose beliefs even interfere with their ability to cooperate with behavioral interventions. Many behavioral psychotherapists have adopted some of these "cognitive" techniques for dealing with such problems (as in the "cognitive–behavioral" therapies), but in the end, what distinguishes a cognitive therapy from a behavioral therapy is the model which is taught to the patient.

The cognitive therapist sees the importance of teaching the patient to elucidate and test underlying assumptions and beliefs as a way of generalizing the gains made in dealing with any specific situation to other current situations in their lives, or situations they have yet to encounter. Challenging these belief systems is particularly important when dealing with Axis II disordered patients. These differences mentioned above are also playing an important role in cognitive therapy's future evolution. In the past, cognitive therapy has been seen merely as a variant of behavioral therapy. But Beck's cognitive therapy also has strong roots the psychodynamic world, which is becoming more apparent as more literature is being published on the cognitive therapy of personality disorders.

The strong emphasis in cognitive therapy on belief systems allows these more active, directed behavioral techniques to be used with individuals usually resistant to them, such as Axis II disordered patients, who have been traditionally treated in more long-term (usually psychodynamic) psychotherapies. Thus, cognitive therapy, in essence, is bridging two schools of psychotherapy that often have been considered mutually exclusive.

The central role of the belief systems in cognitive therapy also allows it to integrate much more easily into two other areas traditionally considered almost exclusively psychodynamic: inpatient psychotherapy units and psychiatric training programs.

COGNITIVE THERAPY AND
PSYCHIATRIC TRAINING

Economic forces are increasing the demand for short-term psychotherapy services. Traditional psychiatric residency programs have been slow in the past to respond to this need, in part because of the difficulty in training beginning therapists in short-term techniques. While some psychodynamic psychotherapists have learned the psychodynamically-based, short-term psychotherapies of Sifneos, Mann, Davenloo, and others, these psychotherapies are often more difficult and require several years of long-term psychodynamic psychotherapy experience before the short-term training can begin. This precludes teaching them to psychiatry residents who have little more than 3 years of training, much of it in areas other than psychotherapy.

Cognitive therapy, on the other hand, is the first standardized treatment method (with the first treatment manual) of any psychotherapy. Its model is simple to learn and yet powerful, and the techniques and their applications follow more easily from the model, once it is understood. It is a highly structured therapy that is well delineated, making it easier for therapists in training to learn, and yet the strong emphasis on belief systems "translates well" to the experiences that these therapists have begun to develop in a long-term psychodynamic training.

This holds true also for nonpsychiatric psychotherapists who have chosen to learn a more directed short-term approach.

COGNITIVE THERAPY INPATIENT UNITS

This ability of the cognitive therapist to "speak the language of beliefs" is well-suited for psychiatric inpatient units. Inpatient psychiatry has felt strong pressures in recent years from the managed health system to lower average lengths of stay. This requires more focused interventions on those problems responsible for precipitating the inpatient admission, rather than just treating the basic disorder in a safer setting. Yet, because some form of psychodynamically-based psychotherapy is the predominant type of psychotherapy in this country, most patients entering psychiatric units will be coming from and discharged to a psychodynamic outpatient therapist.

Cognitive therapy can provide the structure that these more severely disturbed patients require. The inpatient cognitive therapist and the patient can collaboratively and selectively address the distorted perceptions and underlying beliefs responsible for worsening their condition and resulting in their inpatient admission. Since most inpatient admissions are becoming briefer, it is important for the inpatient cognitive therapist to help strengthen the patient's relationship with his outpatient therapist (presuming it is valid), and not entangle the patient in a potentially confusing and maladaptive examination of differences between the inpatient and outpatient therapies.

Take, for example, the situation of the 42-year-old woman who had become increasingly depressed after changes in her job as a school teacher. She had assumed the position as the head of the school's small art department after the former director transferred to another school district. She was performing well and enjoying her job when the former department head moved back to her school. She felt intimidated by him, and offered to allow him to resume his former position, which, to her surprise, he accepted. She felt extremely tense when working with him, and she noticed herself thinking more and more about her emotionally abusive father. She eventually noticed starting to feel depressed, with low motivation and energy, problems concentrating, and withdrawal from many formerly pleasurable experiences.

Eventually, she started to have suicidal ideation, about which she spoke to her family. They encouraged her to enter treatment, and she started therapy with a psychodynamic psychotherapist. Initially, she felt a little better, but when the symptoms of her depression did not abate, she started feeling as though she was "letting him down." Her suicidal ideation returned, but she was finding it more difficult to deal with her therapist about it because of her withdrawal from him. It was at this point that the therapist referred her for inpatient treatment.

The patient and her inpatient cognitive therapist first examined the situations in which she felt particularly depressed, during which her suicidal ideation would begin. From examining her automatic thoughts in various situations, they uncovered the following pattern: The patient would be in an interaction in which she would either have a disagreement or feel misunderstood. She would usually have the automatic thought, "He doesn't understand me," accompanied by feelings of anger and sadness. She and her therapist elucidated the following "downward arrow":

He doesn't understand me;
↓
If he cared about me, he'd understand me.
↓
He doesn't care about me;
↓
He doesn't like me;
↓
He's rejecting me;
↓
I'll be all alone.
↓
There will be nobody to help me with my problems.

She noted that her response to these thoughts was to become angry and sad, and to withdraw somewhat from the person. She described having the following automatic thought when she backed away from the person: "Maybe he'll understand how badly I'm feeling and come after me." She would notice feeling a little more hopeful at this point, but became extremely vigilant for any signs of misunderstanding or rejection in the individual. If she noticed any, the previous set of thoughts would return, but this time she would feel even more angry and sad, and would became even more withdrawn.

She noted that at some point she would have the thought, "Well they'd really know how badly I was feeling if I killed myself. Then it would be too late for them to come and get me." At that point, she would often feel frightened and would usually seek out some other source of support and comfort. However, when this pattern began happening with greater and greater frequency, she noted feeling more helpless and hopeless and having more thoughts such as, "No one will understand me. It's hopeless," followed by even more powerful thoughts of suicide.

The patient and her therapist decided to intervene at the level of the belief, "If people don't understand me, then they don't care about me." They examined evidence for and against this belief, and the patient was able to both describe several instances in which people she knew cared about her didn't understand her but were able to understand her later, and also instances where she was unable to understand someone she cared for. She was also able to uncover those times when people did misunderstand her or not care about her, including occasions involving her relationship with her father. She and her psychodynamic outpatient psychotherapist had been discussing her relationship with her father before her admission, and she was much more aware of her beliefs that he neither understood her nor cared for her. However, she was able to see that not everyone reacted to her as her father did.

The patient and her cognitive therapist focused on helping her to come up with more rational responses to her automatic thoughts when she felt she was being misunderstood, and to learn more direct ways of asking for help and support other than withdrawing and hoping that the other individual would "read her mind." She noted that when she was able to ask for some assistance and receive it from some of the staff on the unit she felt more hopeful and less suicidal. She was able to practice her techniques for testing her distortions about people misunderstanding her in the therapy group on the unit, and to learn appropriate ways for helping the group members to understand her. By observing her automatic thoughts, she was able to notice that when she was in an angry confrontation with someone, she would have the thought, "I can't stand up for myself or they'll abuse me even more, and I won't be able to stand it." She said this was the way she had always felt when dealing with her father in confrontations.

Again, she and her therapist looked for evidence for and against this belief, including times when she had been able to stand up for herself, and times when she had not been able to stand up for herself but had been able "to stand it." She and her therapist set up an assertiveness training program through the rehabilitation therapy staff at the hospital, and together they worked on helping her to come up with rational responses to the self-deprecating automatic thoughts she would have when she would backed down from a confrontation.

They also worked on ways of helping her to structure her work situation to define her and her department head's jobs so that there was less overlap and conflict between them. The patient met several times with her outpatient therapist, while she was an inpatient, and together they examined her distortions of their relationship. The patient's suicidal ideation would still occur when she felt particularly rejected, but it was much briefer and much less intense. She felt her suicidal ideation was much more easily managed, and as she and her outpatient therapist felt that they could work together safely on an outpatient basis, she was discharged.

Six months later, the outpatient therapist reported that the patient was doing well with eventual complete abeyance of her suicidal ideation, resolution of her depression, and an increase in her assertiveness. She and her outpatient therapist continued to work on her relationships with her parents, particularly her father, and on her current relationships.

This example shows how an inpatient cognitive therapist can work with the patient and the outpatient psychodynamic treater to help the patient manage overwhelming affect, control inappropriate behaviors, and deal with important distorted thoughts and beliefs, including beliefs about the therapeutic relationship, without disrupting that relationship. In this setting, because patients only deal with the inpatient therapist on a brief basis, it is important not to set up a conflict in their minds about the two different methods of treatment. This might force them to feel as though they had to choose between investing in their inpatient cognitive therapy or investing in their outpatient psychodynamic therapy, with the possibility that a great deal of guilt, anxiety, anger, and sadness might result.

Because of its pragmatic quality and history of extensive outcome testing, cognitive therapy is often particularly popular on more biologically-oriented inpatient units.

COGNITIVE THERAPY:
OUTLOOK FOR THE FUTURE

Because of its diverse theoretical underpinnings, cognitive therapy has evolved from a short-term therapy for depression to a more broadly-based, and, at times, much longer psychotherapy for a variety of psychiatric disorders and a variety of modalities. Current research is ongoing to validate the newer applications of cognitive therapy in outcome studies, as was done with the cognitive therapy of depression. Research also continues to expand the applicability of cognitive therapy, allowing cognitive therapists to treat the full spectrum of psychiatric disorders.

REFERENCES

Arkowitz, H., & Hannah, M. T. (1989). Cognitive, behavioral, and psychodynamic therapies: Converging or diverging pathways to change? In A. Freeman, K. M. Simon, L. E. Beutler & H. Arkowitz (Eds.), *Comprehensive handbook of cognitive therapy.* New York: Plenum Press.

Beck, A. T. (1976). *Cognitive therapy and the emotional disorders.* New York: International Universities Press.

Beck, A. T. (1988). *Love is never enough.* New York: Harper & Row.

Beck, A. T., & Emery, G,. with Greenberg, R. L. (1985). *Anxiety disorders and phobias: A cognitive perspective.* New York: Basic Books.

Beck, A. T., Freeman, A., & associates. (1990). *Cognitive therapy of personality disorders.* New York: Guilford Press.

Beck, A. T., & Greenberg, R. L. (1979). Brief cognitive therapies. *Psychiatric Clinics of North America, 2,* 23–79.

Beck, A. T., & Rush, A. J. (1989). Cognitive therapy. In H. I. Kaplan & B. J. Saddock (Eds.), *Comprehensive textbook of psychiatry* (Vol. 5). Baltimore: Williams & Wilkins.

Beck, A. T., Rush, A. J., Shaw, B. F., & Emery, G. (1979). *Cognitive therapy of depression.* New York: Guilford Press.

Freeman, A. (1981). Dreams and images in cognitive therapy. In G. Emery, S. D. Hollon, & R. C. Bedrosian (Eds.). (1981). *New directions in cognitive therapy.* New York: Guilford Press.

Hollon, S. D., & Najavits, L. (1988). Review of empirical studies on cognitive therapy. In A. J. Frances & R. E. Hales (Eds.), *Psychiatric press review of psychiatry* (Vol. 7). Washington, DC: American Psychiatric Press.

Young, J. E., & Beck, A. T. (1982). Cognitive therapy: Clinical applications. In A. J. Rush (Ed.), *Short-term psychotherapies for depression.* New York: Guilford Press.

II

THE THERAPEUTIC EXPERIENCE

F·I·V·E

斑

Thoughts on the Nature of the Therapeutic Relationship

THEODORE I. ANDERSON

It is now axiomatic that sexual contact between psychotherapists and patients is nontherapeutic and counter to accepted ethical practice. Nonetheless, it has become more and more apparent that this injunction has not been respected by an embarassing number of therapists. Complaints of sexual involvement by therapists with patients have increasingly been brought before ethics boards, with the results often making front-page news in newspapers. Recent authors (Gabbard, 1989; Pope & Bouhoutsos, 1986; Stone, 1984) have made it abundantly clear that psychotherapists engaged in sexual involvement with *current* patients are in violation of professional ethics, of civil and criminal law in many states, and of standards of good clinical practice in all communities.

What may not be clear is that having such a relationship with a *former* patient is equally problematic. All psychotherapy professions are presently considering extending their ethics codes to include "former" patients, but as of this writing only the American Psychiatric Association (APA) has taken action. The APA Board of Trustees adopted in 1988 an annotation to the code entitled, "Principles of Medical Ethics with Annotations Especially Applicable to Psychiatry." The annotation reads: "Sexual involvement with one's former patients generally exploits emotions deriving from treatment and therefore almost always is unethical" (1989, p. 10).

Given the surge in attention to this problem in the therapeutic relationship, I will discuss in this chapter the specific functions of professional ethics, professional covenants, treatment contracts, and selected aspects of the relationship after the termination of treatment. Then, in order to illustrate the ethical implications of the interaction of these issues, I will present three cases in which a clinician's sexual involvement with former patients became a concern. I will conclude with some ideas about risk factors that make us potentially abusive to our current and former patients, as well as to our profession, and suggest ways by which we can recognize and manage our own unconscious exploitative urges as early as possible in the process.

Since of all the psychotherapy associations only the APA (American Psychiatric Association) has up to now taken a formal ethical position regarding "former" patients, I will be addressing the special ethical dilemmas currently unique to psychiatrists. However, all psychotherapists may find these considerations relevant to their own practices, since professional organizations representing psychologists, social workers, and other psychotherapists and counselors may soon be amending their ethics codes on this aspect of practice.

BACKGROUND

Clinicians have taken both sides of the argument about sexual involvement with current patients. Hippocrates (Edelstein, 1943) had sworn in the time-honored Oath to abstain "from the seduction of females or males" (p. 3). Centuries later, Freud (1915/1968) clearly articulated the reasons why the psychoanalytic "treatment must be carried out in abstinence" (p. 165). However, some clinicians have more recently argued that social and sexual behavior with current patients is often a beneficial aspect of treatment. McCartney (1966) argued that the resolution (often by mutual physical contact) of the "overt transference" was necessray for full adult emotional development. Shepard (1971) also wrote to this effect. Easson (1971) shifted attention to "former" patients, when he described in detail the process by which successfully terminated psychotherapy could be naturally transformed into an egalitarian social relationship, and suggested that a subsequent marriage of the ex-therapist and "former" patient could be a laudable therapeutic outcome. At the Massachusetts Psychological Association annual meeting, Redstone (1978) developed the theme further in a discussion of the "posttermination phase of psychotherapy."

At the same time, professional awareness and concern about relations with patients still in treatment was building in other settings. In 1978, the Ethics Committee of the APA adopted the statement that,

"Sexual activity with a patient is unethical" (American Psychiatric Association, 1978, p. 4), and the American Psychological Association soon followed suit. In the same year Kardener et al. (1973) surveyed physicians, and shortly thereafter Holroyd and Brodsky (1977) surveyed psychologists regarding their behaviors and attitudes toward sexual involvement with patients. Masters and Johnson (1976) had already argued that sexual relationships with patients was seduction, resulting from the abuse of the therapist's power, and should be prosecuted as rape. In 1980, the National Association of Social Work's code of ethics was amended to read, "The social worker should under no circumstances engage in sexual activities with clients." Pope et al. (1986), in a paper presented at the annual meeting of the American Psychological Association, described the diagnosis and treatment of the "therapist–patient sex syndrome," as a variant of post–traumatic stress disorder. Even professional liability insurance companies now often limit or exclude coverage for "undue familiarity."

Concern about sexual involvement with "former" patients was much slower in coming to the attention of ethics committees and state legislatures. When sexual behavior with former patients was considered at all, the argument usually centered on the question of how long after treatment stopped should the therapist have to wait. Debates about the proper length of the waiting period arguments resulted in wide variations among states. In 1986, Florida enacted laws (Chapter 21U-15.004) to the effect that the therapy relationship exists "in perpetuity," while in California (Civic Code 43-93) and Minnesota (148 A.01-.05) the waiting period is 2 years. The ethics committees of our professional organizations were slow to follow with action.

The magnitude of the problem, however, is not small. Gartrell et al. (1986) reported that of 1,442 psychiatrists responding to their nationally distributed questionnaire, 84 psychiatrists reported sexual involvement with patients, and 63% of the incidents happened after the treatment had terminated. Furthermore, 74% of the psychiatrist respondents thought it should be ethical to do so in "some circumstances." Herman et al. (1987) reported that in the same survey 29.6% of the responding psychiatrists believed that therapist–patient sexual contacts are sometimes acceptable with patients after termination of therapy, and some 8.5% had no opinion on the subject at all. Akamatsu (1988), having surveyed 1000 psychologists, reported that only 44.7% of the respondents believed that sexual intimacy with former clients was "very unethical," and of the total respondents, 76% believed that the time elapsed since termination of therapy should be a factor in evaluating the ethics of such behavior. A smaller number of the psychologists surveyed (22%) thought transference issues were relevant to such evaluations. Even fewer psychologists (14%) thought exploitation issues were relevant. Perhaps these diverse attitudes prevented consensus within professional associations of social workers and psychologists and delayed the adoption of formal ethical standards for conduct relating to "former" patients. It was not until December 1988 that psychiatrists took action, as noted above.

This APA ethics code now addresses the goal of protecting "former" patients from harm, but it does not address the need for the profession to be protected from itself. It leaves for case–by–case interpretation the definitions of "sexual involvement," "exploitation," "former patient," and the question of whether "emotions" are always conscious. It does imply that if the patient's emotions were not exploited, no ethical violations have occurred. Further, it implies that the doctor–patient relationship can cease, thereby creating the "former patient" concept. At no time does the APA ethics code mention explicitly other potentially exploitative post-therapeutic relationships (such as financial, recreational, or vocational) between psychiatrists and their "former" patients, and these issues are beyond the scope of our discussion here as well. Also beyond the scope of this chapter are important concerns regarding the differences in ethical covenants distinguishing nonpsychiatric physicians, psychiatrists, and nonmedical psychotherapists, and the personality characteristics associated with clinicians at high risk for unethical sexual behavior.

COMMON STANDARDS OF CONDUCT

Before discussing the application of professional ethics to the issue of sexual behavior with "former" patients, I will consider the ways professional ethics are distinguished from other standards of psychotherapeutic conduct, including morals and personal ethics, law, clinical care, and wisdom. While each of us strives for at least a partial integration of these standards, the standards themselves are quite distinct. As a result we may at times be forced to make difficult, conscious decisions about our own personal and professional behavior.

Personal ethics standards (morals) are derived from the personal relationships one has with significant others (family, friends, religious and cultural leaders) and will vary widely among equally competent psychotherapists. Opinions regarding issues such as abortion, divorce, and truth telling are strongly influenced by personal ethics. Personal ethics are related but not identical to legality. Laws are derived from political entities that generate, monitor, and sanction behavior. Actions (such as civil disobedience) can easily be moral but illegal. Standards of good clinical practice are applied within the community where one professional and can be judged only by one's practicing peers. Personal wisdom guides behavior when these standards become integrated with one's internal conscious and unconscious drives, personal thought patterns, and appreciation of the consequences of action. Naturally, there may be wide disagreement on courses of wise action.

PROFESSIONAL ETHICS

Distinguished from all the above is the code of professional ethics. For each psychotherapist it is defined as that ethical code subscribed to by joining one's professional organization. The ethics code is one of the most significant, distinguishing characteristics of each professional organization. The members themselves create and change the code from time to time, melding collegial opinion and professional idealism. The ultimate sanction for unethical behavior is expulsion from the Association. It is clear, of course, that professional ethics codes never apply to patient behavior or to individuals who are not members of the organization.

A professionally unethical act need not damage a patient or be immoral, illegal, or intentional. But it certainly is always offensive to the profession that has generated the code. The code serves as one of the significant guides to assist professionals in distinguishing impulse from action in the conduct of their work and to mitigate the envy, shame, and rage of those who witness colleagues acting on impulses that they deny themselves. For clinicians, dilemmas in practice often arise when the code cannot be explicitly defined or followed and its intent must be inferred.

COVENANT AND CONTRACT

Covenant

Let me now distinguish two elements of the professional ethics code: the covenant and the contract. The professional covenant (Masters, 1975; May, 1975) is a relationship between the profession and the community. For psychiatrists it is the agreement among psychiatrists and between psychiatrists and the community on what "psychiatry" is. The covenant promises the community an enduring fiduciary relation ship with each prospective patient. In this way it gives hope to those who come for treatment and sustains their trust in the physician. By joining the APA and acquiring the power of the collegial collective, the psychiatrist adopts the covenant and is a ceaseless ambassador for the Association. The covenant can be broken only when the professional ceases to be a member of the Association. The patient cannot release the psychiatrist from the covenant.

Contract

The therapeutic contract, however, emerges in the interaction between patient and therapist and begins with the first contact initiated by the patient. This contract presupposes the obligation to "do no harm." It contains the therapist's own unique "frame" definitions, outlining what the therapist and patient need from each other in order for professional services to take place, and provides an opportunity for the patient, with informed consent, to agree to it. Except in certain situations, it forever constrains the therapist, but never the patient, from talking publicly about their interaction. Although the therapist enters the contract bound not only by law but also by the covenant, the patient does not. Thus defined, the contract is not simply an egalitarian agreement between consenting independent adults.

Whereas guidelines for the ethical management of the initiated contract may be clear, the definitions of what initiates a contract may be ambiguous (Simon, 1988) or idiosyncratic (Social Workers Professional Liability Policy, p. 3). For example, the psychotherapist, while covering for a colleague, may have telephone contact with a patient to provide supportive consultation. At another time a psychotherapist may meet a family member of a patient who has been brought to the emergency room for psychiatric help. Although professional ethics standards are not explicit on these cases, insurance companies may limit coverage for a clinician charged with sexual misconduct "with or to any former or current patient or client of any Insured, or with or to any relative or member of the same household of any said patient or client, or with or to any person with whom said patient or client or relative has an affectionate personal relationship" (Social Worker Professional Liability Policy, p. 3).

ENDING THE TREATMENT

The termination of therapy may lend itself to a wide variety of posttermination arrangements defining what the patient and the therapist may expect of themselves and each other. What ends and what continues?

The therapist and patient may decide either to "suspend" the treatment or to bring it to an "end." To suspend the treatment the therapist might tell the patient, "Under the best of conditions, we will not meet again. On the other hand, if you believe that it would be a good idea to call me again, please do." If the treatment is terminated by suspension, the therapist's obligation is extended after "termination" and explicitly holds open forever the therapist's availability for further service. Clearly, the patient never becomes a "former" patient.

Or, to end the treatment, the therapist might say, "It is important that the inevitable posttreatment phase of your growth takes place alone or with someone else. It is not wise for us to consider me as being available to you in the future." The therapist's recommendation to end the treatment arises within the treatment contract from the ongoing clinical judgment about what is best for the patient. The professional burden of maintaining this aspect of the frame, as with other frame issues, rests on the therapist alone.

If the treatment ends and the patient subsequently "breaks" the contract by calling the therapist for further consultation, the professionally ethical therapist honors the fiduciary relationship, maintains the covenant, and works therapeutically within the "ending" contract. The patient is still a patient: The therapist is not free to abandon either the covenant or the contract. One of the prices paid by the practicing clinician is to forego the pleasure of an uncomplicated extra-therapeutic relationship with a person with whom a professional contract has once been initiated.

DILEMMAS

Three case examples will now illustrate familiar dilemmas. The first one concerns a situation in which the psychiatrist and the "former" patient knew each other socially before treatment began.

> Dr. Adams, a divorced psychiatrist, asks you informally if you think it's ethical for him to go to dinner with Dianne. He tells you the following story:
>
> After his divorce, he met Dianne, a young, attractive single nurse on the inpatient ward. Their relationship was quite informal and friendly, but because she was already committed to a relationship, he never asked her out. He left the hospital and went into practice. One year later, when she was abandoned by her boyfriend, she became

moody and lonely. She recalled that she had liked and trusted Dr. Adams, and she turned to him for therapy. She soon began to feel better and terminated the treatment, not expecting to return. She still liked and trusted Dr. Adams and, knowing that he was not married, one month later invited him to her apartment for dinner. He eagerly accepted since he had liked her for a long time. They have never had physical contact except to shake hands warmly at the beginning and at the end of treatment. He asks you if you think it's all right for him to go to this dinner, since he would have asked her out long ago if she had been available.

The second vignette concerns a psychiatrist and a relative of a "former" patient who are introduced socially, independent of the prior professional relationship.

Dr. Evans is a single psychiatrist who asks your collegial advice on the ethics of his calling Elaine for a date. He describes the situation:

He was invited to a party and met Elaine, an attractive woman who reminded him that they had met once 3 years ago while he was covering the emergency room. She had brought her seriously depressed widowed father for emergency admission and in the course of this event Dr. Evans had spent 2 hours interviewing her about her father, herself, and her family. Her father had been admitted to the care of another psychiatrist and had been billed for the emergency room visit. Dr. Evans recalls really liking her then, and he is now tempted to invite her out socially. He knows he should not convert treatment situations into friendships, but he wonders if she really was a patient of his. In any case, he believes this independent introduction changes things, and gives him a new start with her. He also thinks that the 3-year gap was long enough to make the prior relationship irrelevant, even if it were a professional one, but still he is vaguely troubled. He asks your advice on the ethics of his asking her for a date.

The third situation is one in which therapy turns into a marriage:

Betsy felt mildly depressed after a thwarted romance and the death of her father. For treatment she was referred to Dr. Good, a well-known and respected, divorced male psychiatrist. Dr. Good soon discovered that he was scheduling her as his last patient for the day and was staying late. He was also telling her more about himself than was his custom. He sometimes moved over to sit next to her on the couch and allowed her, without comment, to put her hand on his arm. Finally, their hands touched and with mutual relief they acknowledged their affection for each other. Since she was feeling better, they quickly brought her treatment to an end so that they could enjoy each other socially. Thus began a courtship that ended in marriage a year later. Now 10 years and two children later, they are blissfully happy and he continues his practice in their community. A colleague, in discussing their situation said, "What's wrong with that?"

Now, for an appendix, the story goes on:

When their youngest child entered first grade, Betsy felt abandoned, fell in love with the first grade teacher, and decided to divorce Dr. Good. In the divorce proceedings she alleged that he had abused his power in courting and marrying her. Alleging damages to herself and the children, she filed a malpractice suit in addition to the divorce. In order to bolster her case, she brought it to the attention of the local ethics committee, charging him with unethical behavior.

DISCUSSION

In addressing the ethical aspects of the above situations, we have two categories of concern. The first is the possibility that the treatment contract has been formed and subsequently breached and that, as a result, the patient has been unethically exploited and abused. The second is the possibility that the covenant has been breached and the profession thereby exploited or harmed. Since these concerns are addressed on a case–by–case basis, we can not answer them definitively here, but we should look at some of the specific questions they pose.

Contract Violation

In determining the possibility of contract violation, we must acknowledge ambiguity in the definitions of "sexual involvement," "exploitation," "emotions," and "former patient." The case examples raise questions about the physical and emotional limits of "sexual involvement." The psychiatrist may wonder whether shaking hands, sitting on a couch with a patient, having an extended conversation with a "former" patient at a party, accepting an invitation to dinner, or even wearing attractive clothing might be construed as sexual involvement. Does discussing these actions with the patient, obtaining the patient's permission, and even receiving affirmation of their therapeutic usefulness remove the possibility of sexual involvement? Suppose, as in psychodrama, or in the therapy of children and adolescents, the psychotherapy technique regularly includes physical contact?

The psychiatrist is expected to use the power obtained from the covenant therapeutically. In these examples we will look for possible exploitation and the abuse of power. Is it an abuse of power to accept an unsolicited invitation to dinner from a patient whose treatment has probably come to an end forever? Clinicians may often extend their therapy sessions a minute or two, or talk with their patients about themselves. At what point does this become an abuse of power? Is it use or abuse of power for Dr. Good to agree to bring the treatment to an end so that he and his patient could enjoy a mutually desired social relationship? (*The Psychiatric Times*, 1989).

How conscious must an "emotion" be? If the therapy uses cognitive, behavioral, or other theoretical bases that deny or ignore unconscious transference considerations, does that mean such aspects of treatment don't exist? And if they do exist, can they be analyzed away? Can the patient emerge from therapy without unresolved unconscious feelings for the therapist?

Is the doctor–patient relationship always, in part, an unconscious, permanently unresolvable emotional analogue of the parent–child relationship? Does the covenant not promise this? It is possible that Elaine, the patient's daughter, has an unresolvable dependency on Dr. Evans whom she met professionally once 3 years ago? If Dr. Good's behavior was initially professionally unethical, does the marriage a year later and the happy years of childrearing change the overall ethical nature of his behavior? Was he marrying someone who is still a "patient," or did she release herself from that role by gratefully terminating treatment and marrying him?

Covenant Violation

The covenant has been violated if the psychotherapist's behavior has caused the profession to suffer in the public eye, or if it hinders his or her professional capacity to consistently provide quality services. In any of these cases has the psychotherapist abused the power of the Association, and thereby exploited the profession?

When Dr. Adams accepts the invitation, Dr. Good marries, and Dr. Evans calls for the date, they are sending a message to the community that, under certain conditions, a patient could expect this kind of treatment from an ethical psychiatrist. Would this public belief enhance or hinder treatment efforts with subsequent patients? As members of the ethics committee to which Mrs. Good comes with her complaint, what shall we do with our own envy, shame, guilt, relief, or rage in personally having known Dr. Good while he was happily married? What if we know other psychiatrists who are still happily married to their former patients and whose ethical behavior has never been questioned? It is not impossible that one such psychiatrist sits on the ethics committee.

RECOGNIZING POTENTIALLY UNETHICAL BEHAVIOR IN OURSELVES

With the questions above remaining unanswered, let us shift our attention to ourselves as practicing clinicians in order to better detect our own potentially unethical behavior.

First, we should pay attention to the factors that put us all at risk. The first question is: Are there ways of knowing who among us are especially at risk? Simon (1989) suggested that we are at high risk for developing unethical sexual behavior with *current* patients if we meet the following criteria:

1. Men between 40 and 60 years old.
2. Have teenage children or troubled marriages.
3. Have chronic medical symptoms, depression, disturbed sleep, or problems with drug or alcohol abuse.
4. Have "burned out" practices that are ungratifying.
5. Have young attractive female patients.

In the absence of separate criteria regarding sexual behavior with "former" patients, these guidelines will have to serve us. Although all psychotherapists are vulnerable to ethical indiscretions, there is no comparable literature citing special factors putting women, gay, or lesbian psychiatrists at risk for unethical sexual involvement with either current or "former" patients.

Second, careful consideration should be given to the terms of termination. It is best for the therapist to remember that the posttreatment contract and relationship endures forever in some form, and must be discussed with the patient as a part of the termination. There are many ways to terminate treatment, but it is important to anticipate the possible feelings and wishes of the patient for further contact, and to agree on ways the therapist will respond. The therapist may draw on this discussion later, in order to delay an action that might violate the ongoing termination contract and thereby be abusive to the "former" patient. It is also important for the psychotherapist to anticipate the corollary, his or her own possible wishes for further contact with the patient, either for social, recreational, vocational, or business purposes.

The ethical therapist will recognize that these self-serving wishes are common and that they may derive from knowledge and feelings about the patient that arise during the treatment. If these wishes are acted upon with a current or "former" patient, an abuse of the covenant, if not the contract, is difficult to avoid. It should be noted that I have used quotes in referring to the "former" patient since, in practice, there are no former patients.

Third, it is important to be alert to behavioral clues that indicate that our unconscious forces may be putting the "former" patient at risk for abuse. Insofar as countertransference feelings are, by definition, unconscious, they may motivate behaviors that may seem at the time to be unusual but quite reasonable, and perhaps even creatively therapeutic. After these countertransference feelings have abated, these same actions may appear clearly to have been exploitative deviations from the covenant and from the therapeutic contract normally established by the therapist. Thus, unusual or uncommon behavior on the part of the therapist may be an early clue to unconscious exploitative or abusive motivation.

Fourth, we must be alert to the "fit" of our behavior with professional idealism. Could our creative management of the case be presented at grand rounds without excessive shame? Would our colleagues' professionalism be enhanced by our discovery of new treatment techniques?

Finally, we must continue our work toward agreement regarding the boundary of what behaviors are and are not ethical with current and "former" patients. As experience accumulates within our professions, we will probably continue to evolve guidelines balancing popular opinion and ideal professionalism. Each of our professional associations has yet to address in their ethics codes the ageless concern about the professional covenant and the ongoing fiduciary relationship of the therapist and patient.

OBTAINING CONSULTATION FOR OURSELVES

What steps should we as therapists take upon discovering we may be in a potentially exploitative state of mind? As in other clinical emergencies, the time to act is as soon as action is considered. Here it is imperative that therapists protect the patient, the profession, and themselves by talking it out with another person. Depending on the therapist's initial awareness of concern, the consultant may be a colleague, the ethics committee itself, a therapist, a lawyer, an insurance agent, or a friend.

A collegial consultation might be useful in determining the clinical wisdom of the contemplated action. One's own therapist might be useful in discovering the personal wisdom of it. The fine print of the liability insurance policy should be consulted carefully, and an attorney might guide a therapist on the legal ramifications of any contemplated action. The therapist's religious leader, parent, or family might be an appropriate consultant regarding the moral aspect of his behavior. It is often in the conflicting interaction of these guidelines for behavior that the psychiatrist experiences painful indecision about actions to take with the patient. Exploring this pain with another person often delays the impulse to act and leads to an unforeseen solution to a professional ethical dilemma.

If the situation seems too intimate or shameful to discuss with anyone beside the "former" patient, all the more reason for being uneasy with oneself and getting an outside audience quickly. Proudly handling these situations with self-reliant determination may lead one deeper into self-deception. The "former" patient, of course, is not a good consultant regarding professional ethics. If, at the moment, the therapist and "former" patient are together enjoying a relationship that is harmful or exploitative to the patient, the therapist, or the profession, only the therapist is professionally accountable. Just as we counsel our patients to understand before they act, we should heed that advice ourselves.

SUMMARY

As of this writing, only one psychotherapy professional association (American Psychiatric Association) has adopted an ethical code stating that sexual involvement with a "former" patient "almost always is unethical." Whereas the definitions of sexual involvement, exploitation, emotions, and "former" patient are left for case interpretation, all psychotherapists are cautioned to carefully monitor their own behavior and to seek outside consultation at the first moment sexual or any other potentially self-serving involvement with a current or "former" patient is anticipated.

When professionals join together, a collective professional covenant is established. Psychotherapists, in joining their respective professional associations, subscribe to that ethical covenant. In contrast, it is the patient who initiates the treatment contract by first contacting the therapist. However the treatment ends, the therapist alone must manage the covenant and the enduring posttreatment contract. Even if the therapist and "former" patient meet under other circumstances or have other relationships before or after treatment, their relationship is forever unbalanced by the therapist's unshared responsibility for managing both the treatment and the termination contract and by the unresolvable power inequities promised by the covenant. Both the covenant and the contract continue beyond the treatment. It seems ultimately undeniable that "Once a patient, always a patient."

REFERENCES

Akamatsu, J. T. (1988). Intimate relationships with former clients: National survey of attitudes and behavior among practitioners. *Professional Psychology: Research and Practice, 19*(4), 454–458.

American Psychiatric Association. (1978). *The principles of medical ethics with annotations especially applicable to psychiatry.* Washington, DC: Author.

Divorce–malpractice suit is landmark decision in domestic law and ethics. (1989). *The Psychiatric Times, 6*(10), 31.

Easson, W. M. (1971). Patient and therapist after termination of psychotherapy. *American Journal of Psychotherapy, 25*(4), 635–642.

Edelstein, L. (1943). *The Hippocratic Oath: Text, translation, and interpretation.* Baltimore: Johns Hopkins University Press.

Freud, S (1968). Observations on transference-love: Further recommendations on the technique of psychoanalysis III. In J. Strachey (Ed. and Trans.), *The standard edition of the complete psychological works of Sigmund Freud* (Vol. 12). London: Hogarth Press. (Original work published 1915)

Gabbard, G. O. (Ed.). (1989). *Sexual exploitation in professional relationships.* Washington, DC: American Psychiatric Press.

Gartrell, N., Herman, J., Olarte, S., Feldstein, M., & Localio, R. (1986). Psychiatrist–patient sexual contact: Results of a national survey. I. Prevalence. *American Journal of Psychiatry 143*, 1126–1131.

Herman, J. L., Gartrell, N., Olarte, S., Feldstein, M., & Localio, R. (1987). Psychiatrist–patient sexual contact: Results of a national survey. II. Psychiatrist's attitudes. *American Journal of Psychiatry, 144*, 164–169.

Holroyd, J., & Brodsky, A. (1977, October). Psychologists attitudes and practices regarding erotic and nonerotic physical contact with patients. *American Psychologist*, 843–849.

Kardener, S., Fuller, M., & Mensh, I. (1973). A survey of physicians attitudes and practices regarding erotic and non-erotic contact with patients. *American Journal of Psychiatry, 130*, 1077–1081.

Massachusetts Psychiatric Society. (1989). Massachusetts Psychiatric Society News: Ethical Principles Amended. *Massachusetts Psychiatric Society, 25*(5), 10.

Masters, R. G. (1975, December, 24–28). *Is contract an adequate basis for medical ethics?* (Hastings Center Report 5). Hastings-on-Hudson, New York, Institute of Society, Ethics and the Life Sciences.

Masters, W. H., & Johnson, V. E. (1976). Principles of the new sex therapy. *American Journal of Psychiatry, 133,* 548–554.

May, W. F. (1975, December, 29–31). *Code, covenant, contract, or philanthropy — A basis for professional ethics.* (Hastings Center Report 5). Hastings-on-Hudson, New York, Institute of Society, Ethics, and the Life Sciences.

McCartney, J. (1966). Overt transference. *Journal of Sex Research, 2*(3), 227–237.

Pope, K. S., & Bouhoutsos J. C. (1986). *Sexual intimacy between therapists and patients.* New York: Praeger.

Redstone, J. (1978). *The post-termination phase of psychotherapy.* Paper presented at the annual meeting of the Massachusetts Psychological Society, Boston, MA.

Shepard, M. (1971). *The love treatment: Sexual intimacy between patients and psychotherapists.* New York: Wyden.

Simon, R. I. (1988). *Concise guide to clinical psychiatry and the law.* Washington, DC: American Psychiatric Press.

Simon, R. I. (1989). Sexual exploitation of patients: How it begins before it happens. *Psychiatric Annals, 19*(2), 104–112.

Social Worker Professional Liability Policy. (1990). New York: American Home Insurance Company.

Stone, A. A. (1984). *Law, psychiatry, and morality.* Washington, DC: American Psychiatric Press.

S·I·X

꙰

The Nature of Time and Psychotherapeutic Experience: When Treatment Duration Shifts from Time-limited to Long-Term

TIMOTHY C. ENGELMANN

MAX DAY

STEPHEN DURANT

W ith the introduction of HMOs and the increased effectiveness of refined short-term treatment approaches, there is currently a strong trend in outpatient psychotherapy to shorten the duration of treatment. Explicit factors that influence the shortening of treatment involve a need for patients to experience change more quickly, in order to ameliorate pain and facilitate the production of more healthy behavior. This approach overlooks the fact that the experience of anxiety and sadness are two important warning signals that work to strengthen the patient. A further factor in decreasing the length of treatment is the considerable demand made upon the clinician's available hours in treatment settings, for in many clinics long waiting lists can delay assignment to a psychotherapist. If treatment duration can be reduced, then more patients will be offered help. A less explicit factor, but one that exerts a strong amount of pressure to reduce treatment length, is financial. Patients are often unable to afford long-term treatment, and many insurance companies are eager to support treatment that is cost-effective. An even more subtle factor that influences duration of treatment is societal. Implicitly, there is an assumption that the more efficient the procedure, the better it is. Many people's lifestyles preclude time and resources for long-term involvement. While this type of lifestyle could in itself be a focus of treatment, it is often ignored because urgency for change hints that the more expeditiously available the product, the more fully life can be experienced. These demands, either subtle or direct, place pressure upon psychotherapy to keep the pace moving as rapid as possible. Compounding these pressures are ambivalent feelings carried by the anticipation of change. By shortening treatment duration, the wish to remain the same may predominate. Although there are some aspects of patients' lives that change in short-term treatment, the actual changes may be superficial or short-lived. Although psychotherapeutic "success" will be determined by these changes, other, more fundamental aspects of the patients' lives may remain recalcitrant to change. In short-term treatment selective themes are focused upon and, when resolved or changed, the patient is considered better and treatment is terminated. This approach raises a perennial question as to whether such change is an artifact or will endure over time.

It is the authors' opinion that not taking the time to probe more fundamental material that is decidedly left unexamined in short-term treatment is ultimately detrimental. If deeper material is unaddressed, it will adversely impact upon patients' lives. Given these considerations, it is incumbent upon the therapeutic contract to allow for as long a time as is needed to thoroughly address this deeper material.

By exploring what takes place when treatment duration changes, these and other factors become more explicit. Additionally, changes in treatment duration illuminate aspects of the nature of time within psychotherapy.

TIME CHANGE IN PSYCHOTHERAPY

There are two types of change in the duration of treatment that commonly occur and allow for the assessment of the impact of time on psychotherapy. Correspondingly, when treatment duration changes, the nature of time also changes. One type of change in the duration of treatment is when prescribed *time-limited psychotherapy extends to long-term treatment*. The other type of change occurs when patients who are seen by therapists in training programs *continue treatment with their therapists* after the training is completed. Training programs set an iatrogenetically determined termination date when the therapist completes training. If the therapy continues after this termination date is set, a shift from time-limited to long-term therapy occurs.

There is clinical and theoretical urgency to examine the impact of extending treatment duration on process and change. Clinically, extending treatment duration has many effects. Theoretically, increasing its duration provides opportunity to examine some basic assumptions pertaining to time and psychotherapy.

This chapter reviews aspects of treatment that are affected when the duration of treatment is extended from time-limited or closed-ended to long-term or open-ended. Specifically, transference and countertransference, resistance, the material presented in therapy, and technique are reviewed. Further, certain types of patients are more amenable to successful transition from short-term to long-term treatment and clinical recommendations are offered. Finally, epistemological questions of clinical meaning and proof are reviewed as clinical meaning undergoes fundamental change when treatment duration is extended. Although this chapter does not address the relative efficacy between time-limited and long-term psychotherapy approaches, there is an additional area of importance implied when treatment duration changes. By exploring change in treatment duration, certain contrasts between time-limited and long-term psychotherapy will be evident.

THE ISSUE OF TIME AND EMERGENCE
OF TRANSFERENCE

James Mann (1973) raises the issue of time in presenting his arguments for time-limited therapy. In time-limited therapy, an end is immediately established that evokes awareness, and in his view, conformity to successional or an adult grasp of time. This conformity involves separation and loss and questions pertaining to one's *raison d'être.* Awareness of sequential time is one of the earliest developmental accomplishments, one of the most important to resolve existentially, and the final to master as one approaches death. Mann suggests that time-limited therapy, by definition, highlights an awareness of time as a central ingredient in the psychotherapeutic process. Instead of avoiding awareness of time, time is placed on center stage to facilitate and quicken the process of therapy — and bring the patient's life into greater correspondence with adult time. Although Mann fails to define adult time specifically, it appears to correspond to a sequential understanding of time, or, as he puts it, categorical time. We define *sequential time* in terms of the past, present, and future as measured by seconds, minutes, hours, weeks, years, centuries, and millennia: It is defined by clocks and calendars. An implicit goal of psychotherapy, is to raise patients' awareness of sequential time, and make their lives more congruent with it.

As defined in units of past, present, and future, sequential time orders experience. In time-limited therapy, this ordering is used to bring critical issues of treatment to the forefront. By framing treatment as time-limited, closer correspondence to the present is actively made by the therapist. The patient is less likely to regress, and material is held closer to immediate problems. Transference is handled, but in such a way as to limit the extent of regression by selecting one focal point to work on (cf. Luborsky, 1984). The patient's wish to return to a more childlike experience of time, that is, one that has minimal boundaries (Bonaparte, 1940; Piaget, 1954, 1966), is frustrated as reminders of termination and treatment course are made. It is also curbed by relating specific transference issues to current difficulties through focused, technical maneuvers. Mann argues that this is beneficial as the patient's regression is titrated against the balance of focused current events.

While correspondence to sequential time is a natural result and direct aim of short-term treatment, there is a fuzziness as to how time is conceptualized and used. If transference is the continuation of past relationships into the therapeutic one, it involves concepts of time that are categorically distinct from that of sequential time. The clinical construct of transference, along with the clinical constructs of fixation, developmental arrest, and regression all have in common a continuation of the past into the present. Also, through projection into future expectations, plans, and goals, sequential time becomes subordinated. Further, dream work and other types of unconscious activity do not follow rules corresponding to sequential time. Although they have some correspondence to sequential time, dreams are generally governed by other rules of time. It is our position that understanding clinical constructs such as transference exclusively from the perspective of sequential time is an error, and limits their range and breadth. Other concepts of time need to be introduced to understand these constructs more fully — and how the extension of treatment duration affects them.

Since Einstein's theory of relativity was introduced, striking changes in how we understand the universe have been made. A closed-ended, absolute Newtonian understanding of the world has been replaced by an open-ended, relativistic understanding. Time is no longer posed as a universal and an unalterable given. Rather, time and space are relative, with the only constant being the speed of light. In psychotherapy, time and its experience is relative to treatment duration. All clinical phenomena embedded within the treatment situation are defined by its duration. For instance, sequential time is more salient in time-limited therapy. There is both an explicit and an implicit selection process that filters in clinical material relevant to sequential time. Material is understood more in the focused here-and-now. When the duration of treatment opens into a continuing long-term model, sequential time becomes less salient, allowing for other concepts of time to predominate. As a result, clinical phenomena are reshaped for they are no longer understood from the perspective of sequence, but rather in terms more akin to the open-ended clinical material being presented. Concepts of time that pertain to extending the duration of treatment and the expression of clinical phenomena are epochal time, nonlinear time, and reversibility of time.

Epochal time is defined by events or epochs that have a monumental impact upon history. Epochal events transform sequential time. They occur within the matrix of sequential time, but radically influence all events that precede and are subsequent to the given epoch. Through such dramatic impact, the events that occur in the epoch have a timeless quality as they transcend the constraints imposed on them by sequential time. Therefore, epochal time is categorically distinct from sequential time. For instance, epochal events in Western civilization are such events as the birth of Christ, the signing of the Constitution, and the holocaust, which have duration and significance that exceed the constraints of sequential time. Likewise, the birth of the individual and the continuity of personal identity involve epochal time. They fit within the fabric of sequential time, for it is in sequential time that they are known, but they also transcend sequential time, by both influencing events occurring within sequential time and by lasting beyond its limits. Epochal time also has relevance in personality development. Developmental epochs that follow similar principles involve separation–individuation, the birth of siblings, oedipal events, and loss. The ways in which these are handled persist throughout the sequence of time in individual lives.

Nonlinear time involves the condensation and expansion of sequential time. It is analogous to symbol formation. Symbols form through condensation and expansion of multiple levels of meaning (cf. Ricouer, 1970). For instance, an event occurring during the oedipal period of development condenses previously occurring events and coalesces to form the backdrop that will influence later occurring experiences. Through epochal and nonlinear time, activity taking place during developmental epochs has far-reaching and profound influence both on the organization of events that took place prior to the epoch and on the experience of subsequent events. In the clinical setting, transference, when defined by epochal and nonlinear time, reflects how epochs were initially experienced and continue to influence patients' lives. When transference is interpreted, the epoch is reorganized.

Reversibility of time is perhaps the most important concept in clinical theory, for herein the possibility of therapeutic change through genetic interpretation is achieved. The reliving of memories brought to bear on the present through transference enables a redefinition of the past by traversing the unconscious to the previously unresolved issue.

Epochal time, nonlinear time, and time-reversibility are interdependent and impact upon the individual's world that is ordered by sequential time. An epochal event has impact on certain nodal points in the history of the individual, which develop in a nonlinear fashion and which impact upon previously occurring events. The construct of transference involves these three aspects of time. Epochal time permits the continuation of the transference into the present. It evolves nonlinearly as different developmental levels unfold. Through interpretation, there is the possibility of reversibility, when the manifestation of the past is made conscious in the present relationship. The interpretation will reorganize the influence of the set of past experiences taking place in the transference. Once made conscious and worked through, correspondence to sequential time will occur. The rearranged structure of the past, formed through interpretation of the transference, evolves into a new epoch from which future experiences will be defined. The representations constructed in therapy serve as nodal points for the activation of a new line of epochal time. Through new lines of epochal time, future experiences take on new definitions of meaning.

Unconscious activity presumably has no organization of time. Organization occurs through conscious thought, by placing sequence and order to events. While time-limited therapy enhances conformity to sequential time, it short-circuits the ability to experience and explore other dimensions of clinical experience that are governed by these other aspects of time. For example, transference involves a continuation of aspects of past relationships into the present, where they are relived as if the past relationship is still going on. If taken from the perspective of sequential time, transference is a remnant of the past enacted in the present. From the perspective of epochal time, no time has elapsed from the original relationship to the transferential relationship. We propose that maintaining a working alliance enables the patient to ally with sequential time so that regression into epochal time through the transference can occur without disruption. When the transference relationship becomes interpreted, old ways of relating dissolve and epochal time is given new definition. The resultant change is made manifest through the interlocking sequential time of the patient. The past is no longer operating on the present in a manner that prohibits growth. The old is made new in congruence with sequential aspects of time. For transferential relationships to be more accessible to the present, sufficient access to epochal time is necessary. Such fuller access is achieved in long-term therapy, in which the constraints of sequential time placed by time-limited psychotherapy are less operative. If psychotherapy is bounded by a defined time limit, there is less likelihood that the patient will experience nonlinear time-related events.

The following case illustrates the constriction placed on transference expression when epochal time is truncated by time-limited psychotherapy and the expansion of such expression when treatment duration extends to long-term.

CASE EXAMPLE

Brenda is a 43-year-old divorcee who was seen in time-limited psychotherapy for relief of distress occurring after the breakup of a relationship she had had with a married man. Aspects of this relationship were presented and explored in her initial treatment and the patient felt somewhat improved. However, after treatment had ended, the patient continued with difficulties that led to a referral for long-term psychotherapy.

A bright, articulate, and insightful woman, Brenda had reached the top of her career as a financial consultant for a leading investment firm until severe physical pain had paralyzed her from continuing her job duties. In the course of long-term treatment, it became evident that her physical pain was related to failures in her relationships. Although these difficulties were partially addressed in short-term treatment, that treatment had focused on the relationship she had had with the married man. Perceiving herself as one who must yield to the demands of others, she learned not to show her feelings, fearing that their expression would evoke abandonment. Brenda spent considerable amount of personal resources in taking care of others, rather than attending to her own wishes. In time-limited treatment, this general pattern was overlooked. Caring for others compensated for emotional sustenance that was missing from her relationships. Her organizational abilities and superior intelligence made for much monetary success, but did not provide needed emotional support.

Through the course of long-term treatment, the roots of her

emotional difficulties slowly became evident. With some trepidation, Brenda described her mother as living a rather reclusive life. She lived in constant fear of being harmed by either natural events, such as a tornado hitting the north shore of Boston, or by thieves breaking into her home. From early development on, Brenda gave more to her mother than she received. Throughout her own failed marriage, her relationships with those with whom she had worked, and her affair, a pattern of caring for others emerged. Formed at developmental epochs in her relationship with her mother, this pattern persisted through epochal time, was evident in her daily life through sequential time, and emerged in the transference. Although her pattern of caring for others was pointed out to her in time-limited treatment, full evolution of her transference did not form until she was in long-term treatment, when the constraints on epochal time were lifted. When her transference to her father emerged, markedly vivid aspects of her past became manifested. Brenda relived the feelings of pronounced inferiority she had had when she was about 6 or 7 years old. They became strikingly displayed in the transference, to the point that when she came in after a session of expressing these memories, she stated, "I felt as if I was seven. The experiences were so clear, I was neither my present age nor 7, I relived them here." As her memory of these earlier events became manifest, anger at her father for being weak and ineffectual emerged. It soon became clear that events of the past were being continued into the transference. Also operative in the transference were these earlier occurring experiences now lived out in her present-day relationships. Once interpreted, the course of epochal time was traversed, reversibility of time was encountered, and a new epoch formed in the treatment was subsequently activated. The patient began successfully to assert her needs. With friends she increasingly learned how to receive for herself, significantly reduced her chronic pain, and returned to work.

In Brenda's first treatment, aspects of her relationships with her parents were addressed. However, the change that occurred was not enduring. In long-term treatment, the relationships that had occurred during development persisted into the transference through the course of epochal time. Change was made through interpretation as a new epoch was formed in treatment. Reversibility took place as the new epoch replaced the old one. Her short-term treatment addressed aspects of her relationships, but, as it was more congruous to sequential time, these aspects were not brought into complete analysis. When she entered long-term treatment, the evolution of epochal time took place and successful access to her transference was achieved.

TIME AND TRANSFERENCE–
COUNTERTRANSFERENCE THEMES

The duration of treatment will impact upon the extent to which the patient will manifest transference themes in psychotherapy. In time-limited treatment, the transference may or may not be focused upon. Although transference themes are present, the transference may not be brought to direct and consistent interpretation. It may be left as the "ground" upon which clinical material is the "figure." For instance, a patient comes to treatment for help in establishing and maintaining meaningful relationships. In discussing aspects of the patient's relationships, a transference theme may become evident in which the therapist is seen as a protective, benevolent individual. In long-term treatment, this transference would be traced to aspects of the patient's life involving one or two parental figures and extended to cover other concurrently occurring relationships. In time-limited treatment, the transference theme might be excluded from inquiry as aspects of the patient's relationships with others are addressed. In this latter case, the transference provides the ground upon which presenting symptoms are generated and worked on. Leaving the transference theme exclusively as ground can provide symptomatic relief, but the depth of exploration and treatment of the nature of the patient's interpersonal relationships will not take place.

When time-limited treatment extends to long-term treatment, a figure–ground shift in the importance of the transference will inevitably occur. No longer will the transference be the blackboard upon which symptomatic complaints are drawn. Rather, the transference becomes the direct object of inquiry. With this shift in focus, symptomatic issues gradually recede into the background, allowing transference to become figure. When this occurs, the phenomenological field of inquiry for the patient and therapist expands. The breadth and range of the transference is increased, and there will be more intense affective expression, and *pari passu* an intensification of countertransference reaction. At the juncture between time-limited and long-term therapy, there is greater risk for patients to drop out of treatment. Not only will the focus of inquiry subtly shift, but the intensity of affective expression may drive the patient to abort treatment, rationalizing that what needed to be covered was done under short-term treatment so that long-term treatment is not needed. Continued symptomatic distress coupled with empathically attuned gradual titration of the patient's ability to tolerate increased affective expression will facilitate successful transition to long-term treatment.

A potential artifact of time-limited treatment, and treatment under training programs, is subtle pressure upon the therapist to diminish the expression of transference and countertransference by attending to symptomatic difficulties. Particularly in training programs there is an implicit attempt by the clinician "not to rock the boat." Certain areas of difficulty, thus, may be consciously or unconsciously avoided in order to maximize symptomatic relief. Such an approach will keep treatment from becoming too affectively stimulating, but therapeutic gains will be shortcircuited at the expense of limiting distress. Clearly, when the duration of treatment is extended there will be a considerable impact upon transference and countertransference. If there is a limit to the duration of treatment with a particular patient, certain areas of functioning will be excluded from inquiry. When treatment duration is extended to an open-ended model, then these previously omitted areas will have room for expression. Universal themes involving loss, separation, abandonment, and rejection will be evident toward the known closing of treatment. When treatment is extended, these themes will be mitigated by the continued presence of the therapist, but may be supplanted by fantasies of grandiosity in that the therapist remains, and guilt that wishes are gratified. Further, patients will fear confronting avoided aspects of their world and there will be a potential fostering of dependency on the therapist and the expectation that other wishes will be gratified. The role of the therapist is to monitor and explore these and other themes that are idiosyncratic to each patient who experiences a lengthening of treatment duration. The intensification of affective expression in shifting the transference from figure to ground was observed in the following case.

CASE EXAMPLE

Sean, a 36-year-old manic–depressive patient with an extensive treatment history that occurred primarily in his hometown in southern California, presented to the outpatient clinic for treatment upon arrival to Boston and was assigned to a psychology intern who was to see him for the 2-year duration of his training program.

Overweight, his face scarred from a rare skin ailment, he presented in an often labile, childlike, and devaluing manner. In the first few months of treatment, he displayed doll house furniture that he had habitually collected. Disgust was also presented to the therapist during the early stages of treatment. Sean would either stick his tongue out or make profane gestures at him. At Sean's worst, he was grandiose, devaluing, and entitled; his speech would become pressured and his gesturing more and more obscene. He often lamented his emotional and financial reliance on his parents and feared involvement with his therapist. Whenever it appeared he was becoming attached, he became extremely rude and inappropriate. Often, he directed his tirades at himself, by repeating, "I'm just a fat, crazy nobody who still needs my mother to tell me what to wear."

Through the course of managing his angry outbursts, Sean's history was revealed. Severe physical and sexual abuse prompted several inpatient hospitalizations that began at college during his first attempt at separation from his family. Significant treatment history involved an abrupt and painful termination of therapy with someone he had been seeing for about 9 years. This resulted in a hospitalization that caused Sean to feel manipulated. Feeling flagrantly betrayed and abandoned, he refused to continue with this therapist. His next course of therapy was with a psychology intern, who terminated treatment at the end of the internship.

He began his current treatment after a 6-week delay due to being placed on the clinic's waiting list. Again, the patient felt betrayed and abandoned. His new therapist soon became aware of potential difficulties as he reviewed his very chaotic history. What became implicit in reviewing the patient's potential for difficulty was that he had an extreme vulnerability to disorganization and a propensity for vivid displays of markedly unpleasant affects. With this in mind, the therapist set out initially to offer supportive psychotherapy, for if transference or affects were stimulated, there was considerable risk of hospitalization and very tumultuous treatment.

The supportive approach worked for the first 6 to 9 months of therapy. Sean's life became more organized and he seemed to improve. He obtained a job as a fulltime gardener for a nursery and reduced his acting out. The threat of hospitalization receded into the background. Although his life outside of the therapy improved, he continued to devalue the therapist. Verbal insults replaced his obscene gesturing, and provocative comments about the therapist's personal life commenced. Occasional suspicious and paranoid comments about previous therapists were made. Sean's unpleasant presentation was an attempt to keep the therapist from getting close to him. It became evident that he feared closeness and needed to resort to very primitive maneuvers to keep the therapist distant. Occasionally a glimmer of affective closeness appeared when Sean let down his aggressive manner and revealed a profoundly depressed, helpless, and abandoned side. When the therapist tried to address this, Sean would quickly protect himself through a renewed verbal and gestural assault.

The fluidity of boundaries between Sean and others came to vivid realization when the therapist sustained an accident that left his arm broken and placed in a cast. This exacerbated Sean's difficulties. Distinctions between his anger toward the therapist and reality were blurred. The occurrence of this injury came at approximately a year into therapy. Although the therapist was not aware of this at the time, Sean had mistakenly perceived that this therapist was about to terminate with him, as his past therapist had done at the end of a 1-year internship. As the current therapist's internship was 2 years in length, treatment continued, but not without first being interrupted by Sean's being hospitalized. Severe fear of loss of the therapist, coupled with the reality of the therapist's injury, resulted in Sean's seeking the safety of inpatient treatment.

When it became evident that treatment with this therapist would continue, Sean allowed the therapeutic relationship to deepen in a more positively affective manner. Slowly, Sean verbalized his experience of social isolation, and no longer resorted to his previous profane manner. A mild sense of well-being was emerging. When the end of the 2-year internship approached, there was uncertainty that the therapist would be able to continue seeing Sean. During this time Sean presented with no unusual difficulty. When the decision was made to continue in treatment, Sean's fear of abandonment dissipated and a deepening of the transference relationship emerged.

In the transference Sean had protected from involvement with the therapist because of the realization that this treatment had a fixed termination date. When the treatment became open-ended, increased ambivalence was felt. Once the pressure of time lifted, there was a deeper settling in to the course of treatment. The sense that the therapist was to stay gave "permission" and safety to Sean to reveal deeper, more affectively laden areas of his life. Part of the countertransference involved an acceptance of this material relayed nonverbally through the extension of the treatment duration. As treatment progressed, the lonely, abused, and self-depreciating individual was seen, although vaguely, as someone who was valiantly struggling to carve out his autonomy.

TIME AS FRAME AND THE LOGIC OF CLINICAL MEANING

Psychotherapy process is ordered or framed by different layers of meaning. On a preliminary layer there are realistic features of the therapist and the treatment setting. Along with the duration of treatment, the age and sex of the therapist, and the type of setting in which the patient is seen, pose constraints upon which the transference is formed. Greenson (1976) discusses these features in a general way as the "real relationship," in which the patient relates to the analyst as a person. On a different level, the therapist is seen through the lenses of the transference as the object of transference. Although the real relationship differs markedly from the transference relationship, it can be argued that, in certain respects, the transference is shaped by the real relationship (Gill, 1982). Assuming there is no change in the duration of treatment, the frame in which material is presented in the transference remains constant. When the duration lengthens, a new frame is introduced that will invariably have impact upon the material presented. Such a change will result not only in a figure–ground shift, *it will fundamentally alter the meaning of the material the patient presents.* This change in meaning is not limited to the natural consequences of shifting the focus from symptomatic complaints to transference, but rather, the understanding of the symptomatic complaints themselves will be fundamentally altered.

When the duration of treatment remains constant, changes that take place occur on one level of abstraction. Within this level, material is generated, questions are raised, and the patient's material is understood. The interaction between therapist and patient runs linearly to the frame. Material from one session is continued to the next, connections are made, patterns are evident, and through interpretation these patterns are interconnected into a matrix to form clinical meaning. The generation of material and its understanding are in part governed by the duration of treatment. When the duration of treatment changes to being unlimited, the frame governing the generation and definition of meaning also changes. Changing the frame results in a second-order change that redefines the material generated across previous, current, and future sessions. A new set is introduced that fundamentally alters the meaning of the material produced across the sessions. Watzlawick, Weakland, and Fisch (1974) describe two orders of change that have clear relevance to the changes in duration of treatment. On one level of analysis, events occur and changes take place. Second-order change occurs when the events and changes that take place on the first level are in themselves changed. An example of the two levels of change is seen in accelerating an automobile. With the accelerator depressed, the speed of the car increases. A second-order change occurs when the gears shift, which not only affects the car's speed, but also the action of the accelerator.

When there is a variation in the duration of treatment, a

second-order change occurs. On one plane of analysis, a patient in time-limited psychotherapy presents with material that is juxtaposed against the context of a closed-ended set. This set frames the material presented by ordering it in a linear mode, in which sequential time is most salient. A second-order change occurs when there is a shift to an open-ended set. Such change will reframe the material presented by organizing it differently.

Changing the duration of treatment profoundly influences the meaning of the patient's presentations. Material produced by the patient obtains clinical meaning and logical proof through hermeneutics (Gadamer, 1975, 1976; Spence, 1982; Ricouer, 1970). Through hermeneutics, systematic methods for obtaining meaning and analyzing proof are made. Briefly, these methods involve how specific material is understood by the way it fits into the total context of inquiry. Every aspect of the patient's life unfolds into a story that fits together uniquely. The story and specific information within the story are altered as more and more material is generated, for meaning is derived from the total context from which material is generated. If the context is determined by time-limited treatment, then the meaning of the clinical material will have one context of proof. If that context changes to long-term therapy, then the meaning of that material will also change. New data will be introduced, a broader phenomenological field of inquiry will be achieved, resistances will give way, and more subtle and dynamically charged layers of meaning will emerge. This new meaning does not necessarily negate the meaning obtained under a short-term frame of analysis, for under that frame the meaning has its relevance. The shift in frame does, however, provide new understanding that would not be obtained if treatment were to terminate at the end of training or at the end of short-term therapy. When the set upon which material generated is different, a new baseline for comparison becomes established. Treatment duration provides a context for meaning, upon which clinical material becomes presented, ordered, and understood.

CASE EXAMPLE

An example of the change in meaning of the patient's unfolding narrative when treatment extends from short-term to long-term is found in the case of Nellie. An attractive Ecuadorian woman, Nellie began treatment at 40 when she was hospitalized for a first episode of manic–depression. Upon reaching her 40th birthday, several medical and familial difficulties precipitated a florid mania. A frenzy of extremely intensive affects flooded her. She became very troubled by a deteriorating physical condition. She had a rather thin physique shaped by years of ballet performances, which culminated in her attaining the pinnacle of success in the world of European ballet. This taste of stardom came to a crashing halt, when, in an attempt to push her body to its limit of endurance, she ruptured tendons in her knee. Abruptly, her dancing career was truncated, and her stardom faded.

During Nellie's treatment, her mania subsided to reveal several devastatingly painful experiences. Almost exactly a year before her manic episode her only sister, 2 years her junior, had died unexpectedly of heart failure; her father was diagnosed with terminal polycystic kidney disease; and her fiance broke off his commitment to her. She had just completed recovery from her third knee operation — an operation that proved to be less successful than she had hoped. Her multiple attempts to again reach the heights of stardom in ballet were frustrated, and the realization that she would no longer be able to dance became a vivid reality.

After this initial and troubling history was reviewed, focus on the meaning of the lost function of her leg emerged. Slowly and painfully, her unsuccessful surgeries were described in the difficult context of an evolving recognition that her body would no longer support her aspirations to regain her stardom. Her actual physical pain was the theme for several sessions. Gradually, grief work to deal with the loss of her physical capacity to dance was integrated into her conscious experience. She began to accept her loss and was making plans to choreograph or to pursue other avenues of creative expression. Over the course of about 3 months of treatment, the theme of her leg became less prominent, and the difficulties of daily living emerged. Her mother was painted as a very controlling woman throughout her development, whereas her father was seen as a protective figure. Continued frustrations in several areas of her experience were more and more evident. She began working in a local convenience store and felt powerless to assert herself against a punitive boss. In addition, the intensity of her relationship with her fiance waxed and waned, only to resound with unmet commitment, frustration, and a pervading powerlessness. As these areas of difficulty became more vividly evident, a subtle shift in the transference occurred in which she felt controlled and powerless. When these transference themes were interpreted it became evident that she felt emotionally handicapped and that she did not have "two legs to stand on."

In reviewing this case, it is clear that a fundamental change in the meaning of her symptomatic complaint of her inability to dance occurred during the process of treatment. If treatment had been kept short-term, the significance of her knee injury would have had only one contextual basis for understanding. However, by her engaging in long-term treatment, other aspects of her life became intertwined with her knee difficulties, revealing symbolic meanings of her symptoms that would not have become consciously evident if treatment was short-term. The meaning of the loss of her ability to dance, when kept to the scope of the initial 15 sessions, was circumscribed to everyday matters (surgeries, plans, etc.). Throughout the extended course of treatment, the meaning of the loss of her leg became fundamentally different in her subjective world. It became a symbol of her inability to feel grounded and powerful enough to cause significant change in her life. Her leg was a symbol for the loss of her ability to successfully master the demands of her life. No longer was her injury the focus of the therapeutic process. Instead, its symbolic meaning became known to her. As a result, despite the loss of her dance career, she was able to start new artistic adventures, as she felt empowered to make lasting changes in her life. She learned to communicate constructively with her fiance and did not rely on her weakening father for protection or strength. Through the course of long-term treatment the meaning of the patient's symptomatic complaint fundamentally shifted from specific limitations and frustrations she experienced from the loss of her ability to dance to more widespread difficulties in her overall personality functioning.

TIME, CHARACTER STRUCTURE, CLINICAL PROBLEMS AND TECHNICAL RECOMMENDATIONS

Some patients who undergo time-limited treatment will, by the nature of their problems, need their treatment to be expanded. Clinical judgment is required to evaluate certain patients for extended treatment. First, one must evaluate if treatment goals that are explicitly or implicitly made have or have not been met by time-limited treatment. Second, even if certain goals have been met, do new treatment issues present themselves that require a longer term duration of treatment? Third, to what extent does keeping treatment time-limited prevent working on otherwise avoided aspects of treatment that would be best addressed in long-term treatment? Conversely, to what extent is extending the duration of treatment a resistance to terminating time-limited treatment? Is extending treatment counterproductive to the goals established under time-limited treatment? Will dependency needs be gratified and not treated if the duration of treatment is extended? If short-term goals are not successfully treated, does resistance to changing to long-term treatment suggest the therapist might not want to admit failure of the time-limited approach?

Changes that result from a shift in the duration of psychotherapy from a closed-ended model to an open-ended one take place through *stages*. The *first stage* operates in the realistic concerns of termination versus continuation. The therapist's thought processes involved in such a change are important, as are the patient's wishes not to be rejected or abandoned. The *second stage* begins at the point of decision to continue and involves a transition period between the previous and newly establishing set. The *third stage* involves settling into an extended duration of treatment.

If patients are unable to consistently maintain some connection with sequential time, there will be considerable disorganization when treatment is extended. This is particularly evident with patients who are vulnerable to psychosis, as their hold on sequential time is compromised. Moreover, when the patient regresses through nonlinear aspects of time, there will be a reliving of the past that may come with overwhelmingly intense affect states. Patients with severe character pathology may project their difficulties onto the therapist, in part to defend against their affects, and in part, to link in a pathological way to aspects of sequential time found in the therapist by externalizing their difficulties.

Clearly technical distinctions are evident between treatment that is short-term or closed-ended and treatment that is long-term and open-ended. In some types of time-limited treatments, there is more emphasis on supportive work than on transference. In other types, the therapist actively brings material to focus on a centrally defined transference theme. In short-term treatment comments are more directive. In long-term therapy, comments are less directive and have a broader focus. In short-term therapy, sessions are used as catalytic agents and the technique of inquiry is "associative anamnesis" (Alexander & French, 1946), rather than as freely "associative." In short-term therapy, the central issue of treatment is determined by the therapist, who is assumed to be "all knowing." When regression occurs in short-term treatment, it is more organized, defined, and limited than in long-term therapy. Short-term therapy will reduce dependency and procrastination. In time-limited supportive therapy, there will be less emotional involvement. Also, there is a source of resistance found in the patient's hidden suspicion of the reliability and trustworthiness of the therapist when the duration changes.

Clearly, some problems are more amenable to short-term treatment. Specifically, grief work, situational difficulties, and some types of post-traumatic stress disorders are amenable to treatment that is short-term. When characterological issues emerge as these difficulties are treated, consideration for long-term treatment is urged. Criteria for recommending long-term treatment involves the patient's ability to "regress" into aspects of time other than sequential time, the patient's subjective discomfort resulting from characterological difficulties, and the patient's willingness to work on them.

A difficulty is raised by selecting patients with specific problems to be assigned time-limited or long-term treatment by artifactually raising success rates. By selecting patients who present with focused problems and then selecting problems that are, by meeting operational criteria most amenable to treatment that is short-term, "success" rates become artificially raised. Naturally, certain issues become salient aspects of the treatment that permit focused attention that can be tracked and measured in terms of treatment efficacy. Herein lies an artifact of treatment efficacy literature in that target problems will be the focus of treatment that are clearly defined and treatable within a certain time period. Other variables that may be more vague or less conscious will be excluded from treatment. The measurement of outcome will exclude these other variables and will artificially raise "success" rates. However, if there are areas of difficulty that are left untreated, then the degree of "success" may be challenged. The termination phase of treatment may open up these areas for inspection, but, due to time constraints imposed by short-term therapy, they will be left unattended.

SUMMARY

Time is both experienced and observed. It is a basic and fundamental organizing principle through which conscious experience is ordered. Time offers regularity and predictability. It constitutes part of the frame upon which the adult world is formed and structured. The organization of reality involves an ordering of experience according to structures and operations, fundamental to which is the sense of time. The duration of psychotherapy affects the emergence, intensity, and meaning of all occurrences throughout the psychotherapeutic process. The impact of length of treatment is vividly evident when its duration changes from time-limited to long-term therapy. This chapter traced aspects of time and treatment that change when the duration of psychotherapy is extended. Different concepts of time are offered that best fit many types of clinical phenomena evidenced in long-term treatment. Along with these, both the therapist's and the patient's reactions intensify as the boundary between time-limited and long-term treatment is broached. By changing sets when treatment duration is extended, meaning is altered and special technical considerations are mandated.

REFERENCES

Alexander, F., & French, T. M. (1946). *Psychoanalytic therapy*. New York: Ronald Press.

Bonaparte, M. (1940). Time and the unconscious. *International Journal of Psychoanalysis, 21*, 427.

Gadamer, H. (1975). *Truth and method*. New York: Crossroad.

Gadamer, H. (1976). *Philosophical hermeneutics* (D. Linge, Trans.). Berkeley: University of California Press.

Gill, M. (1982). *The analysis of transference. Vol. 1: Theory and technique*. New York: International Universities Press.

Greenson, R. R. (1976). *The technique and practice of psychoanalysis* (Vol. 1). New York: International Universities Press.

Luborsky, L. (1984). *Principles of psychoanalytic psychotherapy: A manual for supportive-expressive treatment*. New York: Basic Books.

Mann, J. (1973). *Time-limited psychotherapy*. Cambridge: Harvard University Press.

Piaget, J. (1954). *The construction of reality in the child*. New York: Basic Books.

Piaget, J. (1966). *L'epistemologie du temps*. Paris: Presses Universitaires de France.

Ricouer, P. (1970). *Freud and philosophy: An essay on interpretation* (D. Savage, Trans.). New Haven: Yale University Press.

Spence, D. P. (1982). *Narrative truth and historical truth*. New York: W. W. Norton.

Watzlawick, P., Weakland, J., & Fisch, R. (1974). *Change*. New York: W. W. Norton.

Recognition of and Response to Countertransference: Psychoanalytic and Interpersonal Communications Approaches

SHERMAN EISENTHAL

The concept of countertransference withstood revision for nearly four decades. Freud first reported his observations of countertransference phenomena in 1910. He attributed it to the influence of the patient on the therapist's unconscious. In theory, the transference would emerge uncontaminated if the therapist maintained an unobtrusive and detached presence, abstaining from expressing his or her own feelings and presenting him- or herself as a blank screen. The therapeutic paradigm was fundamentally monadic, and the blank screen was its emblem. Countertransference signified failure to meet the ego ideal (Racker, 1968); and personal analysis and ongoing self-analysis became requirements for control.

In the late 1940s a series of critical papers began to appear. The blank screen ideal was challenged, and the interplay between transference and countertransference was reexamined. Countertransference could be informative and not simply a pathological intrusion of the therapist's unconscious. Among the innovators was Heimann (1950), who proposed that countertransference is a creation of the patient that provides unique access to his or her unconscious. In a similar regard, Theodore Reik (1948) characterized the therapist's unconscious reactions to the patient as an invaluable resource to be listened to with "the third ear." Little (1951) saw the complex interactive nature of countertransference when working with severely disturbed patients, and found them to be highly sensitive to it.

Treatment success could hinge on how openly the analyst dealt with the countertransference. Searles (1958) observed that very disturbed patients seemed to absorb his unconscious reactions, postural ones, for example, and then play them back to him in subtle mimicry. One can see that a new model of the treatment process was being fashioned, one that directed the therapist to listen nondefensively to his or her countertransference experience in the unfolding interaction with the patient and to regard it as strategic material for analysis.

Later, in place of the monadic ideal of a "blank screen," there came more interactive interpersonal role models. Langs (1976) proposed that the ideal therapist role was to be a "container." This concept, formulated by Bion (1959), stresses the need for restraint in receiving and processing the patient's affective pressure. However, the "container" concept is ambiguous about the therapist's contribution to the interactive process — what it is and what it should be. A clearer and stronger embodiment of a more interactive position is found in Sullivan's (1953) conception of "participant observer." Hoffman (1983) went a step further, by prefering the emphasis of the more directly interactive concept of "participant," and went on to say that the therapist is not an "empty container," an allusion he feared could obscure the therapist's contribution to the countertransference. The idealized split between the therapist and the patient was breaking down. Racker (1968) asserted that psychotherapy should be construed as an interaction between two personalities, each with internal strife, and not between a sick individual and a healthy one.

One can see the pendulum swing on the therapist's contribution to countertransference. Countertransference has come to represent an amalgam of the patient's objects and the subjective intrusions of the therapist, a totality (Heimann, 1950), a compromise between the patient's interactional pressure and the therapist's unique personality (Sandler, 1976). This totalist view, first proposed by Heimann (1950), has gained dominance in recent years (Kernberg, 1975). How to understand and approach the therapist's role in the countertransference was subject to reconsideration and revision.

The self-experience and reactions of the therapist in the treatment hour became the subject of less defensive and more fruitful inquiry and analysis that was directly relevant to the treatment process. Winnicott's (1949) distinction between objective and subjective countertransference was among the earliest efforts to identify and sort out the patient's transference from the therapist's transference, imprinted in the medium of the countertransference. Both Winnicott (1949) and Searles

(1965) wrote about the "hateful" patient from the perspective of induced "objective" countertransference reactions—namely the impact of the patient's transference. "Subjective countertransference" expressed the therapist's personality.

Another perspective was provided by Racker (1953), who distinguished between direct and indirect countertransference. The direct countertransference response signified countertransference stimulated by the patient—that the patient was either getting into difficulty (the depressive subtype) or becoming an aggressive threat to the therapist (the paranoid subtype). Indirect countertransference signified the impact from nonpatient objects of the therapist's transference, such as colleagues or professional groups who might judge, criticize, or mock. An especially important distinction by Racker (1953) concerned the therapist's identification, whether it was with the patient or his or her objects, that is, whether it was concordant or complementary. This is a refinement of "direct countertransference," and a counterpart of Winnicott's objective countertransference. Deutsch (1926/1953) was among the first to draw attention to the significance of the therapist's identification with the patient's objects. Recently, Giovacchini (1989) distinguished between the homogenized and the idiosyncratic countertransference, his version of the objective versus the subjective.

A more ambivalent early revisionist, Cohen (1952), found anxiety in the analyst to be the common thread in various formulations of countertransference at that time. She dismissed Winnicott's objective countertransference, however, since it did not fit Freud's assertion that countertransference is the converse of transference. She thus took the "establishment line" and eliminated the possibility that the patient's "real" interaction with the therapist had any influence on the transference. Three sources of countertransference anxiety were classified, each a variation of the "subjective" type proposed by Winnicott: (1) situational factors (distractions from the analyst's outside life); (2) unresolved neurotic problems of the analyst (such as treatment distortions due to the tendency of obsessive individuals to be excessively controlling); and (3) communication of the patient's anxiety to the analyst, which she likened to empathy, a sensitivity to subtle cues from the patient that are contagious. In this third category, although she granted the analyst accurate perception, she then claimed that the analyst's empathy was a sensitivity derived from unresolved past problems. Many of the qualities of objective countertransference thus seem to resurface with this third category. From this series of papers one can see that the clinical challenge of countertransference began to shift. Processing the countertransference became more important than preventing it.

An historical review of this process of change in the meaning and utility of countertransference can be found in Epstein and Feiner (1979) and Tansey and Burke (1989). And Kiesler (1982) should be refered to for the perspective from the interpersonal communications approach.

OBJECTIVES

The purpose of this chapter is to describe three approaches to the countertransference that reflect different aspects of current changes in its meaning: one based on the psychoanalytic object relations approach developed by Tansey and Burke (1989), and two based on the interpersonal communications approach, especially the work of Kiesler (1982, 1988) and Cashdan (1988). These three approaches present contrasting ways of understanding and responding to countertransference. Tansey and Burke (1989) illuminate the empathic processing of countertransference while the Kiesler approach clarifies metacommunication strategies for disengagement from the countertransference pressure and Cashdan presents a confrontative strategy for disengagement that incorporates the concepts of projective identification and its underlying metacommunication.

OBJECT RELATIONS APPROACH

Following the lines of the object relations tradition, Tansey and Burke (1985, 1989; Burke & Tansey, 1985) employ a paradigm that is both intrapsychic and interpersonal. They focus on the experiential processes of the therapist, aiming to integrate countertransference with projective identification and empathy. The interplay between the patient's projective identifications and the therapist identificatory responses constitutes the critical interactive unit for analysis. It is in the medium of the countertransference that the therapist's experiences the impact of the projective identification. The challenge is to proceed empathically through the three phases of receiving, processing, and communicating the interpersonal significance of this exchange, given the intense affective pressures that can disrupt the process. Their presentation describes in a step-by-step fashion their procedure to facilitate successful processing.

Projective Identification: The Source of the Message

Projective identification underlies, in theory, the interactional pressure from the patient that induces countertransference. The concept originated in Melanie Klein's (1946) reconstruction of the experience of infants toward their hostile and aggressive impulses. These hateful and destructive aspects of the self are disowned, split off, and projected in fantasies of mother, a means "in fantasy" to both rid oneself of disturbing impulses and affects and to control mother. For Klein (1946) the process was exclusively intrapsychic, with no interpersonal consequences. It has become, however, the "conceptual bridge" linking the intrapsychic with the interpersonal, the inside with the outside (Malin & Grotstein, 1966; Racker, 1953; Kernberg, 1975; Sandler, 1976; Ogden, 1979). Ogden (1979, 1982) elaborated on the link between a patient's fantasized primitive internalized object relationships and the interactional pressure on the therapist to replay the role of these internalized objects, which results in the countertransference. Projective identification is thus a special form of transference communication (Ogden, 1982).

Ogden (1979) theorizes that projective identification occurs in three stages: fantasy, interactive pressure, and reintrojection. Sandler (1987) and Kernberg (1987) prefer to restrict the concept to the interpersonal pressure, the induction of a complementary response. Sandler (1987) clarified the essential distinctions by referring to the interactive pressure as second stage projective identification in order to distinguish it from Klein's original "fantasy" conception, the first stage of projective identification. Ogden (1982) wanted to include the third stage (reintrojection of the processed projective identification) as a critical part of the interactive and integrative process since the patient learns from experiencing the induced therapist response, reintrojecting a more manageable orientation to the other. For the sake of clarity and precision Tansey and Burke (1989) also support the restriction of projective identification to the second stage meaning. The events of this third stage are a critical part of the communication process described below.

Receptive Phase

In this first stage of interactional communication the goal is to receive the patient's projective identifications. Three major tasks are outlined by Tansey and Burke (1989), which they call subphases: being set to receive; having a balanced orientation to the incoming affective pressure from the patient, resulting in an awareness of signal affects signifying a transient identificatory experience.

To receive projective identifications, a passive mind set is required, what Sandler (1976) called free-floating attention applied to the patient *and* one's self. This passive orientation of the therapist to self-experience is analogous to the now standard practice applied by Freud (1912/1953) in listening to the patient's experience. This requirement of the therapist to be in deep and continuous contact with his or her inner experience and reactions was stressed by Racker in his approach to countertransference (1968). The value of a receptive mental set is evident. However, it is very difficult to maintain this evenly suspended attention under certain clinical conditions such as in the treatment of borderline and psychotic patients (Ogden, 1982). Moreover, it is not clear whether this receptive mental set need be so passive. Spence (1982) considers an active mental set more appropriate for listening to complex mental processes.

If one succeeds in maintaining the needed receptivity, then a sense of the patient's affective pressure will be experienced and registered. A good early indicator of this pressure is a sense of anxiety and defensiveness in the therapist (Cohen, 1952). The unprocessed pressure may take many forms — one may be impersonal complaints by the patient that life continues to be miserable despite therapy, a second may be personal accusations of indifference, greed, seductiveness, threats of suicide or aggression against the therapist; and a third may be nonverbal displays of helplessness or dysphoric moods or actions such as coming late, sleepiness, and acting out. Not all the pressures are negative. Some will take the shape of helpfulness, praise, and extensive accommodations to the therapist's needs, such as ingratiating and pleased smiles and looks.

If the therapist is not disrupted by the advent of pressure, then he or she can enter the identification-signal affect subphase, the very goal of this receptive stage. When the therapist starts to sense any of a variety of self-feelings and needs, then an identification may have occurred: Some will be negative such as feeling inadequate, greedy, thoughtless, hostile; some will be more neutral, such as an anxious need to be protective and nurturant, a sense of indebtedness or obligation; and some will be positive, such as love, admiration, and sexual attraction. The challenge is to contain these affective reactions and not give in to them.

Disruptive influences occur at each step of the receptive process. Tansey and Burke (1989) present a useful organization of these influences. Especially important is the constraint of one's own character, which either dulls or oversensitizes one's mind to certain classes of pressure: aggressive, sexual, control, ingratiating, and dependency. One may be predisposed to take defensive positions, either by being too rigid or too loose in receiving particular pressures. That is, one may respond to reasonable requests in a doctrinaire way or to unreasonable ones in a *laissez faire* or permissive way, being overly ready to follow rules or to give in and be nice. The task and challenge is to identify and then use one's "personal equation." Aside from weaknesses in the therapist's character, there are other constraints. Situational factors (unexpected stress, lack of sleep, or illness) can also disrupt receptivity. These influences are of secondary significance when they are contextual and temporary. They become significant when they also reflect enduring characterological influences.

Ways are described to moderate the affective pressure that is so disruptive to the receptive attitude. Expecting the pressure may help. It also helps to aim for a balanced attitude toward controlling the interaction process, avoiding too much or too little control. On the one hand, strong control may be exerted in the case of frame issues where rigid rules are the recommended practice (Langs, 1975, 1976). Tansey and Burke advocate flexibility. They maintain that rigid rules actually stop therapists from listening to the meaning underlying the frame issues. On the other hand, too little control may be applied when a patient acts out in the hour (e.g., screaming and yelling), disruptive effects that should be addressed. Limit setting in such circumstances is essential.

A better case is made by Tansey and Burke on the greater value of knowing one's weaknesses than of the success in overcoming them. When the therapist achieves awareness of the interactional pressure and is able to label the evoked feelings (e.g., being greedy, contemptible, demanding, hopeless, etc.), the stage is set to move to the next phase — the more active and evaluative mental set of the internal processing phase.

Internal Processing Phase

The major objective in this phase is to grasp empathically the meaning of the signal affects and to proceed to make an interpersonal formulation. The process requires a shift from a passive receptive mode to an active reflective one directed at one's affective reactions. Internal processing consists of three tasks or phases. First is containment–separateness from the pressure of the introjective identification provoked by the patient's projective identification. The second phase is developing a working model of the object and self-representations conveyed. The last phase tests the empathic connection between models of the patient and of the self. The aim is to decipher the message embedded in the patient's projective identifications.

This containment–separateness phase is probably the most difficult and crucial one in the empathic processing of countertransference reactions. The affective task is to contain the affective pressure long enough to achieve psychological distance from it. A delicate balance must be achieved between the extremes of cold, mechanical technical neutrality (where empathy is lacking) and indulgent surrender to one's subjectivity. A middle ground of humane and objective control over one's subjectivity is most desirable (Reik, 1948). Several ways are described by Ogden (1979) to gain the needed distance. "The therapist's theoretical training, his personal analysis, his experience, his psychological-mindedness, and his psychological language can all be brought to bear on the experience he is attempting to understand and to contain" (p. 367).

After attaining needed psychological distance, one can proceed with the second task: to reflectively and empathically process the trial identifications. The objective is to develop what Greenson (1960) has called a "working model" of the patient. This is achieved by registering the experience of the patient as if the therapist *were* the patient. It is a cumulative process that produces this "working model," a process that includes the patient's past and present fantasies and defenses, outward appearance, and current mood. Tansey and Burke (1989) also construct a "working model" of the therapist's self-experience in the interaction. That is, the therapist listens to his or her own self representations of the interaction, taking what is ordinarily in the background of attention and bringing it momentarily but regularly to the foreground. The therapist thereby becomes more actively self-aware of the interactive experience: being self-consciously aware, for example, of feeling warm, competent, and at ease with one patient while feeling distant, self-doubting, and tense with another.

The processing of these two models requires attentiveness directed simultaneously at oneself and the patient. This task is demanding, formidable, and highly subjective. These two working models therefore should be regarded as tentative constructions subject to distortion, requiring refinement and validation. They are designed to lay the groundwork for empathic integrations. This brings us to the third phase or task — finding the empathic connection. Ideally the therapist should alternate attending to the working models of the patient and him- or herself to attain awareness of an "empathic connection." The search proceeds by an effort to identify the correspondence between the reactions of the patient and the therapist, whether one is identifying with the patient's self (concordant identification) or the patient's objects (complementary identification). An example of a complementary identification would be one in which a therapist starts to feel distant, cold, and ungiving to a patient and does not know why; feelings that, in fact, match those of a significant object in the patient's life and complement the patient's needy, demanding behavior. If the therapist started to feel needy, alone, and isolated, then the identification would be concordant—what some would call a process akin to empathy. It should be noted that complementary identifications are the expected responses to projective identifications; concordant identifications signify different antecedents according to Sandler (1987). A variety of identificatory experiences thus have to be borne in awareness and integrated in order to carry out the task of finding an empathic connection and making an interpersonal diagnosis. The projective identifications may be a playing out of what Racker (1957) has called the patient's "vicious circle," that is, the patient's recurrent problematic style of relating to others, or it could be a specific reaction, such as the patient's feeling abandoned when the therapist cancels an appointment.

Recognizing and Controlling Disruptive Pressure

The disruptive effects in countertransference are inevitable (Racker, 1953). The therapist's concern may start with damage control. What is challenging for the therapist is to recognize the projected role he or she is being pressured to play, diagnose its meaning, and resist the pressure to act it out. The earlier the recognition of the recurrent themes underlying the countertransference, the easier it is not to play into the patient's "vicious circle." Unfortunately, no signal is emitted at the point of costly defensiveness and acting out. Most agree that disruptive actions are difficult to monitor and detect, except, as Cohen (1952) put it, by an "ear witness." In the reception phase, countertransference is characterized as a loss of attentiveness or receptivity. In the internal processing phase anxiety, irritability, and self-doubt are common indications of empathic disruption. One indication may be a failure to see how one's feelings and behavior toward the patient signify complementary identifications; another may be a failure to generate working models of the patient's experience and the therapist's self-experience in the interaction.

In addition to attending to signs of countertransference anxiety, a number of other resources should be noted. One special resource is the therapist's fantasies and day dreams during or after the hour. Another is the therapist's developing a positive orientation toward containment and the processing of signal affects. When self-scrutiny fails and indicators of disruption persist, the conventional wisdom suggests that the therapist seek consultation and case discussion with peers—if the need is recognized. When dealing with borderline and psychotic patients, ongoing consultation or supervision is essential and not optional (Ogden, 1982).

The internal processing phase is completed when the therapist grasps the meaning underlying the interpersonal scenario provoked by the patient's projective identifications. A sign that the therapist is on track is a subjective sense of a reduction in the interactional pressure. The next phase is communication.

Validation of Inferences: Source and Meaning

Before communicating over the countertransference, Tansey and Burke suggest first validating hypotheses about its source and meaning. They point out the lack of research on this objective. Their model for validation is Roy Schafer's (1954) converging lines of inference, developed to validate Rorschach hypotheses. Confidence in one's judgment grows with the *convergence of different lines of inference*. Five lines of inference are presented for both source and meaning. With regard to testing the source, one line of inference, for example, is to ask: "What is observable in the interaction that may have contributed to the countertransference response?" If the patient's mood seems connected to the therapist actions (indifference, hostility, etc.) then the interactional pressure is not from a projective identification and the signal affect should be read accordingly. A more subtle line of inference is awareness of one's own characterological propensities that may mislead one in reading patient behavior: Is the patient being charming or hostile or idealizing because of the reinforcement they get from the therapist?

With regard to testing the "meaning," there are two basic considerations: one involves identifying the feelings projected onto the therapist, the other involves discovering the purpose being served. This search for the meaning of the projective identification is one of the basic goals of the entire process. Was the patient trying to rid him- or herself of an unbearable feeling? Or was the patient trying to send a specific message about how it feels to be abandoned by the therapist who announced that he or she will have to miss the next appointment? Of the two aspects of "meaning," determining the purpose appears more difficult and demanding. Ultimately the resolution of meaning depends on the scope and adequacy of one's theory of interpersonal communication. Tansey and Burke do not make theirs explicit. Almost the entire burden of the patient's contribution to countertransference appears to be assigned to projective identification. Is this the only means of countertransference communication, the only channel for transference to have a countertransference impact? For this lack of theoretical scope, one has trouble understanding the rationale behind the lines of inference selected for validation. The particular lines presented are useful but lack theoretical coherence.

One line of inference, for example, is to ask "To what extent does the patient appear to be unconsciously creating, in the therapeutic relationship, the same pattern that has characterized prior intimate relationships?" Another is to sort out what Racker (1968) calls one's own "personal equation" as a factor. A third is to establish whether a specific communication is being made regarding events in the hour. They add that validation continues with processing the feedback from the patient's response to countertransference communications. In their validation model, Tansey and Burke (1989) present a unique combination of rigor and clinical practicality to test countertransference hypotheses. The clinical plausibility of their approach is an impressive achievement.

The Communication Phase

Tansey and Burke (1989) regard communication to be a crucial part of the empathic processing of countertransference reactions. The need for empathic sensitivity does not stop when empathic understanding has been gained. The timing and content of countertransference-based communications also requires considerable empathic sensitivity. The boundaries of this communication phase can be confusing and need to be put in perspective. This phase signifies the time when an explicit effort is made to communicate the results of empathic processing of the countertransference experience. This should not be construed to mean that communication has not occurred at every step along the way. Posture, voice, facial expression, and attention continuously communicate reactions to patient. In fact, many therapeutic alliances have been shaken and even foundered over the manner of canceling appointments or in judgmental smiles or frowns. When experiencing interactional pressure from the patient's projective identifications, prior to the therapist's readiness, to make informed communications, Tansey and Burke suggest that one should convey interest and concern but not unconditional positive regard or acceptance in the Rogerian sense. Such "acceptance" of pressure would be misleading and possibly communicate defensiveness, thereby playing into the patient's projective identification. Their suggested stance — somewhere between neutrality and equanimity — appears more an ideal intention than an attainable reality. A Rogerian might counter with the proposition that unconditional acceptance creates a mental set that serves to contain the therapist's affect. Unconditional acceptance does not preclude empathic reflection of the patient's inductive behavior.

During the receptive and internal processing phases, interpreta tion is technically inappropriate and may signal countertransference defensiveness or acting out by the therapist. The appropriate communicative stance is "noninterpretive communications." This signifies exploration and clarification, conveying a sense of interest, reliability, and understanding to the patient. Restraint applies especially to the potent nonverbal level of communication, which is even harder to monitor than the verbal level.

Communications fall into three levels of empathic understanding: first, the noninterpretive; second, either transference- or countertransference-based understanding; and third, an integration of transference- and countertransference-based understanding. Transference-based communications take the form of: "You seem to . . ." statements. Countertransference-based communications take the form of: "This reminds me . . ." statements. Disclosure of the countertransference is controversial. Some feel that it burdens the patient unnecessarily (Langs, 1978; Reich, 1960). Others feel that it redefines expectations, especially by the therapist, as if the patient should know what is expected after interpretive disclosures (Hoffman, 1983). Many feel that it is very potent and should only be used sparingly (Giovacchini, 1972b; Winnicott, 1949). Gill (1983) observed that Sullivan did not interpret the relationship. Herron and Rouslin (1982) examine disclosure in the context of the therapist's narcissism and see therein the potential for rationalizing a lack of restraint as a countertransference communication. One resolution is to be specific about disclosure. Certain preconditions for countertransference communication are spelled out, such as admitting to an error in technique, or responding to a resistance or a crisis (Racker, 1968; Greenson, 1974). There are some who do not feel that countertransference disclosure needs special justification (Little, 1951, 1957; Searles, 1975; Tauber, 1954; Bollas, 1983). Tansey and Burke see a special value in the integration of both frameworks in an interpretation. For them, it communicates the therapist's deepest understanding to the patient.

INTERPERSONAL COMMUNICATIONS APPROACHES

Kiesler's Approach to the Impact Message

The equivalent of countertransference for Kiesler (1979, 1982, 1988) is the therapist's impact message. It signifies the impact on the therapist of the patient's "evoking style." The impact message is multidimensional, comprising four major components: feelings (such as boredom), action tendencies (such as an urge to act protective), cognitive attributions (attributing wants or intentions to the patient such as, "He wants to be special!"), and fantasies (such as "I feel like we are travelling on separate sides of a river). These components are similar to "signal affects" of countertransference described in the psychoanalytic approach. Like countertransference, the impact message is unattended when it is first received.

Patient's Evoking Style

Beier (1966) introduced the concept of evoking style to describe patient communications that are indirect and coercive. This is an elaboration (in the abnormal direction) of Leary's (1957) analysis of the normal, purposeful aim of interpersonal behavior to induce complementary responses from the other in pursuit of consistency. The differences in communication between normal and neurotic is that the normal approach to relationship claims is open, direct, in awareness, and has a persuasive quality, whereas the neurotic approach is covert, inflexible, indirect, and has an "evoking" quality that induces the other to respond in a desired way. Normal communication invites negotiated solutions to differences, whereas evocative neurotic communication invites coercive, manipulative settlements. A basic assumption of this approach is that patients will communicate in the same "duplicitous, self-defeating way" in the therapy relationship as they do with other significant people in their lives. The evoking style is thus a generalized interpersonal response, a duplicitous style of interacting. It is a more obviously behavioral and interactional concept than projective identification, which it resembles.

The motivating force behind the neurotic evoking style is to maintain and confirm the relationship claims of the self-system and to avoid experiences inconsistent with the self-system (Sullivan, 1953). The object is to present the self in a manner that obtains consistent or predictable outcomes. People vary in the inflexibility and narrowness of their style of interaction with others. The pressure of the evoking messages cumulatively result in the therapist being shaped and pulled (like others in the patient's life) into a reciprocal role, identifiable, in theory, as a position on the interpersonal circumflex of inclusion, control, and affection–affiliation (Kiesler, 1983; Schutz, 1958). On the control dimension reciprocal signifies a complementary position—if the client is submissive, the therapist is dominant; whereas on the affiliation–affection dimension reciprocal signifies the corresponding position—if the client is hostile, the therapist is hostile.

Being Hooked

In the communication analytic approach to psychotherapy the objective is to identify and then modify the patient's self-defeating evoking style of interacting with others, especially with the therapist. Kielser describes this process as having two stages from the therapist's perspective: the "engaged" or "hooked" phase, and the "disengaged" or "squirmed loose" phase. The therapist cannot avoid being "hooked," at least initially, since patients go to extremes of intensity and persistence to control the relationship. Furthermore, the interpersonal therapist expects to be "hooked" — it is both an expression of the interpersonal disorder and the medium of change. The process of recognizing the state of being "hooked," of deciphering the impact message is the first stage of disengagement, which can be called "squirming loose." This graphic metaphor aptly describes the required effort and perhaps the affective experience of disengagement.

Different strategies are recommended to achieve this goal. One is to acknowledge the operation of the patient's evoking style and monitor one's impact messages, attending to what one feels, what one wants to do or not do, and to one's attributions and fantasies. The mental set is to self-consciously ask oneself: "What is this client doing to me?" Beitman (1987) suggests asking: "What percentage is me and what percentage is the patient?" In listening to the patient's behavior the therapist should attend to shifts away from "good" role behavior: when the therapy bogs down and progress has stopped, when the patient stops following through and deviates from a working mode (whether it be through humor, moodiness, or withdrawal), and when one senses "resistance." In listening to one's own inner state, signs include: increased anxiety; incongruity between one's actions and feelings; avoidance of certain topics; and deviating from one's usual therapy style. As stated earlier a special resource can be found in exploration of one's fantasies and dreams (Singer & Pope, 1978; Herron & Rouslin, 1982). An external aid for self-exploration is the "Impact Message Inventory" (Kiesler et al., 1985), and, of course, consultation with colleagues.

Disengagement Strategies: Unhooking

The psychodynamic and the interpersonal communications approaches differ in their orientation to recognition and to the processing of the impact message. In the interpersonal communications approach the concepts of receptive attention, containment, and empathic processing of the signal affects are not stressed, nor is thinking in terms of trial identifications and working models to plan appropriate interventions. The objective of recognition is to identify the patient's evoking style (embedded in the impact message) in order to disengage from the reciprocal response and to metacommunicate about the relationship. This strategy employs asocial responses, clarifications, and reflections, but not interpretations.

With attention directed to the patient's "pulling" complementary behavior, the therapist can proceed to actively use disengagement strategies. This means discontinuing reinforcement of such behavior, for example, on noticing that a client recurrently uses humor as a diversion, the therapist stops making the socially expectable contingent response, that is, the therapist neither laughs nor acts amused. This breaking away from the patient's evoking style is what Beier (1966) calls the "asocial response." It deviates from the social norm of reciprocity and it is nonconfirmatory. The aim is to "not reinforce" such evocative behavior. As a consequence the evocative behavior is subject to modification. Another strategy to disengage from the patient's distinct evoking style is to directly interrupt it. Kiesler gives the example of encouraging decisiveness and concreteness from a patient who is always abstract and conditional.

Disengaging is significant for three reasons: (1) it helps to stop reinforcing the patient's self-defeating evoking style; (2) it prevents or, at least, reduces the pressure on the therapist that could result in hostility and alienation; and (2) it behaviorally prepares for metacommunication over the evoking style.

Metacommunication

The last and most powerful strategy for disengagement is metacommunication with the patient about the relationship messages. Metacommunication signifies communicating about the communication. This is done by referring directly to either the patient's evoking messages or to the therapist's experience of the impact message. In his use of metacommunication Kiesler makes a distinctive contribution to managing countertransference. All communications have two levels, the content and the relationship (Ruesch & Bateson, 1951; Watzlawick, Beavin, & Jackson, 1967; Danziger, 1976). The content signifies the denotative meaning, the report, the representation; whereas the relationship signifies the connotative meaning, the command, the presentation. The relationship is mediated most often analogically, in the tone of voice, a look, the emphasis in a sentence. The content is mediated in a digital mode by verbal statements. Compared to content, the relationship level is more likely to be ambiguous and subject to misinterpretation. To resolve the ambiguity and cut short potential misinterpretation, one can metacommunicate over the relationship aspect of the communication. It puts the patient's metacommunications about the relationship "on the table" directly available for discussion, inspection, and revision.

Principles of Metacommunication

Kiesler delineates eight principles of metacommunicating, all serving to facilitate disengagement and to resolve the impact message. These eight principles provide guidance for communicating over relationship messages. The principles shall be summarized in terms of "the therapist's attitude," "when," and "what."

The Therapist's Attitude

Two principles address this issue. Feedback in metacommunicating can be threatening to the patient's self-esteem. Therefore, it is essential to conveying affiliation and respect, especially in how the message is delivered. In giving feedback, Kiesler suggests that one stress the positive intention in the patient's evoking style as well as the negative consequences for the recipient of this behavior. He also stresses that an attitude of shared participation is important in the feedback process and that feedback is tentative, an approximation of the truth.

When

In three of his principles, Kiesler presents preconditions for the timing of the metacommunications. On the one hand, one should not metacommunicate when the patient is working at the tasks of self-exploration and self-disclosure, and when the patient and therapist are in tune with each other. Cashdan (1988) talks about patients being on good behavior during the start of therapy, and during the engagement process. Impact messages are "there" but are hard to fully appreciate and need not be acted on. In addition, one should not give feedback on the relationship when the impact message is experienced intensely since the result is more likely to be disruptive and offensive than helpful. It is the issue of containment. In fact, giving feedback at such times is usually a clue to being "hooked," being pressured into playing the complementary role. For example, pointing out to a patient in a cold and irritated manner the impact of his "whining, hostile, and demanding behavior" is countertransference acting out and confirms the patient's expectation expressed in his or her evoking style. This points to the principle of not letting the affective intensity build up to a disruptive degree. On the other hand, one should metacommunicate when references are made to the therapist or therapist role, whether they be implicit or explicit. For example, if a patient makes one or a series of statements about how little can be expected from treatment, the deficiencies of past therapists, not working well with people of the therapist's age or sex or ethnic background, it is essential to ask ". . . if this applies to working with me?"

What

In three principles, Kielser proposes rules regarding the focus and content of the feedback. One principle in metacommunicating is to pinpoint the actions, especially the nonverbal ones, that evoke the impact message. An example is presented of the distancing and irritating impact of an obsessive patient's silence, and of laughter and dilatory tactics on the therapist and on others in the patient's life. Giving concrete examples of the evocative behaviors in their various and recurrent forms encourages joint exploration of intentions, stimulus value of actions, and consequences. Another principle refers to selecting a particular meaning frame: the evoking style, the impact message (equivalent to countertransference disclosure), the perceived self-reactions of the patient to relationship issues, and the self-reactions of the therapist (the issue of sympathetic self-disclosure — "I too have suffered from . . ."). Kiesler suggests that two meaning frames are basic: the evoking message and the impact message. Metacommunicating over the impact message, he suggests, requires the prior development of solid affiliative feelings. A third principle involves conditional influences: the patients' complaints, problems, and the position on the interpersonal circle that their evoking style places them. Ultimately, selection should take into consideration homogeneous groupings of evocative interpersonal styles — the hysterical, the passive-dependent, the schizoidal patient.

Cashdan's Object Relations Therapy

Cashdan (1988) integrates object relations theory and communications analysis in his "object relations therapy." Key concepts in his approach to countertransference are projective identification, metacommunication, and affective confrontation.

Projective Identification

As a result of disturbed early interpersonal relationships, primarily with mother, the child develops anomalies in "splitting" that generate

projective identifications (Racker, 1968; Grotstein, 1984). These projective identifications generate coercive and manipulative interpersonal
tactics that carry potent metacommunications. In accord with Malin
and Grotstein (1966), Cashdan believes that modifying projective
identifications is the keystone to essential therapeutic change. To help
the therapist anticipate and evaluate patient behaviors that induce
countertransference, he has developed a schema of the relevant
interpersonal dynamics.

Four major projective identifications are identified in this schema:
dependence, power, sex, and ingratiation. In part, they parallel
successive developmental issues. They are placed into an interpersonal
framework of relational stance, inductive behavior of the projector,
induced behavior in the "other," and the underlying metacommunication. For example, in the case of the projective identification of
dependency, the relational stance is chronic helplessness, inducing in
the "other" a number of caretaking feelings and actions. The patient's
inductive behaviors have the quality of statements such as: "What do
you think?" "Tell me what should I do." "I can't make it on my own." At
a nonverbal level, helplessness is conveyed by waiting for direction,
smiling happily when direction is given, frowning and crying and
giving anxious looks when order is not imposed from the designated
helper. The metacommunication that underlies the inductive behavioral messages is that "I can't survive without you." Cashdan stresses
that this metcommunication has a coercive tone: "You must help me or
else. . . ." Sometimes the induction results in a concordant identification (identifying with the patient's self-representation) as opposed to the
more usual complementary one (identifying with the patient's internalized objects). This is a distinction that Racker (1968) made, referred to
previously in the section on the psychoanalytic approach.

Induction of Countertransference

Signs of successful induction of countertransference are found when
the therapist plays the assigned complementary role without being fully
aware of experiencing the disowned feelings and representations of the
projector. This analysis of countertransference is quite similar to that
of both Tansey and Burke (1989) and Kiesler (1982), as described
above. Cashdan's description is distinguished by his placement of the
indications of countertransference within the framework of the four
major projective identifications. In response to dependency inductions,
the therapist will have the urge to help beyond what is appropriate, to
feel obliged to give advice or explanations. In response to power
inductions, the therapist may feel inadequate, emasculated, doubt his

or her ability to help, be convinced someone else could do a better job, show a readiness to terminate treatment, and express an urge for vindication. In response to sexual inductions, signs include an avid interest in details of the patient's sexual experiences, feeling sexually aroused, and having sexual fantasies. In response to ingratiation inductions, signs include feeling in the patient's debt for all the effort expended, ready to excuse the patient from one's baseline expectations.

The recognition and response to countertransference is also placed into the framework of treatment stages. During the start of treatment when the therapeutic alliance is being formed, the task is engagement. At that point patient-induced countertransference is not seen as a notable force. The patient and therapist play their respective roles, often accompanied by the patient feeling encouraged and experiencing symptom relief. However, after this initial stage, the patient starts to look for something more in their relationship, and his or her projective identifications enter the process. Only after the inductions have drawn the therapist into the "desired" role is the therapist aware that a countertransference has occured. Cashdan stresses that it is the countertransference that enables the therapist to "diagnose" the projective identification and its underlying metacommunication.

Containment Strategies

In this process of reacting to the patient's inductions strong and often overpowering affects are aroused. Cashdan suggests several strategies to contain these affects: Regard these experiences as opportunities for self-exploration and growth; immerse oneself in the experiences; enjoy them — the ingratiation, the manipulation, the arousal, react with humor and playfulness, and acknowledge the dysphoria and assaults on the self as part of the job. Most important is to understand these affects as reactions to projective identifications. Cashdan acknowledges the difficulty of the therapist separating her- or himself from the patient in this diagnostic process. The source of difficulty is likely to be the therapist when countertransference reactions are pervasive, persistent, and resistant to being addressed. He does not present a detailed approach to processing and validating the countertransference as Tansey and Burke do.

Confrontational Communication

One of Cashdan's distinct contributions is his incorporation of countertransference in his confrontational approach to treatment. After the first two stages of treatment (engagement and projective identification) comes the third stage, confrontation. The therapist communicates directly about the patient's projective identification and its underlying metacommunication. Effective therapy has to be directed at the prelinguistic nature of projective identifications. Cognitive, intellectually based interpretations of the countertransference dilute the patient's emotional confrontation of the disturbed relationship with the therapist. This stricture against interpretation holds until the termination stage of treatment. The major task for the therapist is not to question the propriety of the underlying metacommunication, not to explore its meaning, not to give explanations, and not to reassure or calm the patient. To engage in such behavior is to yield to the inductive pressure. The task is to say "No!" For example, in the case of a patient who communicates helplessness and tries to induce the therapist as well as others to take over, the suggested response is to say: "I won't give you direction or advice." The specifics of saying "no" is really defined by the context. Cashdan states that it depends on the specific projective identification and the unique demands associated with it. The objective is clearcut: to encourage the emotional reaction by the patient to the exposure by the therapist of his metacommunication. The idea is not to diffuse it with interpretations. However, the specific means of saying "No!" needs more elaboration.

This confrontative approach is a form of asocial response to the patient's metacommunication. The therapist does more than avoid reinforcing the patient's self-defeating interpersonal style. The therapist intends to frustrate the patient by not giving in to the metacommunicated relationship demands embedded in the projective identification. This open opposition to the patient's demands induces the patient to exert intensified pressure on the therapist to relent, and also induces the therapist to feel turmoil over rejecting, hurting, or endangering the patient. In response to such confrontations, patients may threaten to leave and will repeatedly test the therapist's resolve, blaming the therapist, claiming that it is the therapist who is provocative, intimidating, insensitive, or incompetent. This confrontative approach is more likely to intensify the countertransference than less confrontative approaches. Cashdan believes that this reactive approach obliges the patient to drop his or her manipulative and coercive interpersonal tactics for a more direct and honest style of relationship. When the metacommunications about the patient's manipulative tactics are openly discussed, the fourth stage of treatment is entered—termination. It is at this point that the therapist may make countertransference interpretations, helping the patient to understand the interpersonal impact of his or her inductive behavior on the therapist.

EMERGENT ISSUES

Understanding countertransference

The place of the "current relationship" in the dynamics of the transference defines major differences over the role and significance of the countertransference. Three psychoanalytic views of this role seem to be in competition: classical drive discharge, self psychological, and interpersonal-object relational. The drive approach limits the scope of the current relationship to the impact of "reality" factors, such as the therapeutic alliance. The current relationship thus is acknowledged to have an influence on the treatment process but not on the basic root issue in change, the transference. Transference is restricted to the effects of early development, whether it be embodied in repression of unacceptable impulses or in preoedipal or oedipal object relations. Hoffman (1983) points out in his seminal paper that the "asocial conception of the patient's experience in psychotherapy" is retained even by "conservative critics" of the blank screen role such as Kohut, Stone, and Loewald. A corollary of this restrictive view of transference is the "naive patient fallacy," namely that the patient accepts the therapist's behavior at face value (Hoffman, 1983). Wachtel (1980) argues that in reality patients experience their therapist's behavior and motives as ambiguous, open to multiple interpretations. The separation of the transference from current "reality" factors is a major technical issue since it disposes the therapist to assign very different meanings to past and present influences on the countertransference response. The other and more "radical critics" of the blank screen, a viewpoint Hoffman associates with Racker, Gill, Sandler, and the neo-Sullivanians such as Levenson, regard the current relationship as essential to understanding the transference. The countertransference expresses dynamically the influence of both past object relations and the current therapy relationship.

In the interpersonal communications approaches of Kiesler and Cashdan, the significance of the current interaction in treatment is not disputed. Their approaches are consistent with the neo-Sullivanians.

Mitchell (1989) illustrates the different role implications for countertransference in his comparison of the three current psychoanalytic models: drive-discharge, the self psychological, and relational-conflict. It makes a considerable difference in one's approach to processing the countertransference if the objective is to consolidate the therapeutic alliance without losing sight of the primacy of an uncontaminated transference, or if the objective is to facilitate the experience of a holding environment for the healing of a developmental arrest, or if the objective is to facilitate collaborative efforts to share mutual perceptions of the transference and the countertransference, and thereby to resolve interpersonal dysfunctions inside and outside of the therapy session.

Another major issue is the meaning of the therapist's identificatory experience. There have been a whole series of efforts in the past to classify the identificatory experience in the countertransference starting with Racker's analysis of concordant and complementary types of direct countertransference and Winnicott's objective and subjective countertransference. The identificatory model developed by Tansey and Burke (1989) illustrates the promise and complexity of this analysis of interpersonal communication. They elaborate on a model of concordant and complementary engagement. They link the patient's message, the projective identification, with the therapist's reaction, the introjective identification in terms of the patient's and therapist's introjects (pre-existing and enduring interpersonal schema) and the immediate self-experience in the hour. For example, a concordant engagement of a masochistic patient with his therapist would be characterized as follows: on the patient's side, the introject would be that of a victim and the immediate self-experience in the hour would also be that of a victim: on the therapist's side, the interactional introject would be the patient's self-representation of being a victim (as opposed to the complementary engagement, namely the patient's object representation of victimizer) whose immediate self-experience is also that of a victim. The therapist thus has a concordant identification (empathic) with the masochistic patient's experience of being a victim. The dynamics of this influence process is a matter of speculation. Why, for example, in some cases does the patient enact the object's role, that of the victimizer? The participants play interactive roles in this outcome, but the rules for how it unfolds remains obscure. There is promise of elucidation of this interactive process in the work of Benjamin (1982) on her structural model of social behavior, in Kielser's taxonomy for complementarity in interpersonal behavior (1978, 1983) and in Wiggins's (1982) circumflex model of interpersonal behavior. They provide a framework for describing the underlying rules of interpersonal engagement.

Most of the conceptual burden on the patient's side for the induction of the countertransference has been placed on splitting and projective identification. These concepts represent an effort to account for the induction process that seems especially appropriate for severe disorders but not for neuroses.

Recognition and Response

Most agree that countertransference is inevitable but difficult to recognize initially. The validation hypotheses of Tansey and Burke offer a framework for investigation of this elusive problem. As little is known now as in the 1950s about the effect of the therapist's aptitude, theoretical orientation, and training on his or her capacity to recognize countertransference, to contain the affective pressure, and to respond empathically. Although a connection has been observed between countertransference and process events such as resistance and impasse · (e.g., Blatt & Erlich, 1980), further analysis is awaited. A vocabulary of interpersonal interaction, sensitive to both verbal and nonverbal communication is yet to be developed in the psychoanalytic approaches. The timing and nature of communications over the countertransference has stimulated multiple controversies. Communication over countertransference at the outset of therapy is one example. Disclosure of the countertransference is another. The role of interpretation is a third. In part, at issue is the role of affect and cognition (the analogical vs. the digital) in the treatment process but also the nature of the dysfunction: repressed ideas and impulses versus developmental arrest versus self-defeating interpersonal styles of communication and relationship. Cashdan, for example, proposes that the only effective early intervention is confrontation of the metacommunication underlying the patient's projective identification. Finally, one can wonder when there will be an exchange of information between psychoanalytic and interpersonal communications approaches. This absence of communication is a disquieting metacommunication.

REFERENCES

Beier, E. G. (1966). *The silent language of psychotherapy: Social reinforcement of unconscious processes.* Chicago: Aldine.

Beitman, B. D. (1987). *The structure of individual psychotherapy.* New York: Guilford Press.

Benjamin, L. S. (1982). Use of structural analysis of social behavior (SASB) to guide interventions in psychotherapy (pp. 190–212). In J. A. Anchin & D. J. Kiesler (Eds.), *Handbook of interpersonal psychotherapy.* New York: Pergamon Press.

Bion, W. R. (1959). *Experience in groups.* London: Tavistock.

Blatt, S. J., & Erlich, S. (1980). Levels of resistance in the psychotherapeutic process (pp. 69–132). In P.L. Wachtel (Ed.), *Resistance: Psychodynamic and behavioral approaches.* New York: Plenum.

Bollas, C. (1983). Expressive uses of countertransference. *Contemporary Psychoanalysis, 19,* 1–34.

Burke, W. F., & Tansey, M. J. (1985). Projective identification and counter-transference turmoil: Disruptions in the empathic process. *Contemporary Psychoanalysis, 21,* 372-402.

Carson, R.C. (1969). *Interaction concepts of personality.* Chicago: Aldine.

Cashdan, S. (1988). *Objects relations therapy: Using the relationship.* New York: W. W. Norton.

Cohen, M.B. (1952). Countertransference and anxiety. *Psychiatry, 15,* 231-243.

Danziger, K. (1976). *Interpersonal communication.* Elmsford, NY: Pergamon Press.

Deutsch, H. (1953). Occult processes occurring during psychoanalysis. In G. Devereux (Ed.), *Psychoanalysis and the occult* (pp. 133-146). New York: International Universities Press. (Original work published 1926)

Epstein, L., & Feiner, A. (1979). *Countertransference.* New York: Jason Aronson.

Freud, S. (1953). The future prospects of psychoanalytic therapy. In J. Strachey (Ed. and Trans.), *The standard edition of the complete psychological works of Sigmund Freud* (Vol. 11, pp. 141-151). London: Hogarth Press. (Original work published in 1910).

Freud, S. (1953). Recommendations to physicians practicing psychoanalysis. *The standard edition of the complete psychological works of Sigmund Freud* (Volume 12, pp. 111-120). London: Hogarth Press. (Original work published in 1912)

Gill, M.M. (1983). The interpersonal paradigm and the degree of the therapist's involvement. *Contemporary Psychoanalysis, 19,* 200-237.

Giovacchini, P.L. (1972a). The analytic setting and the treatment of psychosis. In P. L. Giovachinni (Ed.), *Tactics and techniques in psychoanalytic psycho-therapy* (pp. 222-235). New York: Science House.

Giovacchini, P.L. (1972b). Technical difficulties in treating some charactero-logical disorders: Countertransference problems. *International Journal of Psychoanalytic Psychotherapy, 1,* 112-128.

Giovacchini, P.L. (1989). *Countertransference triumphs and catastrophes.* North Vale, NJ: Jason Aronson.

Greenson, R. R. (1960). Empathy and its vicissitudes. *International Journal of Psycho-Analysis, 41,* 418-424.

Greenson, R. R. (1974). Loving, hating, and indifference towards the patient. *International Review of Psychoanalysis, 1,* 259-266.

Grotstein, J.S. (1981). *Splitting and projective identification.* New York: Jason Aronson.

Heimann, P. (1950). On countertransference. *International Journal of Psycho-Analysis, 31,* 81-84.

Herron, W. G., & Rouslin, S. (1982). *Issues in psychotherapy.* Bowie, Maryland: R. J. Brady.

Hoffman, I. (1983). The patient as interpreter of the analyst's experience. *Contemporary Psychoanalysis, 19,* 389-422.

Kernberg, O. (1965). Notes on countertransference. *Journal of the American Psychoanalytic Association, 13,* 38-56.

Kernberg, O. (1975). *Borderline conditions and pathological narcissism.* New York: Jason Aronson.

Kernberg, O. (1976). *Object relations theory and clinical psychoanalysis.* New York: Jason Aronson.

Kernberg, O. (1987). Projection and projective identification: Developmental and clinical aspects. In J. Sandler (Ed.), *Projection, identification, projective identification.* Madison, CT: International Universities Press.

Kiesler, D. J. (1979). An interpersonal communication analysis of relationship in psychotherapy. *Psychiatry, 42,* 299–311.

Kiesler, D.J. (1982). Confronting the client–therapist relationship in psychotherapy. In J. A. Anchin & D. J. Kiesler (Eds.), *Handbook of interpersonal psychotherapy* (pp. 274–295). New York: Pergamon Press.

Kiesler, D.J. (1983). The 1982 Interpersonal Circle: A taxonomy for complementarity in human transactions. *Psychological Review, 90,* 185–214.

Kiesler, D. J. (1988). *Therapeutic metacommunication: Therapist impact disclosure as feedback in psychotherapy.* Palo Alto, CA: Consulting Psychologist Press.

Kiesler, D. J., Anchin, J. C., Perkins, M. J. Chirico, B. M., Kyle, E. M., & Federman, E. J. (1985). *The impact message inventory.* Palo Alto, CA: Consulting Psychologist Press.

Klein, M. (1946). Notes on some schizoid mechanisms. *International Journal of Psycho-Analysis, 33,* 433–438.

Kohut, H. (1977). *The restoration of the self.* New York: International Universities Press.

Langs, R. (1975). Therapeutic misalliances. *International Journal of Psychoanalytic Psychotherapy, 4,* 77–105.

Langs, R. (1976). *The therapeutic interaction: Volume II.* New York: Jason Aronson.

Langs, R. (1978). *Technique in transition.* New York: Jason Aronson.

Leary, T. (1957). *Interpersonal dialogue of personality.* New York: Ronald Press.

Levenson, E. A. (1972). *The fallacy of understanding: An inquiry into the changing structure of psychoanalysis.* New York: Basic Books.

Levenson, E. A. (1981). Fact or fantasies: The nature of psychoanalytic data. *Contemporary Psychoanalysis, 17,* 486–500.

Little, M. (1951). Countertransference and the patient's response to it. *International Journal of Psycho-Analysis, 32,* 32–40.

Little, M. (1957). "R"--The analyst's total response to his patient's needs. *International Journal of Psycho-Analysis, 38,* 240–254.

Malin, A., & Grotstein, J.S. (1966). Projective identification in the therapeutic process. *International Journal of Psycho-Analysis, 42,* 26–31.

Mitchell, S.A. (1989). *Relational concepts in psychoanalysis.* Cambridge: Harvard University Press.

Ogden, T.G. (1979). On projective identification. *International Journal of Psycho-Analysis, 60,* 357–373.

Ogden, T.G. (1982). *Projective identification and psychotherapeutic technique.* New York: Jason Aronson.

Racker, H. (1953). A contribution to the problem of countertransference. *International Journal of Psycho-Analysis, 34*, 313–324.

Racker, H. (1957). The meanings and uses of countertransference. *Psychoanalytic Quarterly, 26*, 303–357.

Racker, H. (1968). *Transference and countertransference.* New York: International Universities Press.

Reich, A. (1960). Further remarks on countertransference. *International Journal of Psycho-Analysis, 41*, 389–395.

Reik, T. (1948). *Listening with the third ear.* New York: Farrar, Strauss, & Young.

Ruesch, J., & Bateson, G. (1951). *Communication: The social matrix of psychiatry.* New York: W. W. Norton.

Sandler, J. (1976). Countertransference and role-responsiveness. *International Review of Psycho-Analysis, 3*, 43–47.

Sandler, J. (1987). *Projection, identification, projective identification.* Madison, CT: International Universities Press.

Schafer, R. (1954). *Psychoanalytic interpretation in Rorschach testing.* New York: Grune/Stratton.

Schafer, R. (1975). The patient as therapist to his analyst. In P. Giovacchini (Ed.), *Tactics and techniques of psychoanalytic therapy* (Vol. 2, pp. 95–151). New York: Jason Aronson.

Schutz, W. C. (1958). *FIRO: A three dimensional theory of interpersonal behavior.* New York: Holt, Rinehart, Winston.

Searles, H. (1958). The schizophrenic's vulnerability to the therapist's unconscious processes. *Journal of Nervous and Mental Disease, 27*, 247–262.

Searles, H. (1965). Transference psychosis in the psychotherapy of schizophrenia. In *Collected papers on schizophrenia and related subjects.* New York: International Universities Press.

Searles, H. (1975). The patient as therapist to the analyst. In P. Giovachinni (Ed.), *Tactics and technique in psychoanalytic psychotherapy* (Vol. 2). New York: Jason Aronson.

Singer, J. L., & Pope, K. S. (1978). The use of imagery and fantasy techniques in psychotherapy. In J. L. Singer & K. S. Pope (Eds.), *The power of human imagination.* New York: Plenum.

Spence, D. P. (1982). *Narrative truth and historical truth.* New York: W. W. Norton.

Sullivan, H. S. (1953). *The interpersonal theory of psychiatry.* New York: W. W. Norton.

Tansey, M. J., & Burke, W. F. (1985). Projective identification and the empathic process. *Contemporary Psychoanalysis, 21*, 42–69.

Tansey, M. J., & Burke, W. F. (1989). *Understanding countertransference: From projective identification to empathy.* Hillsdale, NJ: Academic Press.

Tauber, E. S. (1954). Exploring the therapeutic use of countertransference data. *Psychiatry, 17*, 331–336.

Wachtel, P. S. (1980). Transference, schema and assimilation: The relevance of a Piagetian concept for the psychoanalytic theory of transference. *Annual of Psychoanalysis, 8*, 59–76.

Watzlawick, P., Beavin, J. H., & Jackson, D. D. (1967). *Pragmatics of human interaction.* New York: W. W. Norton.

Wiggins, J. S. (1982). Circomplex models of interpersonal behavior in clinical psychology. In P. C. Kendall & J. K. Butcher (Eds.), *Handbook of research methods in clinical psychology.* New York: John Wiley.

Winnicott, D. W. (1949). Hate in the countertransference. *International Journal of Psycho-Analysis, 30,* 69–75.

E·I·G·H·T

Interpretation, Empathy, and the Future of Psychoanalytic Psychotherapy

PAUL HAMBURG

During the middle of the 20th century, two schools of psychoanalytic theory, separated by a geographic and ideologic ocean, have claimed to rediscover the heart of psychoanalysis. In the United States the contributions of Kohutian self psychology have sought to broaden the understanding of the two-person field, as epitomized by the concept of "empathy," to encompass a complex landscape of connectedness between analyst and patient.

Meanwhile, continental psychoanalysis (especially the school of Jacques Lacan) recommitted itself to Freud's radical appreciation of unconscious processes, especially their linguistic representations. Lacan's work emphasized the alienation of human consciousness from self-knowledge, and the corresponding margin of separateness that characterizes even the most profound connections between persons.

These two expansions of psychoanalytic practice, one emphasizing the two-person field, the other the inner world and the triangularity of human experience, proceeded in an atmosphere that could most sympathetically be described as mutual bewilderment. On the American side, there was understandable reluctance to appreciate a literature that is deeply idiosyncratic and steeped in a literary–philosophical tradition proud of its own inaccessibility. It was easy to proceed from perplexity to disparagement. On the European side, there was a tendency to overvalue the narrowly intellectual, and to dismiss American insight as lacking textual sophistication. On both sides, a difficulty in cultural translation was interpreted as proof of no value. During the past

167

decade, largely because of mounting acceptance of poststructuralist European thought by American literary critics, philosophers, artists, and feminists, American psychoanalytic theorists began to notice Lacan and try to place his work within current psychoanalytic praxis. They still lag well behind European and American academic familiarity with this subject. Lacanian psychoanalytic theory has been read, debated, taught, and revised for a decade in faculties of literature, literary criticism, women's studies, and philosophy at universities around the United States; these academic thinkers are often surprised at their psychoanalytic colleagues' unfamiliarity with Lacanian and post-Lacanian thought.

The possibility of a fruitful encounter between the self-psychological theory of "empathy," and the Lacanian discourse about the "word" has only recently received any serious attention. Muller (1989) explored Kohut's "Two Analyses of Mr. Z" from a Lacanian perspective, launching a quest for common ground between these two theories whose proponents heretofore emphasized their obvious and severe differences.

> Both [Lacan and Kohut] criticized making the ego the criterion for truth and reality. . . . Both men emphasized disintegration anxiety and put mirroring phenomena in the forefront of processes of identification that shape subjective experience. Both challenged the accepted notion of the patient's "resistance" and instead stressed the clinical importance of recognition. (1989, pp. 393–394)

My aim in this chapter is to describe a plane of contact between self psychology, seen as an elaboration of the empathic two-person, presymbolic function of psychoanalysis and Lacanian theory, seen as an elaboration of its linguistic, triadic, symbolic, and interpretive function. The approach will be a critical reading of theoretical approaches to mirroring and to interpretation in Kohut and Lacan. At stake are two essential functions of the psychotherapy: empathy and interpretation.

THE MIRRORING FUNCTION IN
SELF PSYCHOLOGY

Self psychology redefined the psychoanalytic concept of transference to denote the internal experience of a sustaining connection with the therapist. Proceeding beyond transference seen merely as the distorting impact of unconscious desire upon the therapeutic relationship, Kohut delineated the intricate ways that relatively stable "selfobject" transferences meet the psychological needs of narcissistically wounded patients. For these patients, the analyst temporarily assumes an internal existence that supplants missing psychological functions. Selfobject transferences take several forms including twinship (someone in the world is like me), idealizing (there is someone that I can look up to), and mirroring (someone completely understands me). By attempting to match his or her position to the patient's experience of need, the analyst is able to sustain an aspect of the patient's deficient psychological structure. Much of self psychology has explored the difficulty of maintaining the therapist's stance so as to minimize the difference between the analyst's word–actions and the patient's sustaining experience of the analyst. Establishing and maintaining such an "empathic" position become the main themes in Kohutian psychoanalytic practice. The empathic analyst acknowledges the need for his or her words to remain close to the patient's interior experience. Experience-distant interventions are limited to a range that still permits the patient to experience a relatively continuous connection in the face of separateness.

Principal among the sustaining functions of stable transferences is that of mirroring. Mirroring casts a reflected validation upon the patient to the degree that the analyst can maintain an empathic position toward the patient's experience and need. According to the self-psychological perspective, the patient's desire to be reflected does not *distort* the therapeutic connection; rather, it helps to *constitute* it. The analyst does not merely name that desire, nor elucidate its vicissitudes in memory or daily life, but actually becomes a container for it. The facilitating container of the analyst's mirroring activity permits interpretive work to take place. As the patient's internal psychological structures mature, the range of interpretive possibilities widens, and the selfobject connection becomes more complex. Mirroring creates a reflective relationship that mitigates the patient's aloneness, and confirms the truth of the patient's feelings, memories, and conceptual frameworks within a particular context of past experience and distress. Seen in this way a mirror transference is a stable two-person matrix for psychoanalytic action.

Although empathy is an insufficient curative factor in psychoanalysis (a position repeatedly stated by Kohut but at times forgotten by some of his followers), it is the necessary context for therapeutic work. Kohut saw all effective therapeutic action as taking place in a field of empathy. Only the analyst's intricate, thoughtful activity can sustain an empathic position, recognize its temporary breakdowns, initiate the subsequent moments of needed repair, and thereby permit "transmuting internalization," whereby optimal breaks and repairs of the empathic field build psychological structure.

"Transmuting internalization" is a term that seeks to describe how structural change happens in psychoanalytic treatment. Kohut defines change as a result of a series of optimal disappointments (empathic failures) that do not reproduce trauma, but gradually shift a burden from the analyst (as internal selfobject in the patient) to the patient's more autonomous self. The important implication of this theoretical view is that structural change results from moments of difference, not from the consistent identity of therapeutic attunement. It is also of note that the notion of "structure" is somewhat loosely applied in self psychology, as indeed it is in other forms of object relations theory.

For this process to unfold, the analyst must first make sense of the seemingly senseless demands of the patient to maintain an appreciation of the patient's experience, a task that requires an ongoing struggle to discover and match the patient's need for understanding. In this view empathy is a difficult *project* for the analyst, an active, though quiet, attempt to build a matrix of emotional and cognitive understanding sufficient to keep psychoanalysis from falling into a repetition of the traumatic, fragmenting, empathic failures of the patient's childhood. Far from just "being nice" to the patient, or enacting a futile attempt at a corrective emotional experience, therapeutic empathy is a complex struggle that forms the basis of difficult interpretive work. Interpretation in self psychology most often takes place in inevitable moments of disrupted empathy (empathic failure).

For Kohut, in clear contrast to Lacan, the intimacy of a mirroring relation between analyst and patient does not freeze the therapeutic relationship into an undifferentiated realm of symbiotic illusion. "[T]he quietly sustaining matrix provided by the spontaneously established selfobject transference to the analyst . . . is disrupted time and again by the analyst's unavoidable, yet only temporary and thus nontraumatic, empathy failures—that is, his 'optimal failures' " (1984, p. 66). In this respect Kohut is fully consistent with Freud's own view that ego "precipitates" form in response to *frustrated* attachments to the libidinal object; change occurs in turbulence, not from absolute satisfaction.

Throughout psychological development, human life according to Kohut (1984) is characterized by the persistence of a matrix of connection. "[A] move from dependence (symbiosis) to independence (autonomy) is an impossibility. . . . the developmental moves of normal psychological life must be seen in the changing nature of the relationships between the self and its selfobject." (p. 52). Kohut distinguished two lines of relational development, that of selfobject relationships that concern sustenance, understanding, and validation, and that of object relations and their economy of desire.

THE MIRROR FUNCTION IN
LACANIAN PSYCHOANALYSIS

The hermetic labyrinth of Jacques Lacan's discourse would appear to be far removed from the mirror world of empathy. In his mathematical formulas and intellectually perverse style, Lacan belittled the imaginary world of empathic resonance between analyst and patient as just so much illusion. Lacan's style has been explained variously as a reflection of the "language of the other" that he calls the unconscious, an expression of power, a deliberate attempt to torture readers, and an inevitable accompaniment of a discourse designed to promote nonmastery. Even his most devoted followers concede that reading Lacan can be painful.

He returned time and again to the "alterity" of the Freudian unconscious to remind us that we are all embedded in a fabric whose symbolic forms resist mastery, whether as knowledge of another person or knowledge of ourselves. Alterity is a term used in French poststructuralist philosophy and psychoanalysis to denote the quality of otherness (*alter*-other), the force of difference that separates subject from object. Lacan promotes the concept that this alienating force of difference is just as operational in self-knowledge as in knowledge of another, and reflects the irreducible effect of the unconscious. We encounter ourselves as fundamentally other. Freud's concept of the id (the *it*) implies the same experience of a part of our being about which we must say, "that couldn't possibly be me."

In a summary aphorism, Lacan (1977) stated, "The unconscious is the discourse of the other" (p. 172). This "other" represents the absolute otherness (alterity) of the subject and of desire. The "other" is always a third term, a "guarantor of good faith" that transcends and structures the intersubjective relation between two subjects. It is a symbol of the decentering of the subject in Lacanian theory. It is neither me nor you, but the context that permits us to say something to each other, the field of discourse itself.

Lacan reserved the study of symbolic forms as monuments of alienation from self-consciousness and full knowledge of the other for psychoanalysis. One could go so far as to say that his theory emerged from the impossibility of absolute empathy within a therapy room where language was the medium of discourse. There *is* no two-person field, except as an illusion that becomes dangerous if shared by the analyst. "This is the field that our experience polarizes in a relation which is only apparently two-way, for any positing of its structure in merely dual terms is as inadequate to it in theory as it is ruinous for its technique" (p. 56). Lacan's field of interest lay beyond the reach of empathy, if by empathy we mean full understanding; in his explorations the two-person field always revealed its hidden complexity. Whenever it appeared that the intersubjective realm was occupied by two mutually knowable subjects, Lacan named the invisible participants in the discourse. In other words, beyond the two speakers lay an unconscious realm that was irreducible to a dialogue; the unconscious wrote in its own language, which we as psychoanalytically interested persons must learn to read.

Despite his pessimism concerning human understanding, Lacan placed considerable theoretical weight upon the mirror function in early psychological development. The illusion of oneness in reflection established by the mirror function is the origin of all connection. Lacan (1977) postulated that the template of the mirror relationship was the "jubilant assumption of his specular image by the child at the *infans* stage, [*infans* literally means 'without language'] still sunk in his motor incapacity and nursling dependence . . ." (p. 2). Lacan labeled the realm of intrapsychic experience constituted by mirroring the "imaginary," because it is dominated by images and hence a boundariless, presymbolic world. The "imaginary" is one of three registers of human experience in Lacanian theory. The others are the "real" (moments of unmediated encounter with the world that are often traumatic and almost unbearable, as when the solid ground beneath one's feet shakes violently during an earthquake) and the "symbolic" (experience mediated by signification, especially through language).

Although the "imaginary" connection was defined by a relative lack of symbolic mediation, it was nonetheless predicated upon the infant's first experience of desire as the desire-of-the-other. The *mother's* desire to meet the infant's need is the first desire experienced by the infant. The infant wants to *be* the object of the mother's desire, to become whatever it is that she lacks; in Freud's metapsychological language, the infant represents the mother's missing phallus. Even in this presymbolic, mirrored, imaginary world, desire is already defined as being the desire of something other than the self. And lack, discontinuity, incompleteness, and an irreconcilable splitting (*Spaltung*) have already manifested themselves. Lacan writes (1982), "[W]hen one is made into two, there is no going back on it. It can never revert to making one again, not even a new one" (p. 156).

And from this moment on, Lacan (1972) warned us, there will never be an object of which desire can ever say, 'that's it; *that's* what I want.' Desire, a function central to the whole of human experience, is desire of nothing nameable. As he wrote in *Feminine Sexuality* (1982), "This is manifest in the primordial relation to the mother, pregnant as it is with that 'other' to be situated *some way short of* any needs which it might gratify . . . the very satisfactions of need which it obtains are degraded (*sich erniedrigt*) as being no more than a crushing of the demand for love (all of which is palpable in the psychology of early child-care to which our nurse-analysts are so dedicated)" (p. 80).

Although Lacan assigned a critical developmental significance to the mirror function, his interest lay beyond it, in the symbolic relation and alienation of subject and self, self and object, desire and its aim, that result from the intrusion of the "name of the father" into the mirroring relationship between mother and infant. Lacan emphasized the overwhelming importance of the father's symbolic interruption, because it is in this moment, and through its language, that the dual mirroring relationship of mother and infant is transformed into a symbolic structure. The "name of the father" (nom du père) is a crystallization of the moment that language and the reality principle supervene to disrupt the sensual continuum symbolized by the nursing pair. This moment constitutes the speaking subject, albeit in perpetual exile and nonidentity. The speaking subject (the I) and the observed object of self-consciousness (the me) emerge in tandem from the imaginary landscape of the mirror stage. What presents itself as readily accessible to analytic discourse is this symbolic realm of subject, object, and signifiers that has largely replaced the imaginary world of connections and reflected images over the course of early development.

Lacan was much less interested in the intricacies of the imaginary. In part this was because he was convinced that its dimensions were inaccessible to the linguistic explorations of psychoanalysis. He defined his own task as exploring the postimaginary world. In the analytic scene, the echoes of the imaginary seemed like a perpetual siren song luring the analyst away from a proper position of listening to the symbolic expressions of triangular structure; if the analyst strayed toward a mirroring dual relationship with the patient, confusion and disillusionment were certain.

From a Lacanian perspective, mirroring selfobject transferences would fall into the realm of the imaginary, that portion of experience dominated by images and characterized by the absence of clear structural boundaries between self and other. The imaginary realm had an atavistic onus in the Lacanian view. As important as it may be to the rest of human life, it is a stage to be gotten past, a first step along the path of psychological development. The degree to which human connectedness, particularly between mother and infant, was suppressed in Lacan's writing is one of its most astounding features. *The Four Fundamental Concepts of Psychoanalysis,* (1981) a volume of some 280 pages, contained only two references to "mother," mentioned only, "let us say, by illustration." Sarcastic references to "nursemaid" American analysts, who are naively concerned with object relations and hence supportive of their patients, capture the force of Lacan's devaluation of mothering and anything in psychoanalysis that resembles it. Close to his death Lacan spoke about the joy of "speaking of love" and even went so far as to say, "speaking of love, in analytic discourse, basically one does nothing else." The bearer of this love, Lacan (1982) went on to say, topologically beyond the symbolic domain, is the *soul,* "whatever enables a being—the speaking being to call him by its name—to bear what is intolerable in its world, which presumes this soul to be alien to that world, that is to say, fantasmatic." (p. 155) Perhaps the direction implied by Lacan's late shift in emphasis can be seen as lending justification for efforts like the present one to incorporate the two-person field of empathy into his theoretical framework.

Lacan held that psychoanalysis (and most other human experience) must be understood from the symbolic realm, beyond the mirror relation of early psychological life. Part of Lacan's contempt for the empathic, sustaining, two-person function of the analyst stemmed from his relentless privileging[1] of the symbolic function, his insistence that the therapist's "word" was divider and definer of psychological difference. Part may have reflected a complex misogyny disguised in layers of paradox. His misogyny consists of claiming that the "name of the father" and the "phallus" refer to something neither male nor anatomical, and that naming the phallus as primary signifier was not inherently gender-biased; its complexity has enabled it to maintain an extraordinarily loyal feminist following in the face of these positions.

While the adequacy of a humane connection between analyst and patient may be an assumed prerequisite for therapy to proceed, its vicissitudes occupy a remarkably restricted place in Lacan's map of

---

[1]"Privilege" is used in poststructuralist French criticism to refer to the power accorded to certain dominant discourses in traditional philosophy. Often this means one side is emphasized in a duality, as in male–female, monotheism–polytheism, objective–subjective, etc. These conceptual privileges, often unconscious in practice, are the marks that indicate the ideologic substrate of a culture. A similar implication is contained in the deconstructionist term *-centrism,* as in logocentrism (the privileging of the word as full speech), phallocentrism (the privileging of the phallus), and theocentrism (the privileging of the deity).

psychoanalytic practice. The closest Lacan (1977) came to a definition of an empathic context is: "In order to know how to reply to the subject in analysis, the procedure is to recognize first of all *the place* where his ego is . . . in other words, to know *through whom and for whom the subject poses his question*. So long as this is not known, there will be the risk of a misunderstanding concerning the desire that is there to be recognized and concerning the object to whom this desire is addressed" (p. 89).

Like many traditional psychoanalysts, Lacan discounted the complexity of empathy, which he apparently assumed is an easy precondition to interpretive work, something that we all simply do. The maternal function in all of its manifestations, whether in psychoanalysis or in relationship to an infant, was regarded as neither a difficult task nor an interesting subject, whereas the father's interruption of the symbiotic continuity of infant and mother was both complex and fascinating, to be at the very center of psychoanalysis.

In a late, enigmatic essay, "God and the Jouissance of the Woman"[2] Lacan (1982) may have come closest to a belated recognition that there is something in human relationship of importance, connected to maternal love, that is not engraved inside the symbolic order of logos and phallus. He acknowledged the existence of "filia" — that love of a friend for another that is not appropriately subsumed into a sexual economy of privation, demand, and alienation, and linked his own concept of the "other" to the concepts of God and feminine love. Lacan's split subject thus had final recourse to two reparative mechanisms, the ineffable object of religion and the mystified object of woman.

But if the *jouissance* of woman lies outside the sexual economy that is governed by the logos of phallus, desire, and privation, then can it speak? Having situated love and the particular *jouissance* of the feminine beyond knowledge, Lacan wondered whether there could be any knowledge within such love. Can a woman know if her love plays outside the symbolic order? He so carefully defined *sexual* loving as a phenomenon attached to the symbolic (phallic) order, and therefore available to knowledge. If God as absolutely "other," or woman as absolutely "other," can love in a different way, then she cannot know (anything). Woman cannot be the name of something, because that would declare a positive existence for the feminine other, which, strictly speaking, within the phallic economy, cannot be. Hence the barred

---

[2] *Jouissance* is a Lacanian term that denotes joy (a concept for which Lacan and Kohut share a particular fondness) along with orgasm (*jouir*-to come), marking a state of affective transcendence.

article: La Femme; castration always has the last word. Love finds itself (if at all) in exile from the dominant discourse of the symbolic function, and with no room for knowledge in its new marginal realm. For all the brilliance of its intellectual journey, there may also be insufficient room for love *inside* the confines of interpretive discourse as defined by Lacanian theory.

Naming what is repressed in the Lacanian structural schema is a perilous step. A glance at Kohut's description of the empathic milieu, suggests that a vast realm of human experience is missing in Lacan. A conceptual register suggests itself: the maternal function; empathy, connection; intersubjectivity; love; filia; bonding. But these are not concepts that fare well in the phallocentric critical discourse, where they might all be relegated to the imaginary. There is a barrier to naming a powerful maternal presence. The mother's completeness (unlike the father's) seems to be forbidden even as a signifier; she only may appear in the Lacanian schema once she has been discovered to be "castrated," because in her incompleteness, she then occupies her place in a chain of desire that plays around the phallus as the veiled, never-possessed object of desire. The legacy of mother-and-infant outside the phallic economy, the experience of maternal sufficiency, must remain repressed in a system that allows only one signifier, under whose operating system the feminine is "other," outside naming, and subordinate.

INTERPRETATION IN SELF PSYCHOLOGY

Although Kohut (1984) clearly valued interpretation in psychoanalysis, his formulation of change de-emphasized interpretation. Instead, he saw change as a series of structure-building optimal lapses in the selfobject connection between analyst and patient. The building of a "healthy self," which he defined as one "not prone to become fragmented, weakened, or disharmonious during maturity . . ." (p. 70), begins with the spontaneous mobilization of archaic selfobject needs in the analysis, and the internalization of the analyst's response to these needs. In contrast to Lacan's interpretations, which seek to place disharmony and division within a symbolic structure, Kohut's seek to reconfirm wholeness. The valued goals of self-psychological treatment are wholeness, becoming embedded in a matrix of sustaining relationship, and cure.

A successful analysis is one in which the analysand's formerly archaic needs for the responses of archaic selfobjects are superseded by the

experience of the availability of empathic resonance, the major constit-
uent of the sense of security in adult life. Increased ability to verbalize,
broadened insight, greater autonomy of ego functions, and increased
control over impulsiveness may accompany these gains, but they are not
the essence of cure . . . the essence of cure resides in a patient's newly
acquired ability to identify and seek out appropriate selfobjects — both
mirroring and idealizable — as they present themselves in his realistic
surrounding and to be sustained by them (p. 77) . . . contrary to his
experiences in childhood, [the patient realizes that] the sustaining echo
of empathic resonance is indeed available in this world. (p. 78)

Interpretation is subordinated to this system of value. The analyst's principal concern is to understand the vicissitudes of the two-
person field constituted by the selfobject transference.

[S]ince the essential driving force of the analytic process in the
disturbances of the self is provided by the reactivation of the thwarted
developmental needs of the self, since, in other words, the renewed
search of the damaged self for the development-enhancing responses of
an appropriately empathic selfobject always occupy center stage in the
analysand's experiences during analysis, it follows that the analyst's
pivotal communications to the analysand are those that focus on the
psychic configurations to which we refer as selfobject transferences. (p.
192)

Interpretation is made as nearly a part of the two-person field as
possible. Its form almost always begins by acknowledging the analyst's
disruption of empathy, and only proceeds to the genetic material by
analogy and legitimation (e.g., "When I was late to the last session, you
felt disappointed in my sudden unreliability, which reminded you of
the extreme unreliability of your parents for whom you were forever
waiting," etc.). Both need and affect are validated in this form of
interpretation, with special care to acknowledge the validity of the
patient's current experience, no matter how peculiar it might seem were
it observed from a nonempathic viewpoint. Empathy is the attunement
that allows a peculiar transferential experience to become understandable to the analyst, and thus to the patient.

Interpretations of this kind create structure by means of their
subtle acknowledgment of the difference between a legitimate expectation and a disappointing reality. By interpreting inside this restricted
framework, the analyst (as representative of the environment) bears the
burden of difference, which it is assumed that the patient could not
bear without retraumatization. The form of these interpretations
reassures the patient that difference never means having to renounce
the empathic milieu. By contrast, in the example above, a more

traditional interpretation ("You often betray an exaggerated sensitivity to small disappointments like my lateness, because you are still enraged at your father for the way he disappointed you long ago") places the burden of difference on the patient. It is the patient who expects too much, wants the impossible, and is excessively sensitive. The currently mobilized experience of disappointment is misunderstood, despite the accuracy of the interpretation, because its legitimacy is not acknowledged. Nonempathic interpretations of this kind are subtly retraumatizing.

In this respect Kohut demanded that the mobilized selfobject transference be treated as a contextually valid experience, and that difference be introduced in ways that neither invalidated it nor placed the burden of disruption upon the patient. Within these constraints, Kohut claimed that there remained ample room for interpretive intervention, as long as it came from a place very near the edge of the empathic connection between analyst and patient. However, Kohut's narrow focus upon the two-person field creates a larger problem. Not every interpretation concerns selfobject transference. Not all human experience can be so readily subsumed under the predominance of empathy in the analytic scene, even if we accept that human connection is the "psychological oxygen" that Kohut told us it is. By attending with such sensitivity to the vicissitudes of the two-person dynamic, self psychology subtly devalues whatever falls outside it.

These idealistic aspects of self-psychological interpretation form a disturbing blind spot. In particular, self psychology assumes without question that all experience can be empathically shared, that complete understanding between subjects is possible, and that the milieu of human kindness makes possible the wholeness, identity, and harmony of full selfhood. Vast regions of human experience are suppressed in any therapeutic discourse that so privileges the relational field. Disconnection, disharmony, disruption, desire, aggression, hatred, and schism cannot simply be neutralized by a selfobject connection or explained as a consequence of its temporary disruption. Self psychology is at a loss when it must empathize with disconnection.

It is possible to argue that only the continuity of human connection makes endurable the divisions of self from object and self from self that characterize adult life, and justify the closest possible attention to this realm in psychoanalytic discourse. There remains nevertheless a realm of nonidentity that demands understanding on its own terms, which necessarily lie beyond a committed quest for wholeness. By insistently seeking resonant understanding, self psychology devalues the inner world as well as the world of symbolic forms, which are seen only in terms of their reflections in the selfobject relationship. Kohut's privileging of the empathic dimension in effect precludes an empathic response to human alienation, which would require at moments a more metaphoric language, a different respect for distance, and even a movement toward analytic silence in the face of the absolutely other.

Kohut's interpretive framework sought to normalize every instance of alienation or aggression and each encounter with the uncanny within the empathic field. Having decided that aggression, alienation, division, and drive were "disintegration products," mere manifestations of a breakdown in attunement and empathic grounding, he relentlessly refused to consider them as legitimate phenomena in their own right. For Kohut every aggressive impulse could be translated into a story of disappointment; conflict was always a misunderstanding. Aggression was never regarded as a fundamental human attribute, something that must astound most survivors of the 20th century. Whatever the technical merits of this clinical search for the disappointment behind every aggressive or rageful moment, a psychology that has convinced itself that human aggression is always soluble in love is deeply immersed in the imaginary.

Left outside the center of interest in self psychology is the purely personal language and fantasy life of the inner world. Also excluded are massively disillusioning encounters with death, incompleteness, and the "real." Kohut's "healthy self" was supposed to confront these realities without fragmenting. But how does the "whole" self face the truth of its own inevitable, already manifest fragmentation? The cocoon concept of the whole self embedded in its fabric of selfobjects left out a harsh world, both exterior and interior, and promised a fullness of being that has little resemblance to the prevailing chronicles, even the most optimistic ones, of life in our times. In this respect self psychology is a profoundly nostalgic theory.

From the point of view of language, self psychology, like Lacanian theory, has been an enigma to noninitiates. One source of bewilderment is the slipperiness that characterizes the word "selfobject." Despite Kohut's frequent disclaimers to the contrary, the location of this structure seems to wander between the intrapsychic and environmental. Selfobjects are defined as internal representations of significant people or parts of people. The selfobject is a functional part of the patient's self, therefore clearly something internal. Lacan would have had considerable difficulty even with this formulation, since it implies that an internal object is formed by a simple, undynamic, representational act, one that preserves the identity of the thing represented. This violates the symbolic order of representation, which has always barred the signifier from full equivalence with what is signified.

However, in his clinical vignettes, Kohut exceeded his intrapsychic formulation, berating "selfobjects" from patients' childhoods for their failures, and the reader had to assume he was referring to persons that constituted the human environment of the subject. In these instances it seemed that selfobjects were little more than the relational aspects of the people in the patient's life: "—the actual content and form of the nuclear self are often decisively determined by the selective responses of the parental selfobjects" (p. 186). In (1977) he wrote, "rage and destructiveness . . . arise in reaction to the faulty empathic responses of the selfobject" (p. 123).

What is the missing dynamic of Kohut's formulation? How does the parent (or the analyst) become a selfobject? Where are the differences, gaps, additions, subtractions that characterize the creative activity of intersubjectivity? Kohut stated that the unclear locus of the selfobject concept was "harmless and excusable." To explore this process of mutual relationship, full of difference and complexity, would have diverted Kohut from the functional dimension that he sought to isolate in the idea of a selfobject. He had to pretend that these differences do not exist, and proceed as if the two sides of the mirror were to all intents and purposes equivalent. Kohut attempted to write from the position of the imaginary, a two-person field that is largely presymbolic and pre-Oedipal where difference is always minimized as a threat to wholeness. But language in its very substance represented another structure, that of the symbolic function, where imaginary relations are reorganized according to a different principle. So the conceptual difficulties revealed by the slipperiness of the selfobject concept are not easily overcome; to some degree they may afflict any attempt to use language, a symbolic form, to describe the imaginary relation.

Although it is appropriate to examine Kohut's theory from the perspective of its contradictory conceptual language, it is necessary to recall that other attempts to describe the preverbal connections that animate human life have been fraught with similar linguistic difficulties. One has only to think of Buber's I–thou and I–it distinction, of Heidegger's conception of a "thing thinging" to appreciate the philosopher's struggle to find words that capture the lost intimacy of presymbolic existence without mystification or exaltation. Whereas the transcendental aspects of such efforts must remain open to criticism, one needs to avoid the trap of banishing this realm of experience simply because it is almost impossible to speak about. Perhaps only the poet can speak about the ineffable human bond that lies almost beyond words. That it is hard to speak about, however, does not prove its nonexistence or that its manifestations are limited to an obscure period of early childhood.

THE INTERPRETIVE FUNCTION IN LACANIAN THEORY

Lacan's radical statement defined the unconscious as structured like a language. In this way he emphasized the importance of unconscious processes in all discourse, especially psychoanalytic discourse, and established interpretation as the linguistic act *par excellence*. Interpretation is the operation of an active word (the logos) upon the discourse between unknowable subjects in the therapy room. In psychoanalysis it is never clear who speaks, nor to whom speech is addressed. The subject who speaks represents a measure of self-awareness and self-expression, but he or she also speaks from the language of the unconscious, which cannot be mastered. The subject addresses the analyst not only as real object, but also as transferential object, and the therapist's unconscious is hidden object and subject in their discourse. Therapy is the discovery of the other's language, a radical recognition of the double decentering of subject and object. It is in the unconscious aspect of the discourse that meaning remains embedded, awaiting interpretation. Interpretation is the unveiling of the signifier, which Lacan, influenced by structural linguistics, saw as the symbolic organizing principle underlying representation, language, and analytic discourse.

The signifier is a concept adapted from structural linguistics. In Lacan's theoretical matrix, the signifier is the bearer of unconscious meaning within the act of symbolic signification. The signifier calls to someone, and bears a meaning whose content is only partially subsumed by any intentionality. The remainder bears witness to the cultural inheritance in language and to the impossibility of self-knowledge or self-expression as truth. The signifier operates in a chain of meaning that can be traced back to the oedipal "name of the father" that establishes the symbolic order. All signifiers bear some relation, through the structure of the unconscious as language, to the transcendental signifier that Lacan (1982) labels the *phallus*. The phallus, "the privileged signifier of that mark where the share of the logos is wedded to the advent of desire" (p. 82) is one of Lacan's more perplexing but most important theoretical constructs. It represents the structure of symbolic signification, as well as the oedipal interruption by the father of infant–maternal unity. The phallus is not seen in a simple equivalence to the penis, but rather as the symbol of that-which-is-never-possessed. Castration is always an essential aspect of the signifying function of the phallus, because it always represents a lack. This lack links the aspect of desire that yearns for predifferentiated unity (restoration of a symbiotic world) with the desire for the other as symbolic carrier of that which is missing. The phallus can only function "as veiled," since it is a pure signifier that represents nothing real.

The phallus organizes all experiences in terms of lack (castration). It establishes the unconscious movement of desire as a desire for that which is lacking. Because the phallus is not an organ or any other real thing, it cannot ever be possessed, mastered, or attained; its function is limited to that of a signifier, and a model for all signification — the signifier of all signifiers. Desire is inevitably an enactment of alienation, because what is desired cannot by definition be had. The phallus as signifier operates under a veil; once seen and placed in action, it loses its power. It represents the enigmatic nature of power and desire, always displaced in time and space, never entirely realized.

Every act of signification (1982) conceals a displacement of the signifier. In this sense, castration (the division of the fullness of the subject) is reflected in every utterance.

> The signifier has an active function in determining the effects in which the signifiable appears as submitting to its mark, becoming through that passion the signified. This passion of the signifier then becomes a new dimension of the human condition, in that it is not only man who speaks, but in man and through man that it [ça][3] speaks, that his nature is woven by effects in which we can find the structure of language, whose material he becomes, and that consequently there resounds in him, beyond anything ever conceived of by the psychology of ideas, the relation of speech. (p. 78)

Not only is the unconscious a discourse of the other, but this language of the other can belong to no speaking subject.

> "It [ça] speaks in the other, I say, designating by this other the very place called upon by a recourse to speech in any relation where it intervenes. If it speaks in the other, whether or not the subject hears it with his own ears, it is because it is there that the subject, according to a logic prior to any awakening of the signified, finds his signifying place." (p. 79)

Once need is translated into demand, that is to say, put into a "signifying form," then the subject becomes alienated from need, and finds that it is "from the place of the other that his message is emitted." All demand is for a presence or an absence. The power of the other to deprive or to meet one's needs guarantees that no desire can be fulfilled. This privilege of the other thus sketches out the radical form of the gift of something which it does not have, namely, what is called its love (p.

---

[3] ça refers to the alterity of the speaking subject, and also to the It (*Das Es,* the id), Freud's designation for the portion of the desiring subject that is unconscious.

80). The hierarchy of need, demand, and desire represents an increasing complexity of libidinal relationship, along with an ever-growing barrier to fulfillment.

Transference means that the patient never addresses a demand to the analyst as simple object. The patient's demand is to the other as *represented* by the analyst. Analysis begins when the analyst experiences the difference between the manifest discourse of the patient and the unconscious creation of an other, whose substance cannot be demarcated as being composed exclusively of the therapist's unconscious contributions or the patient's. It is this not-fully-knowable transferential creation, the third person in the therapy room, that is placed in question by the therapist's interpretations. Language dispels the illusion that there are two persons in the room, the seductive mirroring illusion of the imaginary realm. As soon as the patient addresses someone in the room who is and is also not the analyst (i.e., as soon as transferential discourse through language has begun), a cleft has formed between the patient and the analyst as fully knowable subject and object; a corresponding cleft alienates the patient as subject from objective self-knowledge.

For Lacan, the fracturing of full selfhood and full mirrored relatedness is an inevitable aspect of the human condition. It is manifest once the developing child enters the realm of symbolic forms (language, discourse, relationship) that transform him or her into a desiring person. In Ecrits, Lacan (1977) wrote: "It is always at the juncture of speech, at the level of its apparition, its emergence . . . that the manifestation of desire is produced. Desire emerges at the moment of its incarnation into speech—it is coincident with the emergence of symbolism" (p. 273). Psychoanalysis is the process whereby symbolic forms establish themselves as playful contexts for the exploration of desire; to the extent that the patient is frozen in transferential repetitions, the world of images still dominates and serves as a relentless source of disappointment. Only by recognizing the paradoxical forms of human desire and alienation, by accepting the limitations of a "castrated" state of nonidentity and the unattainability of desire does anyone achieve that limited measure of freedom available to mortals.

Language establishes a third term in psychoanalytic discourse as it abolishes the illusion of perfect understanding, unequivocal intent, and total empathic connection. Language initiates this displacement regardless of the content of the therapist's speech. It is the very nature of linguistic signs, as reflections of the symbolic structure of the unconscious, that establishes the indeterminacy of all human communication. So the therapist's word of interpretation, as a linguistic function, always interrupts the experience of identity in the therapeutic space, both the identity of self-knowledge and that of being fully known by the other. By killing identity, the therapist's word introduces death as a force within the therapeutic relationship. Death arrives in several forms, in the act of naming, in the multiple fragmentations of self from self-awareness, of the object from its name, of the other from desire. The very form that permits communication, establishes dialogue, and serves as a vehicle for relation *also always* recalls death, disconnection, and solitude.

Lacan thoroughly confirmed the tragic picture of the human condition that Freud painted earlier in the century. Where Kohut described a pattern of increasingly complex, continuously sustained selfobject connections that allowed for a joyful human existence, Lacan saw instead the renunciation of the mirror stage to gain entry into a complex alienated world of symbolic transactions that confront the unknowability of the other, the paradoxes of desire, and the irreducible power of the unconscious. It is hard to invent two more disparate re-readings of the Freudian legacy. And yet in such seemingly irreconcilable differences may be hidden a submerged complementarity between empathy and interpretation.

BARRIERS BETWEEN EMPATHY
AND INTERPRETATION

The image of a perfect mirror holds a special fascination for self psychologists. It represents the empathically attuned therapeutic instrument responding to the patient's (only partially expressible) need as if in a seamless maternal–infant dyad. Although Kohut himself was careful to emphasize that empathy is a *context* for therapeutic action rather than an autonomous curative agent, self psychology has nevertheless abetted a vision of therapy as an obsessive search for the ultimate empathic response.

But mirroring is never perfect. Relationship, even the *specular*[4] relationship of the mirror stage, always implies difference. Despite opposing attitudes toward mirroring in the analytic relationship, both Lacan and Kohut inferred a maternal–infant dyad that transcended difference. For self psychology the recapture of perfect mirroring became the holy Grail in the analytic quest, melding nostalgia with perpetual hopefulness. For Lacan (1977), the mirror stage was a

---

[4]A term used in French psychoanalysis to denote the mirror function (*speculum* = mirror), and its extensions toward imagination (speculation), investigation (the speculum), and the multiplicity of the image (aspects).

developmental throwback confined to an atavistic place before and beyond adult discourse and subtly trivialized. It has no place in analytic practice. "If one confines oneself to an imaginary relation between objects there remains only the dimension of distance to order it" (p. 246). "If it is a question of ripening the Object in the hot house of a confined situation, the analysand is left with only one object, if you will pardon the expression, to get his teeth into, and that's the analyst" (p. 245).

Kohut minimized the dynamic tension of the difference that is always already present, whether in the form of an intruding and fascinating outer world that interrupts the maternal–infant dyad, or as a private inner world beyond connection and empathic understanding. Lacan underestimated the relational complexity of mirroring, the intrusion of difference and unknowability that antedates paternal interruption. He failed to consider the intricate manifestations of difference that precede the linguistic and oedipal symbolic order. He attempted to sunder the mirror function from the intimacy of the maternal–infant dyad, preferring to see the specular moment as an encounter with a literal mirror rather than a human one. In his neglect of the nonverbal, presymbolic, relational richness of maternal connection, Lacan misplaced an entire world of experience, the very same world that Kohut privileged as if it could become the whole world.

While the triangulation represented by the "name of the father" may codify a symbolic order that is oedipal, linguistic, and fundamentally structure-building, it does not launch difference. Maternal–infant symbiosis is best understood as a retrospective construction that *may* accurately portray an adult's nostalgic wish for a joyful annihilation of identity, but not a developmental reality. Modern feminist psychoanalytic critics and researchers in infant development have converged upon a profound skepticism concerning the myth of predifferentiation and unity.

Jacques Derrida criticized the philosophical idealism embodied in Lacan's search for origins beyond difference (Derrida, 1980, 1978). For Derrida, the mythology of the imaginary union of mother and child, later given form and structure by the name of the father, privileged the paternal, phallic world of symbolic forms ("phallo-logocentrism") even as it alienated the maternal function by locating it in a transcendental, prestructural, purely spontaneous, and amorphous space. Locating the maternal function outside our conceptual reach, Lacan perpetuated a mythology of the feminine that incorporated yearnings for unity and the erasure of difference that abound in diverse religious and metaphysical traditions. The feminine, in its manifestation of empathy and attunement, is placed beyond discourse, and linked inextricably to a regressive fantasy. This maneuver sets in motion a paternalistic privileging of femininity (that warm place beyond complexity and adulthood) along with an inevitable, though concealed violence. An aspect of the (male) self is cast out, projected upon the "other," and declared alien, desirable, mysterious, and strange.

In alternately mystifying and erasing maternal connection from the field of discourse, Lacan fell into the same metaphysical idealism he had promised to leave behind. Lacan's *declared* project was to ground psychoanalytic theory beyond the metaphysical lures of mastery, full knowledge, experience, or meaning. In the context of this goal, the concealed fantasy of maternal–infant enclosure, beyond the reach of difference, becomes especially problematic. Lacan's slippage toward traditional metaphysics has extensive implications regarding the psychoanalytic understanding of gender. These considerations have occupied an expanding corpus of post-Lacanian feminist writing, which sets for itself the goal of relocating the feminine in a new intersubjective discourse that supersedes Cartesian knowledge (the dire mastery of subject over object, masculine over feminine).

Two aspects of Lacan's dualism are of special concern here. One links the maternal function with a predifferentiated, presymbolic organization of the mind. The other links the paternal function with a privileged signifier (the phallus) as organizer of the differentiated symbolic order. If the maternal function is bound to presymbolic images, it lies beyond discourse, because discourse (as language) belongs to the symbolic order. Further, the maternal function can have no proper discourse of its own; knowledge falls outside its way of being. Mothering, empathy, and love are barred from self-knowledge. If the realm of interpretation is exclusively associated with the "name of the father," then it is split from the realm of empathy that emerges from maternal mirroring. The double barrier is one of conceptual structure and gender.

Having assigned mirroring and interpretation to radically different discourses, Lacanian psychoanalysis cannot find a way to reconcile them. And Kohutian psychoanalysis has so privileged the mirroring function and so limited the scope of interpretation that it, also, cannot provide a reconciliation of empathy and interpretation.

THE COMPLEMENTARITY OF EMPATHY
AND INTERPRETATION

Psychoanalysis occurs precisely at the intersection of these two worlds, each stubbornly irreducible to the other. Lacan named the world repressed in *his* therapy room when he wrote that almost every word spoken there was "speaking of love." Kohut named the other world, repressed from self psychology's cocoon of empathy, when he wrote that disruption is at the heart of therapeutic change.

In the scene of psychoanalysis empathic connections are made, disrupted, modified, experienced, named, and held. Although they are created in verbal exchanges, these connections are not just equivalent to their discursive text. In the same scene, an interpretive discourse occurs that signifies desire, alienation, incomplete knowledge of self and other, and strangeness. The intersubjective realm created by analyst and patient always contains both worlds, in words that convey love even as they remain captives and representatives of the symbolic order.

Although it is the interpretive world that is explicitly accessible to discursive language, this should not be taken for proof of its pre-eminence. While it is the empathic world that opens up discourse, sustains hope, and ultimately makes separateness bearable, its permeation of the work should not be taken for proof that the Lacanian topology of symbolic forms can be dismissed as incidental disruptions in the empathic field. When either world is privileged, and their intricate relationship to one another thereby forgotten, psychoanalysis becomes a caricature: When the empathic world is forgotten, it becomes an arid, intellectual desert; when the interpretive world is forgotten, it becomes two wanderers adrift without oars upon an uncharted sea.

Like other dualities that inform psychoanalysis, that between love and the Lacanian phallo–logos has a rich intersection. That intersection does not mark a prior state of undifferentiated union—that would be an idealized myth of origins. Nor can psychoanalysis promise a reintegrated wholeness of being—that would be a myth of the whole self as unity. Both the Kohutian and Lacanian projects fail when they become mired in their own idealism; Kohut's in the myth of two becoming one, and Lacan's in the myth of two never connecting again in the world of three.

A deconstructive approach to philosophic dualism, that bedrock of Western language and thought, takes each dual pair, whether male and female, Eros and Thanatos, inner world and environment, or Love and phallo–logos, and reflects upon the hinge that joins them, upon the repression that separates them, the unconscious language that parallels their dual structure, and the desire for reunion that animates them. Such an approach guards against privileging either side of a dualism; indeed it explores the history of such privilege from a psychoanalytically informed perspective, recognizing (and this is the particular contribution of Derrida) that the language we ourselves must use already contains and conceals the very assumptions that we wish to challenge (Derrida 1980, 1978). So one could see Lacan's expulsion of the mother from the center of the psychoanalytic scene as an occurrence of "phallocentrism" (the dominance of the male signifier in a patriarchal culture), and seek words that would permit the play of signifiers to resume, rather than remain arrested at the instant when the phallus is crowned signifier of all signifiers. This aspect of Lacan's theory would be seen as an instance of privilege, a rigid embodiment of cultural and personal norms that shuts off further exploration. Much like the interpretation of a symptom, the repetition compulsion of phallocentrism would be explored in search of a more spontaneous and open understanding of the signifying system. Deconstruction sets out to re-establish the play of signifiers, where Lacan sought to identify the ultimate signifier in a fixed chain of signification. It is beyond the scope of this paper to explore the striking parallels between the deconstructive project of opening up concealed rigidities in philosophical thought and the psychoanalytic project of opening complexity in the face of repetition. The "centrisms" explored by Derrida include logocentrism (the privileging of the full, spoken word), theocentrism (the privileging of a spiritual unity), and ethnocentrism (the cultural malady of the West). Like the interpretation of a symptom, these explorations must take place both inside and outside the systems that they investigate.

Some theorists have proposed that psychoanalysis escape its metapsychological swamp by recognizing itself to be exclusively a science of interpretation. Hermeneutics would particularly emphasize the historical exploration of the patient's life, as an activity analogous to the writing and exegesis of a text. Whereas psychoanalysis has a substantial hermeneutic aspect, as patient and analyst collaborate to write and rewrite a historical narrative, psychoanalysis essentially remains a *clinical* method of inquiry. Its opening of new ground for human understanding came about from a dual commitment: to respect the unconscious as a meaningful realm of human experience, and to establish a therapeutic relationship with a suffering fellow being. As a clinical method psychoanalysis always bespoke therapeutic action. In a sense, it is the ethical dimension of its clinical work that grounds and binds psychoanalysis. A purely hermeneutic reading of psychoanalysis would privilege the purely textual aspects of the work, while marginalizing empathy, speech–action, and the alterity of the unconscious.

These elements of psychoanalysis represented by Kohut and Lacan—let us risk calling them love and the uncanny—seem destined to be repressed and re-repressed, probably because they are the source of such intense discomfort. So they may need to be rediscovered, together, time and again. Challenges face anyone who would speak from the scene where empathy and interpretation intersect: to find words for the experience of being understood, and words for the structure of understanding. It is difficult to write about the connection between patient and analyst; while concepts like "selfobject" are fraught with problems, it is hard to invent better ways of "speaking of love." The words chosen to describe it (love, the maternal function, mirroring, empathy, understanding, connection, the selfobject, friendship, Eros, therapeutic alliance) all hint at its meaning while leaving much room for misunderstanding. These words can re-evoke the "whole self," and full knowledge of one person by another. They can be misinterpreted as replacing a cognitive dimension with something unknowable, mysterious, and unnameable, a return to metaphysical or theological first principles. They can acquire an exalted quality that generates legitimate discomfort, evoking pulpit or cult. These difficulties must be faced by any theory that would speak about the loving aspect of human understanding.

It is especially difficult to find a place for empathy within the angular interpretive structure that surrounded Lacan's language of the "other." It is as if much effort had gone into precluding such a possibility. And although Kohut's exploration of connectedness and its essential place in adult life suggested a necessary counterweight to the ponderous dialectics of desire and alienation, it will never be easy to speak of empathy and the unconscious simultaneously. What makes this goal so worthwhile regardless of the difficulty is that the experience of sitting with patients in psychoanalytic therapy always contains both worlds, one extraordinarily intimate and the other uncannily alienated. Thus, representing psychoanalysis-as-therapy always means a search for a metaphoric language that does justice to this complexity.

This chapter has explored difficult texts from two psychoanalytic movements, both seeking to reaffirm an essential part of Freud's discovery. Self psychology, as developed by Kohut, legitimized the loving relation within psychotherapy, explored its paradoxical dimensions, and sought to find a vocabulary to represent a field of human connectedness that is not fully described by a dialectics of desire. Lacanian psychoanalysis, in contrast, drew heavily from the sophistication of structuralist philosophy, anthropology, and linguistics to rediscover the radical nature of the Freudian unconscious. The two discourses have defined themselves as divergent, and each have made claims to a certain privilege, one for "empathy" and the other for "alterity." And yet it has become evident that neither discourse can claim total access to psychoanalytic truth. As complex and perplexing as these issues are, they remain at the core of the psychoanalytic enterprise as it prepares to enter a new millenium. The future of psychoanalytic psychotherapy depends upon a continued struggle to define the place of empathy *and* interpretation in the therapeutic field.

REFERENCES

Derrida, J. (1978). *Writing and difference* (A. Bass, Trans.). Chicago: University of Chicago Press.

Derrida, J. (1980). *La carte postale*. Paris: Flammarion.

Felman, S. (1987) *Jacques Lacan and the adventure of insight*. Cambridge: Harvard University Press.

Grosz, E. (1989). *Sexual subΛersions*. Sydney: Allen & Unwin.

Kohut, H. (1971). *The Analysis of the self*. New York: International University Press.

Kohut, H. (1977). *The restoration of the self*. Madison: International University Press.

Kohut, H. (1984). *How does analysis cure*. Chicago: The University of Chicago Press.

Lacan, J. *Écrits*. Paris: Éditions du Seuil. 1966.

Lacan, J. (1977). *Écrits* (a selection). (Alan Sheridan, Trans.). New York: Norton & Co.

Lacan, J. (1981). *The four fundamental concepts of psychoanalysis*. New York: Norton & Co.

Lacan, J. (1982). *Feminine sexuality*. New York: Norton & Co.

Muller, J. P. (1984). Lacan and Kohut. In D. W. Detrick & S. P. Detrick (Eds.), *Self Psychology: Comparisons and contrasts*. Hillsdale, NJ: Analytic Press.

A Group Therapist Examines Psychodynamic Factors in Alienation and Detachment

SAUL TUTTMAN

THE CONTEMPORARY SCENE

Here we are, in the last decade of the 20th century overcoming obstacles of time and space, jetting around the world at incredible speed, sending messages from here to anyplace in seconds, retrieving banked data at the touch of a finger. All of this was inconceivable a few years ago. The technology of communication has provided the means to connect with others in quality and efficiency never before achievable. In conducting business, one can phone or Fax at any hour to clarify account balances, recapitulate transactions, and (hopefully) resolve difficulties. But there is one crucial question: Do these developments facilitate fuller, richer communication or does such technology somehow contribute to alienation and distancing? All too often, the computer is "down" or a noncaring, invisible (perhaps demoralized or frustrated) technician does not want to be bothered, hangs up the telephone, perhaps impersonally hides behind a screen of ambiguity and indifference. Further, the data in the computer's memory, although readily retrievable, is only as good as the accuracy of the information fed the machine. Clearly, the use of equipment in this age of electronics and specialization can alienate us or bring us closer together.

In recent years, I have attempted to find treatment centers to which I might refer young adults who need psychotherapy and residential treatment away from their families. All too often, despite the good intentions of professionals and administrators, the results are not as effective as hoped. Just this week, I came across an advertisement in a psychiatric journal that had as its main message: "Are your young patients caught in a vicious cycle? Are they going through hospital and center and then soon on to the next facility?" A series of arrows going around in a circle represents the patient being shuffled from place to place because problems are not being solved. Although the message contends that the problem may be the result of treatment of insufficient time to succeed in stabilizing patients, I wonder if there are not other elements in these cases that interfere with positive results.

I have observed at least seven cases of family pathology and treatment of the identified patient over time and I believe that there is a meaningful way of conceptualizing the problem, which I attempt to do in this chapter.

The purpose is to examine how we can overcome alienation and detachment, not only in our patients but also in ourselves in the course of our work when we function as group leaders and members of psychiatric treatment teams in hospitals and clinics. In attempting to carry out such functions, like in other complex systems in contemporary society, the team (as a group), despite constructive intent, all too often "acts out" with countertherapeutic behavior. By explaining why this happens and by considering some case illustrations of the interaction between therapist and patients, we shall seek clarification of that which contributes to pathological behavior on the part of both patients and therapists. We will explore those conditions necessary to increase the possibility of successful, therapeutic "working through," involving the therapists who compose the mental health team and their patients.

HOW GROUP THERAPY DEALS WITH THE PATIENT'S ALIENATION

Let us begin by examining a treatment milieu that is so devised as to encourage communication and the "working through" of alienation. Group psychotherapy usually involves a special type of interaction among individuals who work together in a group over a period of time. Such treatment situations generate (to greater or lesser degree depending upon the leader's orientation and the potentialities of group members) a sense of cohesiveness, empathic resonance, and bonding. As members of a psychotherapy group, we learn about one another's histories, hopes, dreads, and fantasies. Usually the processes of mirroring; making comparisons; respecting and reacting to one another's perceptions, patterns, and styles serve to facilitate and catalyze relatedness. The "facilitating environment" (Winnicott, 1958), the "mother group" (Scheidlinger, 1974), the "group-as-a-whole" (Stein & Kibel, 1984; Horwitz, 1991; Pines, 1975), and the "work group" (Bion, 1959) all relate to this process. From this vantage point, we can appreciate the potential productive power of the group, when skillfully organized along therapeutic lines (Rutan & Stone, 1984; Tuttman, 1991). But there is something paradoxical here, since there is also a powerful negative destructive force potentially at work in the group. Many lessons can be gleaned from history regarding the unleashing of dangerous group processes. Among numerous examples, we might mention the inquisition, the holocaust, wars, and riots where hysterical masses wreak havoc. The writings of LeBon (1895) and McDougall (1920), referred to by Freud (1921/1955) in his monograph on group psychology, as well as the psychoanalytic papers of Peto (1975) and Greenacre (1972) explored such issues. Bion (1959) described primary process manifestations in group behavior (which he called underlying "basic assumptions"). Unless harnessed by the rationality of the "work" group assumption, unconscious drives may be *acted out*. We see many potentialities in our instrument. One variable is the manner, persona, and training of the therapist who conducts the group. It is also important to consider how the social climate at any particular time can influence the motivations and insights of mental health professionals and thereby affect their work.

ALIENATION IN MENTAL HEALTH TEAMS

Traditionally, psychotherapists of all theoretical persuasions have dealt with alienation and disconnectedness in patients. Therapists have attempted to facilitate a more object-related, positivistic, humane process within patients. Although some social scientists believe there are increasing opportunities for open expression in our culture, others contend that the qualities of detachment and noninvolvement permeate much of current society beyond the prevalence of such psychopathology in individual personalities, such that the norm reflects greater alienation. Could such trends impact upon the present day functioning of the mental health practitioner and the psychiatric team?

Perhaps among the problems that may be responsible for the generally less effective functioning of the contemporary mental health professionals are: the increasing complexities of professional functioning, given intramural conflicts between the disciplines and problems in health care administration (insurance, government regulation, budget cuts, malpractice threats, conflicting and competing models of health care, etc.). In addition, the issues of alienation and disconnectedness seen in many patients are also prevalent in administrators and therapists. The focus on behavior modification and the use of pharmacologic agents, etc., may be (aside from the inherent value of these approaches) part of the mechanistic trend prevalent in contemporary society that leads to emotional isolation. The neglect of the psychodynamic perspectives and the concomitant minimizing of transference–countertransference and resistance factors at work in both patients and therapists may limit the effectiveness of both individual and group treatment. I recognize the economic realities that work against more expensive and time-consuming methods; nevertheless, I believe that a conscientious application of a modified psychoanalytic focus can be vitally important today in helping achieve more relatedness and cost-effective treatment. Psychodynamic issues need to be "worked through" if treatment is to be effective. This can be demonstrated by clinical examples. Before presenting such case illustrations, there are other matters to address: First, it is necessry to confront the tendency to resist a greater focus on feelings in treatment. Many individuals and groups are motivated by anxiety to avoid painful awareness and therefore disconnect bonds between ideas and feelings that might heighten subjective experiencing. Bion's (1959) paper, "Attacks on Linking," explores this means of avoiding painful thoughts and feelings. Such depersonalizing processes may be involved in institutionalized mistreatment, which occurs all too frequently. Similar alienating processes in groups (e.g., scapegoating) have been described by Scheidlinger (1982) and others (Gadlin, 1991; Mack, 1991). One example is to be noted in groups of professionals who staff the treatment teams of hospitals and clinics. For our purposes in this chapter, it is important to relate the problems potentially inherent in the "team approach" that may sometimes unfortunately parallel the characteristics of the psychopathology and defensive mechanisms of our patient populations who require the services of the psychiatric team. I detect a trend among today's mental health care providers to seek efficient systems that promise immediate and tangible results. For one thing, insurance companies require it. Do the personalities of today's clinicians as well as the "modern" patient-consumers demand immediate concrete and efficient results. Panaceas in the form of medication ("magic pills") and "new" techniques often appear as instant "get well" methods. The progression of a therapeutic relationship, by its very nature usually offers slower, less tangible proof of dramatic effectiveness. A "quick fix" may be the order of the day in contrast to a subtle "working through" of delicate relationships.

It is my plan to further explore the pressures leading to alienation and detachment within the psychiatric treatment team when the treatment "group" deals with the challenging task of interacting with seriously disturbed patients — usually in the hospital and clinic. It is my opinion that the work of the therapists who treat such patients benefits from psychoanalytic training and understanding. Such training is especially helpful when applied selectively in treating the transferences, countertransferences, and resistances which are ever present, especially in the relationships of seriously disturbed, challenging patients and their therapists. These patients often "act out" their problems with a great inclination to utilize the mechanisms of displacement, projection, projective-identification, and splitting. Dealing effectively with this population requires an analytic perspective that is most likely to have been achieved when the therapist has been psychoanalyzed and well supervised in terms of analytic principles and concepts, especially those applied to the seriously ill. It is not my belief that formal, classical psychoanalytic treatment is always indicated with severe pathology, including psychoses, although selective use of related insights is often invaluable. Those versed in psychodynamic theory and practice can often more effectively avoid acting out with patients and can frequently provide enlightened, pragmatic, therapeutic care.

PSYCHOPATHOLOGY IN THE TREATMENT DYAD AND TEAM

Observations of the psychoanalytic psychiatrist Main (1957) caused him to reach similar conclusions to my own regarding the group dynamics of the mental health hospital team. We have all experienced how reassuring it is for the individual psychotherapist and the group of staff members when a patient gets better. There is a sense of personal potency and reassurance when we are effective, and our self-esteem grows and pleasure in work increases. A good patient, from the hospital doctor's point of view, is one who has experienced great suffering and danger to life and sanity, who then responds quickly to a treatment method valued by his doctor and who thereafter remains completely well. Unfortunately, such success is very rare when working with the more difficult patients who make up our practice population. Those who recover slowly or incompletely are less satisfying and only the most mature therapists are able to encounter such frustration without developing ambivalence toward the patient. Think of the strain that may arise in the insecure doctor or team whose patients get even worse despite long and devoted care. Frequently, therapist and team involvement varies with the patient's response. Certainly therapists undertake the work of relieving suffering because of deep personal unconscious motives. When human needs are not satisfied, they sometimes become more passionate and often their expression is accompanied by aggression. At other times, frustrated needs lead to withdrawal. It is clear that hopelessness in the patient tends to create "in ardent therapists something of the same gamut of feeling. . . . [T]he sufferer who frustrates the keen therapists by failing to improve is in danger of meeting primitive human behavior disguised as good treatment" (Main, 1957).

An important finding on response to pressure and anxiety in the hospital setting concerns the administration of sedatives by experienced treatment nurses. It seemed that, despite the rationale for sedation, the nurse would tend to give sedatives when she had reached the limit of her resources and was no longer able to tolerate the patient's problems without developing anxiety, impatience, guilt, anger, or despair. The sedative would alter the situation, producing a more desirable, that is, quiet patient which the nurse "needed." Since, nurses and other professionals often work in a team setting, we must examine the group dynamic aspects of the mental health team's means of coping with anxiety and pressure. The presence of a "therapeutic team" leads to a shared responsibility on the part of a specialized group, who are ostensibly there to serve the needs of patients. But we know how threatening and powerful the patient's "acting out" of needs can be and how that patient's unconscious mechanisms (i.e., projective identification) can generate high levels of apprehension and anxiety in staff-team members. There can be an "acting out" collusion on the part of the therapeutic team-group to protect professional narcissism. (This collusion can be constructive in that it may provide insulation for members of the team that enables them to avoid a sadistic response to the patient. On the other hand, patient and staff–group collusion can create pathological acting out behavior in both patients and team.) I have found it helpful to provide a group therapeutic milieu for teams of professional staff workers. In such settings, team members can often "work through" reactions to patients, leading to more realistic and constructive therapeutic team behavior. (See pages 12-14 of Main [1957] for an example of such "group treatment" of the therapeutic team.) Similarly, Main (1957) noted that by encouraging professional personnel to recognize their ordinary fallible human emotions they became more able to tolerate their own feelings, so that the use of sedatives in the hospital decreased. Clearly, there is an ongoing need for the therapist and the team to examine their motives as a necessary though painful safeguard against undue intrusions from unconscious forces. When therapists recognize within themselves, the arousal of primitive feelings they have the opportunity to work on what in the patients" behavior may disturb them. Some observations of Main (1957) are consistent with the work of Stanton and Schwartz (1949, 1954) with regard to tensions in a staff that strongly affect patient well-being. There are many possibilities for antitherapeutic acting out in terms of group identifications. It is important to appreciate and "work through" interactions within the psychiatric team, as well as interactions between an individual patient, or a group of patients, and individual members of the mental health team, the team-as-a-whole, or subgroupings. Those team members who are in agreement with regard to treatment policies often come to experience and to define themselves as an "in-group." In contrast there are those who disagree with these policies, the "out-group" team members. For example, it may happen that in a particular setting the "out-group" regards the "in-group" as overindulgent, collusive, and unrealistic. In such a situation if during the course of treatment, as the patients come more in contact with archaic underlying conflicts and symptoms develop, the "out-group" staff may press for serious interventions (such as ECT, lobotomy, etc.). I have also observed that patients with unusual, not generally accepted, needs often cause attitudinal splits in the staff that, when covert and unresolved cause distress. (Main and others have noted that tensions and differences in staff attitudes really occur along lines of allegiances that had existed prior to the patients coming to the hospital.) Some patients have the unusual capacity to induce feelings of massive responsibility out of a sense of guilt on the part of the attendants who become involved with and concerned about them. Does the guilt in the staff members at least partially relate to belonging to an inconstant, untrustworthy, harsh world? Is it sometimes induced by the patient's projective identifications? Staff guilt, when it becomes intolerable, is often dealt with by denial and by projections onto the "out-group" of critics. Often, "in-group" members make compulsive efforts to be ideal and omnipotent. These efforts, of course, fail to quiet the patient's reproaches and distress, and so further efforts are made at "super-therapy." As a persecuting but damaged object, the patient receives frantic benevolence until increased hatred and guilt in the staff make constructive treatment impossible. At such times sedation and other extreme treatments are often employed. Staff goodwill becomes split and eventually such patients are transferred or abandoned. Each professional blames the others and reinforces the validity of their own viewpoint. Clearly, the only antidote for such unfortunate scenarios comes from attending to staff interaction, communication, and the "working through" of the strong countertransferences that are aroused within the treatment team members. This might best be accomplished in a "facilitating" group experience where supportive safeguards area-available to work through unconscious countertransferences. It is for such reasons that I firmly attest to the ongoing value of utilizing psychoanalytic insights and endeavoring to understand group dynamics and relate to the underlying needs and feelings of the therapeutic teams members. I recognize how anxiety provoking it can be when one is both "in touch" with the suffering of patients and yet feels sometimes irrational rejection of these same patients. I have written about this in a paper (Tuttman, 1987) concerning the observation of inexperienced group leaders dealing with a very needy and disturbed patient group. It can also be helpful to therapists to appreciate the psychodynamics operating in a group of severely suffering, decompensated, masochistic patients. With such patients one sometimes sees an angry response by the same staff members, and a readiness for suffering by other staff members, reflecting sadistic and masochistic responses to the sadomas-ochism of the patient who rages for nurturance. Main (1957) contended this is often the case. His patients searched for material tokens of love but developed "eventual insatiability, passion and ruthlessness with which these were pursued. They used oppression, flattery, seduction and searched for reassurance against retaliation." Main described how those patients "isolated and controlled the behavior of their objects and counter-attacked by savage suffering and appeal when the revengeful potential of their damaged objects seemed great," while underlying this was a "simple, basic expectation . . . that someone other then [oneself] should be responsible for [oneself]" (Main, 1957, p. 129).

I have described the importance of examining and "working through" transference and countertransference conflicts and resistance when working with the seriously disturbed patient, and I have attempted to highlight both the value and problems in team approaches to the treatment of those patients as well as the importance of group support and perspective for the therapy team members. Sadomaso-chistic unconscious impulses tend to get "acted out" when there is no constructive staff perspective and when there is alienation and other defensive mechanisms at work that tend to interfere with the therapist's functioning. I find that staff functioning and patient care can be enhanced by both psychoanalytic and group dynamic supervision and training. I should like to report an example from my own clinical experience where the use of psychoanalytic group perspectives helped the treatment of a difficult patient, by letting me empathize with and treat the therapeutic team, rather than focus solely on the patient.

Case Example A

In the course of beginning to supervise at an experimental program for treating physically disabled patients in New York City, I observed on the ward the unfolding of a tragic sequence. The patient was an elderly French woman. In her youth, she had been a successful concert pianist and in later years the accompanist of a world renowned soprano. She was a stoical, highly principled, somewhat snobbish, dedicated woman, who probably had always been socially isolated but was very proud of her skills and reputation and the quality of her musicianship. She never married and had no children or other family members. She developed breast cancer and this required a mastectomy and axillary lymph node dissection. The resulting swelling in her arm did not subside and her piano work was seriously compromised. Despite a lifelong habit of saving, she gradually became impoverished. Poverty and charity, and association with poor and indigent people, was intolerable to her. She was sent to the rehabilitation center, Where her critical attitudes and irritability, related to her character structure, frustrations, and difficult circumstances, made her disliked by other patients and staff. She was very demanding and critical of those who tried to help her. While hospitalized, she suffered a stroke on her "good" side, and her remaining working arm and hand as well as one of her legs became paralyzed. She was now aphasic—utterly helpless and completely defeated. All she could show was an indignation that made her more unbearable to others. I was not involved directly in her care and perhaps this helped me feel compassion for her plight. Those who had the responsibility of working with her became increasingly belligerent and unsympathetic. My job at the time was to be a consultant to the staff, not a supervisor or teacher. As the unofficial group-team leader, I was careful not to criticize or direct the attitudes of the staff. In the course of discussing all the patients currently being served, her name eventually came up. The power and the wisdom of the group began to manifest itself. First there was ventilation—how irritating, ungrateful, demanding, hostile, unbearably haughty, and superior she was. I expressed empathy for the staff members but said little more. One by one, over time, each staff member offered observations, reported the rumors and the experiences with this patient. One nurse had actually attended a concert some years before when the patient played professionally. Concern was expressed that she had no visitors. One nurse had been proudly shown a letter by this patient from the singer she so faithfully served and who wrote to her from Paris. One physical therapist expressed some pity for her plight; someone else spoke sadly about how she negated the goodwill she clearly needed so much but rejected. I mentioned what a difficult situation this was for all of us and for her: "Who is immune from criticism — who does not need appreciation and reassurance?" Somehow the group process succeeded in converting the counterattack launched automatically by the ward staff in response to the pathetic assaultiveness of this angry, anguished patient. We were becoming a more concerned group who began to reject both the roles of persecutor and victim of persecution. This group therapeutic interaction helped the staff-group to stop "acting out" a reactive role that was harmful for the staff as well as for the patient.

Case Example B

The following illustration may be profitably considered from the vantage point of the interactions in family-groups, the hospital treatment group, and the intrapsychic group of mental representations within the designated patient's personality. One can apply a general system theory focus (Bertalanffy, 1966) to this complex situation. The family group experience of Mr. and Mrs. Z and Jonathan certainly involves group dynamics. In addition, the "role suction" this patient "applied" to various members of psychiatric hospital teams involved at different times in his care demonstrates the importance of monitoring group psychodynamics at play between patients and hospital professionals.

As a psychoanalytic psychiatrist in the New York City area, I had treated, many years ago, two unrelated young adults who happened to have been referred to me within a 12-month period. After initial consultations and periods of individual treatment, I placed these patients in the same psychodynamic psychotherapy group. I report their subsequent family interaction in this chapter, because having treated both patients (before they even knew one another), having then worked with them in a therapy group, and, later, having observed their own son interact with them and subsequently with several therapists and teams, I was in a unique position to learn about the insidious, psychic identifications at work that were "acted out" by the professional team as well as by the patient (now the son) and his family.

Over the course of participation of the young adults in group, he and she became emotionally entangled and began a private relationship. I saw this as "acting out." In my opinion these struggling, highly intelligent but immature and emotionally isolated individuals believed each had found in the other a potential companion-caretaker. Each was socially inept and had little confidence or feelings of self-esteem. Each came from a rejecting family background that had contributed to serious problems. Clearly, neither had received adequate nurturance or emotional support in early life. They gravitated toward one another in the group and offered and sought symbiotic support from the idealized objects they created of one another. The group and I noted this and interpreted it to both of them; however, in the course of summer vacations when the group was not meeting, they continued their alliance and eventually married. I will call them Mr. and Mrs. Z. Since neither had worked through or resolved their respective developmental issues, they ended up enmeshed in a hostile and ambivalent relationship, each needing the other to serve as "self-object," each bitterly disappointed in how little they were getting, and reach resenting the pressure from the other one to supply nurturance. This struggle resulted in an ongoing intense, frustrating, and confusing interaction that was not meaningfully gratifying to either, and reenforced for each a sense of hopelessness that protected them from the risk of intimacy. After losing a child shortly after birth, Mrs. Z managed to conceive once again, and Jonathan was born. He turned out to be a highly intelligent, healthy, and precocious youngster. When he twice developed a serious and dangerous illness in early life, his mother reacted with intense concern and pain. The family situation was tense, since these parents constantly and openly attacked one another, and showed mutual contempt, especially at times when life situations felt overwhelming and neither could cope adequately or respect the partner's capacities. Despite their efforts to engage in a constructive relationship, the atmosphere was frequently charged with rivalry and criticism, if not rejection and sadistic confrontations. Later, Mr. and Mrs. Z adopted a young female child, to whom Jonathan reacted with great ambivalence. He was already an adolescent who was having problems in high school, including an involvement with marijuana, alcohol, and perhaps other drugs. There is some question as to the degree and timing at which he first became active in buying and selling drugs and perhaps in other quasi-illegal activities. His parents would confer with me from time to time. It looked as though Jonathan was "acting out" in a manner that can be construed as a call for help. He expressed a certain dread of leaving home. It was apparent that he did not feel emotionally prepared for life as a college student who could separate from his parents. He was under considerable pressure from family traditions and from his peers to excell educationally since most of his fellow students were ambitious and preparing for out-of-town colleges. As a very gifted and intelligent youngster, Jonathan had previously impressed teachers with his creativity and capacities; nevertheless, he did not develop good study habits and "got by" on his native gifts. This became increasingly difficult as he entered the higher classes where work demands (in a school for gifted children) increased. His involvement with drugs further interfered with ego functioning, and hence with his school work. As a result, I believe, he chose to surround himself with the more disturbed and less intellectual youngsters in the neighborhood who maintained a pseudotough and independent veneer and engaged in antisocial acting out. He became increasingly unable to focus on schoolwork; which resulted in his not being accepted by the college to which he had applied. He was extremely disappointed and expressed antagonism, especially toward his mother, who he blamed for all his emotional troubles. He disdainfully described his father as passive and too readily overwhelmed by his mother's hysteria and assertiveness. Basically, Jonathan had considerable academic ambition—two uncles had been renowned scholars. His parents also had a history of difficulties in formal school achievement probably due to their own emotional conflicts. They were nonetheless sophisticated, well read and informed, despite primitive emotional acting-out propensities—a confusing amalgam of qualities. Having grown up in a family household in which each family member felt contempt toward the other (and secretly toward themselves) and continually attacked one another, there was little opportunity for Jonathan to internalize any harmonious constructive identification or develop a stable sense of identity. His parents were continually shrieking at each other and were, at times, physically assaultive. Jonathan heard his mother describe his father's impotence, inadequacy, and inability to make decisions. Equally devastating was his father's contempt for his mother's appearance. He described her as a fat, manipulating liar, sloppy, dirty, and a miserable housekeeper. In addition he accurately mentioned her addiction to tranquilizers and diet pills.

Jonathan had several disappointing love affairs, much conflict with his friends and family, and potential difficulty with legal authorities. It looked as though he might have become a "runner" for a counterfeiting ring. Although his parents did not engage in criminal activity, they continually lied to one another and acted deceitfully and disrespectfully. Eventually, at my recommendation, he went to a nearby private hospital for detoxification and treatment. At that time he was abusing marijuana, alcohol, and crack. Although he was successfully detoxified, his acting out propensities and (in my opinion) the apparent lack of a psychodynamic perspective at this hospital, resulted in a situation in which the psychiatric team succumbed to the patient's manipulations and repeated many of the patterns of Jonathan's initial family relationships, countertransferentially induced. This impressed me as countertherapeutic. Furthermore, Jonathan's sadomasochistic propensities encouraged an antitherapeutic interaction between himself and the hospital treatment staff. I believe that, in Jonathan's case, my long-term knowledge of the family and my psychoanalytic training perspective (permitting me to avoid countertransferential pull) protected me from being invoked into a protagonist role. I could dispassionately study the acting out of Jonathan, family, and staff members at these institutions. I visited him in the hospital and found that he shrewdly and maliciously "sized up" the professionally competitive social worker who undermined the inexperienced psychiatric resident. Jonathan also accurately sensed the rigidity and righteousness of the nursing staff, and correctly noted the conflicts between attendants. The staff wanted to talk with me and I noted to myself that Jonathan's observations probably had some basis in reality. I attempted to communicate tactfully and openly with them. I told them how he had spent his whole life in psychological combat with the divisive forces around him. Although the patient did not know it , the doctors told me their unit chief had recently died in an auto accident and how chaotic the service had become. Clearly Jonathan was exploiting this situation. He was also sensitive to the confusing contradictions between staff workers — some used reward and punishment systems, some focused on psychodynamic interpretations. The rituals and rules of the hospital were dismissed by Jonathan as irrational. Having survived a jungle at home and having had long experience in avoiding inner chaos, which resulted from poor ego controls, by shifting his focus onto the overt problems of others, he felt the victory of uncannily spotting deep insecurities and playing one against the other, feeling stronger by arousing vulnerability and confusion in others. To feel powerful, he lied to the staff, telling them of the murders he had committed and other exaggerations; he somehow seemed to enjoy the pyrrhic victory of the confusion and chaos he generated, as well as the prestige and notoriety. Clearly, Jonathan was not getting the help he needed.

After searching for possible places for further care, a famous midwestern center was recommended. I did not know much about the current situation there, aside from the reputation of some of the directors. Through a colleague in the field, I contacted one of their psychiatrists. He offered to provide treatment and constructive maintenance care. Unfortunately, it soon became apparent that the particular service team at this prestigious center was not sufficiently intact or sophisticated in regard to psychodynamic understanding dealing with transference/countertransference issues. Although formerly psychoanalytic in orientation, the institution was now operated as a private-practice center, and behavior-modification, pharmacology, and the twelve step AA program (or its equivalent approach re: narcotics) were used primarily. Jonathan easily figured out how to "expose" the contradictions between these approaches. Although I find value in these modalities, it was clear to me that without working through his identifactory processes psychoanalytically, and without being confronted sensitively but firmly about his psychopathic machinations, Jonathan would not have a meaningful therapeutic engagement. Unfortunately, this turned out to be the case. Carefully observing treatment approaches there, I had to conclude there was a basic lack of engagement or a consistent "holding environment" that proved essential for this patient. I realize that he provoked an atmosphere that was counterproductive; however, it was my hope that his transference provocations could be contained by an experienced and knowledgeable staff. Typically, measures involving periods of silence, confinement to a "quiet" room, removal of shoes, deprivation of privileges were employed. A treatment situation at a more sophisticated psychodynamically oriented facility was indicated, although hard to find.

I consider that Jonathan suffers from features of both narcissistic and borderline personality disorders. He has significant psychopathic trends. I believe he is potentially capable of making a therapeutic relationship and alliance; however, he requires calm, firm, reality-oriented, consistent handling in response to his provocative and testing-out behavior, by a therapist and staff who can face his maneuvers with him and work through together the countertransferential reactions that Jonathan readily masterminds whenever he has the opportunity to "wedge" his needs in a manipulative manner between himself and authority figures. In that sense, he is a challenging patient and the prognosis is guarded. This negative outcome may have been underwritten also by what appeared to be his compulsive need to end up in hopeless situations, quite similar to his parents' masochistic styles.

Although it had been my hope that he could get more effective treatment at an appropriate center, I was disturbed to find that one of the most prestigious psychoanalytic treatment centers for the disturbed patient now had trainees who did not undergo training analyses! The most senior staff members had retired, and pending the appointment of a new, experienced director, the care of patients was under the guidance of a relatively inexperienced psychiatrist, primarily trained in the treatment of more traditional patients. Jonathan was assigned to a novice trainee who was clearly insecure and unable to cope with him therapeutically.

Anticipating disaster, I finally recommended a senior psychiatrist in another city who would be available to work with him privately in intensive treatment while he stayed at a half-way house. I hope that he will be able to return to community living, when ready.

Personally I have treated psychotic patients in my office despite occasional risks, when suitable alternatives were unavailable. I have had considerable success, in some instances, although I believe a well-functioning hospital team approach can be the most valuable one, but only when conditions for "working through" are favorable. Unfortunately such services are almost extinct—for several practical reasons. Despite his bravura, I still believe Jonathan's acting out tendencies can be contained. His more constructive objectives can be realized—but only if he is engaged by appropriate treatment. I also believe that the family crisis has mustered his parents who also have the potential for constructive therapeutic engagement, when met by a firm, realistic therapeutic staff. I believe that it is important for Jonathan's parents to be involved with his therapists, but in a new way, without their having the opportunity to exercise control over his care.

CONCLUSIONS

After teaching and supervising psychoanalysts, psychiatrists, and psychologists over many years, and serving as a consultant and supervisor, I have generally found hospital staffs to be devoted and well meaning. This is also true of the supervisees and students I have encountered at graduate and professional schools and at postgraduate training programs. However, in the light of the above case examples, it strikes me as unfortunate (though perhaps inevitable given the present system of care and education) that: (1) The least experienced clinicians are often responsible for the most disturbed patients; (2) the quality of training mental health professionals is deficient too often, especially with regard to work with the personality of the novice therapist. This factor (personality of the therapist) is probably the most important "therapeutic instrument." Concepts can be taught in the classroom and through readings, but the working through of personality dynamics, such as countertransferential responses, personal and emotional ways of dealing with resistances, therapeutic failure, etc., is vital in the treatment of such patients; (3) cutbacks in financial support resulting in shorter hospitalization and fewer beds for intensive psychotherapy have become all too standard. Those who work with the seriously disturbed where there is role suction and projective identification at work, do best when they are very well trained and supervised, in settings with staff support structures in place (Reister, 1991). It interferes with optimal work when the therapists have had little opportunity (or motivation) to "work through" their own personal issues via treatment. The main therapeutic instrument, I repeat, is the personality of the "treater." Excellent supervision as well as treatment and training in group is invaluable for the members of a psychotherapy team.

As we get to know the inner lives of our patients, their histories, and the circumstances with which they have had to contend, it is no surprise that they have detached and alienated themselves from their own fears, fantasies, and memories. It is very important that, as dynamically oriented therapists, we work through our resistances, personal conflicts, and patterns that block our own availability and understanding. There is little hope for our helping those difficult to treat patients if therapists cannot become attuned to both their own histories, patterns, defenses, and needs, and their reaction to such qualities in their patients. The problems become even more complex these days because of interdiscipline rivalries and clashes between theoretical orientations. Of even greater importance is the prevalence of specialization amongst hospital staff members and the organizational complexity of the treatment team. Although these factors can promote efficient use of personnel, the very organizational structure can interfere with good rapport and understanding between a patient and a staff member — unless special measures are taken to encourage communication and the relationships.

The issue of alienation and disconnectedness in so many patients on the contemporary scene is of great concern. I believe that those psychotherapists who neglect the psychodynamic emphasis, given the recent focus on behavior modification and pharmacologic agents, etc. (which can also be very valuable), may be contributing, albeit inadvertently, to the trend toward emotional isolation. Therapists who appreciate that the power of unconscious dynamics is always involved may be more effective in facilitating greater relatedness and involvement instead of alienation and detachment.

REFERENCES

Bacal, H. A. (1991). Reactiveness and responsiveness in the group therapeutic process. In S. Tuttman (Ed.), *Psychoanalytic group theory and therapy.* Madison, CT: International Universities Press.

Balint, M. (1968). *The basic fault.* London: Tavistock.

Bertalanffy, von L. (1966). General system theory and psychiatry. In S. Arieti (Ed.), *American handbook of psychiatry* (pp. 705–721). New York: Basic Books.

Bion, W. R. (1962). *Learning from experience.* New York: Jason Aronson.

Bion, W. R. (1959a). Attacks on linking. *International Journal of Psychoanalysis, 40* (Pts 5-6).

Bion, W. R. (1959b). *Experience in groups.* New York: Basic Books.

Ferenczi, S. (1955). *Final contributions to the problems and methods of psychoanalysis.* New York: Basic Books.

Foulkes, S. H. (1964). *Therapeutic group analysis.* New York: International Universities Press.

Freud, A. (1966). The ego and the mechanisms of defense. *The Writings of Anna Freud* (Vol. 2). New York: International Universities Press. (Original work published 1936)

Freud, S. (1955). Group psychology and the analysis of ego. In J. Strachey (Ed. and Trans), *The standard edition of the complete psychological works of Sigmund Freud* (Vol. 18, pp. 69-143). London: Hogarth Press. (Original work published 1921)

Gadlin, W. I. (1991). On scapegoating: Biblical-classical sources, group psychotherapy, and world affairs. In S. Tuttman (Ed.), *Psychoanalytic group theory and therapy.* Madison, CT: International Universities Press.

Gay, P. (1988). *Freud: A life for our time.* New York: Basic Books.

Greenacre, P. (1972). Crowds and crisis: Psychoanalytic considerations. *Psychoanalytic Study Child, 27,* 136-155.

Horwitz, L. (1991). The evolution of a group-centered approach. In S. Tuttman (Ed.), *Psychoanalytic group theory and therapy* (pp. 275-286). Madison, CT: International Universities Press.

James, D. C. (1982). Transitional phenomena and the matrix in group psychotherapy. In M. Pines & L. Rafelson (Eds.), *The individual and the group — Boundaries and interrelations. (Vol. I: Theory* (pp. 645-661). New York: Plenum Press.

Jones, E. (1953-1955). *The work and life of Sigmund Freud.* New York: Basic Books.

Kibel, H. D. (1991). The therapeutic use of splitting: The role of the mother group. In S. Tuttman (Ed.), *Psychoanalytic group theory and therapy* (pp. 113-132). Madison, CT: International Universities Press.

Kibel, H. D., & Stein, A. (1981). The group as a whole approach: An appraisal. *International Journal of Group Psychotherapy, 31,* 409-427.

Klein, M. (1975). *The psychoanalysis of children.* New York: Delacorte Press. (Original work published 1932)

Kosseff, J. W. (1991). Infant and mother and the mother-group. In S. Tuttman (Ed.), *Psychoanalytic group theory and therapy* (pp. 133-156). Madison, CT: International Universities Press.

LeBon, G. (1895). *The crowd: Study of the popular mind.* London: Fisher, Unwin.

Mack, J. E. (1991). Ideology and technology: Lessons from the Nazi doctors for the nuclear age. In S. Tuttman (Ed.), *Psychoanalytic group theory and therapy* (pp. 45-70). Madison, CT: International Universities Press.

Mahler, M. S., Pine, F., & Bergmann, M. A. (1975). *The psychological birth of the human infant.* New York: Basic Books.

Main, T. (1957). The ailment. *British Journal of Medical Psychology, 30*(pt. 3), pp. 129–145.

McDougall, W. (1920). *The group mind*. Cambridge, England: Cambridge University Press.

Peto, A. (1975). On crowd violence: The role of archaic superego and body image. *International Review of Psychoanalysis, 2,* 449–466.

Pines, M. (1975). Group therapy with 'difficult patients.' In R. Wolberg & M. L. Aronson (Eds.), *Group therapy 1975: An overview*. New York: Grune/Stratton.

Reister, A. (1991). Supervision and support structures for group leaders and therapists. In S. Tuttman (Ed.), *Psychoanalytic group theory and therapy*. Madison, CT: International Universities Press.

Rutan, J. S., & Stone, W. N. (1984). *Psychoanalytic group psychotherapy*. New York: MacMillan.

Scheidlinger, S. (1964). Identification, the sense of belonging and of identity in small groups. *International Journal of Group Psychotherapy, 14,* 291–306.

Scheidlinger, S. (1968). On the concept of regression in group psychotherapy. *International Journal of Group Psychotherapy 18,* 3–20.

Scheidlinger, S. (1974). On the concept of the mother group. *International Journal of Group Psychotherapy, 24,* 417–428.

Scheidlinger, S. (1980). *Psychoanalytic group dynamics: Basic readings*. New York: International Universities Press.

Scheidlinger, S. (1982). *On scapegoating in group psychotherapy*. New York: International Universities Press.

Schlachet, P. (1985). The clinical validation of therapists interventions in group therapy. *International Journal of Group Psychotherapy, 35,* 225–238.

Schorske, C. (1981). *Fin de si cle vienna*. New York: Vintage Books. (Original work published 1961)

Stanton, A. H., & Schwartz, M. S. (1949). Management of a type of institutional participation in mental illness. *Psychiatry, 12,* 12–26.

Stanton, A. H., & Schwartz, M. S. (1954). *The mental hospital*. New York: Basic Books.

Stein, A., & Kibel, H. D. (1984). A group dynamic-peer interaction to group psychotherapy. *International Journal of Group Psychotherapy, 34,* 315–333.

Tuttman, S. (1980). The question of group psychotherapy from a psychoanalytic viewpoint. *Journal of American Academy of Psychoanalysis, 8,* 217–234.

Tuttman, S. (1986). Theoretical and technical elements which characterize American approaches to psychoanalytic group psychotherapy. *International Journal of Group psychotherapy, 36,* 499–515.

Tuttman, S. (1987). My reactions to the videotape of a difficult group. *Group, 11,* 222–228.

Tuttman, S. (1991). Group Dynamic Treatment. In I. L Kutash & A. Wolf (Eds.), *Group Psychotherapists Handbook*. New York: Columbia University Press.

Winnicott, D.W. (1965). The capacity to be alone. In *The maturational processes and the facilitating environment* (pp. 29–36). New York: International Universities Press. (Original work published 1958)

Winnicott, D. W. (1968). *Collected papers: Through pediatrics to psychoanalysis.* New York: Basic Books.

Winnicott, D. W. (1958). Ego distortion in terms of true and false self. In *Collected papers: Through pediatrics to psychoanalysis* (pp. 140–152). New York: Basic Books.

Winnicott, D. W. (1969). The use of an object and relating through identifications. In *Playing and reality.* New York: Basic Books.

Winnicott, D. W. (1971). *Playing and reality.* New York: Basic Books.

III

TRENDS IN THERAPY FOR WOMEN, CHILDREN, AND FAMILIES

T·E·N

🕉

Contemporary Child Psychotherapy

MICHAEL JELLINEK

How has the clinician's approach to child psychotherapy evolved over the past decade? The core skills and the need for empathy have not changed. The fundamental nature of children is the same whether described by philosophers, painters, parents, or child therapists. Thus much of the literature on child therapy focuses on differences in interpretation of behavioral observations or, even more commonly, differences in emphasis. The goal of this chapter is not to diminish the value of any particular perspective, as most experienced therapists will acknowledge that they draw from multiple sources to find what is most clinically relevant for each of their child patients. Instead this chapter will note several evolving trends and recent research directions that may supplement the clinician's perspective in outlining a treatment plan or conducting a course of psychotherapy.

FAMILY

Divorce

The structure and nature of the American family continues to change. The divorce rate has risen dramatically over the past 30 years so that currently over one million children experience the divorce of their parents every year. Combining the rate of divorce, death, and abandonment, over 40% of all children by the time they are 18 will have spent time being raised by a single parent, and for approximately 90%

of these children, the single parent is the mother. Although the social stigma of divorce has possibly been eased by its prevalence, the experience is searing for every child. Divorce shatters the sense of trust between children and the only structure they know — the family. The change in the child's relationship to each parent and between the parents is too often compounded by ongoing parental hostility and severe economic consequences (both because of the absolute decrease in disposable income and in the disproportionate decrease for the mother). Despite increased emphasis on the role of the father and on joint custody arrangements, most children see their fathers much less after to the divorce.

The consequences of being raised by a single parent are largely unknown but are likely to affect the therapeutic relationship, as more children must deal with the "joint custody," "visitation schedules," and "step" relationships. The shocking reality and seemingly voluntary nature of divorce compounds other reasons children may have for withholding or limiting information, trust, and intimacy — the critical elements of a therapeutic relationship. These children will be conflicted since they are in desperate need of a secure relationship, yet reluctant to make any commitment. On a practical level the therapist will have to deal more often with two households, complexities of scheduling, and in struggles based on postdivorce financial pressures and unresolved hostility between the parents. Therapists should negotiate carefully with both parents to assure the agreement, support, and stability of the therapeutic relationship. If the divorce is not final or if there is a likelihood of legal disputes in the future, then the therapist should also reach some understanding as to his or her potential role in court.

Loss of Extended Family

Even the intact family is more isolated from the traditions communicated across generations by grandparents. In addition to the practical and emotional isolation of the parents, fewer children have the unconditional acceptance and availability of a grandmother or grandfather. The increasing mobility of each generation is evident by the rate of turnover in homes and jobs as well as surges in population, largely driven by economic forces, to one part of the country or another. As a result, during these stressful times, there are fewer relatives to offer support by recounting potentially helpful, value-laden family myths. One aspect of therapy with the child or family may be to play a supporting and accepting role that previously was performed by the extended family.

Day Care

More children (over 50%) are spending more hours at younger ages in day care. Maternity and paternity leave policies are commonly measured in weeks (the company's time frame) rather than months or years (a developmental time frame). The economic consequences of supporting a child and single-income household, especially after having functioned with dual incomes previously, often forces an early return to work and to more hours. The impact of day care on very young children is unknown. Statistics derived from questionnaires show little effect other than an earlier ability on the part of children to socialize and relate to other children in group settings; in-depth studies are generally longitudinal and are confounded by intervening variables that make it impossible to discern what may be the direct effects of day care. Day care itself is not a simple variable. What is the quality of the day care? What is the individual child's temperament, needs, wishes, place in the family? What is the mother's temperament? Needs? Wishes? In terms of psychotherapy, does an extensive positive day-care history help foster socialization and the initial relationship to the therapist, or does extensive day-care only encourage faster but more superficial, less intimate relationships? Will some children emerge from day-care more autonomous or more needy? What is the effect of "quality time?" Do parents who used or did not use day-care feel more or less guilty concerning their child's difficulties?

Despite increased use of day care, much is unknown, so that the impact of day care on the psychotherapeutic relationship is highly speculative. For some children extensive use of day care, possibly a type of day care that compliments the family's style or philosophy, may have a substantial impact. For example a child, especially one whose temperament would best be served by individualized, sensitive handling, might be placed in an achievement-oriented daycare setting that reflects the family's emphasis on high performance. For such a child the day-care setting may provoke a feeling of neediness and a sense that his or her acceptance is based almost solely on accomplishment. Alternatively, another child, raised by a highly career-oriented mother or a depressed mother may thrive in a day-care setting, especially one chosen to reflect the child's temperament and needs. Therefore, given the increased likelihood that more young children will be placed in day care, every therapist should take a thorough history of early mothering and the child's capacity to separate, as well as his or her temperament. In general, the impact of day care on a particular therapeutic relationship will vary widely.

Achievement Orientation

Family life, reflecting our culture's values, prioritizes achievement and good health: Get above average grades, "hit the ground running;" exercise; don't watch television; eat a balanced diet, no soda, no sugar, no fat, no additives, etc. Taken as a whole, these combined goals create a pressured world for the child. Achievement is valued, relaxed play or "senseless fun" may well be criticized as a "waste of time." Parents may well be in their career "boom" period during their child's school age years. The parental sense of urgency, economic striving, career advancement, and attendant frustrations all lend support to valuing achievement at the expense of fun.

Time should be "quality time." Increasingly children enter kindergarten later so that they have an edge throughout elementary school. As part of every therapeutic evaluation the clinician must assess the extent and rigidity of the family's commitment to any particular lifestyle, especially if the parents' values preclude setting reasonable expectations and hinder their capacity for empathy. The therapist will hear of elaborate plans to meet parental goals that make little sense for the child. There may be unnecessary extra tutoring, supplemental coaching, and parent overinvolvement in the child's private life. By early adolescence parents will increase their efforts at control so as to help their competent child avoid mistakes. Therapists who may be blind to their own drive for achievement and perfection can assess this possible bias by examining their own behavior, lifestyle, and attitudes — especially about their own children and personal "senseless fun."

School

Although school continues to be a valuable resource by which one can assess the child's cognitive and social functioning outside of the home, interpreting this information from the school, and accessing treatment services, has become more complex. The society's mandate to schools has broadened. Schools are expected to meet on a more individualized basis a variety of traditional academic needs, increasingly for children at earlier ages. Schools are also expected to cover more subjects, many oriented to long-term prevention of self-destructive behaviors. Courses on sex, substance abuse, and AIDS are now available. There is pressure to lengthen the school day and to add extensive after school programs, partly to enhance the child's experience, partly to promote achievement, and partly to accommodate many of the families' needs for day-care services. For children with special educational and emotional needs, federal and state legislation requires schools to have comprehensive evaluations and treatment services.

Unfortunately, much of this enlightened legislation was passed without funding so that individual school districts must provide the support to fulfill these newly imposed legal mandates. School budgets are being cut, and there is a reluctance to evaluate children's needs for special services. Thus the free flow of information from the school to the therapist may be impeded because of the concern that any negative data will lead to new, costly demands for services. However, despite some possible administrative ambivalence in providing information, the overall expansion of school-based services for both learning disabilities and emotional disturbance has been a major benefit to special needs children — there are resource rooms, after school programs, tutoring, and, if necessary, substantially separate classrooms as well as partial support for day or fully residential placements.

Therapists should be in contact with the school, even if this communication is funneled through a special needs administrator, so that there is a consistency of approach and overall coordination of whatever services are needed and available. One of the most helpful interventions is to visit the school and ask for a team conference. Such visits should be supported by parents and often are key to implementing a comprehensive treatment plan. Clinicians should be aware that working with the schools may not be straightforward, as there are serious financial implications for the local school budget; however teacher–therapist communication is essential and may require persistence and a gentle form of advocacy.

Genetics and Biology

The debate between nature and nurture has a long tradition. Given Freud's training as a neurologist, his early writings emphasized the source of the instincts as biological. However, the clinical emphasis of psychodynamic treatment has been on environmental or nurture issues, especially the character of the parents. Much work has been done to clarify the nature–nurture question. Although most of the recent findings support the nature perspective, therapy is primarily directed at what can be modified, namely the nurture.

One of the first major efforts to broaden both the developmental and the therapeutic perspective were the studies defining children's temperament. Chess and Thomas (1977) were able to describe nine temperamental characteristics that were relatively stable from the third week of life through infancy and into toddlerhood. For example, some "easy" infants had an initially positive approach to new events, made transitions easily, were naturally able to keep a schedule in terms of eating, sleeping, diaper changes, etc. Others were "difficult" in that they were more negative, irregular, easily upset by transitions, harder to calm down, etc. Since parents had well-established temperaments and styles, Chess and Thomas felt that some emotional and behavioral problems arise because of the "poor fit" between parent and child, the source of the problem being interactional rather than intrapsychic. Although longer term studies of these temperamental characteristics demonstrated that most characteristics were unstable and changeable by early school age, temperament theory added a dimension to the range of potential etiologies of child psychiatric disorders.

Current research is studying the stability of selected temperaments and the temperamental profiles of the children of parents with anxiety disorders. Work by Biederman and colleagues (1990) indicates that the children of parents with anxiety disorders are more likely to have a "behavioral inhibition" trait, as defined by the independent work of Kagan et al. Thus the young children of parents with anxiety disorder tend to be shy and take about 20 minutes to feel comfortable in new situations. After this adjustment period they are indistinguishable from children that needed no time to explore their new setting. However, the implication of this genetic link between an adult disorder and early childhood trait highlighted the need to integrate genetic and environmental approaches to understanding behavior.

A growing list of neurological, genetic, and epidemiological studies has demonstrated the clear, at times, overwhelming impact of genetics. Whether studying schizophrenia, depression, anxiety, or attention-deficit hyperactivity disorder, the role of genetic factors is substantial; nevertheless the environment has an impact on the expression of the biological and the clinical presentation is still very much modified by child rearing, ability to maintain self-esteem, events such as divorce, and protective factors — poverty, warm relationship with adults, special competencies, etc. (Jellinek & Murphy, 1991).

The information regarding inborn characteristics such as temperament and the data supporting the contributions of genetics to child psychiatric disorders should put into context narrow psychodynamic views, and humble any therapist overcommitted to a single theoretical model. In terms of individual treatment, the therapist should take a careful family history. Treatment efforts should give a high priority to supporting self-esteem and pick target areas based on what is most likely to be modifiable, while, at the same time, respecting the potential of biological interventions such as psychopharmacology.

At times this new biological–genetic data can be used to pressure therapists to value their descriptive, diagnostic categories of DSM-

III-R and even to take a "cookbook," essentially linear approach to treatment. Since most of the research is directed at what can be reliable and validly measured, Axis I, character issues and the clinical reality of multiple diagnosis tend to be devalued. Maintaining the balance between scientific method and the individual patient's clinical realities and complexities will be an ongoing challenge.

Information

Children are being exposed to an unprecedented quantity of information. Some of this information is real: The television news is packed tight with stories of war, death, famine, disease, and tragedy. The images are sharp and explicit, the tone is engaging, and the program fast paced. Other information comes from fictional television characters and movies. Although there is controversy as to whether there is a causal relationship between fictionalized violence and children's behavior, there is little doubt that children must adapt to more of everything.

Although not all of this information is necessarily harmful to the therapist's work, it must be taken into account. When asked about how the child or adolescent understands major news events, when asked about their favorite television shows, and what they feel about how any information they hear relates to their personal concerns, children's responses will vary. Some will identify and gain perspective from a situation comedy, others, facing divorce of their parents, will feel less alone and stigmatized, and still others will find their maladaptive defenses are reinforced by negative identifications.

Who Do You Serve?

Therapists of children and adolescents frequently must ask who they are serving. The adult patient may be self-referred but have limited insurance; the therapist may be working within a setting such as an employee assistance program or health maintenance organization that has bureaucratic or economic goals quite apart from an individual patient's needs. The child is always referred by an adult, usually a parent or teacher, who may have goals that are beyond the child's perspective. The adolescent, also usually referred, may raise more complex issues of consent and autonomy. Treatment planning can be greatly influenced by these outside forces. Sometimes therapy becomes "sectored" to define a shorter course and limited goals. Other times adolescents may be admitted to an inpatient unit prior to subsequent outpatient treatment. Parents may be too slow to take appropriately effective action or else deprive their adolescent of a chance for reasonable autonomy. Clinicians need to be thoughtful in noting the various familial, administrative, legal, economic, and social forces that interfere with a clear view of the patient's wishes and best interests.

CONCLUSION

The past decade has highlighted the complex and changing character of the psychotherapeutic relationship. Theoretically, therapists must be open-minded as new information about human development, genetics, and psychopharmacology indicates a multifactorial basis for psychopathology. Therapists may need to be more creative in developing comprehensive treatment plans that integrate the realities of the child's life. How can a busy family's life be adjusted to meet the child's needs? What do schools now offer because of expanded services? Administratively, therapy is more likely to take place in group practice settings, and under clearer, external cost controls. The patient will be functioning in an evolving social setting that includes drastic changes in family life, day care, divorce, information systems, etc. Patients are in a competitive world of ever increasing expectations for health, wealth, and achievement. And, of critical importance, is that clinicians themselves are subject to these trends and forces.

REFERENCES

Biederman, J., Rosenbaum, J. F., Hirshfeld, D. R., Faraone, S. V., Bolduc, E. A., Gersten, M., Meminger, S. T., Snidman, N., Reznick, J. S., & Kagan, J. (1990). Psychiatric correlates of behavioral inhibition in young children of parents with and without psychiatric disorders. *Archives of General Psychiatry, 47*, 21–26.

Chess, S., & Thomas, A. (1977). *Temperament and development.* New York: Brunner/Mazel.

Jellinek, M. S., & Murphy, J. M. (1991). Patients who are parents: Approaches to screening of psychiatric disorders in the children of adult patients. *Comprehensive Mental Health Care, 1*(1), 57–68.

E·L·E·V·E·N

※

The Current Face
of Family Therapy

LOIS SIMS SLOVIK
JAMES L. GRIFFITH

The theory and practice of family therapy has changed markedly since its inception. What we call family systems therapy is, at any moment in time, a marriage of theory and clinical need. While theoretical family-system paradigms continue to evolve in conjunction with the current scientific and philosophical thinking, the foci of clinical interest and the creation of techniques evolve in conjunction with societal need. Family therapy as it is practiced today appears simultaneously similar to and different from the family therapy that was conceived in the late 1940s. To best comprehend the current practice of family therapy, it is important to have an understanding of its development.

HISTORICAL PERSPECTIVE: THE FIRST WAVE

The Scientific Backdrop

Family therapy has evolved in conjunction with the scientific thinking of the day. In the 1940s, simultaneous with the inception of family therapy, biologist Ludwig von Bertalanffy first developed what he called the General Systems Theory (1968). This theory was an attempt to provide a comprehensive theoretical model that would embrace all living systems and provide a framework for looking at seemingly unrelated phenomena and understanding how together they represented interrelated components of a larger system. A system is regarded as a complex of component parts in mutual interaction. Each part is seen as being in relationship to the other parts, with the various components best understood as functions of the total system. According to this theory, to best understand how something works, one must study the transactional process taking place between the components, rather than just adding up what each part contributes (Goldenberg & Goldenberg, 1980). Emphasis is on multiple, circular causality (A causes B, B simultaneously affects A, which in turn affects B) rather than linear causality (A causes B, B causes C, etc.). Other aspects of this theory include the concept that the whole being greater than the sum of its parts and that all systems have structure with hierarchically arranged parts. Over time, these communicating, interacting parts create sequences of interaction which, when repetitive, form the system's "rules" (expectations of anticipated events). A system is considered to always be in dynamic balance between homeostasis (stability) and transformation (movement).

The Clinical Perspective

As a consequence of World War II, there was significant emigration of psychoanalytic European psychologists and psychiatrists into the United States. As a result, at the conclusion of the war, psychoanalysis had become the dominant ideology in American psychiatry. Freud, the father of psychoanalysis, understood the importance of the family. He viewed it as the context within which the child learned particular ways of coping and adaption. Unlike family therapy, which views simultaneously and with equality all members of the system, Freud's theoretical and clinical attention was focused on the effects that other family members had on the individual. From his perspective, the individual was seen as carrying forward childhood attitudes and behaviors that were transferred to others. These previously formed childhood perceptions were seen as interfering with adaption in the changed situations of adulthood. The job of the therapist, who operated as a "blank screen," was to interpret the interpersonal "distortions" (transference) that occurred in therapy, clarify them, and encourage better reality testing.

Although whole families were being seen therapeutically by social workers as early as the late 1800s (Broderick & Schrader, 1980), the family movement as we know it today emerged in the late 1940s. With the sudden reuniting of families at the conclusion of WWII, a number of problems emerged — social, interpersonal, cultural, and situational, for which the public turned to mental health professionals for help. The focus of the request was interpersonal, and came at the family level.

The problems included marital discord, divorce, delinquency, and emotional breakdowns in family members (Goldenberg & Goldenberg, 1980). Although many of the psychoanalytic clinicians continued to offer help to the individual, others began to look at family relationships. To work within the psychoanalytic frame, protect the patient's confidentiality, and prevent the "contamination" of the therapy, clinicians developed the concept of orthopsychiatric, interdisciplinary teams — with one member working exclusively with the family.

A marriage between scientific theory and clinical need occurred when the clinicians who worked with family systems viewed them through the lens of General Systems Theory. This resulted in a focus of clinical attention that was concentrated on the interpersonal interaction between the individual family members. It was a significant theoretical shift to define symptoms in terms of what people were doing in the context of human relationships and not as defects existing within individuals.

The epistemology of these visually oriented family theorists was further reinforced by the discovery of the usefulness of the one-way mirror as a means of observing families. Psychologist Charles Futwiler (Simon, 1982) had been using the one-way mirror as a way of offering live supervision for psychological testing. One day Futwiler was asked to psychologically reevaluate a 16-year-old runaway adolescent whom he had, by clinical assessment and psychological testing, diagnosed as being normal. During the reevaluation he serendipitously observed her in the context of her family. Suddenly her pathologic behavior made sense!

Through the use of the one-way mirror, individuals were seen as "fitting" within the communicational dynamics of the family. Moreover, the mirror allowed multiple therapists to simultaneously observe the family. As the therapists focused on different aspects of the communication processes between family members, they clinically confirmed the validity of the concept of circular causality.

During the late 1940s and early 1950s isolated pockets of family therapy practitioners proliferated across the United States. These included Jackson, Haley (who was profoundly influenced by Milton Erikson), Weakland, Watzlawick, Satir and Bateson in California, Whittaker and Napier in Wisconsin, Ackerman and Minuchin (who later moved to Philadelphia) in New York; and Bowen (who later moved to National Institute of Mental Health in Maryland) in Kansas. The focus of clinical attention during this time was on schizophrenia, delinquency, and multiproblem families. Each group brought its own unique perspective to the observation of families, and from each a distinct "school" of family therapy developed. With the invention of the video camera the groups were able to videotape their family sessions, encouraging crossfertilization of ideas.

The 1950s and '60s were exciting years for the family movement. In 1956, the Mental Research Institute team of Bateson, Jackson, Haley, and Weakland generated a major paper, "Toward a Theory of Schizophrenia" that had tremendous impact on the field. In it they introduced the concept of the double-bind, a situation in which a person receives contradictory messages from the same individual, and is called upon to make a response. The person in such a situation is doomed to failure whatever he or she chooses, since to heed one message is to ignore another. The group theorized that in order to escape hurt and punishment the child learns to respond with equally incongruent messages. The MRI team believed that over time the child lost the ability to understand the true meaning of his or her own or others' communications.

The following is a poignant example of the double-bind as described in this landmark study:

> A young man who had recovered fairly well from an acute schizophrenic episode was visited in the hospital by his mother. He was glad to see her and impulsively hugged her, whereupon she stiffened. He withdrew his arms and she asked, "Don't you love me any more?" He then blushed and she asked, "Dear, you must not be so easily embarrassed and afraid of your feelings." According to the authors the patient, upon returning to the ward, became violent and assaultive. (p. 259)

HISTORICAL PERSPECTIVE:
THE SECOND WAVE

The Scientific Backdrop

During the 1960s family therapists viewed families through the combined lenses of General Systems Theory and cybernetics. Cybernetics, as described by Norbert Wiener (1961), is "the science of communication and control." It focuses on patterning and describes the activity of feedback cycles. For example, a stimulus that encounters positive feedback increases, whereas one that encounters negative feedback, depending upon the situation, either decreases, remains the same, or disappears. Family theorists, who had already observed the mutual interaction among family members, began to apply the concepts of cybernetics to the domain of human affairs. As they began to observe family interaction from the position of patterning and control they began to notice how verbal and nonverbal feedback within families served to reinforce or extinguish behaviors.

The Clinical Perspective

Family therapy was born into a visually-oriented culture in which movies were popular and each home had a television. The evening news and shows like "Father Knows Best" or "Leave it to Beaver" mirrored to the family either who they were, or who they should be, the family ideal.

During this time an important shift occurred in the clinical use of the one-way mirror. Instead of being just observers of family interaction, clinicians now became the family therapists. The team became a powerful nonobservable force that asked questions, made interpretations, and gave important messages to the family. During this time the teams were also used for "live" supervision. In most family programs, trainees were required to treat families under the observation of their supervisors. Clinical vision had become panoramic, like the movie screens of the day.

Family therapists now saw themselves as keen observers who viewed and tracked the repetitive sequences and cycles of family interaction. Symptoms were no longer seen as contained within the individual. Rather, they were seen as a series of actions or behaviors that were interpersonal in nature and existed within the circular feedback of a cybernetic loop. The composite of the loops then fit within a pattern that constituted the whole. Each person's verbal and nonverbal behavior was considered to be simultaneously caused by, and causing, the behaviors of the other family members. Adopting the cybernetic model to their clinical experience these early family therapists viewed symptoms as serving the function of maintaining the stability (homeostasis) of the family.

Consistent with the cybernetic model, an individual's symptomatic behavior was seen as co-evolving in concert with the behaviors of other family members. That is, if a spontaneous action done by an individual received repetitive positive or reinforcing feedback by others it became integrated within the fabric of the family's pattern of interaction. An example of this might be that of a young child who goes to nursery school for the first time and cries, not wanting to leave his mother. His mother, ambivalent about leaving him, and perhaps not wanting to go to work herself, unintentionally acts in a way to reinforce his crying. The other children and the teachers have their part in the dance, and may also act in ways that reinforce the child's crying, further reinforcing the mother–child action. Mother goes home that night and talks with her husband who disagrees on how she should handle their son. In this scenario, father has been working late every night, and has not been available to the family. Their son's "problem" now forces the couple to dialogue. Over time, if this repetitive dance escalates, the couple may, like magnets, be drawn into conversing about this problem. The parents may then be told that their son is "not ready" for school and therefore mother will have to stay home with him. The simple act of the child's crying, his solution to not wanting to separate from his mother, could be seen as serving as a "solution" to other problems within the family system. But now, particularly if the child is labeled as school phobic, the solution to the problem, as Watzlawick (1974) has been noted to say, can become an even bigger problem!

Traditionally, the position of the family therapist was one of a skilled observer who looked for, diagnosed, and disrupted the family's pathologic cycles so that it could move on. Depending upon his particular epistemology, he would use various techniques to accomplish this task. Various schools of family therapy proliferated during the 1960s and 1970s. These included Structural Family Therapy, exemplified by the work of Minuchin, Montalvo, and Fishman (1974); Existential Family Therapy, exemplified by Carl Whittaker (1978); Bowenian Family Therapy (1978); Strategic Family Therapy, exemplified by the works of Jay Haley (1976) and Cloe Madanes (1981); the MRI (Bodin, 1981); and Systemic Family Therapy, exemplified by Selvini-Pallazoli and her Milan team (1978), and the Ackerman team (Stanton, 1981).

Short-Term Therapy

By intervening at the family level, therapists saw themselves as able to effect changes both faster and more efficiently than ever before. Perhaps aided by the growing resistance of insurance carriers to cover extensive, long-term psychotherapy, various brief problem-focused therapies arose. These included the MRI group (Bodin, 1981) and the Brief Systems Group, led by Steve de Shazer and Insoo Berg (1986). Selvini-Pallazoli's Milan group was considered to be "brief, long-term therapy," as families were seen approximately once per month, with the treatment averaging 1 to 2 years.

The emphasis of short-term family therapy continued to be on communication, action sequences, and the team approach. For the Milan group, therapeutic intervention was spearheaded to dissolve problems by putting the family into a "therapeutic" double-bind. (This was an interesting innovation of the use of the "pathologic" double-bind). The team would send the family (either via the therapist or by letter) a message that was constructed in such a way that the family was encouraged to view their interactions as supporting the symptomatic behavior of the identified patient. They were then told that what the family was viewing as a problem was its own "best solution" to an even greater problem. The family was then told (paradoxically) not to change.

The Advent of Self-Help Groups

The 1960s and 1970s saw the proliferation of self-help groups. Many were modeled after Alcoholics Anonymous (Kurtz, 1988), whereas others such as eating disorder groups developed to meet the need for peer support; still others developed in response to what was perceived as an attitude of family blame created by the mental health profession, which included family therapy.

THE HISTORICAL PERSPECTIVE: THE THIRD WAVE

The marriage of constructivism and cybernetics marks the third wave of the family therapy movement. The constructivist perspective emphasizes the observer's participation in constructing what is observed. This idea is not new: Constructivism comes from a European tradition that includes Kant, Wittgenstein, and Piaget. Constructivism has as its central tenet the eradication of the idea of objectivity. Human beings are considered to be closed systems. Information is not considered to be representational. "Reality" is not discovered through objective means, but rather is agreed upon consensually through social interaction (Real, 1990). In the late 1970s and early 1980s constructivism enjoyed a resurgence of popularity in both the sciences and in literature, where it was called deconstruction theory.

It was once believed that a description of a family system would provide an explanation of the family. Applying constructivism to family therapy assumes that a description of a family system provides information mostly about the observer or the observing system. Clinically, the idea of multiple perspectives (or multiple realities) was a normal outgrowth of the team approach. During the previous wave, the therapy team was seen as multiple observing eyes that were able to see different aspects of the family's cybernetic circles. It now became a simple but important leap to accepting the fact that there were multiple "truths" that could be noted about the family, as seen by the different members of the therapy team. Emphasis during this phase moved away from the idea of a "real" description of the family and toward the concept of interpreted realities brought forth by the observing system.

The team was a natural vehicle by which clinicians were able to learn by observing "the masters" treat families. As part of this process, an interesting thing happened. Trainees who flocked to become part of training teams were more interested in what the therapist did than what the family did! As a result, the focus of their attention was riveted on the part of the therapeutic "loop" that included the therapist. From this vantage point they noted that how the therapist viewed the family, and what the therapist did, was an integral part of the feedback loop that served to co-create the family's response and therefore the therapeutic reality.

The Scientific Backdrop

In the 1980s many family theorists who were already interested in the theories of Gregory Bateson (1972) now became interested in the theories of biologist Humberto Maturana (1987), cognitive scientist Francisco Varela (1980), cybernetician Heinz von Foerster (1981), and cognitive psychologist Ernst von Glaserfield (1987). Most of these scientific theories were consistent with the information-based ideas of Bateson, particularly that of his "double description" (1979). Double description refers to the arrival at pattern through the superimposition of view upon alternative view. Bateson referred to the intersection of these patterns as "information" (1979).

Constructively speaking, how one knows and what one knows are interrelated and inseparable. According to both Bateson and Maturana, the basic act of knowing is through the creation of a difference. It is only by distinguishing one pattern from another that humans are able to know their world. Individuals draw distinctions in order both to observe and to describe what they observe. To draw a distinction is to delineate one pattern from another, draw a boundary around it, and give it meaning. The recursive operation of drawing distinctions upon distinctions is consistent with the world of cybernetics (Keeney, 1983).

Maturana (Efran & Lukens, 1985) described living systems as "structure-determined." That is, their operation is a function of how they are built, arrayed, and put together. He postulated that individuals do not perceive an objective universe, as the objects they think they see are products of their own nervous system. That is to say, each person's picture of, or knowledge about the world, is the basis for what they see, how they feel, and their attitude toward it. Translated to humans, their biologic and previously constructed cognitive maps (the composite of distinctions that have been drawn) determine how they view the world, and how they respond to what they see.

As a child develops, he learns to distinguish and punctuate streams of experience and give them meaning (Freud's transference). This meaning becomes described in language. Language is the tool for imposing distinctions upon our world. Language and meaning are also the tool for coupling. According to Maturana (1987), organisms survive by fitting with aspects of their surrounding medium and with one another through the process of becoming "structurally coupled." Humans structurally couple with each other through the creation of compatible perceptions that have co-created meanings in language. Viewed in this way, the family unit is composed of structurally coupled persons that have compatible but not identical perceptions.

The constructivist position implies that all interaction between human beings takes place between what Maturana calls "informationally closed" nervous systems that can only influence each other in indirect ways (Efran & Lukens, 1985). For each individual the acquisition of new knowledge occurs in response to either external or internal stimuli. As a result of these perturbations a shift in an individual's structure occurs. This leads to the recoupling of information that is now seen as "new" information. An organism does not create something out of nothing. It uncovers, selects, reshuffles, combines, and synthesizes already existing facts, ideas, and skills.

Adopting the scientific perspective in this phase, the clinical thrust of family therapy became that of creating a therapeutic environment in which each individual would be able to share his perceptions, ideas, and beliefs. This would result in the evolution of multiple perspectives that would intersect with one another and create new information for family members.

The Clinical Perspective

The scientific epistemology of constructivism and second-order cybernetics has had a tremendous affect on the family therapist's clinical perspective. Most family therapists now acknowledge that in the process of doing family therapy several individuals are present, each of whom is responding to his own reality and his own description of (his) family. In other words, there are as many families in the room as there are observer description of families! Each member has his or her own family, and each is entirely separate and legitimate. Family therapists no longer considered one person's view to be a distortion of some presumably correct interpretation. In place of one objective universe waiting to be discovered or correctly described they echo Maturana's "multiverse" (Efran & Lukens, 1985), where many observer "verses" co-existed, each valid in its own right. "What is the true version of reality?" was replaced by "Which version of reality is most useful?"

Given the constructivist epistemology, the position of the family therapist was now more different than ever before. Embracing the concept of multiple realities, each autonomously and individually constructed, the therapist no longer operated as if he could reveal "the truth" about the family or the problem. He could only propose or make available other sets of distinctions by creating an environment that could provide people with the opportunity to have new and different perceptive experiences for which they were ready. Therapy became the creation of a context in which each family member was stimulated to put forth his or her reality in the presence of the other family members. The hope was that new information would be made available at the junction of these alternative perspectives. The therapeutic focus became the creation of questions and a therapeutic milieu that would accomplish this task.

In 1980 during the second wave the Milan (Palazzoli) Systemic team (1980) published a seminal paper called "Hypothesizing, Circularity and Neutrality." The concepts they espoused became an important foundation for the development of questions used in the third wave. In this paper they described a new form of questioning, which they referred to as "circular questioning." Questions of this type were designed to enhance "the capacity of the therapist to conduct his investigation on the basis of feedback from the family in response to the information (that) he solicits about relationships and, therefore, about difference and change" (p. 8). By inviting each member of the family to describe how he or she sees the relationship between two other members of the family, circular questions operationalize Bateson's concept of double description, and a "binocular" perspective (one in which new information occurs at the junction of alternative perspectives) is achieved. An example of this circular questioning includes: (to Pam's brother) "When Pam is asked to do something she doesn't want to do, how does she respond? (ans: "She becomes angry and threatens mother"). "When Pam threatens mother, what does your father do?" (ans: "Father looks up from the football game and comes to my mother's aid"). "How does your mother react?" "How does your brother react?" "If you're around, what do you do?" "Who in the family would agree with this description?" "Who would disagree?"

Initially, circular questions helped therapists to evaluate and build systemic hypotheses and plan interventions. But as they played with different variations of circular questions therapists became aware that the questioning itself was a powerful therapeutic tool. It in itself created a therapeutic environment that facilitated changes in perception. This wave of family therapy is marked by the creative development of questions (Penn, 1982, 1985; Tomm, 1985; White, 1988) designed to help people create perceptual changes and enhance healing.

If the distinctions that human beings make create what they see, they also obscure alternative distinctions, that they cannot see. That is, once the focus of our attention is drawn to a particular pattern, it can obscure our ability to see alternative patterns. For example, when we look at the well-known figure–ground picture of faces and vases, we either see the faces or the vases.

If our focus is on a particular problem, then we will be open to noticing when the problem might be expected to occur, but will not notice it when it does not occur. For example, when we say, "Johnny never listens," we become exquisitely sensitive to noticing when he doesn't listen, but not when Johnny does. There is important, healing, therapeutic information in those exceptions to the rule. Steve deShazer (1985) and Michael White (1986) are known for their therapeutic focus on the unexpected "positive" outcome.

The Impact of the Changing Social Context

Family structure is changing. By the year 2000 the nuclear family will be in the minority. During the 1970s and 1980s there has been a dramatic rise in the rate of divorce and remarriage. Currently each year, approximately 1.5% of the U.S. population is involved in the process of divorce (Statistical Abstract, 1987). Presently, about one-half of all first marriages will end in divorce. Approximately 16 percent of all families with children under 18 years of age are one-parent families created by separation or divorce. Of those adults who divorce, 75% of all women, and 80% of all men remarry, usually within 3 years (Hetherington & Tyron, 1989). Of these second marriages, approximately 60% will end in divorce (Glick 1984). Only about half of all children living in the United States will reach age 18 having lived continuously with both biologic parents (Furstenberg et al., 1983). When working with divorcing or blending families, therapists are called upon to work with various aspects of the system and must be able to entertain multiple perspectives.

THE CURRENT WAVE

The cutting edge of family therapy is marked by the epistemologies of second order cybernetics, constructivism, and social construction theory. Second order cybernetics places the *observer in that which is observed*, and highlights the fact that all description is self-referential. Unlike the therapists during the first wave, the "cutting-edge" family therapists of today do not see themselves as standing outside the family system. Previously, the idea of being an outside observer was reinforced by standing behind the one-way mirror. Cutting-edge family therapists see themselves as an equal and recursive part of the therapeutic system. First order family therapists believed that they knew what a "normal" family was, and assumed that they could influence family members predictably by using certain techniques or strategies. Second order family therapists see family therapy as a co-creation between therapist and family members that results in the potential creation of changes. Unlike the earlier therapists they do not believe that they can predict what changes will occur as a result of their interventions.

Second order cybernetics, constructivism, and social construction theory are similar in that they dismiss the idea of an objectively known truth existing outside of the observer. But unlike constructivism which places its emphasis on the operations of the nervous system, social construction theory places emphasis on social interpretation and the intersubjective influence of language as a determinant of meaning. It is based upon the concept that as we navigate our way through the world, we build up our ideas about it and ourselves, in relation to it. For example, these ideas would evolve from conversing with other people. Social construction theory (Hoffman, 1990) sees the development of knowledge as a social phenomenon in which perception can only evolve within a cradle of communication.

Unlike the biologically based constructivists who see meaning as existing autonomously within each individual, social construction theory sees meaning as a fluid process of constantly changing narratives that are socially derived and exist in language. Gergen (1985), whose emphasis is on the texts that create identity, says, "Social constructionism views discourse about the world not as a reflection or map of the world, but as an artifact of communal interchange" (p. 266). Consistent with this is the idea that it is those stories that we create for ourselves in the context of our conversations with others that serve to constitute our identity. Hoffman (1990) advises us, "I think it particularly helpful for the therapist to think of problems as stories that people have agreed to tell themselves" (p. 3).

Whereas the first wave of family therapists were visually oriented, the current wave appears to be more language-focused. Language, its role in determining meaning and its function as a form of social participation influenced by history and culture, is currently understood as combining to create the social construction that each of us calls reality (Gergen, 1985). If, according to Goolishian and Anderson (1987), language can only take on meaning in the context of human action, then meaning is considered to be interactional, local in nature, and always changing.

The Scientific Backdrop

The scientific backdrop to the current "cutting edge" epistemology of family therapy resides in the scientific findings of Prigogine and Stengers (1984) who describe "order out of fluctuation," Thom's (1975) catastrophic theory, which offers a mathematical description for discontinuous change, and Gleich's (1987) version of chaos theory, which depicts the order to be found in turbulence. These scientific models propose an analogue for describing the shifting, nonpredictable trajectories of human groups as opposed to the more static cycles of cybernetic theory (Hoffman, 1990).

The Clinical Perspective

The Effects of Changing Cultural Roles

Currently, family therapy is being strongly influenced by the recent writings about gender bias in psychological research and clinical practice (Goldner et al., 1990). As a result of the feminist movement, there is a growing body of material (Heatherington et al., 1976; Erkel, 1990; Hersch, 1990) questioning the world view associated with male value systems, particularly the male emphasis on autonomy, independence, and control. These values are in marked contrast to what appears to be the normal female values of relationship and connection. Moreover, the application of developmental schema based on studies of male maturation that are then applied to all human development tend to devalue qualities such as dependency and caretaking that are normally associated with women. Traditionally, the heterosexual, patriarchal family has been taken as the norm. Most of the early family therapists were charismatic, patriarchal men who held fixed, male-oriented perceptions of the "normal" family. In many cases the resultant epistemological gender bias created pathology out of normalcy. Family therapists are now passionately dialoguing about the ways in which this bias has affected therapy — and what to do about it.

The first wave of family therapy emphasized power and control, particularly in the structural and strategic schools, where the therapist was expected to take a hierarchically superior stance. The therapist was seen as a master director or manipulator. The earlier structural models held a normative bias toward a male-dominated system. A family was noted to be dysfunctional if hierarchy, power, and status lines were not clear and if generational lines were not enforced (Aponte & Van Deusen, 1981). Embedded in this epistemology (which the therapist was expected to uphold) is the support of inequality (Hoffman, 1990). In part, the focus of attention on gender bias and the evolution toward a social constructionist view of therapy, is a backlash against the authoritarian, manipulative, and controlling positioning of the structural and strategic therapies.

Social Problems

Currently there is great concern regarding domestic violence and sexual abuse (Gellels & Straus, 1989). Given the power differential involved in abuse, there has been much unhappiness with the cybernetic model (Hoffman, 1990). The cybernetic model de-emphasizes the concept of power and contains within it terms like "circular causality" and "complimentarity" as a way of designating the reciprocity of elements that exist in a relationship. Moreover, the cybernetic view asserts that everyone participates in a mutual-causal pattern of behavior that results in the violent episode. Feminists have vociferously objected to this when it is applied to the relationship between men and women. They view it as an epistemology that tends to victimize the victim. They point to the fact that in the case of unequal or abusive relationships these words can mask both the responsibility of the man who is physically stronger, and the vulnerability of the woman. They highlight the fact that power does exist in human relations, as do personal responsibility and moral judgment (Hoffman, 1990).

Current family clinicians are struggling with issues of power and control, particularly in the domain of sexual and physical abuse. Many family therapists are struggling to develop an epistemology for effective treatment. Although some clinicians are faced with the necessity of doing something about a criminal or quasi-criminal situation in a family and are forced to fall back on linear or reformist models of family therapy when they feel that they need to intervene to stop violence (Hoffman, 1989), others (Lane & Russell, 1987; Goldner et al., 1990), have been experimenting with nonpejorative systemic approaches. Unfortunately, there has been mixed results.

The roles of men and women in our society are in transition. This has created a cultural shift within the family. More women have entered the work force. In many cases, difficult economic times have necessitated that both parents work in order for the family to survive.

Although the majority of child caretakers are women, more men are increasing their contact with their children. In the 1970s as the rate of divorce began to increase, an alarming number of fathers either markedly decreased or cut off contact (Heatherington et al., 1976) with their children. As a result, other fathers felt that they were unable to have adequate access to their children, resulting in a backlash for father's rights. Increasing numbers of divorced men began demanding joint custody and more say in the rearing of their children. The result has been that both men and woman are beginning to speak out for a more balanced cultural system (Erkel, 1990).

The stresses resulting from divorce, remarriage, families in which both parents are working, gender role confusion, decreased community connection, rising drug abuse and violence, affect all people of all ages, but particularly children and even more so the adolescent (Hersch, 1990)). Currently, there is an increasing focus in family therapy on working with the "problem adolescent."

THE CONTEXT OF CURRENT CLINICAL PRACTICE:

Theory Translated into Therapy

Cutting edge family therapists are concerned with their participation within the therapeutic system. They see themselves as facilitating change through their participation in, and active engagement with, each system member's perceptions and experience. The therapeutic system is considered to be complex. Moreover, the behaviors of client and therapist are seen as "interventions" that attempt to alter, modify, transform, or change each other in a way that will solve his problems (Penn, 1982).

Karl Tomm (1987) has coined the phrase "interventive interviewing" to describe "a perspective in which the range of therapeutic opportunities is extended by considering everything a therapist does during an interview to be an intervention" (p. 4). This perspective accepts the idea that, although the actual effect of any intervention with a family member is always determined by the family member, it is impossible for a therapist to interact with another individual without potentially intervening in his or her autonomous activity. Moreover, it accepts the fact that although many deliberate therapeutic interventions do have their desired effects, the intentions and consequent actions of the therapist do not determine or guarantee a particular response.

Many of today's family therapists conduct their therapy from a position of "not knowing." This is not to say that the therapist is not knowledgeable or does not possess therapeutic skills — rather, it means he or she does not have any set ideas about what should or should not change. Ideally, the family and the therapist through their co-created meetings come up with understandings or ideas for actions that are different than those previously held. The therapy then takes its shape according to the emergent qualities of the conversation that inspires it.

There are some therapists that work on a micro level of conversation with regard to the problem. When a family comes in with a problem, systems therapists like Goolishian and Anderson (1987), will choose to work with what they call "the problem determined system." The problem determined system is made up of those people who constitute the social system who are "talking" about the problem. The therapeutic meeting–conversation is made up of all, or some, of these people. It can include family members, teachers, social systems, etc. In this theoretical framework, change comes about by dialoguing about the problem, often in "minute" detail, so that new perspectives, with their corresponding new meanings, may evolve. When this happens, new solutions arise — and the problem "dissolves."

In most outpatient departments, the prevalent therapeutic stance in family therapy contains elements of second order cybernetics, constructivism, social construction theory, and a growing appreciation for the linguistic creation of reality. Family therapy developed from various different roots, and most "schools" still retain elements of their origins. How they each interpret and incorporate the new epistemologies in their theories or practice varies. A common similarity that is still retained is the fact that some form of "family" is in the room. Yet, since the focus of attention is on the elements that are maintaining the problem, who the therapist chooses to work with is more flexible. This means that partial or multiple generations, or various blood-related groups, may be included in the therapy room. The expanded range of attention has also come full circle as the integrity of the individual has regained attention. In response to the monumental shift in the family therapy range of attention, Hoffman (1990) has suggested that the phrase "systemic practice" replace the old label of "family therapy."

THREE TECHNIQUES OF
CURRENT IMPORTANCE

Family therapists who are oriented toward focusing on their own behavior and its effect within the therapeutic system have became very sensitive to the questions that they construct. Most family therapy interviews currently contain variations of circular questioning. Originally designed as a tool for observing family interaction and structure, circular questioning is now being used as both an information-gathering and a change-inducing technique.

In studying the construction of questions, clinicians have became aware that a question, by proposing a distinction, sets limits on the construction of an answer (Keeney, 1983). They also have noticed that questions can have therapeutic effects on family members, either directly through the implications of the questions and/or indirectly through the verbal and nonverbal responses of family members. Conversely, some questions can have countertherapeutic effects (Tomm, 1987).

Circular and Reflexive Circular Questions

Karl Tomm (1987) has devoted a great deal of attention to the construction of what he calls circular and reflexive circular questions. These questions have been found to be very useful in enabling family members to generate new patterns of cognition and behavior on their own. Tomm describes reflexive questions as attempts to deliberately trigger a change in the system being investigated. Reflexive questions encourage family members to mobilize their own problem-solving resources. Tomm believes that the mechanism for the resultant change is the reflexivity between levels of meaning within an individual's own belief systems. The questions are considered to be reflexive in that they are formulated to trigger family members to reflect upon the implications of their current perceptions and actions, and to consider new options.

Tomm 91987) has constructed eight groups of reflexive questions: (1) *Future-oriented questions*: These questions are designed to help people break out of their present-bound monologue by either stimulating them to consider the future implications of their current behavior, or by cognitively projecting them into the future in order to open up alternative behaviors for the present. Examples of this type include: "If in the future, the two of you had a better relationship, what would you be looking for that you don't see right now?" or "If Mary continues to play hooky from school, what do you think she'll be doing in three years? How do you think she'll feel when her friends are all going on to college?" In asking these questions the therapist is less interested in the content of the answers than in the fact that family members entertain the questions and begin to experience the implications that the answers might have. (2) *Observer-perspective questions*: These questions help people become observers of their own behaviors so that they recognize their roles as links in the ongoing pattern. An example of this type includes: "What do you do when he feels criticized and withdraws?" (3) *Unexpected counter-change questions*: These questions are constructed to either alter the context in which a particular action is viewed, thereby changing meaning, or to make apparent that which has been previously masked. To a couple who complain of fighting all the time, the therapist might ask: "What do you do when you're not fighting?" or "Which of the two of you experiences the passion and energy the most in what you are calling a fight?" (4) *Embedded-suggestion questions*: These questions allow the therapist to include some specific content that points in a direction he or she considers therapeutically useful, such as: "If instead of withdrawing and appearing angry when you felt hurt, you gently told him how you felt, how do you think he'd respond?" (5) *Normative-comparison questions*: Individuals or families that see themselves as having a problem tend to experience themselves as abnormal. This can result in isolation and the reinforcement of the problem. To compare or connect the problem with the lives of others can interrupt this judgment-laden cycle and allow openings for health. A question of this type might be: "Since all parents eventually have to struggle with the sadness, pain or loneliness of their children growing up and no longer needing them, who do you know of that would understand your situation most readily because they've most recently gone through it?" (6) *Distinction-clarifying questions*: These types of questions are useful in separating components of a pattern, thereby decreasing vagueness or in connecting elements into a pattern, thereby creating new units of distinction. An example of this type is: "Which is more important to you, to get even with your father by failing the test or passing the test, graduating, and getting on with your own life?" (7) *Questions introducing hypotheses*: These questions postulate that the very same clinical hypotheses (tentative explanations) that serve to orient and organize therapeutic behavior may also serve to orient and organize the healing behavior of family members. An example of this type is: "If when you get angry he withdraws as a way of protecting himself, making you feel vulnerable, encouraging you to forget your anger and run after him. . . . What do you think would happen if the next time you didn't pursue him?" (8) *Process-interruption questions*: These questions create a sudden shift in the process of the session. For example, when a couple suddenly begins to viciously fight, the therapist might ask: "Do you think that I may have initiated this fight by appearing to take your husband's side?"

Externalizing the Problem and the Use of Relative Influence Questions

Michael White (1988/89) has developed the process of questioning in a related but different direction. In the process of questioning, White invites family members to construct a new and externalized description of the problem. This is an approach to therapy that encourages persons to objectify, and at times to personify, the problem that they experience as oppressive. In the process the problem becomes a separate entity and thus external to the person who was ascribed the problem — in essence, it, not the person, becomes the problem.

Normally when a family presents a problem in therapy, their presentation is demoralized. This is a result of taking, as a reflection on themselves, each other, and/or on their relationships, the ongoing existence of the problem and their failed attempts to solve it. They present with what White calls a "problem-saturated description" of family life. That is, conversations about the problem have developed into a monologue, and all aspects of life have become colored by the fabric of the problem. Through a process of "externalization" they discover new, successful solutions to dealing with the problem and "re-author" a healthy self-description.

White has constructed a process of questioning that he calls "relative influence questioning." Relative influence questioning invites family members to come up with two different descriptions of their association with the problem (that then become externalized and objectified) that they present for therapy. The first is a description of their current association with the problem in relation to their lives and their relationships with family members. The second is a description of their influence and that of other family members in the life of the problem.

After the problem has become externalized, patients and their families are helped to create alternative stories by attending to facts about their lives and relationships that could not be perceived in the morass of the problem-saturated description. Through the use of what White calls "unique outcome questions," the therapist helps the family co-create alternative stories, by asking them to locate exceptions to the influence of the problem in their lives and their relationships. By changing the focus of attention new knowledge, skills, and competencies emerge. According to White, "In response to the invitation to attend to unique outcomes, family members entertain new descriptions of themselves, others, and their relationships (White, 1988/89).

The Reflecting Team

The reflecting team, as described by Tom Anderson (1987), is a recent innovation that is becoming widely used in many outpatient family therapy programs. It contains many of the aspects of previous family therapy team approaches but with a new difference: The one-way mirror has evolved into a "two-way mirror." The theory behind this technique is consistent with the ideas espoused by both Bateson and Maturana—it is enormously respectful and supports the idea of multiple perspectives.

The format of the reflecting team is similar to a systemic interview but with some interesting innovations. Unlike the earlier Milan interviews, midway through the sessions, the interviewer does not go behind the mirror to consult with the team. Rather, after a period of time (ranging from 10 minutes to 45 minutes and occurring one or more times during the interview), the interviewer requests comments from the team from behind the mirror, now called the reflecting team. In order for this to occur, the light and sound systems are reversed between the interviewing and team rooms. The family and the therapist then become the observers of the team's conversation (amongst themselves) about the family's conversation (family interview). Although there are reflecting team rules to guide the discussion, the positions taken or comments made by the team are not preplanned or strategically determined. The "reflections" begin when the members of the team first spontaneously present their ideas. Some ideas are then elaborated upon. As a rule, everything is said as speculative ("I am not sure, but . . . ," "I had the feeling that. . . ."), and has the feeling of tentative offerings, not pronouncements, criticisms, interpretations, or supervisory remarks.

The task of the reflecting team is to offer new ideas for the family, even though some of those ideas may not be seen as interesting to the family, or may even be rejected. What is considered to be important is that the family be able to select those ideas that "fit" and are found to be useful. It is hoped that the reflections will trigger a change in the family's perception so that new dialogue will occur and new solutions evolve.

At the conclusion of the team's "reflections," the sound and lights go off in the team room, and are turned on in the therapy room, where the interview continues. Circular questioning is then resumed as the family is asked by the interviewer "What, if anything have you found helpful, not helpful, etc."

SUMMARY AND CONCLUSION

Family therapy, although still recognizable, is very different now than it was at its inception. The current forms of family therapy practiced in many outpatient department still contain theoretical and clinical elements of their initial roots, but most contain some elements of second order cybernetics and constructivism, and reflect a growing appreciation for the linguistic creation of reality. The evolution and current integration of theory and clinical need has created a therapy that is more collaborative, respectful, and less hierarchical than the earlier family therapy. Therapeutic attention is more focused on strengths and resources and less on pathology. There has also been a marked change in the positioning of the therapist. Family therapy is currently perceived as an ongoing co-creation between therapist and family that takes its shape from the emergent qualities of the shared conversation. The therapist is no longer considered to be the one who holds the truth, yet clearly he or she continues to strive to entertain ideas and skills that are useful for healing.

REFERENCES

Andersen, T. (1987). The reflecting team: Dialogue and meta-dialogue in clinical work. *Family Process, 26*, 415–428.

Aponte, H., & VanDeusen, J. (1981). Structural family therapy. In A. Gurman & D. Kniskern (Eds.), *Handbook of family therapy*. New York: Brunner/Mazel.

Bateson, G. (1972). *Mind and nature: A necessary unity*. New York: E. P. Dutton.

Bateson, G. *Steps to an ecology of mind*. (1972). New York: Ballantine.

Bateson, G., Jackson, D., Haley, J., & Weskland, J. (1956). Towards a theory of schizophrenia. *Behavioral Science, 1*, 255–264.

Bertalanffy, von L. (1968). *General systems theory: Foundation, development, applications*. New York: Brazillier.

Bodin, A. (1981). The Interactional view: Family therapy approaches of the Mental Research Institute. In A. Gurman & D. Kniskern (Eds.), *Handbook of family therapy*. New York: Brunner/Mazel.

Bowen, M. (1978). *Family therapy in clinical practice*. New York: Jason Aronson.

Broderick, C., & Schrader, S. (1981). The history of professional marriage and family therapy. In A. Gurman & D. Kniskern (Eds.), *The handbook of family therapy*. New York: Brunner/Mazel.

deShazer, S. (1985). *Keys to solution in brief therapy*. New York: W. W. Norton.

DeShazer, S., Berg, I., Lipchik, E., Nunnally, E., Molnar, A., Gingerich, W., & Weiner-Davis, M. (1986). Brief therapy: Focused solution development. *Family Process, 25*(2), 207–223.

Efran, J., & Lukens, M. (1985, May-June). The world according to Humberto Maturana. *Family Therapy Networker, 9*(3), 22–29.

Erkel, T. (1990). Men nurturing men: The birth of a movement. *Family Therapy Networker, 13*(3), 26–35.

Furstenberg, F., Jr., Nord, C., Peterson, J., & Zill, N. (1983). The life course of children of divorce: Marital disruption and parental contact. *American Sociological Review, 48*, 656–668.

Gellels, R., & Straus, M. *Intimate violence: The causes and consequences of abuse in the American family.* New York: Touchstone.

Gergen, K. (1985). Social constructionist theory: Context and implications. In K. Gergen & K. Davis (Eds.), *The social construction of the person.* New York: Springer-Verlag.

Gergen, K. (1985). The social constructionist movement in modern psychology. *American Psychologist, 40*, 266–275.

Gilligan, C. (1982). *In a different voice: Psychological theory and women's development.* Cambridge: Harvard University Press.

Gleich, J. (1987). *Chaos.* New York: Viking Press.

Glick, P.C. (1984). Marriage, divorce and living arrangements. *Journal of Family Issues, 5*, 7–26.

Goldenberg, I., & Goldenberg, H. (Eds.). (1980). *Family therapy: An overview.* Monterey, CA: Brooks/Cole.

Goldner, V. (1988). Generation and gender: Normative and covert hierarchies. *Family Process, 27*, 17–31.

Goldner, V., Penn, P., Sheinberg, & Walker, G. (1990). Love and violence: Gender paradoxes in volatile attachments. *Family Process, 29*, 4.

Goolishian, H., & Anderson, H. (1987). Language systems and therapy: An evolving idea [Special issue: Psychotherapy with families]. *Psychotherapy, 24*, 529–537.

Haley, J. (1976). *Problem-solving therapy.* San Francisco, CA: Jossey Bass.

Hare-Mustin, R. (1987). The problem of gender in family therapy theory. *Family Process, 26*, 15–28.

Heatherington, E.M., Cox, M., & Cox, R. Divorced fathers. *Family Coordinator, 25*, 417–28.

Hersch, P. (1990). The resounding silence. *Family Therapy Networker, 14*(4), 19–29.

Hetherington, E., & Tyron, A. (1989). His and her divorces. *Family Therapy Networker, 13*(6), 58–62.

Hoffman, L. (1990). Constructing realities: An art of lenses. *Family Process, 20*, 1–13.

Keeney, B. (1983). *Aesthetics of change.* New York: Guilford Press.

Kurtz, E. (1988). *AA: The story.* New York: Harper & Row.

Lane, G., & Russell, T. (1987). Neutrality vs. social control: A systemic approach to violent couples. *The Family Therapy Networker, 11*(3), 52–56.

Madanes, C. (1981). *Strategic family therapy.* San Francisco, CA: Jossey-Bass.

Maturana, H., & Varela, F. (1980). *Autopoisis and cognition: The realization of living.* Boston: D. Reidel.

Maturana, H., & Varela, F. (1987). *The tree of knowledge: The biological roots of human understanding*. Boston, MA: Shambhala Publications.

Minuchin, S. (1974). *Families and family therapy*. Cambridge, MA: Harvard University Press.

Penn, P. (1982). Circular questioning. *Family Process, 21*, 267–280.

Penn, P. (1985). Feed-forward: Future questions, future maps. *Family Process, 24*, 299–310.

Prigogine, I., & Stengers, I. (1984). *Order out of chaos: Man's new dialogue with nature*. New York: Bantam.

Real, T. (1990). The therapeutic use of self in constructionist/systemic therapy. *Family Process, 29*, 255–272.

Selvini-Palazzoli, M., Bjoscolo, L., Cechin, G., & Prata, G. (1978). *Paradox and counter paradox: A new model in the therapy of the family in schizophrenic transaction* (E.V. Burt, Trans.). New York: Jason Aronson.

Selvini-Palazzoli, M., Boscolo, L., Cecchin, G., & Prata, G. (1980). Hypo-thesizing–circularity–neutrality: Three guidelines for the conductor of the session. *Family Process, 19*, 3–12.

Simon, R. (1982). Behind the one-way mirror: An interview with Jay Haley. *Family Therapy Networker, 6*, 18–28.

Stanton, M.D. (1981). Strategic approaches to family therapy. In A. Gurman & D. Kniskern (Eds.), *Handbook of family therapy*. New York: Brunner/Ma-zel.

Thom, R. (1975). *Structural stability and morphogenesis*. Reading, MA: Benjamin.

Tomm, K. (1987). Interventive interviewing: Part I. Strategizing as a fourth guideline for the therapist. *Family Process, 26*, 3–14.

Tomm, K. (1987). Interventive interviewing: Part II. Reflexive questioning as a means to enable self-healing. *Family Process, 26*, 1967–1983.

U.S. Department of Commerce/Bureau of the Census. (1987). *Statistical Abstract of The United States 1988 National Data Book and Guide to Sources* (108th ed.). Washington, DC: U.S. Department of Commerce/ Bureau of the Census.

von Forester, H. (1981). *Observing systems*. Seaside, CA: Intersystems Publica-tions.

von Glasersfeld, E. (1987). *The construction of knowledge*. Salinas, CA: Intersy-stems Publications.

Walters, M., Carter, E., Papp, P., & Silverstein, O. (1988). *The invisible web*. New York. Guilford Press.

Watzlawick, P., Weakland, J., & Fisch, R. (1974). *Change: Principles of problem formation and problem resolution*. New York/London: W. W. Norton.

Weiner, M. (1961). *Cybernetics*. Cambridge, MA: MIT Press.

Whitaker, C., & Napier, A. (1978). *The family crucible*. New York: Harper & Row.

White, M. (1988, Winter). Negative explanation, restraint, and double description: A template for family therapy. *Family Process, 25*(2), 169–184.

White, M. (1988, Winter). The process of questioning: A therapy of literary merit. *Dulwich Centre Newsletter*, 8–14.

White, M. (1988/89, Summer). The externalizing of the problem and the re-authering of lives and relationships. *Dulwich Centre Newsletter*.

T·W·E·L·V·E

⬛

Women on the Borderline

ANNE ALONSO

All theory is, after all, a metaphor, a story organized around observations and educated guesses to explain human behavior. One of the more prominent theoretical concerns in the field of psychopathology and psychotherapy currently is the diagnosis of borderline personality disorder. This chapter emerges from my conviction that the borderline diagnosis is deeply flawed, and, used as such, serves a pervasive cultural bias. The goal of this chapter is to explore a number of problems with the diagnosis and to clarify some of the criteria of the borderline syndrome as they apply to women and to men. This exploration should help clinicians improve the ways we treat women who do indeed suffer from a number of symptoms that loosely come to be identified as "borderline." If we can think more clearly about this problem, we should be in a position to separate fact from bias, to use the diagnosis of severe pathology in an appropriate and precise way, and to avoid the excesses of polemics that lead to the abuse of our patients and do violence to the clinical profession. Finally, I will suggest some clinical options based in psychodynamic theory and technique that I believe serve this population well.

To keep us focused on the concrete realities of the people we are treating and attempting to understand, I offer two cases from my practice, disguised a bit for the protection of the individuals, but accurate in the matters that count. I offer the cases of Jill and Jack.

JILL

Jill was referred to me by the inpatient unit where she was hospitalized following an overdose of antidepressant medication—her first, and gratefully, her only to date. She was 40-years-old at the time, the mother of four sons, the last of whom is autistic. She has been married to a fairly successful lawyer for over 20 years and has worked in her home; her autistic son, of course, presents great challenges to the whole family. She has maneuvered with remarkable success with the public school system to have him placed in one and another classroom, doing her best to keep him mainstreamed, with questionable value for him. Her older sons were in the throes of very difficult adolescences, and she was fighting valiantly to keep the lid on "the disasters," as she put it. Her husband worked all the time, and she involved herself in the care of his disabled mother, with whom there seems to be a reciprocally hateful attachment.

Jill's family history was replete with physical and sexual abuse at the hands of both alcoholic parents and their friends: Mother was cold, father loving to a fault. She was the oldest child. As a student she was understandably distracted by her developing sexuality given the unsafe female management of sex. She became pregnant at age 18 after an adolescence of some promiscuity, and married her present husband who was the father of the baby.

She had been in treatment with a woman who had, by her own and the patient's account, been extremely involved in the patient's life, visiting her home often, meeting her for lunch, discussing her own plans to meet and marry an eligible man, etc. It was during this treatment that the patient was hospitalized. She was then referred to me for group psychotherapy by the family therapist who attempted to work with the couple, but that treatment came to a screeching halt when the husband threatened to sue him after he dared to suggest the husband might have something to do with the situation.

Jill is a very attractive and well-groomed woman, although she is painfully thin, and had in the past suffered from anorexia nervosa. She has no friends, although she has many acquaintances who mostly depend on her in overwhelming ways. What socializing her family did was with other family members, all of them ambivalently held. I will discuss more about her treatment later.

JACK

Jack was also about 40 when he arrived at my office self-referred. His chief complaint was that he smoked too much! I suggested smoke-enders, and explained that my work is analytic. He then told me that perhaps he drank a bit too much. Again, I suggested Alcoholics

Anonymous. It was clearly a busy week, and I was apparently clearing the decks. He went away and came back a month later, expressing some interest in "your kind of work." Perhaps I could help with his night terrors, and the prodrome which included frank visual and sometime auditory hallucinations. This got my attention, and we began to work.

He was and continues to be a very successful business executive. He told me proudly that his work was indistinguishable from his leisure, and that he spent about 20 hours a day at the office, "maybe some less on Saturday and Sunday." Beyond his original problems of smoking and drinking he was troubled by his responsibility for the care of his psychotic brother, whom the family had hospitalized in his town, although the family lived out of state. The brother would occasionally be discharged or leave against medical advice, and would come to live with him, much to his concern. The patient would care for him as best he could, however, and refer him back to his hospital system in an appropriate way.

He too was the oldest child in his family, which was prominent in the community, as was Jill's. The father was seen as distant, the mother as loving to a fault, that is, she clung, demanded attention, and was seen as "silly" by the patient. The father told him that it is a man's obligation to take care of the women, but at the same time, to never weaken his life with undue emotional attachments.

He had no friends or time for friendship. He had never married, but had a series of women who lived with him, and on whom he seemed unconsciously dependent, in that he ended each relationship after some real or perceived abandonment by the woman.

Of interest is that each night, he would come home, sit in a chair, and purposely drink himself into oblivion. He described this as a period of unwinding from the many important business decisions that had preoccupied him all day.

He was also an attractive man, although he dressed more like an undergraduate, as though he'd forgotten to buy any new clothes since then, and looked strangely inappropriate for his milieu.

I offer these two cases to illustrate a number of points that I believe are relevant to this discussion, and will come back to them from time to time in this chapter.

These two cases have more similiarties than differences at the level of intrapsychic reality. Both struggle with excessive anxiety, and both try to modulate this anxiety by oral compulsive means. She starves or overdoses; he drinks and smokes and works to excess. Both try to manage their dependency in unsuccessful ways, she by prostituting herself in order to keep a relationship that will gratify her directly or vicariously; he by avoiding them in an emotional anorexia, lest he "weaken his life." Both have real strength and real vulnerability, masked by a false self of apparent maturity. Both are profoundly disappointed by people.

She is referred to me as a "bad borderline." I suppose he meets the DSM-III-R criteria for narcissistic character disorder. Or are they substantially different? Are we seeing, among other things, an example of gender bias? Does the world react accordingly? Do we shut down some options when we think about Jill, and are we unrealistically optimistic about Jack in our first impressions?

Let us now return to theoretical considerations. Over the past 15 years or so, we have read about a dominant character description loosely called borderline personality disorder, and second only to that, we have read about narcissistic character disorder. In fact, we have arrived at the shorthand usage of terms that refer to the sufferers as "borderlines" and "narcissists"—a deplorable situation whereby we define the whole patient by her or his weakest character traits, as though there were no other parts to the complex human being we are invested in understanding and helping. The criteria are subjective and nonspecific, and cut a wide swath across a cluster of behaviors with little proven validity or reliability. We know what this usually means. To be a "card-carrying borderline" a patient must have low levels of frustration tolerance, high levels of aggression; must use splitting as a major defense, and must have made a suicidal move at some point, or been trapped in an addiction of some sort. Apart from its scientific weakness this kind of generalizing means that almost anyone in a state of primitive regression can be considered "borderline" at one time or another. The diagnosis ends up being applied to those patients— usually female patients—whom most clinicians, especially novices, hate to treat. This is natural enough given the intensity of the furies that soon emerge from both parties in the transaction. The logical consequence is that for primitively defended patients who are notoriously difficult to help, the therapist becomes the sufferer and the patient the pariah in the clinical system.

The strands of the discourse are confusing and numerous, and leave more questions unanswered: How is it that there is a preponderance of people with borderline pathology now? Are we seeing an epidemic of a new disease? Are we encountering an old phenomenon in modern clothing? Are we swept in a backlash related to the feminist movement (as suggested by the temporal coincidence of the rise of the "borderline")? Or are we confounded by the use of a cross-sectional categorical nomenclature to define what is a longitudinal developmental problem? And finally, are we, in the era of quick fixes and short-term interventions, simply getting sloppy clinically, using the term to define a broad general style of relating, while failing to separate the use from the abuse of the diagnosis? Diagnosis is a very important aspect of our work as psychodynamic clinicians. We are reliant on the use of the transference to facilitate the resolution of conflict. This means that the therapist is dependent on an in-depth understanding of the etiology of the problems the patient and he or she will encounter — so that the therapist can know what it is that is being transferred. However, the diagnosis must be able to describe the here and now as it evolved from the there and then, and to facilitate predictions about the course of treatment. Finally, it should suggest a prognosis for the patient. This implies that over the course of a successful treatment the diagnosis should evolve and change. Absent any concern with etiology, it becomes very difficult to project a map for growth and continued development that can lead to an altered diagnosis.

THE BORDERLINE DIAGNOSIS

The problems presented by this group of patients are not new to the psychodynamic literature. Anna Freud (1936) was initially concerned with the ego's ability to defend itself against overwhelming anxiety — the hallmark of those people we consider to now be struggling with borderline defenses. Over the years, Helene Deutsch (1944, 1945), Frieda Fromm-Reichman (1950), Hannah Segal (1981), Donald Winnicott (1975), Edith Jacobsen (1964), Otto Kernberg (1975), to name just a few representative authors, have attempted to understand the dynamics of these patients and, especially, to devise ways to treat them without ourselves merging with them in their dilemmas. The essential criteria for people with predominantly borderline defenses are seen as the following:

1. High levels of chronic and diffuse anxiety, beyond what the situation apparently calls for.
2. Low levels of frustration tolerance.
3. A narrow range of sublimatory channels, mostly primitive (taking the form of acting out or derealization).
4. A tendency to lose contact with reality intermittently when under great pressure.
5. Splitting as a major defense.
6. A yearning for and a simultaneous terror of merger with another person.

If one considers the two cases now, it can be seen that both patients exhibit virtually all these symptoms, although in different arenas. Jill has few sublimatory channels besides her involvement with people; Jack can work remarkably well, but that's about all. Her frustration tolerance for intellectual involvements is minimal, as is his with interpersonal. She splits her world into good and bad people based on their capacity to be emotionally gratifying; he adulates people whom he considers to be intellectual peers, and scorns the rest.

If we can agree that these are defenses, then it stands to reason that each individual man or woman will employ them in his or her own personality style. Defining one's personality style, however, is not a simple matter. It is derived from an integration of several factors, including one's biology, intrapsychic dynamics, interpersonal competence, and the culture's support or impingement on any individual's opportunities to express the self. Thus, the manner in which I display my borderline defenses will give evidence to my personality traits; if my personality is primarily obsessive–compulsive, then my management of overwhelming anxiety will probably appear as a set of rigid, constricted, and impersonal habits that in their extreme may be viewed as "schizoid" or may appear in the compulsive use of anxiety managers such as substance abuse or workaholism (like Jack). If, on the other hand, my personality style is hysterical, then the chances are that I will manage undue anxiety by seeking instant and intense attachment to others, either through sexual promiscuity or clingy, help-rejecting complaints about my physical symptoms (like Jill). In the former case, attachments are seen as endangering one's equilibrium and to be avoided. In the latter, they are sought after as life-saving.

It is at the level of the unconscious that both Jill and Jack are plunged into an identical paradox—both desperately need people and attachments. With Jack, the absence of others causes him to people his world with artifacts and hypnogogic hallucinations. Jill is willing to try suicide and risk her life to call attention to her need to be loved.

If we can agree that for the time being the problem can be reduced to the management of undue anxiety, then we can see all the familiar and dread-inducing demonstrations we attribute to the borderline spectrum as a solution to this overwhelming anxiety. We can proceed to consider women's development in terms of biological, psychological, and socio-political perspectives.

Biological

Freud said that "biology and destiny" (1931); in a sense, of course, he was correct, although not specifically for women any more than for men. It seems irrefutable by now that there are constitutional strengths and weaknesses, and that these predispose us, for better and for worse, toward certain physiological and psychological reactions throughout the life span. It may well be that a certain body chemistry will contribute to immoderate reactions to stress, or make it difficult for the individual to modulate affect. I do not question the pathophysiology of certain severe emotional conditions, and this includes the more severe borderline syndromes. I see the similarity to manic-depressive disease or cyclothymic disorders, and am cautious about broad generalities. However, I do find myself curious about the apparent mind–body split that is generated in the clinical literature around causality. The preponderance of the current literature would have us believe that the genesis of serious mental problems lies in the body chemistry and genetic endowment, and that the emotional state of these patients is *an effect* of the biology. The evidence is sparse. There is no persuasive study to illustrate what is cause and what is effect. It is true that in the first and briefest encounters, psychopharmacology seems to offer the quickest relief for some; it is not evident at all that this is true in the long run, and in fact there is evidence to the contrary.

What always occurs between mind and body, and to consider that this is a circular process: If I worry, I will probably develop physical symptoms; and if I have difficult physical symptoms, I will probably worry. If I have both for a long time and cannot easily be healed, and if I complain, and if I am a woman, the chances of my being labeled a borderline are pretty high.

Modern literature's consideration of women's bodies as vulnerable to borderline states sounds suspiciously like Hippocrates's "wandering uterus." We are, as a field, still in the "dark continent" about the more sophisticated considerations of the pathogenesis of severe mental illness, and need to avoid tautologies, such as female predominance for an illness characterized by symptoms that are caricatures of female traits and defensive styles.

Women's Developmental Psychology and the Borderline Dilemma

We've come a long way since Freud's deficiency theory of development for women. He saw women's development in the context of male development, and in setting male-ness as the norm, viewed women as clearly deficient in body structure (they lack a penis) and in moral fiber, since the persistent attachment to the mother was seen to preclude Oedipal resolution. The latter led to an immature conscience, in Freud's schema. By the end of his life, Freud was acknowledging that women's development was a dark continent and exhorting the women in his inner circle to write about and study the lives of women and children. Since then, we have come to respect the value of attachments throughout the life span and, in particular, many analysts are writing about women in relationships as the norm. Gilligan (1982) with her concept of a separate voice for women, and Miller (1976) and the Stone Center Group with their self-in-relation theory are continuing the work of pioneers such as Karen Horney (1933), Clara Thompson (1964), and a host of others who decried the model of health as "independence and individuation," while pathologizing attachment and dependency for healthy women and men, for that matter. Certainly object relations theory and self psychology stress the importance of the continuing tie to others, as did the Sullivanians and other interpersonal theorists in this country and abroad.

The climate for definitions of health, then includes and requires lifelong attachments, and it is in this realm that we begin to encounter the confusions around the diagnosis and treatment of borderline conditions. When we try to understand these women, we are left with a view of women who attach too much, too readily, or too indiscriminately. What do we mean exactly when we say "too much"?

One thing we mean is that the anxiety with which the attachments are experienced overwhelms the capacity of the woman to still feel intact, lovable, and to be alone at times without feeling bereft. The hyper-vulnerability to separation seems to strike at the heart of what defines healthy development for women, that is, the sense of self-in-relation. However, we haven't yet quite arrived at the reasons for this fragile equilibrium.

Psychodynamic theory informs us that children are propelled by two primary instincts (libido and aggression), or attachment and the aggression subsequent to the real or fantasied loss of attachment. But if it were that simple, we would not expect Jill to be so troubled, since her world is full of attachments. But they do not save her.

I am indebted here to Dr. Arnold Modell (1990) for his clarifying essays on two major concepts that have particular importance to this work today: (1) the mind remembers categories of experience, rather than simply actual facts, and (2) memories are re-contextualized according to subsequent and present experience. This means, in simplified form, that if I misunderstand something Jill said, she is apt to recall all the nonempathic understandings of the past as a category of pain that generates accumulated affects, which find expression in her "unreasonable" rage at me. She cannot see that her present terror is a repetition of a cycle of loss and re-attachment, and cannot discern the reality of the now, since the past is perceived by her as ever present. Suffice it to say that for now we are not speaking about physical separations, except insofar as they act as current triggers for re-experiencing past abandonments that were indeed life-threatening.

But there is a special quality to that rage: It is passionate, and also evokes the earliest attachments; it is sado-erotic, in the sense that it both attacks and attaches simultaneously. To give it up is to really threaten the patient with ineluctable loss. Paradoxically, this rage takes on the force of a pleasurable perversion, with some of the same life-saving fantasies that underlie all perversions. Surely the target of those passions is hardly inured to a similar primitive set of temptations, as any seasoned clinician will recognize when trying to treat the patient in this state without retaliating or withdrawing from the arena.

We are, I believe, talking about a set of experiences early in life that separated the child from reality, that imposed a separate reality could not be assimilated with the reality that the parents offered the child. In essence, a psychotic-like split occurred in which the child held on to her sanity by keeping a secret reality hidden within herself, and simultaneously lived another reality to accommodate the parents long enough to survive in their care. This externally accommodating reality is what Winnicott was to refer to as the false-self (1975), which I believe constitutes the core of the borderline dilemma for these women.

The false self serves remarkably well to protect the vestigial real self from destruction by the nonprotective environment, like a cast does a broken leg; the problem is, that like the cast, it is necrotic and lifeless, and leaves the patient feeling hollow and worthless.

The cost of maintaining this internal split into adulthood is colossal. For one thing, authenticity is dangerous, and must be subdued or transformed into an hysterical, manic-like defense, often histrionic, infantile, and generating scorn and ridicule from the audience. When this fails, the depression that follows is a free-fall into despair that the patient tries to survive by grasping onto any available object—the more familiar, the sooner grasped. But now the patient is caught in a paradox; to attach authentically is to risk exposing the real self to another possible hostile and destructive source of nurturance, but to fail to attach is to die—and so we have the help-rejecting style that is so often the hallmark of this defense.

In a sense the propensity to define the self in relation to other people is a double-edged sword, especially when it interferes with the capacity to be alone, to work, to take risks in relationships, and to enjoy solitude. But for these women what is really compromised is the very capacity to feel alive, with or without the tie to another. And so they simultaneously seek and repudiate the important other.

This same help-rejecting defense interferes with the ability to learn from another person, and often the woman's academic life and work options have been delimited because it's too hard to accept another's ideas and take them in without endangering the integrity of the self.

When we consider how the real self find expression normally, we think about authentic emotional contact, intellectual work, affectionate mutual sexuality, and vigorous and imaginative play. All these avenues are constricted for the individual in the throes of the borderline dilemma. Nonetheless, people try to move forward, and to get well. In the repetition compulsion that is an attempt at mastery as well as a self-defeating cyclic process, the patient attempts to re-contextualize her past reality.

The Cultural Dimension

The socio-politics of female development contribute to confusion about the diagnosis of borderline for women. Most women in Western culture are socialized in ways that are more similar than different, and yet most women are not locked into intransigent borderline defensive operations. So what here distinguishes the healthy from the sick woman?

The Commonalities

Women are brought up to be docile, polite, accommodating, and pleasing to the eye. In particular, most women are brought up to value relationships, to want to be mothers and wives, and to place the greatest primacy on these roles. Societal factors such as limited options for birth control and abortion, tolerance of physical assault on women and children, and the glass ceiling that professional women encounter even in the most successful professional milieus are only the more current manifestations of a pervasive set of cultural values. In our own field, we see the medical problems of women, problems like premenstrual syndrome (PMS), being defined as psychiatric, and we hear serious debate among the architects of the DSM-IV on this issue. Can anyone imagine the DSM-IV listing urinary urgency and frequency secondary to prostatism as a psychiatric condition?

Should women protest, they are perceived as angry, combative, nonfeminine, manipulative, bitchy. Should they accept these mores, they are defined as masochistic, hyper-emotional, or guilty for the harm that may befall their loved ones. When her son was arrested on drug charges, we heard Geraldine Ferraro, in her anguish, state that her family would not be in this mess were it not for her political aspirations. It takes a lot of stamina and health to maintain one's authenticity, one's intimate commitments, and one's capacity to work at full tilt in a constraining society where first-class citizenship is still far from stably assured for women. In short, the real self has to push hard against the pressures to assume an appeasing false self.

If these pressures are common to the healthiest women, what then can we expect of the pressures on the sicker women in our culture? If the real self is not robust, if the split in the culture resonates with and reinforces the intrapsychic splits in these patients, might we assume that the personal and political conflicts deepen the dilemmas for a greater number of women than ever before? Could it be that with the increasing options for women, with the successes of the feminist revolution, we have plunged a great number of women into more conscious conflicts than ever before? If so, then *good for us and for them* because the alternative to conscious conflict is a life of quiet despair, and the unexamined life is not much worth living. We have the opportunity to offer a large group of previously underserved women a chance to fight the good fight and move on in their lives. It is at this juncture that psychoanalysis adds a great dimension of hope to the condition of women, and of sick women in particular. It is not enough to say that women are culturally oppressed. We need to acknowledge that all of us, men and women, have somehow lived with and continue to live with this repression, and that to move beyond the historic accommodations we must finally come to an active and creative source of working through the conflicts that beset us and our patients. Psychoanalysis, with its insistence that the unconscious needs from the repressed past serve to fuel and maintain neurotic solutions in the present, at the same time insists that the resolution of the unconscious trap moves the individual to an active, creative stance toward changing a life. This is the fundamental optimism that Freud alludes to when he said "where id was, let ego be."

So, no, we're not seeing more borderline problems than we used to see. We are, I believe, living in a climate where cultural repression is being seen for what it is, and its influence on psychological development is beginning to be understood — much like in Freud's day, by the way, where sexual repression was seen as the conflictual norm. Would Dora, Anna O., and the Wolf Man be diagnosed as borderline personalities today?

I do not mean, in this integration, to diminish the very real pathology of groups of women who suffer from the severe and life-threatening problems subsumed under the borderline pathologies. But I believe, along with Nancy Chodorow (1989) and my other feminist colleagues, that the personal is political, and that we cannot seriously address ourselves to a psychodynamic understanding of sick women without taking into account the cultural definitions in which they and we play out our developmental options.

Treatment Implications

The psychotherapy of women with primarily borderline defenses must begin with a careful diagnosis of the extent and pervasiveness of the anxiety and an identification of the unconscious sources of her terror coupled with her sado-eroticism, directed either toward others or toward herself. This is no easy task since, as we have reviewed, her memory for the past is merged with her present experience. Perhaps this is one reason for the vagueness of the diagnosis. We note, for example, that depression, another vague affect, is defined in terms of chronic, acute, endogenous, related to unresolved grief, etc. The only distinctions for borderline problems seem to be more morally tinged, that is, there are "good" borderlines, "as-if" borderlines, and "bad" borderlines. Perhaps one of the reasons for this difference is that the diagnosis of borderline defenses, absent a good history, is derived primarily from the patient's behaviors, the therapist's impulses and fantasies, and from the intersubjective field between patient and therapist.

If a patient frightens or repels the clinician, or seduces her into overinvolvement, this patient will be called a "bad" borderline, just as she will if her behaviors threaten the helping system with failure, or endanger her children. Can we help but identify with the child whose mother is out of control? Is this not a universal and atavistic fear, a fantasy of the Medea, that lies at the root of much of the terror of women in our culture?

Once we arrive at an interpretation of the three arms of data — historical, behavioral, and inter-subjective — then the patient's borderline defenses take on a human dimension that allows the work to proceed.

The treatment of any patient with early and severe developmental problems begins with a need to help the patient enter several levels of reality in the clinician's office. We must return to the patient's internal splitting of reality, value it for the life-saving defense it once was, and help her eventually to recognize that indeed several levels of reality are going on at the same time. The playing field for this activity is in the transference relationship.

Modell (1990) refers to the "dependent/containing transference" (p. 5) which he defines as the "frame" of the therapy. He, as does Winnicott, describes creativity and healing as occurring in the play space between analyst and patient, in the safe context of the containing environment. So the rules of the therapy, like the rules of any game, are what allow the play to happen. The limit-setting that we often refer to in the treatment of people who have trouble containing their own anxiety is in essence the rules of the game of recontextualizing one's own experience. The safer and more consistent the therapeutic hour, the sooner the patient will dare to look at several realities at once, without feeling a loss of her personal reality testing. When she can see several realities in an hour (i.e., the external reality of the trusting alliance; the as-if parental/dependent reality of the patient role; the consistency of the clinician's professional behavior; the intrinsic asymmetry of her and the therapist's positions in the clinical hour; and the equality of the two individuals in the world at large outside the hour), then she can begin to move beyond the defense of splitting to more mature defenses for dealing with contradictions, ambivalence, and human disappointments. The consistency of the rules of the game of psychotherapy, as it were, become internalized by the patient into a memory of an expected past, a safe present, and a likely future that was not available to her as an infant. Similarly, she can begin to know and believe that her interactions with people in the present recycle her past in ways that can now be emotionally remembered and separated from the reality of the present. Now when the therapist goes away, she has some observation on the two realities — the feeling categories that my departure evokes from the past as well as her adult conscious awareness that I will probably return, and even if I don't, she will be able to survive as she could not have as an infant.

The novelist Italo Valvino (in Modell, 1990) observes that "each level of reality acts upon another level of reality and transforms it" (p. 5). I believe this is what we mean when we say that our patient has "worked something through" from the past, namely that the monstrous danger of past reality is relived in the play space of the transference situation, and in the re-living transforms an infantile terror into an adult fear of human dimension. The anxieties of the present are also transformed and made more manageable when we integrate them with the anxieties of the now-remembered past.

The work of the transference is critical for healing, but that healing can only occur in the context of a safe and respectful holding environment. Further, the transference is in part the very atmosphere of the clinical room, in part the nonspecific aspects of the relationship between patient and therapist, and in part the patient's sense that the therapist can survive her separateness and her rage without retaliating or, worse, demanding that she paper it over to be "good." I say rage because the patient in this dilemma can neither love nor hate. She can rage, but this rage is about as futile as howling at the moon. Hatred, on the other hand, is an act of separation from the archaic fantasy of the maturational environment that failed to acknowledge the reality of the child's real self, and demanded, instead, a pseudo love. The capacity to hate and have the object of one's hatred survive means that the authentic expression of the child's feelings is safe for both the child and the other. The reassurance of a safe separateness allows for love and intimacy without fear of the loss of self.

The intensity of love and hate as they begin to emerge in these patients is impressive, and it is a rare clinician who is not tested periodically by the waves of highly personal and specifically pointed affect coming her way. It can be very difficult to contain these feelings, to metabolize them and give them back in measured amounts in a way that the patient can tolerate hearing. But even more importantly, the patient may find it too dangerous to risk the one benevolent relationship she has been able to make, and so the false self maintains in the therapy hour while the outside remains unchanged. For many, the dyadic relationship fails because it promises more than it can deliver, or the patient cannot risk the gratification inherent in it to make necessary changes.

THE CLINICIAN, THE PATIENT, AND THE BORDER—WHERE IS THE LINE?

If one could count the number of words written about the feelings these patients arouse in the therapist, they would probably equal those written about the patient, at least in level of passion if not in volume. Let me acknowledge that the primitiveness of these defensive operations presents me and most of my colleagues with a challenge akin to walking on hot coals. I too have forgotten appointments, talked too much, helped too much, been insulted by forgetting important data, and lost empathy any number of times during a given hour. What's important, it seems to me, is to think further about the meaning of these common and ubiquitous lapses in even the most dedicated and experienced among us. Put another way, why do we lose our capacity to maintain contact with several levels of reality ourselves when we are deeply involved with such a patient at such a moment?

In addition to the usual explanations regarding the need to empathize with patients by partially fusing with their experience, it is possible that these patients regress to levels of primitiveness that we clinicians are too ashamed to maintain in our consciousness; we may in turn split off those aspects of ourselves, and in our own projective identifications with these patients resort to fearing and scorning them or, in a reaction formation, to patronizing them by overreaching and overprotecting. Once we have split off from consciousness certain important aspects of ourselves, then indeed we compromise our own capacity to maintain several levels of reality along with our patients.

The implications seem to be several: There is never a substitute for the clinician's own self-examination and personal therapy. However, consultation with colleagues, a blended caseload, and familiarity with the research are all important protections against the multiple pressures that result from working at analyzing that level of characterological defense.

SUMMARY AND CONCLUSIONS

The path to recovery from psychological distress is the same for all human beings. We all must overcome the anxieties that beset and overwhelm us now and then. We do so by knowing ourselves better, by finding and developing more loving relationships, and by engaging in work that is gratifying and commands our respect in one way or another. The diagnosis of mental distress has some common dimensions for all people and, then, some very distinct and particular aspects that apply to that individual based on her biology, her psychology, and her cultural context. This is no less true when we apply ourselves to the treatment of seriously disturbed people who primarily utilize defenses that fall into the borderline spectrum.

In this chapter I have attempted to describe and differentiate some of the characteristics of these sicker patients and have sought to do so by setting aside what is often a carelessly applied and overgeneralized diagnosis. In a discussion of the clinicians' difficulties in working with these patients, I have tried to illuminate some of the pitfalls that, when overcome, offer those of us who have the privilege of working with them a unique opportunity for our own growth and healing as well as theirs.

REFERENCES

Baker-Miller, J. (1976). *Toward a new psychology of women.* Boston: Beacon Press.

Calvino, I. (1986). *The uses of literature* (P. Creagh, Trans.). New York: Harcourt, Brace & Jovanovich.

Chodorow, N. (1989). *Feminism and psychoanalytic theory.* New Haven: Yale University Press.

Deutsch, H. (1944, 1945). *Psychology of women* (Vols. 1 & 2). New York: Grune/Stratton.

Freud, A. (1936). *Ego and the mechanisms of defense.* New York: International Universities Press.

Freud, S. (1949). Female sexuality. In J. Strachey (Ed. and Trans.), *The standard edition of the psychological works of Sigmund Freud* (Vol. 21, pp. 223–243). London: Hogarth Press. (Original work published 1931)

Fromm-Reichman, F. (1950). *Principles of intensive psychotherapy.* Chicago: University of Chicago Press.

Gilligan, C. (1982). *In a different voice.* Cambridge: Harvard University Press.

Horney, K. (1933). Psychogenic factors in functional female disorders. *American Journal of Obstetrics and Gynecology, 25,* 694.

Jacobsen, E. (1964). *The self and the object world.* New York: International Universities Press.

Kernberg, O. (1975). *Borderline conditions and pathologic narcissism.* New York: Jason Aronson.

Luborsky, L. (1988). *Who will benefit from psychotherapy?* New York: Basic Books.

Modell, A. (1990). *Other times, other realities.* Cambridge: Harvard University Press.

Segal, H. (1981). *Melanie Klein.* New York: Penguin Books.

Thompson, C. (1964). *On women.* New York: New American Library.

Winnicott, D.W. (1975). *Through paediatrics to psychoanalysis.* London: Hogarth Press. (Original work published 1948)

IV

TREATMENT ISSUES
FOR THE 1990s

The Denial of the Risk of AIDS in Heterosexuals Coming for Treatment of Sexual Disorders

LINDA SHAFER

T he number of AIDS deaths in the United States continues to rise, with higher numbers of female and pediatric cases. The incidence of AIDS in the heterosexual population is increasing, primarily through contact with IV drug users and bisexual men. Clinicians treating patients with sexual disorders often see patients exhibiting risky behaviors and showing lack of knowledge about AIDS. The role of today's sex therapist has expanded from the treatment of sexual disorders to the prevention of the spread of AIDS through education and the fostering of long-term intimate relationships.

A group of heterosexual patients presenting with sexual problems was evaluated through in-depth interviewing for the effects of the threat of AIDS on their sexual behavior and for current sexual problems. Denial was considered to be the major psychological mechanism involved in their coping with the risk of AIDS. Denial helped explain why this group did not consider the threat of AIDS a factor in the etiology of their sexual problem or a reason to change their sexual behavior to any significant degree. If these results hold true for the general heterosexual population, we can expect a significant increase in new AIDS cases among this supposedly low-risk group.

As of January 1, 1991, there have been over 100,000 confirmed AIDS deaths in the United States. With over 1 million Americans believed to be infected with HIV, there will continue to be an increase in AIDS deaths each year. Approximately 90% of AIDS victims in the United States are male, with 75% between the ages of 25 and 44 years. The groups highest at risk for AIDS are gay and bisexual men and IV drug users of both sexes. Since AIDS cases among IV drug users are split almost equally between males and females, the percentage of female AIDS victims is rising. This is also leading to an increasing number of pediatric AIDS cases, primarily through perinatal transmission.

Holmes et al. (1990) found that the incidence of AIDS from heterosexual contact had increased from 0.9% in early 1983 to 4% in 1988. Although the numbers are small, the rate of increase is substantial. By gender, heterosexual contact accounted for 1.4% of AIDS cases in males in 1988 compared to only 0.1% in males in 1983, and 28% compared to 13% in females. When these statistics are analyzed according to racial background, the percentages are more startling. Black and Hispanic men and women have a much higher incidence of AIDS from heterosexual contact than the total population. It is assumed that this is due to the high incidence of IV drug abuse in major urban centers where minority populations tend to aggregate.

Although the incidence of HIV spread through heterosexual contact is quite low among the middle class, Glaser et al. (1989) found that it is spreading through IV drug abuse. They found a need for greater education, since people who knew that they had high-risk partners still generally avoided the use of condoms or other precautions. Thurman and Franklin (1990) found that, although college students seemed to be fairly well informed about AIDS and recommendations for reducing the risk of spread of the disease, they were reluctant to modify their sexual behavior.

With the incubation period for HIV now believed to be as long as 10 to 12 years, there will continue to be considerable growth in the number of AIDS cases, even if the spread of the disease among HIV-infected individuals is somehow controlled. The long incubation period also increases the possibility of an explosion of AIDS cases in the heterosexual population.

The sexual revolution paved the way for increased sexual freedom and experimentation. Sexual intercourse is no longer linked to marriage or to a committed relationship. Heterosexual intercourse begins at younger and younger ages, with many individuals becoming sexually active in early teen years. Moreover, data indicate that people are having an increased number of heterosexual partners before marriage.

According to Cobliner (1988), evidence from reliable sources indicates that the sexual lifestyle of contemporary college students has undergone some fundamental changes during the past 25 years.

Heterosexual partners engage in multiple, short-term sexual relationships without commitment and make a conscious effort to suppress romantic and intimate feelings. The situation is closely associated with the women's liberation movement, newer, more effective methods of contraception, the increased mobility of the population, and changes in child-raising patterns.

How has AIDS affected our expression of affection, commitment, sexuality, and quest for overall interpersonal intimacy? AIDS is very integrally tied to the most intimate parts of human lives. The sexual climate has shifted dramatically during the current AIDS epidemic. Advocates for sexual freedom have changed their tune and are now preaching sexual restraint and sexual caution. Programs promoting "safe sex" are underway. Finding a suitable partner, communicating sexual needs, fears, issues of trust and commitment have all become much more complex issues since AIDS began to have an influence.

Many support a blanket recommendation of condoms and nonoxynol 9 containing spermicide (Francis & Chin, 1987) for all sexual exposures, except for longstanding and mutually monogamous relationships in which both partners have tested negative for HIV. The addition of condoms and spermicide should not entail great expense, loss of pleasure, or risk of adverse reaction to either individual.

However, many people do not want to be burdened by what they perceive as rules and regulations regarding sex. For example, those who do not use condoms cite as reasons decreased feeling, decreased pleasure, inconvenience, and their use not being romantic. Some people do not want to give up sexual freedom and spontaneity.

Trocki (1990) studied sexual risk taking in a general, largely heterosexual population. The preliminary analysis showed that 20% of the adult population had taken some sexual risk in the past 12 months and that only a few people used condoms with new or occasional partners.

As a sex therapist working both prior to and during the current AIDS era, I have had the vantage point of observing and influencing sexual behaviors and treating sexual disorders. I have felt gratified that I could help people experience the joys of sex, alleviating guilt, fear, myths, and misconceptions. More recently, I have felt concerned that those sexual freedoms might lead to unnecessary death from AIDS. I feel obliged to help stop the spread of AIDS, and counsel those individuals I see about the risks, especially targeting those I consider to be in high-risk groups. I also try to educate those health care professionals with whom I am in contact about how to take a good sexual history, including how to talk about AIDS risks with patients.

I am also concerned about a new syndrome, FAIDS (Leif, 1986), or fear of AIDS. Not only can this cause sexual activity to be phobically avoided, it can also be the root cause of prejudice against those with AIDS. Thus, in efforts to help stop the spread of AIDS by education and by targeting high-risk behavior, there is a danger that the rights of those inflicted with AIDS could sometimes be violated.

As a clinician treating sexual disorders, I feel compelled to help promote safer sex behaviors by emphasizing what is safe and enjoyable, rather than focusing on what is risky. Individuals who come for consultation may range from those patients who fear that they are infected with the AIDS virus to those from high-risk groups who are considering testing, to those who are HIV-positive, to the partner of an HIV-positive person, to those with AIDS and their partners or families. Of course, there is still a predominance of low-risk heterosexuals coming in for treatment of their sexual disorders. The whole field of sex therapy increasingly involves more complex ethical and moral issues.

The AIDS epidemic has caused an enormous amount of human suffering and loss of life. People in some high-risk groups, particularly gay men, have made a commitment to change their lifestyle, and results have been encouraging. Results for IV drug users are less satisfactory, and programs such as needle exchange need to be explored more vigorously. It seems clear, given the threat of AIDS exploding into the heterosexual population, that this low-risk group needs to modify its behavior as well. There needs to be some tempering of the sexual freedom resulting from the sexual revolution of the 1960s. A return to more intimate long term relationships would not only be a positive factor in fighting AIDS but a positive influence on society as a whole.

While working as a sex therapist, I have become increasingly interested in the effects of AIDS — knowledge of AIDS, fears of AIDS — on people coming in for treatment of sexual disorders. I have speculated that AIDS would indeed be a factor in the etiology and treatment of new sexual problems.

In taking a sexual history to help determine the etiology of the sexual problem at hand, I routinely ask about a past history of venereal disease, unwanted pregnancy, abortion, rape, and incest, as well as about a host of other possible traumatic events or fears connected with sexuality (See *Assessment of Sexual Function*, 1973). I also routinely ask questions about AIDS — thoughts, feelings, and experiences.

The patient population with sexual problems that I usually see falls into a wide range of categories, from single heterosexuals in uncommitted relationships at higher risk for AIDS due to multiple partners, to married heterosexuals having extramarital affairs at moderate risk for AIDS due to multiple-selected partners, to married or monogamous heterosexuals at low risk for AIDS. I also see a small number of homosexual and bisexual men in the high-risk category for AIDS. In addition, I see a number of individuals with AIDS phobia, people with a relatively low risk for AIDS who are obsessed with fear of catching the disease because of a real or imagined past experience. The majority of individuals coming in for treatment are Caucasian, but there is also a high number of Hispanics and a lower number of blacks. IV drug use, and drug use in general with the exception of alcohol, do not seem to be factors in my present population. The individuals have a varied educational background, most having a high school education or higher.

In the homosexual and bisexual groups, AIDS has definitely been a factor in changing sexual behavior and creating new sexual problems. The changes in behavior range from limiting the number of partners to changing the types of sexual practices, including decreased anal intercourse and judicious use of condoms. The sexual problems that have developed in this group include increased impotence related to fears of contracting AIDS, as well as both an increase and a decrease in libido. Actually, for some, the fear of AIDS has contributed to a sense of excitement in what is dangerous and forbidden and thus has led to increased sexual activity (Master et al., 1988).

In the AIDS phobic group, the fear of AIDS takes the form of an obsession, and many individuals with this fear meet the criteria for DSM-III-R obsessive-compulsive disorder. They are often treated successfully with antidepressant drugs such as imipramine, clomipramine, and fluoxetine targeting their obsessive-compulsive symptoms (Jager, 1988).

However, it is the heterosexual group that has caused me the most surprise and alarm. With few exceptions, individuals in this group coming in for treatment of sexual problems denied that AIDS was at all a factor in the etiology of their problem. They further implied that AIDS did not influence their sexual behavior or current sexual practices, except as a passing thought. Some implied that they thought about AIDS in the selection of their partners, thus indicating a change in sexual behavior. However, on further questioning on how they choose partners, they said they "just knew" or "just had a sense" about whom they should be careful with or keep away from.

Then, I began to carry out detailed interviews of single heterosexual individuals who had come in for treatment of sexual problems to evaluate their understanding of the threat posed by the AIDS epidemic. This included questions about any sexual inhibitions or problems caused by adapting to a new "safe sex" behavior. Some of the screening questions used in these in-depth interviews were taken from the

Masters and Johnson 1987 study of current sexual behavior. Examples of these questions are as follows:

1. How many sex partners have you had in the preceding year?
2. If you are living with someone, do you think your partner has been faithful to you during the entire relationship? Have you been faithful to your partner during the relationship?
3. How often have you and your partner used condoms during the past year?
4. Do you think your awareness of AIDS has contributed to your current sexual problem?
5. Do you think that you can recognize someone who is infected with the AIDS virus?
6. Do you think that there is any real risk of AIDS among heterosexuals who don't use IV drugs?
7. Do you think it is possible that you have been exposed to the AIDS virus in the past year?

As a sex therapist, I am ideally situated both to obtain information about current heterosexual behavior in this population and to help educate these people about issues of "safe sex" and the spread of AIDS. On occasion, the questioning and educating has had the reverse effect of creating more anxiety and fear of AIDS, thus exacerbating the current sexual problem.

Some sample comments I obtained in the interviews were:

"Isn't AIDS just for gay people?"
"I know I should use a condom, but who can bother?"
"I'm sure my girlfriend is clean."
"I wanted my partner to put on a condom, but I thought he'd be insulted."
"If I had to think about putting on a condom, I'd never get it up."
"Women expect you to get it up on demand. Who can think about safe sex?"
"I'm pretty careful about who I pick for a partner. They're not gay and they don't use drugs."

The conclusions I reached from these interviews were as follows: (1) Heterosexuals at risk for developing AIDS because of multiple partners did not consider this important in the etiology of their presenting sexual problem. (2) These same heterosexuals, with few exceptions, were informed about transmission and spread of AIDS and had some knowledge about safe sex, acquired largely through media exposure.

(3) Despite this knowledge, individuals chose to ignore the dire threat of AIDS in their sexual practices.

What psychological mechanism explains this group's disregard of the AIDS threat? The majority of individuals with sexual problems come in with widespread anxiety. It is certainly possible that this anxiety about performance (Masters & Johnson, 1970) causes them to use denial in handling the threat of AIDS. If they focused on AIDS, it is possible that these individuals would not be able to function sexually.

Denial is an unconscious defense mechanism in which an aspect of external reality is rejected. At times, this reality is replaced by a more satisfying fantasy or piece of behavior. In its extreme, denial may reach psychotic proportions, but it usually stops short of this (Mahl, 1971).

Freud's first published discussion of denial was in 1894. Freud (1894/1962) wrote about a woman who became psychotic by denying that a man who came to her house to see someone else didn't love her. Anna Freud (1946/1966) *The Ego and the Mechanisms of Defense* made the first classification of defense mechanisms including denial. She emphasized that defenses are not of themselves pathological, but may serve to maintain normal psychological well-being. Thus, denial may be both adaptive and dangerous.

Beisser (1979) studied patients with life-threatening illnesses and found that those who used denial had a better chance of survival. Levenson, et al. (1989) in a study of the medical outcome in unstable angina, found that a higher level of denial correlated with an improved chance of recovery. Hackett and Cassem (1968), in a study of how acutely ill Myocardial infarction (MI) patients coped with stress, found that those with the greater level of denial had the better survival record in the Coronary Care Unit.

However, denial can be a dangerous defense in situations involving a risk to one's self. Yellowlees and Ruffin (1989) found that patients with high levels of denial were at greater risk for death following a life-threatening asthma attack. Fields (1989) found that inappropriate denial can delay MI sufferers from seeking immediate medical attention, thus increasing the mortality rate for coronary artery disease. Goldsmith (1988) developed a rating scale for alcoholic denial, emphasizing that denial is a serious obstacle to the treatment of an alcoholic.

During the current AIDS epidemic, it is important to consider the denial of risk-taking behavior. In 1985 O'Reilly et al. studied sexually active teenagers who denied they were at risk for sexually transmitted diseases. Kegeles et al. (1989) found that sexual practices among teenagers (frequency and condom usage) changed little in response to increasing knowledge about AIDS. Logsdon et al. (1989) in a study to evaluate preventive medicine campaigns to reduce risky behavior, found that antismoking campaigns, educating the public about seat belt use, and educating women about breast self-exams have all been hampered by denial. Finally, Jewell and Jewell (1989) have shown that denial and anxiety can also interfere with health care providers' ability to initiate discussions about safe sexual practices with their patients. Thus, both patient and physician may collude to minimize the perception of one's individual risk for AIDS.

There is some evidence that the conclusions I have reached about heterosexuals in my practice can be applied to heterosexuals in the general population. For example, Turner (1989) in a study of heterosexual men and women from a national sample who reported nine or more sexual partners in the past year, reported that 45% of the men and 65% of the women indicated that they had never purchased condoms. Sixty percent of the sample rated their own personal risk of contracting AIDS at the lowest possible level on the interviewer's risk scale. If this is true, then the danger of AIDS spreading beyond the original high-risk groups into the general heterosexual population is real and higher for those individuals with many sexual partners. We, as health care professionals, must not "deny" that the heterosexual population may yet be an important vehicle for the transmission of AIDS.

REFERENCES

Beisser, A. R. (1979, August). Denial and affirmation in illness and health. *American Journal of Psychiatry*, *136*(8), 1026–1030.

Cobliner, W. G. (1988, Spring). The exclusion of intimacy in the sexuality of the contemporary college-age population. *Adolescence*, *23*(89), 99–113.

Fields, K. B. (1989, Feb.). Myocardial infarction and denial. *Journal of Family Practice*, *28*(2), 157–61.

Francis, D. P., & Chin, J. (1987). The prevention of AIDS in the United States. *The Journal of the American Medical Association*, *257*, 1357–66.

Freud, A. (1966). *The ego and the mechanism of defense*. New York: International Universities Press. (Original work published 1946)

Freud, S. (1962). The neuropsychoses of defense. In J. Strachey (Ed. and Trans.), *The standard edition of the complete psychological works of Sigmund Freud* (Vol. 3). London: Hogarth Press. (Original work published 1894)

Glaser, J. B., Strange, T. J., & Rosati, D. (1989, March). Heterosexual human immunodeficiency virus transmission among the middle class. *Archives of Internal Medicine*, *149*(3), 645–49.

Goldsmith, R. J. (1988, Oct.). A rating scale for alcoholic denial. *Journal of Nervous and Mental Disorders*, *176*(10), 614–620.

Group for the Advancement of Psychiatry. (1973). *Assessment of Sexual Function: A Guide to Interviewing*. New York: Jason Aronson.

Hackett, T. P., Cassem, N. H., & Wishnie, H. A. (1965). The coronary care unit: An appraisal of its psychological hazards. *New England Journal of Medicine, 279,* 1365.

Holmes, K. K., Karon, J. M., & Kreiss, J. (1990, July). The increasing frequency of heterosexually acquired AIDS in the United States, 1983-88. *American Journal of Public Health, 80*(7), 858-63.

Jager, H. (Ed.). (1988). *AIDS phobia, disease pattern and possibilities of treatment.* Chichester, England: Ellis Horwood.

Jewell, M. E., & Jewell, G. S. (1989, July). How to assess the risk of HIV exposure. *American Family Practitioner, 40*(1), 153-61.

Kegeles, S. M., Adler, N. E., & Irwin, Jr., C. E. (1988, April). Sexually active adolescents and condoms: Changes over one year in knowledge, attitudes and use. *American Journal of Public Health, 78*(4), 460-61.

Leif, H. I. (1986, Fall). Editorial: Preventing the spread of AIDS. *Journal of Sex and Marital Therapy, 12*(3), 159-61.

Levenson, J. L., Mishra, A., Hamer, R. M., & Hastillo, A. (1989, Jan.-Feb.). Denial and medical outcome in unstable angina. *Psychosomatic Medicine, 51*(1), 27-35.

Logsdon, D. N., Lazaro, C. M., & Meier, R. V. (1989). The feasibility of behavioral risk reduction in primary medical care. *American Journal of Preventive Medicine, 5*(5), 249-56.

Mahl, G. F. (1971). *Psychological conflict and defense.* New York: Harcourt Brace Jovanovich.

Masters, W. H., & Johnson, V. E. (1970). *Human sexual inadequacy.* Boston: Little, Brown.

Masters, W. H., Johnson, V. E., & Kolodny, R. C. (1988). *Crisis: Heterosexual behavior in the age of AIDS.* Boston: Little, Brown.

Masters, W. H., Johnson, V. E., & Kolodny, R. C. (1988). *Crisis: Heterosexual behavior in the age of AIDS.* Boston: Little, Brown.

O'Reilly, K. R., & Aral, S. Q. (1985, July). Adolescence and sexual behavior: Trends and implications for STD. *Journal of Adolescent Health Care, 6*(4), 262-70.

Thurman, Q. C., & Franklin, K. M. (1990, Jan.). AIDS and college health: Knowledge, threat, and prevention at a northeastern university. *Journal of American Collegiate Health, 38*(4), 179-84.

Trocki, K. (1990). Preliminary results on sexual risk-taking in a general population sample. *Progress in Clinical Biology of Research, 325,* 21-25.

Turner, C.F., et al. (1989). *AIDS, sexual behavior and intravenous drug use.* Washington, DC: National Academy Press.

Yellowlees, P. M., & Ruffin, R. E. (1989, June). Psychological defenses and coping styles in patients following a life-threatening attack of asthma. *Chest, 95*(6), 1298-1303.

F·O·U·R·T·E·E·N

妝

Treatment of the Shame
Involved in the Experience
of Incest

SAMUEL R. JAMES

A s society moved into the permissive era of the 1970s and 1980s theoreticians and clinicians alike began to explore in more detail the painful consequences of shame. Until this time shame had been theoretically overshadowed by Freud's (1933) work on guilt. Historically, patients burdened with pathological shame have tended to evade the pain of exposure and recognition, and the clinician has had to pursue the material in order to help the patient reveal its source. Furthermore, the patient's resistances to issues surrounding shame have in many instances proven to be quite formidable, ranging from passive withdrawal to rebellious acting out. Consequently, as adults, such patients have been easily misdiagnosed, seen as depressed or, at best, considered very hard to treat.

Many of the disorders of our age are founded on the experience of shame. As we view more and more symptom complexes (e.g., eating disorders, adult children of alcoholics, etc.) and develop treatments specifically for them, we need to revise our thinking about the importance of shame as a central affect in our patients. Victims of incest, for example, are a group for whom shame is frequently overlooked as an important aspect of their recovery. This chapter is a review of the shame literature and its clinical application. Though many symptom-complexes are founded on shame, adult survivors of father–daughter or stepfather–daughter incest will be the population considered. (For readability the use of the word "father" will include stepfathers as well.) Attention will be given to a theoretical understanding of shame that is clinically applicable to the trauma of incest.

SHAME LITERATURE REVIEW

There are many definitions of shame. It has been described as a perception of the self as bad, diminished, secret, concealed (Thrane, 1978), a triad of weakness, defectiveness, dirtiness (Wurmser, 1987); inclusive of such emotions as shyness, bashfulness, modesty (Nathanson, 1987); as an emotion experienced alone (Alonso & Rutan, 1988); a fear of loss of love (Lewis, 1971); and a defect or failure of the self leading to a decrease in narcissistic self-esteem (Morrison, 1983).

In effect the individual experiences the need to hide or avoid at all cost the singeing experience of being known and/or seen by others. This does not mean that shame-related issues always promote withdrawing behavior. Often shame issues produce aggression as a defense against the anxiety of being exposed.

Freud did not advance early psychoanalytic understanding of shame. His interests were in the area of guilt, and he often used the term shame generically with guilt. When he did separate shame from guilt he understood it as inadequacy or as consisting of feminine qualities (1933). The discussion of such a topic in the Victorian era would not have been as well received as guilt. Thrane (1978) believed that Freud chose guilt out of the longstanding Christian emphasis upon guilt and logic.

Erikson (1950) directed attention to shame when he named the second of his eight "ages of man:" autonomy vs. shame and doubt, and defined the critical conflict as the will to be oneself as compared to shame and doubt about the self. The child was faced with a choice to "stand on his or her own two feet" and deal with the developmental crisis. The refusal to do this meant that psychic energy was turned against the self, which in turn led to a feeling of shame. One was visible, exposed, and conscious of being seen. According to Erikson, the child could become confused, depressed by his or her lack of self-definition and begin to experience a sense of badness, inferiority, and a fear of a loss of love if discovered.

Wurmser (1987) differentiated shame and guilt both theoretically and clinically. Guilt centered around actions — the seeking of confession and forgiveness for wrongdoing — and was connected with secondary process. Shame was centered around the self and the way the self was experienced as bad, defective, a failure. It was a more primitive painful emotion and thus part of primary process.

For Thrane (1978) shame has an important and perhaps useful function in the socialization process. This can be seen in the child's attempt to be socially acceptable in the parent's eyes and thereby master the developmental tasks leading to self-control and power. However, when the child is a mere extension of the parent and is denied the opportunity for self-development, the shame is debilitating. Kinston (1987) poignantly describes the way in which the child is caught in a painful bind of either pursuing self-interests and development or being a narcissistic extension of the parent.

> The interpersonal interactions are painful, horrible and traumatic. Should she exist as him/herself the child is subjected to rejection and invalidating attitudes and finds that s/he causes pain, depression, rage or resentment in the parent. Should the child comply with the parental projection s/he must destroy his/her own experience. The former course is clearly associated with low self-esteem and identity disturbance and problems of self-regulation. The latter course results in a spurious sense of well-being due to the receipt of (false) approval and love, and the absence or psychic destruction of personal need, frustration or conflict. (p. 223)

When a child achieves socially acceptable behavior with his or her parents without developing a sense of mastery and self-control, the child becomes empty, lacking in direction and in an internal understanding of how to succeed or be related in an autonomous way. The child loses an opportunity to develop self-esteem because of the conflict between being him- or herself and being what the parent wishes him or her to be. Taken together, these elements contribute to the development of shame.

Demos (1983) describes three components necessary for healthy self-esteem that are often missing in the shame-prone child: (1) a sense of competence; (2) a willingness to trust his or her own inner experience; and (3) a feeling of relatedness or lack of isolation. When a child does not develop these qualities, he or she struggles with shame and/or a lack of a sense of self. Object relations theorists (e.g., Klein, 1946) have provided a helpful way of thinking about how children either gain or fail to gain the above. According to object relations theorists the child is believed to introject the parents and seek to be like them. At the same time they have to contend with the parents' role as both the good and bad objects, resulting in a great tension due to trying to come to terms with the dynamics between the two.

Lewis (1987) points out that identification with the threatening parent stirs an "internalized threat" that is experienced as guilt.

> Identification with the beloved or admired ego ideal stirs pride and triumphant feelings; failure to live up to this internalized admired image stirs shame. The pain of shame is the loss of love and the loss of the feeling of unity. (p. 23)

Piers and Singer (1953) add that shame is produced by the inability to reserve the tension between the self and the ego ideal. The self is not worthy of being related to and the child fears abandonment, the threat of shame.

With positive self-esteem the child does not fear loss of love and abandonment. He or she can afford to look at the whole self. But negative self-esteem leads to hiding from the self, parents, friends, and therapists. According to Morrison (1983), shame anxiety "drives the individual into irrational flight covering or hiding of the exposed vulnerability, or into denial of that defect or vulnerability" (p. 299).

Since psychotherapy involves self-recognition and shame involves a fear of self-exposure, the potential for conflict in the course of treatment is inevitable. The self-recognition required by treatment can be experienced as a failure with respect to an ideal or identity. The self is experienced as bad, evil, no good. Hence, any action on the part of the therapist can be viewed with suspicion by the patient. The movements toward self-exposure produce anxiety. Wurmser (1987) describes how "any form of self-expression, e.g., looks, physiognomy, words, or gestures means self-surrender" (p. 79).

There has been a failure in seeing and being seen that is especially poignant in light of Tomkins's (1982) assertion that the child learns through seeing the face, the "communications center for sending and receiving information of all kinds . . ." (p. 376). Consequently, one for whom being seen is shameful finds allowing another to see the inner self as nearly impossible.

SHAME AND INCEST

Concomitant with recent explorations of shame, several issue-specific groups have emerged that appear to have shame as a common denominator. Adult Children of Alcoholics, eating disorder groups, incest and Incest Anonymous groups, Substance Abuse groups, etc., all deal with the impact of shame on the lives of their members. All work to break the isolation of shame so that it can be normalized and discussed. According to Alonso and Rutan (1988), "Reduction of shame sets the stage for better integration of self and a subsequent increase in self-esteem that is crucial in furthering development" (p. 5). The goal of treatment is to work through the different aspects of the patient's shame so that self-development and esteem can return to a healthy functioning level. The focus of this chapter will be on how attention to the shame involved in incest victimization is an essential element in the successful treatment of the survivor. This focus can easily be used with the myriad other populations for which shame is a fundamental affect.

Understanding the family of the incest survivor is integral to appreciating the sense of shame in the victim. Herman (1981) argues that the horror of incest is not in the sexual act but in the corruption of parental love. It is the failure to recognize the daughter as separate and to treat her instead as a selfobject of the father; thus, she is robbed of the opportunity for healthy psychosexual development. Erikson (1950), too, believed that the combination of a loss of self-control and a foreign overcontrol led to a lasting propensity for doubt and shame. She is robbed of an opportunity to develop a sense of self. Intrapsychically, incest victims are forced into a shame-laden developmental path that results in performance behavior that lacks genuine spontaneity, desire, and warmth.

Classical theory postulates that children develop sequentially through defined stages of psychosexual development, each of which must be experienced and mastered for healthy functioning. The child frequently uses sexual fantasies for the parent as an expression of the libidinal energy to help master each stage. This energy helps secure a bond between the parent and child so that the child can attend to her own maturational development. When a daughter, however, is thrust into an incestuous relationship, she can be overwhelmed by unsuitable stimulation (Sgroi et al., 1982). Anna Freud (1981) describes it this way:

> The child cannot avoid being physically aroused and this experience disastrously disrupts the normal sequence in her sexual organization. She is forced into premature phallic or genital development while her legitimate needs and their accompanying mental expression are bypassed. Thus, the child is forced into premature ego development and must abandon the ordered psychosexual development of childhood. (p. 33)

Hence, development becomes based upon confusion in terms of relationships with the self and others and her role as daughter or lover–pseudowife. The intensification of the relationship will confuse her in terms of expression of libidinal energy, causing a loss of valuable resources in her attachment to her parents. Although she may wish parental encouragement in order to be spontaneous and risk exploring her own life, she more likely than not feels the need to distance herself and flee the involvement. This distancing often produces a sense of the "bad or dirty me" who is defective and needs to hide for fear of exposure. There can also be excitation of the incest, and the fear of having seduced father leads to shame.

This set of circumstances also produces internal reality confusion as the child struggles with her normal sexual fantasies for the parent and her own sense of appropriate limits. Upon the father's violation of the appropriate father–daughter sexual boundary, the daughter learns early (and quite destructively) that fantasies of union with the parent can be realized. The boundary violation violates the ego ideal, which in turn produces fusion of libidinal and aggressive energies for the daughter, generating great potential for confusing or inhibited sexuality in adult life.

At the same time, the incest survivor has often had to deal with all of this internal confusion and arrested development while living in a family that is consumed by emotional poverty. Whereas these families quite often perform and look normal in public, privately they interact with isolation, secrecy, and misuse of power and love. Neediness and chaos appear to have imploded within the family.

Groth (1982) tells us that the fathers of incest victims were "passive, dependent and child-like or aggressive–dominant" and suffered from a "deep-seated core feeling of helplessness, vulnerability and dependence" (p. 225). The stresses of adult life created regressive behavior marked by feelings of intense shame, overwhelming insecurity, and neediness. Such fathers usually came from backgrounds of emotional deprivation (Mrazek, 1981) and "one in three were abused themselves" (Groth, 1982). Power became a primary way to deal with their internal inadequacies and shameful feelings. The overriding need of these fathers was to meet their own needs first and to maintain control within a closed family system (Sgroi, 1982).

The families of incest victims generally comply with the father's demand for social isolation. Many times the social skills of the family are poor to begin with, so that outside social relationships are not well developed. Managing the family's dependence and insularity is an important gain and the daughter serves an important function in upholding the family cohesion. She frequently does not have many resources outside of the family and fears the further demise of her own family. Since she is ultimately frightened of the desertion of her father and the emotional collapse of her mother (Herman, 1981) she enters the conspiracy of silence to try to save her family (Butler, 1978). Thus, the isolation from outside scrutiny serves to encourage and exacerbate sexual involvement (Finkelhor, 1979), and thrust a sense of shame upon the daughter that is traumatic.

The mothers of incest victims are mostly housewives (Herman, 1982), who were sexually abused themselves (Butler, 1978), have difficulty supervising their children (Finkelhor, 1978), and are often absent emotionally and physically from the family. In short, they are weak, ineffective women at the mercy of the rageful oppression of their husbands.

Many maternal duties are reassigned to the oldest daughter, who is also the most likely incest victim (Finkelhor, 1978). The daughter becomes a pseudoadult whose desperate attempts to keep the family together prevents her from leaving the family scene for fear of total disintegration of the family unit.

Since the mother is seen as an ineffective protector, many daughters are frightened to go to her for help. Some mothers, however, are able to provide adequate protection and do remove the daughter or oust the father upon disclosure (Herman, 1981). Mothers who do not provide adequate protection for the daughter are generally thought to be lacking in resources (e.g. financial, familial, friendships) that they could draw upon. As a result, they discount their daughter's revelation. In these instances the daughter is left on her own. When the daughter feels, whether real or imagined, that she can not go to her mother (or anyone else) for help, she is helplessly caught in a destructive family web that is impossible to work with productively. As part of an intricate triangle with her parents, she struggles with the fear of the loss of love (Lewis, 1971), while feeling powerless and defective (Wurmser, 1987) if she defends herself. This is experienced as a failure to live up to her ego ideal.

The ego ideal is further sacrificed when the daughter realizes the sinister elements of the father's actions, but at the same time depends on the father as her primary source of love and affection. The longing for closeness is strong. In cases when the father is not violent, some even find comfort in the relationship with him (Butler, 1978; Herman, 1981). The closeness, however, is experienced through sexual involvement, not verbal acknowledgment of the daughter's issues in life and her wish to master them.

Additionally, any feelings of pleasure also produce great loathing and strong fear that *she* is in fact responsible for the sexual nature of the relationship. This kind of conflict manifests itself in a sense of shame that one is dirty, bad, and needs to hide from potential exposure.

The shame involved in incest underlines how lost the daughter becomes within herself, family, and social world. And as a lost child, she takes on the trauma as something deserved, thus a certain level of masochism is born. Often, victims of incest assume Winnicott's (1963) "as if" qualities in an attempt to belong while not risking the real self to come forth. The constant struggle is to relate and have emotional needs met but not get so close that exposure would be necessary to belong.

The delicate dance between attachment and withdrawal is not only painful but impossible to successfully negotiate.

TREATMENT OF THE SHAME INVOLVED IN INCEST

The treatment of shame is similar to clinical work with any regressive affect. Morrison (1984) provides a treatment strategy for shame that can easily be applied to incest victims.

> The first step is to recognize shame and shame anxiety in the patient's material. Once recognized, the relevance and the importance of the shame experience to the patient's dynamics and to hiding and withdrawal of material from analysis must be acknowledged. The analyst must be able to communicate that he accepts the patient's shame experience. (p. 501)

In summary Morrison recommends that the clinician "recognize, acknowledge, accept, and investigate the patients' shame" (p. 503).

While this approach provides a clinical strategy, the real encounter is fraught with dilemmas. The intensity of the need to hide, even repress to the point that the patient has no conscious recall, is quite severe. The fear of being placed under the "gaze" of the clinician is very frightening. The years of repressed fear and hatred can be projected upon the clinician with a conviction that he or she will reject the patient because of her history. Most incest survivors are very skilled at distracting attention away from this material.

Consequently, the clinician needs to be able to accept the incest survivor's need to hide, but to look for a cluster of characteristics that may suggest that incest occurred in her past. These are: a lack of basic trust, substance abuse, isolation, low self-esteem, difficulty with close relationships, history of unempathic mother or overwhelming father, fear of exposure, shame and guilt, depression, and loss of pleasure associated with sex. Focusing upon the shame component is critical since it is the intrapsychic mechanism that actively attempts to prevent these characteristics from surfacing in treatment.

The task of assessment is further complicated since most clinicians, trained to treat depression, miss the way in which shame tends to be covered by depression. As Lewis (1987) points out, "Acute unidentified or unacknowledged shame is often hard to distinguish from its rapid transformation into depressive ideation" (p. 107). When the depression is seen as the goal of treatment, the work can last for a long period of time without significant movement. The depression is a psychopolitical attempt to maintain a relationship with the selfobject father.

The assessment can be facilitated by asking empathic and thoughtful questions about the depression, raising the possibility that it is a cover for incestuous conflict. If there is a history of incest, the patient may respond by withdrawing into lack of recall, denial, or a gradual revelation of parts of the experience. The depression at this time gives way to anxiety, excitement, and relief. In acutely depressed patients, the depression could worsen at disclosure since the loss of the selfobject father would be too intense. Consequently, it is better to wait until her depression is better managed to begin this line of exploration.

The primary task of the intervention is to introduce the material in such a way that the patient feels safe enough to acknowledge it. Many patients will admit that it occurred but will refrain from discussing the incest event. Wurmser (1987) reminds us that: "The careful analysis of shame requires great tact and patience. We have to respect the patient's need to hide behind layers of silence, evasion, omission and intellectualizations as dictated by intense anxiety about exposure" (p. 90).

It is important that the therapist establish a "holding environment" (Winnicott, 1963), whereby the clinician conveys an understanding and accepting of the patient's anxiety and pain, a missing ingredient in the development of the incest survivor. The forceful entry into premature ego development left her without adequate holding, mirroring, and protection; this ultimately produced the anxiety that worsened into shame.

Self psychologists (e.g., Kohut, 1971, 1977; Morrison, 1983) have discussed the use of empathic mirroring as a technique to help "hold" the patient while exploring the material. This mirrors the loss of the exhibitionistic self and the wish for the lost merger in early life. It provides an opportunity for joining the selfobject therapist, who provides the necessary support to return to a healthy psychosexual developmental process.

Empathic listening and engagement provide the necessary mirroring that allow for the development of the self. The work is made difficult by the patient's multiple defenses. But even when the patient is in an active state of defense and having difficulty holding on to the shameful affect, the empathic bond will continue to hold and reassure her.

In order to preserve the therapeutic relationship the patient believes she must hide. Her admiration for the clinician makes revealing delicate matters about herself especially painful. Consequently, the hiding becomes a boundary to distinguish the self's and the other's experience (Lewis, 1987) and helps to preserve separate identity and emotional relatedness. At times the impasse is the only way the patient can feel related and bounded at the same time. To rush her through the impasse may come at the price of destroying the relatedness and insisting that the patient be an extension of the therapist. It may be experienced as yet another boundary violation. The clinician's countertransference unwittingly reproduces the selfobject relationship with the father. The clinician must be able to carefully acknowledge the involvement expressed by the impasse and help the patient move from a passive to an active understanding of relatedness.

The key to treatment is acceptance of the shame. Although acceptance is essential to all forms of psychotherapy, it is especially true for shame affect. Guilt, by contrast, seeks forgiveness (Thrane, 1978), whereas shame seeks acceptance (Lewis, 1971). Yet the acceptance quite often is not readily accepted. Often it produces feelings of paranoia, especially if the clinician is male and the patient's father had used kindness to lure her into sexual involvement. It can also produce self-loathing if she does not feel worthy of kindness and understanding. Mostly it elicits anxiety and suspiciousness since the empathic mirroring produces a dilemma. For on the one hand, feeling accepted produces the warmth from a selfobject that she has been seeking, but this same warmth can be confusing.

The pressure of this dilemma can produce acting out. Ganzarian and Buchele (1987) provide insight into the acting out by describing it as a side effect of treatment. Patients "need to master their traumatic pasts by compulsively repeating them through actions, often quite dramatic. A central portion of the repetition is 'keeping the secret' by not talking" (p 185). The loyalty to the father is not easily surrendered. Although the event was traumatic, it still offered some, albeit negligible warmth and acceptance.

Acting out is an attempt to address the inherent pain through behavior instead of words. When the clinician tries to help the patient use verbal communication, the patient may use the only language she has at her disposal, for example, acting out. Unless the acting out appears to be dangerous, the clinician needs to allow it as a precommunication about a shameful trauma she is trying to address. It contains intense, painful affect that more clearly than words expresses the horror and rage of her experience. Through acceptance and working through the acting out, there is the opportunity for the behavior to be translated into words.

In time the suspiciousness is transformed into basic trust and verbal cooperation within the treatment, whereupon the clinician may suggest the use of outside supports to assist and advance the work. Incest groups have proliferated in the past 10 years (Tsai & Wagner, 1978; Herman, 1981; Goodman & Nowak Scibelli, 1985; Herman & Schatzow, 1984). These groups are time-limited and carefully designed to help patients deal with the most common concomitants of incest: shame and guilt, low self-esteem, impact of the incest upon current relationships, coping difficulties, and difficult relationships with family members.

The groups are useful in the treatment of shame since they help to establish a sense of universality (Yalom, 1975) as the unique wretchedness of incest victims gives way to communal involvement and affirmation. The recovery of any shameful affect requires going public and being able to discuss the incest in detail, thus breaking the secrecy and isolation. This is a valuable asset in group treatment since it provides the public component in a safe, supportive community that can tolerate the intensity while accepting the patient.

The working-through phase does not have to focus exclusively upon shame. Many issues of the trauma of incest need attention and must to be addressed. Shame, however, is the foundation of the other various themes surrounding the event. Understanding shame helps us understand the patient and the need for active, empathic work to facilitate recovery. Attention to the shame component allows for an empathic return to the arrested developmental state so that preoedipal and oedipal issues can be addressed. It behooves the clinician not to become lost within the patient's defenses and acting out, and to continue to focus upon the impact of the shame within the incestuous experience.

SUMMARY

This chapter has reviewed the pertinent material in the shame and incest literatures to illustrate the usefulness of exploring the shame affect with incest survivors. Father–daughter incest is a trauma that forces the daughter into premature psychosexual development. This produces feelings of withdrawal into isolation and a sense of self that is dirty, bad, evil, and a failure. If left untreated, it can produce difficulty with regulation of self-esteem and sexual development, closeness with others, and intense shame and fear of being discovered.

Clinicians have long been involved in the treatment of incest survivors but often the attention has been on depression—the disguised agent of shame. Depression is more socially acceptable but fails to acknowledge the horror, rage, and violation that elicits shame. By addressing shame, the patient in time is enabled to more actively resume her life with a sense of self-esteem, responsibility, and healthy relatedness to others.

The attention to shame also allows for the exploration of loyalty to the father and the fear of differentiating from him. This often leads to acting out and feeling overwhelmed by regressive affect. Through the acting out part of the work, the clinician can hold and accept the patient as she tries to communicate the pain of this trauma until it can be symbolized in words that adequately represent her feelings. Since it is shame that drives a patient into hiding, the exploration of and working through of shame should allow the patient the opportunity to move from the isolation of the conspiracy of silence to a more dynamic participation in her life.

REFERENCES

Alonso, A., & Rutan, J.S. (1988). The experience of shame and the restoration of self-respect in group therapy. *International Journal of Group Psychotherapy, 38,* 3–13.

Butler, S. (1978). *Conspiracy of silence.* San Francisco: New Glide Publications.

Demos, E.V. (1983). A perspective from infant research on affect and self-esteem. In J. Mack & S. Ablon (Eds.), *The development and sustaining of self-esteem in childhood* (pp. 45–78). New York: International University Press.

Erikson, E. (1950). *Childhood and society.* New York: W.W. Norton.

Finkelhor, D. (1979). *Sexually victimized children.* New York: The Free Press.

Freud, A. (1981) A psychoanalyst view of sexual abuse by parents. In P. Mrazek & C. Kempe (Eds.), *Sexually abused children and their families* (pp 33–34). New York: Pergamon Press.

Freud, S. (1964). *New introductory lectures on psychoanalysis.* In J. Strachey (Ed. and, Trans.), *The standard edition of the complete psychological work of Sigmund Freud* (Vol. 22, pp. 58–182) London: Hogarth Press. (Original work published 1933)

Ganzarian, R., & Buchele, B. (1987). Acting out during group psychotherapy for incest. *International Journal of Group Psychotherapy, 37,* 185–200.

Goodman, B., & Nowak-Scibelli, D. (1985). Group treatment for women incestuously abused as children. *International Journal of Group Psychotherapy, 35,* 531–544.

Groth, A.N. (1982). The incest offender. In S. Sgroi (Ed.), *Handbook of clinical intervention in child sexual abuse* (pp. 215–239). Lexington, MA: Lexington Books.

Herman, J. (1981). *Father daughter incest.* Cambridge, MA: Harvard University Press.

Herman, J., & Schatzow, E. (1984). Time limited group therapy for women with a history of incest. *International Journal of Group Psychotherapy, 34,* 605–616.

Kinston, W. (1987). The shame of narcissism. In D. Nathanson (Ed.), *The many faces of shame* pp. 214–245. New York: The Guilford Press.

Klein, M. (1946). Notes on some schizoid mechanisms. In M. Klein (Ed.), *Developments in psychoanalysis.* London: Hogarth Press.

Kohut, H. (1971). *The analysis of the self.* New York: International University Press.

Kohut, H. (1977). *The restoration of the self.* New York: International University Press.

Lewis, H.B. (1971). *Shame and guilt in neurosis.* New York: International University Press.

Lewis, H.B. (1987). Shame and the narcissistic personality. In D. Nathanson (Ed.), *The many faces of shame* pp. 93–132. New York: The Guilford Press.

Morrison, A.P. (1983). Shame, ideal self and narcissism. *Contemporary Psychoanalysis, 19,* 295–318.

Morrison, A.P. (1984). Working with shame in psychoanalytic treatment. *Journal of American Psychoanalytic Association, 32,* 479–506.

Mrazek, P.B. (1981). Group psychotherapy with sexually abused children. In P.B. Mrazek and C.H. Kempe (Eds.), *Sexually abused children and their families* pp. 199–218. New York: Pergamon Press.

Nathanson, D. (1987). A timetable for shame. In D. Nathanson (Ed.), *The many faces of shame* (pp. 1–63). New York: Guilford Press.

Piers, G., & Singer, M. (1953). *Shame and guilt.* Springfield, IL: Thomas.

Sgroi, S.M., Brick, L.C., & Porter, F.S. (1982). A conceptual framework for child sexual abuse. In S. Sgroi (Ed.), *Handbook of clinical intervention in child sexual abuse.* Lexington, MA: Lexington Books.

Thrane, G. (1978). Shame and the construction of the self. *Annual of Psychoanalysis, 7,* 321–341.

Tomkins, S.S. (1987). Affect theory. In P. Ekman (Ed.), *Emotion in the human face* pp. 353–395. Cambridge, England: Cambridge University Press.

Tsai, M., & Wagner, N. (1978). Therapy groups for women sexually molested as children. *Archives of sexual behavior, 7,* 417–427.

Winnicott, D.W. (1962). Ego integration in child development. *Maturational Processes,* 56–63.

Wurmser, L. (1987). Shame: the veiled companion of narcissism. In D. Nathanson (Ed.), *The many faces of shame* pp. 64–92. New York: Guilford Press.

Yalom, I. (1975). *The theory and practice of group psychotherapy.* New York: Basic Books.

F·I·F·T·E·E·N

※

Group Psychotherapy for Eating Disorders

HELEN RIESS

No volume examining modern currents in the practice of psychotherapy would be complete without a section on the eating disorders. Although anorexia nervosa and bulimia nervosa are not newly described syndromes, their preponderance in today's young women suggests that our modern culture fosters and perpetuates these syndromes as never before documented in the history of eating disorders. Eating disorders are but one of many specific pathological responses to the pressures of the modern world. A frantic pursuit of thinness was certainly not present in previous times or cultures. The painters Titian and Giorgione in the early 16th century depicted women with very substantial figures luxuriating in their femaleness. Rubens in the 17th century glorified the massive proportions of breasts, abdomen, and thighs of his models who would be considered obese by today's standards. The hourglass figure was fashionable in the 19th century. There was a strong emphasis on outward appearance where women forced themselves into confining corsets and added bustles to accentuate their hips. These fashions gave way to the pencil-thin slimness of the flapper era in the 1920s, a time when the women's emancipation movement was underway and stereotyped female roles were being questioned. The androgynous slenderness of women reflected a turn away from women's role as provider of sexual pleasure for men and marked a new statement of independence. This coincided with the first outbreak of eating disorders in western civilization. The outbreak was short-lived but made a recurrence in the late 1960s and early 1970s. By taking a look at what was happening in the women's movement, where traditional sex roles were being challenged as well as the general unrest and lack of certainty that has been the hallmark of the 20th century, some clues can be found to help explain why anorexia and bulimia have reached epidemic proportions in the late 20th century. Is it the role confusion with ever increasing pressures on today's women to maintain traditional expectations as well as compete in what has traditionally been a man's world that foster these disorders, or is the anomie of today's society leaving women anxious, isolated, and uncertain? Is today's woman literally "starving for love" in a world where others' self-preoccupation leaves young women with little confidence of their own self-worth? If so, group therapy would provide support for individuals' finding their own particular roles in society, a sense of connection to others, and a forum in which to explore what each member is yearning for.

It is generally agreed upon that eating disorders arise from a combination of risk factors, including sociocultural factors, psychological factors, biological vulnerabilities, and familial predispositions. The fact that our society has the highest number of reports of these disorders suggests that there is something idiosyncratic about our particular time in history that increases the risk of eating disorders in modern women. The ever growing number of young women suffering from self-starvation and deprivation makes it incumbent upon us to find therapeutic measures to treat and cure these all too pervasive disorders.

This chapter will provide a brief overview of the eating disorders anorexia and bulimia nervosa. The historical roots of the disorders will be described. The definitions of today's eating disorders will be given, along with information about their epidemiology and etiology. The bulk of this chapter will describe group treatment options with a particular emphasis on a step-wise approach using group therapy. Group therapy has emerged as a favored treatment modality for patients with bulimia (Herzog, 1988).

HISTORICAL ROOTS

Medical reports of anorexia nervosa date back to the 17th century (Morton, 1694/1985), and bulimic symptoms have been described in the medical literature since the late 19th century. The first documented account of bulimia as a disorder in its own right, and not a symptom associated with other illnesses, was not published until the mid-20th century. A marked surge of patients presenting with bulimia nervosa occurred in the 1970s with reports of this disorder and anorexia nervosa reaching epidemic proportions in the 1980s. We continue to see a rise in the numbers of patients presenting with these illnesses. It is estimated that from 5–10% of young women meet criteria for eating disorders (Pope, Hudson, & Yurgelun-Todd, 1984). Some reports show that as many as 5–19% of female college students have the essential symptoms of bulimia nervosa (Halmi, Falk, & Schwartz, 1981; Pyle, 1984).

Although the eating disorders are not new, their incidence and prevalence are such that they cannot be overlooked in reports of psychiatric illness in our current culture. Clearly we must examine why these disorders are so prevalent today, particularly when bulimia was scarcely recognized in the early part of this century and anorectics were considered oddities of past centuries. Brumberg (1988) maintains that self-starvation has had different meanings in different times and cultures. Medieval ascetics such as Catherine of Sienna were elevated to the ranks of sainthood because of their severe austerity and "miraculous" ability to fast. Women in the 19th century used not eating as their own form of control and protection from a society that thrust them into roles for which they were unprepared, that is, the sexual role of wife and mother in a society where sex remained shrouded in mystery and fear for young girls. The "delicacy of the thin bourgeois girl also became a status symbol, a sign of aristocracy and good breeding, whereas a healthy appetite was considered vulgar." Brumberg's point is that over the last two centuries "appetite became less of a biological drive and more a social and emotional instrument." Twentieth-century anorectics are using this instrument to combat their own sense of role confusion and conflicting expectations that modern society and their female heritage dictate (Brumberg, 1988). Today, thousands of young women are dedicated to fasting and dieting, but these behaviors are not seen as abnormal until drastic physiological or mental changes indicate that the dieter has gone overboard.

Modern women are obsessed with thinness. Were this not true, the diet industry with its weight loss clinics, diet books, and exercise plans guaranteed to shed unwanted pounds would not be a million dollar business. Surely not everyone who goes on a weight loss diet has an eating disorder, but the diet culture has contributed to the pervasive problem of eating disorders. The current emphasis on slimness provides modern women with an unattainable goal that is used to measure self-worth and self-love. If we accept the modern tenet that "One can never be too rich or too thin" it is no surprise that so many young women dedicate themselves to lives of rigid self-control and the torture of denying their appetites in order to feel attractive and acceptable.

DEFINITIONS

The latest diagnostic criteria for anorexia nervosa as described in the DSM-III-R are: a refusal to maintain normal body weight with weight loss leading to body weight 15% below that expected for age and height; a morbid fear of fatness; marked disturbance in body image (the anoretic feels "fat" even when emaciated); and loss of menses for 3 consecutive months. Interestingly, the 1982 DSM-III set weight loss at 25% lower than expected body weight. This meant that only severely starved persons met the criteria for anorexia nervosa. The change in criteria to 15% makes more patients meet the criteria for this disorder, which may partially account for the growing numbers, but also increases the probability that a person suffering from anorexia will be diagnosed and treated before starving herself to a life-threatening weight. Bulimia nervosa is characterized by binge eating followed by a number of different efforts to counteract the resultant weight gain (Russell, 1979). The DSM-III-R criteria include: recurrent episodes of binge eating (rapid consumption of a large amount of food in a discrete period of time); a feeling of lack of control over eating behavior during the eating binges; regular engagement in either self-induced vomiting, use of laxatives or diuretics, strict dieting or fasting, or vigorous exercise in order to prevent weight gain; a minimum average of two binge eating episodes a week for at least 3 months (DSM-III-R, 1987). These criteria are the most recently revised to distinguish the symptom (binge eating) from the diagnostic syndrome (bulimia nervosa). Both anorexia and bulimia nervosa are serious disorders that can place those afflicted at risk for sudden death. Anorectics can literally starve to death while bulimics may lose vital electrolytes through purging behaviors that result in cardiac compromise. When the two disorders coexist in the same person she is particularly at risk for serious medical complications.

EPIDEMIOLOGY

Anorexia nervosa is predominantly an illness afflicting young women, as 90–95% of the anorectic and bulimic populations is female. There have been reports of anorexia in males as well as in prepubescent girls and middle-aged women. Original reports of anorexia nervosa associated the disorder with the upper middle socioeconomic class, but there has been a decline from 71–52% in this stratum, indicating a more equal distribution across social classes (Garfinkle & Garner, 1982). The onset of anorexia tends to occur at an earlier age than bulimia. In anorexia the onset occurs between the ages 12–25 years with a bimodal peak at ages 14 and 18 (Eckbert, 1985). Bulimia nervosa is primarily a disorder of young adult women, beginning between 17 and 25 years of age (Halmi et al., 1981). Most bulimics are within a normal weight range but as many as 50% have a history of being overweight (Johnson & Connors, 1987). Cases of bulimia are much more difficult to detect because of the secretive nature of the disorder and the apparently normal physical appearance of the affected person. It is not uncommon for bulimics to be symptomatic for 5–8 years prior to seeking treatment.

The incidence of anorexia nervosa has doubled over the past two decades. A New York study showed an increased incidence from 0.35 per 100,000 in 1960–1969 to 0.64 per 100,000 in 1970–1976 (Jones, Fox, Babigian, & Hutton, 1980). The prevalence of bulimia nervosa is widespread with reports varying between 5–20% of college students (Strangler & Priutz, 1980; Herzog, 1988). The prevalence is lower in the nonuniversity setting.

ETIOLOGY

The etiology of the eating disorders involves an interplay of psychological, sociocultural, familial, and biological factors.

Psychological Factors

Psychoanalysts in the early history of treating anorexia believed that self-starvation was a defense against sexual fantasies of oral impregnation or against ambivalent sadistic fantasies (Herzog, 1988). Today ego psychologists and object relations theorists maintain that eating disorders are a result of early defects in ego structure and object failures. Hilda Bruch (1973), a leading authority on eating disorders, maintains that self-deficits originating from the lack of appropriate responses from the mother to the child lead to a sense of ineffectiveness, helplessness, and self-hatred. She believes that mothers who use feedings primarily to quiet the child rather than to respond to the child's hunger do not help the child to distinguish his or her own needs from those of others. When older, the child feels a connection with her mother by attending to the mother's wishes and needs rather than her own. Bruch argues that this is what underlies the anorectic's overwillingness to comply to others' wishes and become overly perfectionistic in areas that appeal to parents, such as high scholastic achievement, athletic prowess, and development of other special skills. When the child turns to the pursuit of thinness as a way to achieve self-control and perfectionism, the distorted sense that she can never become thin enough leads to self-loathing and depression. Researchers show that between 25–50% of eating disordered patients have major depression at some time in their illness. The exact relationship between affective disorders and eating disorders is unclear and is presently the subject of much research.

Sociocultural Factors

The present sociocultural milieu in western societies fosters the notion that physical attractiveness in women necessitates a slender, lean body. Although the recent fitness culture promotes exercise primarily for healthy bodies, the emphasis on slimness as well as muscle tone prevails. Magazine and television models continue to portray extremely thin bodies as the norm for today's women. The effect of these models is twofold: some women try to imitate them by rigorous exercise routines and dieting, while others feel inadequate and depressed that they can never reach this thin ideal. According to Boskind-Lodahl and White (1979), one of the effects of our male-dominated society is that women's perception of themselves are influenced by the way men see them. Young women learn that thin is desirable, and in an effort to be loved and held in high esteem they will starve themselves to feel acceptable.

Familial Factors

More often than not, the patient with an eating disorder is a member of a dysfunctional or troubled family. The problems in the family are usually not talked about and thus remain unresolved so that the eating disordered member becomes the targeted problem child. For example, when the threat of divorce is not verbalized, the child becomes symptomatic, and the problem is refocused on the child, thus keeping the parents together. Should the child recover, the threat resurfaces. As a result, the child becomes stuck in a static role, impairing her own development and warding off her own fears about maturation and sexuality. The typical anorectic family is characterized by rigidity, overprotection, enmeshment, lack of conflict resolution, and use of the child to mitigate parental conflicts (Minuchin, Rosman, & Baker, 1978).

Biological Factors

Abnormalities of the hypothalamic-pituitary-adrenal axis appear in both depression and eating disorders (Doerr, Fichter, Pirke, & Lund, 1980). Certain neurotransmitter levels are abnormal in anorectics even after weight recovery (Gold, Kaye, Robertson, & Ebert, 1983). This suggests that there may be underlying neurochemical disturbances in anorectic patients leading to their disorder. Researchers of bulimia suggest that there may be a central neurochemical abnormality of the serotonergic and noradrenergic systems. Serotonin causes the sensation of satiety, and the low level of this neurotransmitter in bulimics may predispose them to binging behaviors (Kaye, Ebert, Gwirtsman, & Weiss, 1984). Further evidence of a biological component in the etiology of eating disorders is the ameliorating effect of the antidepressant medications that act on noradrenergic and serotonergic receptors.

TREATMENTS

Treatment of eating disorders is extremely difficult and problematic because of the multi-axial etiologies and the denial of illness present in both anorexia and bulimia nervosa. Several promising treatment modalities have emerged but no single treatment has been shown to be universally effective. Inpatient treatment is usually reserved for medically unstable patients, suicidality, or patients whose family situations are so chaotic that temporary separation from the family is necessary. Among the outpatient treatments that have been reported to be useful alone or in combination are individual psychotherapy (psychodynamic, cognitive–behavioral, behavioral), family therapy, nutritional therapy, pharmacotherapy, and group psychotherapy. This chapter will focus on group therapy, which is a natural form of therapy for patients struggling with interpersonal issues. Although the other forms of therapy are often used in conjunction with a group, no format offers a better context for patients to work out their interpersonal conflicts. Group therapy addresses the four etiologies of eating disorders: the sociocultural context; each member's psychological and familial constellation; and a forum to discuss the benefits of or disappointments in medications, thus addressing the biological etiology. There are five major models of outpatient group therapy for eating disordered patients: psychodynamic psychotherapy groups; cognitive–behavioral groups; psychoeducational groups; self-help groups; and combinations. The combination groups may have special areas of focus such as sexual abuse (increasingly commonly found among eating disordered patients), body image issues, or family relationships, where parents may be part of the group.

As stated previously group therapy is emerging as a favored treatment for patients with bulimia nervosa. Furthermore, there are many types of group therapy available for eating disordered patients. Deciding which type of group to recommend for patients is difficult because many different forms are touted to be effective. Time-limited psychoeducational groups and cognitive–behavioral groups have received wide acclaim for results in decreasing bulimic symptoms, while open-ended psychodynamically oriented groups are reported to repair the gaps in ego structure necessary for long lasting recovery (Browning, 1985; Barth & Wurman, 1986). This chapter will present different types of group therapy and suggest a specific sequence that may benefit some patients and increase the likelihood for successful outcomes.

Although the literature is replete with reports of success using time-limited cognitive–behavioral groups and psychoeducational groups, the lack of long-term follow-up studies makes it difficult to determine how lasting the reported decreases in symptomatology will be. Although bulimic symptoms such as binge eating and purging are easy to measure, and weight gain or loss in the anorectic can be a concrete sign of progress or relapse, it is far more difficult to measure the extent to which the underlying psychopathology has been diagnosed and treated. The chronic nature of anorexia and bulimia nervosa, with frequent relapses during periods of stress, suggest that underlying gaps in ego structure must be addressed and corrected before complete healing can occur.

Group therapy provides eating disordered patients with a safe environment to disclose and discuss their illness — usually a well-guarded secret shrouded in shame, guilt, and self-hatred. The isolation that develops around this disorder can be profound: Bulimic patients often have symptoms for 5–8 years before presenting for help (Herzog, 1988). A psychodynamic group helps patients explore their inner experiences and their interpersonal relationships by functioning as a paradigm for relationships in the outside world. Group therapy also helps patients examine the potential relationship between family dynamics and their eating disorders. As the group process develops, patients learn to appreciate the unique role that their eating symptoms served for themselves as individuals as well as for their families (Brotman, Alonso, & Herzog, 1986). Focusing on eating symptoms is not the task of a psychodynamic group. The connections made between past life experiences, current interpersonal relationships, and dynamics between members and group leaders provide the understanding required to promote healing.

If psychodynamically oriented group psychotherapy is in fact a powerful and useful tool in the recovery from eating disorders, why is relatively little written on the subject, especially in comparison to time-limited treatments? There are many practical considerations that make psychodynamic groups more difficult to study and hence to write about. They are often of long duration and do not lend themselves to quick research studies. Because it is the process that promotes the cure, it is difficult to base progress on a measurable factor such as exposure to education or the behavioral techniques that are used in time-limited treatments. Open-ended groups may last for years, during which individual therapy, pharmacotherapy, behavioral and cognitive therapy may have all played a part, making it difficult to conclude that psychodynamic group therapy alone made a difference. It is unrealistic to deprive a patient suffering from an eating disorder other treatments to perform the pure kind of research that would be necessary to study the effects of open-ended group therapy. This type of control is much more feasible in a short, time-limited model.

There may be another important factor involved in the relative paucity of information available on open-ended psychodynamic group therapy for eating disordered patients. Our own observations in the Eating Disorders Unit as well as The Center For Group Psychotherapy at the Massachusetts General Hospital show that the act of forming an open-ended psychodynamic group for eating disordered patients is extremely difficult. This difficulty was corroborated by participants of a workshop on eating disorder groups at the 1990 meeting of the American Group Psychotherapy Association. The authors below have expressed similar findings in their reports on psychodynamic group psychotherapy.

Browning (1985) warns against the "unwarranted optimism" that is generated in therapists by bulimic patients being evaluated for group therapy. Their eagerness to please authority figures—cultivated for years by the development of a false self—makes these patients very skillful at telling you what you want to hear. Typically, bulimic patients will accept referrals to groups with great enthusiasm, presenting themselves as compliant candidates for group therapy. However, it is not uncommon for them to come for two sessions and then drop out, or to make endless excuses for absences without stating that they have no intention to continue. Despite well-articulated group contracts about the importance of group continuity, announcements, and group discussions about plans to leave, these patients tend to drop out prematurely for unclear reasons. Are bulimic patients by nature deceptive and unable to keep commitments? More likely it is their profound sense of "badness" and a sense of shame at being unable or unprepared to take a step that makes them unable to remain in treatment. These patients would rather disappear than tell us that they think the recommendation is wrong for them.

Another reason why psychodynamic groups are difficult is their lack of focus on eating and weight issues. Although there may be resentment that group leaders are withholding magic answers, these patients have difficulty expressing disappointment or hostility toward a leader. It is easier to leave than to express those feelings. It is also difficult to come to terms with the feelings of dependence on a group, since such feelings are often associated with enmeshed entanglements from conflicted family relationships. Anorectic patients generally have great difficulty even agreeing to join a group because of their tendency to deny their illness and shun close interpersonal relationships.

Barth and Wurman (1986) observed that long-term psychodynamic group psychotherapy was extremely helpful for bulimic women, even for those who had the disorder for many years and for whom other forms of treatment had been unhelpful. They also observed that patients were difficult to engage and that they often left precipitously. They instituted a short-term (10–12 week) group as a prerequisite to open-ended group therapy. The members of the open-ended group were graduates from the short-term group who elected to continue in group treatment. The authors observed that feeling a part of the group increased self-esteem. They hypothesized that members utilize a group to complete a structural gap in their psychological makeup. In addition to building support and external structure, the psychodynamic group was important in building internal structures such as self-soothing, self-regulation, and modulations of affects. The authors imply that a preliminary time-limited group was necessary in order to identify those patients who were able to use an open-ended psychodynamic model.

An integrated group treatment approach was taken by Roy-Byrne, Lee-Benner, and Yager (1984). They combined components of cognitive–behavioral techniques with psychodynamic psychotherapy in a year-long therapy group. The group initially was modeled on an "insight–support framework," but behavioral techniques were added later in response to requests made by the group. These authors also describe months of difficulty forming the group, with eight members dropping out before a core of 11 members was finally formed. They report that for several members the increasing use of behavioral techniques was confusing, while others demanded more behavioral prescriptions from the leaders. This combination of dynamic and behavioral approaches created anger and hostility in members who wanted to use insight and support as a means to improvement. Those members refused a request to keep food diaries, which they felt was a demeaning requirement. Some members balked at strict behavioral approaches; others, however, wanted structure around which they could organize themselves.

The authors cited above corroborate our experience that open-ended psychodynamically oriented groups for eating disordered patients are difficult to form, but also that this type of treatment is extremely helpful to those patients who are ready for it or prepared for it. In our experience, it is not difficult to form a time-limited group. Reports of time-limited groups in the literature also show that forming such groups is not difficult (Connors, Johnson, & Stuckey, 1984; Kirkley, Schneidler, Agras, & Bachman, 1985; Lacey, 1983; Schneidider & Agras, 1987; Stevens & Salisbury, 1984; Wolchik, Weiss, & Katzman, 1986). In our own experience at Massachusetts General Hospital we have seen far fewer drop outs in time-limited groups, whereas it takes 9 months to a year to form a stable core of members in an open-ended group. Based on this observation, group entry as a step-wise process was conceptualized by making time-limited treatment the first step. The time-limited treatment can be used as a preparation, a screening device, an educational tool, and a demystification for open-ended dynamic group therapy.

Indeed it is worthwhile speculating whether there are two separate populations of patients presenting with eating disorders: one group that is symptom-focused, wanting a quick cure, and another that appreciates that there are underlying psychological complexities for which eating symptoms provide temporary relief. Certainly not all patients who participate in time-limited treatment are ready for or interested in open-ended treatment at the end of the short-term group. It is also possibile is that we see patients at different stages in their illness. A patient who is convinced that all of her problems would be solved if she stopped binge eating and purging at one stage in her illness may be the same patient who is ready to explore the meaning of her symptoms some years later. Whatever the mechanism that makes some patients able to make use of psychodynamic group treatment, it is important to identify the "readiness" of such individuals before recommending open-ended treatment. In light of the difficulties mentioned above in assessing these all too eager-to-please patients for group therapy, some specific considerations may help.

Patients tend to opt for the least threatening, least commitment-demanding treatment when presented with recommendations for therapy. The high acceptance rate for short-term treatments may reflect several factors: a clear beginning and end (i.e., a clear way out); allowance for the fantasy that there is a quick cure; a sense that less commitment is less risky; lower cost. In addition, a time-limited program makes successful completion appear more likely to the patient. In the author's experience of leading eight different time-limited groups, patients are unanimously disappointed that the group is ending so soon and express the wish that the group would continue. About halfway through the highly structured psychoeducational groups most members begin to feel comfortable enough to express feelings, to share personal experiences, and to sense that their eating symptoms have a great deal to do with their inner life. It appears that the initial nonthreatening nature of the time-limited group enables members to bond around food issues and develop enough group safety to allow deeper aspects of themselves to emerge.

It is not unusual for group members to request referrals to ongoing psychodynamic groups at the end of a time-limited group. This is not true for all patients, however. Some feel that they have been helped by the education they have received and the behavioral and cognitive techniques that they have learned. One anorectic patient stated that learning that laxative use did not decrease caloric intake was the most useful part of group. Her laxative use ceased completely as a result of this knowledge. She did not feel that group process was helpful to her. Two examples of patients who decided to continue in an open-ended group while in a psychoeducational group are Carol and Jane. Carol grew up in a large family with two handicapped siblings. Her role was to be mother's helper and minimizing her own needs was her unspoken script. While in the time-limited group, she became aware of her competitive feelings for the group leaders' attention. She realized that she wanted to be special and her way to achieve this was to become the group member that needed the least. When she was able to recognize and verbalize these feelings, she realized that she had underlying feelings of anger and resentment toward the "less able" members of the group, who reminded her of her handicapped siblings. She wished to explore and understand these feelings and elected to join an open-ended psychodynamic group when the time-limited group ended. She has been able to use the open-ended format very successfully. Jane, a 48-year-old woman had been secretly bulimic for 30 years and no one knew her secret until she joined a time-limited group for bulimics. She thought her bulimia was all about appearance and weight. During the group she heard others talk about their feelings of inadequacy. She related her dread of social engagements because of her fear of sounding stupid if she joined a conversation. She realized that during her childhood no one in her family ever talked about their feelings. Her family played lots of games together, and though she was quite skilled at various board games, she had no confidence when it came to talking. In the psychoeducational group she discovered how sad and isolated she had felt as a chubby girl and adolescent; an experience that she came to mourn. She decided to join an open-ended group to discover more about the feelings she had never before articulated. She revealed to the group she would never have joined if she had known that the group would talk about feelings. She came to focus on food and weight issues, and it was a surprise when she discovered the deep-seated feelings that surfaced in the open-ended group format.

Most time-limited groups for eating disordered patients are modeled after cognitive–behavioral or psychoeducational treatments. One could argue that not only is the time-limited nature of the group a more appealing entrance into therapy, but that the highly structured sessions with planned agendas offer an organizing focus that reduces the psychological chaos that accompanies eating disorders. Didactic information about the nature of eating disorders, their etiology, medical consequences, nutritional concerns, and the psychological and cultural aspects of the disorders are all valuable information for patients to receive. Bulimia and anorexia nervosa can result in severe medical consequences and even death. Behavioral strategies such as goal setting, meal planning, food diaries, and planning activities that are incompatible with binge eating are all valuable tools that may give the patient a greater sense of control. Certainly there are some patients who are so deeply entrenched in their symptoms that insight into the underlying problems is impossible before the behaviors are brought into some degree of control. Thus, time-limited groups may be an entrance into treatment for the new patient, an adjunct to individual therapy or an introduction to open-ended group therapy. Rather than regarding the different types of group treatments as mutually exclusive or incompatible, the author suggests using time-limited treatment as a preliminary treatment before recommending open-ended group therapy. In so doing the intensive experience of psychodynamic group therapy becomes an even more powerful tool in the treatment of this very challenging and multifaceted disorder.

REFERENCES

American Psychiatric Association. (1987). *Diagnostic and statistical manual of mental disorders* (3rd ed., rev.). Washington, DC: Author.

Barth, D., & Wurman, V. (1986). Group therapy with bulimic women: A self-psychological approach. *International Journal of Eating Disorders*, 5(4), 735–745.

Boskind-Lodahl, M., & White, W. C. (1979). Cinderella's step-sisters: A feminist perspective on anorexia nervosa and bulimia. *Signs: Journal Womens Culture*, 2, 342–355.

Brotman, A. W., Alonso, A., & Herzog, D. B. (1986). Group therapy for bulimia: Clinical experience and practical recommendations. *Group*, *9*(1), 15–23.

Browning, W. N. (1985). Long-term dynamic group therapy with bulimic patients: A clinical discussion. In Emmett (Ed), *Theory and treatment of anorexia nervosa and bulimia: A biomedical, sociocultural and psychological perspective* (pp. 141–153). New York: Brunner/Mazel.

Bruch, H. (1973). *Eating disorders: Obesity, anorexia nervosa and the person within*. New York: Basic Books.

Brumberg, J. J. (1988). *Fasting girls*. Cambridge, MA: Harvard University Press.

Connors, M. E., Johnson, C. L., & Stuckey, M. K. (1984). Treatment of bulimia with brief psychoeducational group therapy. *American Journal of Psychiatry*, *141*, 1512–1516.

Doerr, P., Fichter, M., Pirke, K. M., & Lund, R. (1980). Relationship between weight gain and hypothalamic pituitary adrenal function in patients with anorexia nervosa. *Journal of Steroid Biochemistry*, *13*, 529–537.

Eckbert, E. D. (1985). Characteristics of anorexia nervosa. In J. E. Mitchell (Ed), *Anorexia nervosa and bulimia: Diagnosis and treatment* (pp. 3–28). Minneapolis: University of Minnesota Press.

Garfinkel, P. E., & Garner, D. M. (1982). *Anorexia nervosa: A multidimentional perspective*. New York: Brunner/Mazel.

Gold, P. W., Kaye, W., Robertson, G. L., & Ebert, M. (1983). Abnormalities in plasma and cerebro-spinal fluid argenine vasopressin in patients with anorexia nervosa. *New England Journal of Medicine*, *308*, 1117–1123.

Halmi, K. A., Falk, J. R., & Schwartz, E. (1981). Binge eating and vomiting: A survey of a college population. *Psychological Medicine*, *11*, 697–700.

Herzog, D. B. (1988). Eating disorders. In Nicholi (Ed), *Harvard guide to modern psychiatry* (pp. 4344–445). Cambridge, MA: Harvard University Press.

Johnson, C., & Connors, M. E. (1987). *The etiology and treatment of bulimia nervosa: A biopsychosocial perspective*. New York: Basic Books.

Jones, D. L., Fox, M. M., Babigian, H. M., & Hutton, H. E. (1980). Epidemiology of anorexia nervosa in Monroe County, New York: 1960–1979. *Psychosomatic Medicine*, *42*, 551–558.

Kaye, W. H., Ebert, M. H., Gwirtsman, H. E., & Weiss, S. R. (1984). Differences in brain serotonergic metabolism between nonbulimic and bulimic patients with anorexia nervosa. *American Journal of Psychiatry*, *141*, 1598–1601.

Kirkley, B. G., Schneider, J. A., Agras, S. W., & Bachman, J. A. (1985). Comparison of two group treatments for bulimia. *Journal of Consulting and Clinical Psychology*, *53*(1), 43–48.

Lacey, J.H. (1983). Bulimia nervosa, binge eating and psychogenic vomiting: A controlled treatment study and long term outcome. *British Medical Journal*, *286*, 1609–1613.

Minuchin, S., Rosman, B. L., & Baker, L. (1978). *Psychosomatic families: Anorexia nervosa in context*. Cambridge, MA: Harvard University Press.

Morton, R. (1985). Phthisiologica: Or a treatise of consumptions. In A. E. Anderson (Eds.), *Practical comprehensive treatment of anorexia nervosa and bulimia.* Baltimore: The Johns Hopkins University Press. (Original work published 1694 in London by S. Smith and B. Walford)

Pope, H. G., Hudson, J. L., & Yurgelun-Todd, D. (1984). Anorexia nervosa and bulimia among 300 women shoppers. *American Journal of Psychiatry,* *141,* 292–294.

Pyle, R. L., Mitchell, J., Hatsukami, D., & Goff, F. (1984). The interruption of bulimic behaviors. *Psychiatric Clinics of North America,* *7*(20), 275–286.

Roy-Byrne, P., Lee-Benner, K., & Yager, J. (1984). Group therapy for bulimia: A year's perspective. *International Journal of Eating Disorders, 3,* 97–116.

Russell, G.M. (1979). Bulimia nervosa: An ominous variant of anorexia nervosa. *Psychological Medicine, 9,* 429–448.

Schneider, J.A., & Agras, S.W. (1987). A cognitive behavioral group treatment for bulimia. *British Journal of Psychiatry. 146,* 66–69.

Stevens, E. V., & Salisbury, J. D. (1984). Group therapy for bulimia adults. *American Journal of Orthopsychiatry, 54,* 156–161.

Strangler, R. S., & Printz, A. M. (1980). DSM-III: Psychiatric diagnosis in a university population. *American Journal of Psychiatry, 137,* 937–940.

Wolchik, S. A., Weiss, L., & Katzman, M. A. (1986). An empirically validated short-term psychoeducational group treatment program for bulimia. *International Journal of Eating Disorders, 5*(1), 21–34.

Psychopharmacology Today

MAURIZIO FAVA
MARY MCCARTHY

The field of psychopharmacology has changed dramatically over the past three decades. Since the introduction into clinical use of a huge number of safe and efficient chemical compounds with antidepressant, antimanic, antianxiety, and antipsychotic properties, great effort has been made to treat various psychiatric conditions with psychotropic drugs and to find new applications for the same compounds. Given the fairly high responsiveness to drug treatment of psychiatric disorders that are quite prevalent, such as anxiety and affective disorders (Myers et al., 1984), it is not surprising that psychotropic drugs account for a large proportion of all prescription drugs. Nor is it surprising that there has been a combined effort by industry and federal funding sources to develop strategies to explore and maximize the benefits of pharmacotherapy in psychiatry.

Even the psychiatric nosology of the DSM-III-R has taken into account the responses to pharmacological treatment in establishing diagnostic categories and their validity. The characteristic clusters of symptoms in the panic and major depressive disorders are now well known among clinicians because of their great responsivity to drug treatment. Due to the progressive broadening of the psychiatric pharmacopeia, psychiatrists have been encouraged to stay abreast of the pharmacological characteristics and the side-effect profiles of psychotropic drugs. Practitioners also must practice under the increasing threat of legal action if they do not know or anticipate potential problems with medications. This has led to a flourishing of review courses that often offer updated perspectives on the field of psychopharmacology. Participation in such courses often mitigate the stress of psychiatrists having to master an ever-widening body of knowledge about medications.

This chapter will examine some of the relevant aspects of practicing psychopharmacology in psychiatry today, after more than 3 decades characterized by exciting discoveries of either new molecules or new applications of older compounds. It will also discuss some of the unwanted effects such developments have had on the way psychopharmacology is practiced.

THE PATIENT

Has the profile of the patients who are treated with drugs for their psychiatric symptoms changed over time? It certainly has. In the early years of pharmacology in psychiatry there was a tendency toward prescribing medications only or mostly to severely ill patients. Mildly disturbed or neurotic patients were often thought not to need or benefit from drugs. However, this view has been drastically changed by a number of studies that demonstrate the efficacy of drug treatments in psychiatric conditions such as dysthymia and social phobia, which used to be treated only with psychotherapy.

Are drug-treated patients different from those who respond to psychotherapy? In general there are no true distinctions between these two groups for most diagnostic categories. The same depressed patient who markedly benefits from pharmacology can do well after a course of interpersonal, psychodynamic, or cognitive psychotherapy.

It does seem true, however, that many patients (e.g., those with major depressive disorders) who receive only psychotherapy could have been better served if medications had also been prescribed (Keller et al., 1982). Sometimes the setting where the patient is seen influences the treatment prescribed, so that patients who are self-referred to psychotherapy clinics may be less likely to receive medication than those self-referred to psychopharmacology clinics. On the other hand, patients who self-refer to a psychopharmacology clinic may not receive psychotherapy to supplement their medication even when such conjoint treatment might have been helpful. The reality is that only a minority of patients who could benefit from pharmacological treatment receive it in adequate dose and duration.

What is the degree of public acceptance of psychotropic drug treatments today? If we consider that the presence of certain stigmas can still be observed about psychiatric treatments in general, we should not be surprised by the resistance displayed by some patients toward taking medications for their psychological symptoms. First of all, taking a medication often involves an acknowledgment that "there may be something wrong with my mind or brain," which is exactly what certain patients fear the most. Second, the perception that being on medication is indicative of greater sickness than seeing a therapist may be anxiety-provoking for a patient. Third, for some patients, taking a medication feels like a loss of mastery, since they can take no "credit" for feeling better even if the medication works. Lastly, the fear of either physical or psychological dependency may function as a deterrent against the use of pharmacological approaches to psychiatric symptoms.

Other patients, however, demonstrate the opposite attitude. For some, taking a medication can be soothing, since our culture has long trusted in the ability of medication to heal. For others, taking a medication can represent an opportunity to gain more active control over incapacitating symptoms, or can be relieving since the problems can be conceptualized as physical rather than psychological. In rare instances individuals may demand and expect too much of medications, leading to unreasonable requests of the psychiatrist. In general, a fairly pragmatic approach is used by both patients and psychiatrists, with an open discussion of the treatment goals and time frames.

THE PHARMACOTHERAPY PROVIDER

There have been few changes over the years in who provides pharmacotherapy and where it is provided. Specialized mental health services have continued to represent only a fraction of the providers of pharmacotherapy, as the majority of patients with mental illness are actually treated by nonpsychiatric physicians (Regier et al., 1978). Primary care physicians often treat both anxiety and depressive disorders with drugs; however, only 50% of patients with depressive disorders and other psychiatric conditions are detected by general and family practitioners (Sharp & Morrell, 1989). Even when patients do receive drug treatment in the general health sector, they do not necessarily receive the best possible medication, as nonpsychiatrists may fail to recognize psychiatric co-morbid conditions that can contribute to treatment resistance.

In the past few years, some changes have occurred in the mental health field. Many drug treatment providers are now psychiatrists who have subspecialized in the field of psychopharmacology and who work in tertiary care facilities where patients are treated mainly with drugs.

Psychopharmacology clinics are often settings where research and clinical practice mix together, where psychiatrists do consultations with primary care and other physicians. In these clinics, psychopharmacologists also medicate patients who are treated in psychotherapy by other mental health specialists such as psychologists, social workers, and nurses. In some cases the patient is referred to the psychopharmacologist by another psychiatrist, since monitoring the clinical response to and discussing the side effects of medication may interfere with the psychotherapy and give the patient an opportunity to avoid dealing with painful or upsetting issues.

Another important source of treatment is represented by psychiatrists who practice both psychotherapy and pharmacotherapy. These are clinicians whose type of practice often depends on their patient population. For example, those who follow chronic psychotic patients are likely to use drug treatment more frequently than those who follow patients with character disorders. While some psychiatrists treat patients with either pharmacology or psychotherapy, depending on their diagnostic assessment, others use pharmacology as an intrinsic part of the overall treatment plan and combine it with psychotherapy. The distinction between these two approaches is arbitrary, since even in a medication clinic there may be important psychotherapeutic elements involved.

The combination of psychotherapy and pharmacotherapy is a commonly prescribed treatment for a number of psychiatric conditions, including major depressive disorder, bulimia nervosa, and panic disorder with agoraphobia. In the case of depression, a review by Conte et al. (1986) of the studies published in this field revealed that the combined active treatments (drugs plus psychotherapy) were appreciably more effective than the placebo condition but only slightly superior to psychotherapy alone, pharmacotherapy alone, or either of these combined with a placebo. These results do not support the popularity of a combined approach in depression. However, most of the studies cited used as outcome measures instruments that focus on target symptoms of depression and may not necessarily include other aspects of treatment response, such as improved quality of life or interpersonal relationships.

Finally, there has been a recent press among some psychologists and psychiatric nurses to gain the right to prescribe medications, a practice that would put into question the current assumption that whoever prescribes psychotropic medications has full knowledge of their potential side effects, the neurophysiology of mental disorders, and the physical illnesses that mimic psychiatric disorders.

MONITORING THE CLINICAL RESPONSE

In theory, close monitoring of patients in the early phases of treatment should be the standard of practice. The potential emergence of serious side effects from the prescribed medications requires a careful screening of patients' complaints, management of bothersome side effects, and reassurance about the overall safety of such an approach. Patients who cannot afford treatment without third-party assistance may pressure the clinician to decrease the frequency and length of the visits, even when this may be counterproductive for the patient in the long run. Phone calls often become the substitute for office visits, though there is a marked decrease in accuracy of clinical judgment when the patient is not actually seen. This is particularly true when the psychiatrist does not have a great deal of experience with the prescribed drug or with the patient.

Before beginning the pharmacologic treatment of any patient, the psychiatrist should obtain a full history and complete a thorough assessment of mental status, suicide risk (most drugs used in psychiatry are lethal in overdose), and possible co-morbidity. Once a diagnosis is made of one or more psychiatric disorders for which there is evidence that drug treatment can be useful, the clinician must then decide which medication to prescribe. At this point he or she should carefully discuss with the patient the risks, benefits, and potential side effects of the medication. Although probably not the standard of care, it is helpful to obtain a complete physical examination and to assess cardiac and metabolic state through laboratory tests prior to starting drug treatment. However, when the decision to treat a patient with drugs occurs in the context of a psychotherapy relationship, it is not advisable for the clinician to perform the physical examination. Rather it should be delegated to a colleague. The presence of certain physical conditions may be a contraindication to the use of some medications (e.g., tricyclics in patients with severe heart conduction disturbances), while other medications should be used cautiously in patients with certain psychiatric histories (e.g., benzodiazepines in patients with a history of alcohol or drug abuse) (Fava & Borofsky, 1991).

The importance of closely monitoring clinical response has been emphasized over the past few years. This need is only enhanced because of the legal liabilities that psychopharmacologists bear. Psychiatrists who underestimate the seriousness of somatic complaints in patients who go on to develop serious side effects or who fail to make appropriate changes in drug treatment when confronted with clinical deterioration face potential litigation.

COMPLIANCE AND ADHERENCE

The term "compliance" usually refers to the extent to which patients obey and follow the instructions and prescriptions of the psychiatrist in terms of taking their medication. It has been argued that such a term connotes a passive role for the patient, with the term "adherence" proposed as a substitute to imply a more active and collaborative involvement on the part of the patient (Eisenthal et al., 1979). Treatment adherence includes starting and continuing treatment, keeping follow-up appointments, avoiding health risk behaviors (e.g., drinking alcoholic beverages), and maintaining a correct consumption of the prescribed medication. Noncompliance or nonadherence represent the opposite concepts.

The incidence of treatment nonadherence is likely to vary with diagnostic groups: In particular, 24%–63% of schizophrenic outpatients take less than the prescribed dosage of antipsychotic medication (Van Putten, 1974) and 9%–57% of bipolar patients terminate lithium carbonate medication at some point against medical advice (Cochran, 1986). As Meichenbaum and Turk (1987) point out, there are different forms of treatment nonadherence involving drug errors, ranging from failure to fill the prescription, filling the prescription but failing to take the medications, not following the frequency or dose instructions, to taking medications that were not prescribed.

The behavioral measure of adherence represented by pill count is used only in drug studies, whereas patient self-report and biochemical measurements of drug blood levels are commonly used to monitor adherence in psychiatry. Some of the most important factors affecting nonadherence in psychopharmacology are bothersome side effects, lack of reassurance by the physician about the patient's anxieties and about the effects of treatment, lack of continuity of care, and a poor quality of doctor–patient relationship. Coleman (1985) has suggested that there are four factors that may enhance compliance with treatment regimens: compassion, communication, activating patient self-motivation, and shared responsibility with the patient. In psychopharmacology it is often useful to provide patients with a simplified explanatory model of their illness: Spending extra time to explain why a certain drug has been chosen to treat their symptoms helps patients feel that there is a clear rationale for pharmacological intervention.

One of the decisions regarding drug treatment that psychiatrists have to make is whether it is best to prescribe only one drug. While prescribing only one medication may increase compliance and facilitate the monitoring of clinical response in some patients, the presence of co-morbid conditions in other patients can complicate the course of treatment. The latter patients can benefit most from a combination of drug treatments.

Over the past decade there has been an increased awareness among psychopharmacologists that the relationship between the provider and the patient is a key factor in obtaining treatment adherence. Fortunately, it is increasingly rare to find a physician displaying a "doctor doing to a patient" mentality. Modern psychopharmacologists favor a more open and collaborative approach with patients.

EFFECTS OF DRUG STUDIES ON CLINICAL PRACTICE

Studies on the use of drug therapy in psychiatric conditions, particularly those published in well-known journals, have had an increased impact on how psychiatrists practice over the past few years. The broad documentation of treatment efficacy, accompanied by fewer side effects and increased safety in case of overdose, of an antidepressant called fluoxetine (Prozac) has made this drug a best seller. At this writing almost four million people have been exposed to fluoxetine (Prozac). However, when a report on six patients who became preoccupied with suicide while taking fluoxetine (Prozac) appeared in a major psychiatric journal (Teicher et al., 1990), it caught the attention of the media and practitioners. Suddenly there was enormous concern about the potential for suicidality among users of this benign drug, even though very little clinical evidence specifically linked fluoxetine to suicide (Fava & Rosenbaum, 1991). Some patients who were safely responding to this antidepressant were asked to discontinue its use lest they become suicidal, and other patients who had heard of the report asked their doctors to prescribe another drug. In extreme cases, psychiatrists who judge that fluoxetine is the treatment of choice may decide to protect themselves from potential litigation by prescribing a different, and perhaps less effective, medication.

These are clear examples of how the perception that one drug is uniquely linked with a particular risk or side effect, even when based on uncontrolled reports, coupled with concern about legal liability, has profoundly affected the practice of pharmacotherapy.

On the other hand, well-controlled, rigorous studies supporting certain types of pharmacologic approaches to psychiatric patients may be totally ignored by some clinicians. This phenomenon is often justified on the basis that the results of these studies do not always generalize to all groups of patients with a particular diagnosis; that these studies may assess outcome using scales focusing on neurovegetative symptoms rather than on quality of life or relationships; or that they do not take into account the issue of co-morbidity. In spite of the fact that all of the above criticisms may indeed apply to most drug studies, psychiatrists can still derive from them useful information that may help them choose the appropriate treatment for their patients. A clear example of this is that, in spite of the evidence that lack of response in depressed patients may simply be due to insufficient dosing (Simpson et al., 1976), only a minority of patients with major depression receive adequate doses of antidepressants for what is considered an adequate duration (McCombs et al., 1990).

CONCLUSION

The practice of pharmacotherapy has become increasingly complex. In a field that is continuously challenging its limits, where either new drugs or new clinical applications of old drugs continue to emerge, psychiatrists have to keep up with this tremendous flow of new ideas and information. Clinicians also have to struggle daily with medicolegal issues or third-party payment policies that attempt to modify their practices. They must also attempt to enhance adherence among their patients, taking into account the importance of the practitioner–patient relationship and aspects of treatment that may reduce adherence.

In this ever-changing field, psychiatrists must make therapeutic judgments that are independent of media or religious campaigns against particular drugs (e.g., psychostimulants in attention deficit disorder) or of pharmaceutical industries' marketing strategies. They must also consider "the customer's request," the expectations and beliefs of the patients in order to build an alliance that permits stable and productive cooperation between doctors and patients.

Finally, it would be very helpful if research were to have a greater impact on the practice of pharmacotherapy. In order to accomplish this there is a need for more studies that examine issues which are both relevant to clinicians and deal with those populations presenting elements of both Axis I and II disorders—problems closer to what most clinicians face in their everyday practices. Research also needs to develop algorithm protocols for patients who do not respond to standard treatments and newer pharmacologic strategies for patients whose treatment adherence has been poor because of disabling side effects.

REFERENCES

Cochran, S. D. (1986). Compliance with lithium regimens in outpatient treatment of bipolar affective disorders. *Journal of Compliance in Health Care*, *1*, 153–170.

Coleman, V. R. (1985). Physician behavior and compliance. *Journal of Hypertension*, *3*, 67–71.

Conte, H. R., Plutchik, R., Wild, K. V., & Karasu, T. B. (1986). Combined psychotherapy and pharmacotherapy for depression. *Archives of General Psychiatry*, *43*, 471–479.

Eisenthal, S., Emaery, R., Lazare, A., & Udin, H. (1979). Adherence and the negotiated approach to parenthood. *Archives of General Psychiatry*, *36*, 393–398.

Fava, M, & Borofsky, G. F. (1991). Sexual disinhibition during treatment with a benzodiazepine: A case report. *International Journal of Psychiatry in Medicine*, *21*, 99–104.

Fava, M, & Rosenbaum, J. F. (1991). Suicidality and fluoxetine: Is there a relationship? *Journal of Clinical Psychiatry*, *52*, 108–111.

Keller, M. B., Klerman, G. L., Lavori, P. W., Fawcett, J. A., Coryell, W., & Endicott, J. (1982). Treatment received by depressed patients. *Journal of the American Medical Association*, *248*, 1848–1855.

Meichenbaum, D., & Turk, D. C. (1987). *Facilitating treatment adherence*. New York: Plenum Press.

McCombs, J. S., Nichol, M. B., Stimmel, G. L., Sclar, D. A., Beasley, Jr., C. M., & Gross, L. S. (1990). The cost of antidepressant drug therapy failure: A study of antidepressant use patterns in a medicaid population. *Journal of Clinical Psychiatry*, *51* (Suppl. 6), 60–69.

Myers, J. K., Weissman, M. M., Tischler, G. L., Holzer, C. E., Leaf, P. J., Orvaschel, H., Anthony, J. C., Boyd, J. H., Burke, J. D., Kramer, M., & Stolzman, R. (1984). Six-month prevalence of psychiatric disorders in three communities. *Archives of General Psychiatry*, *41*, 959–967.

Regier, D. A., Goldberg, I. D., & Taube, C. A. (1978). The de facto US mental health services system. *Archives of General Psychiatry*, *35*, 685–693.

Sharp, D, & Morrell, D. (1989). The psychiatry of general practice. In P. Williams, G. Wilkinson, & K. Rawnsley (Eds.), *The scope of epidemiological psychiatry: Essays in honour of Michael Sheperd*. London: Routledge & Kegan Paul.

Simpson, G. M., Lee, J. H., Cuculic, Z., & Kellner, R. (1976). Two dosages of imipramine in hospitalized endogenous and neurotic depressives. *Archives of General Psychiatry*, *33*, 1093–1102.

Teicher, M. H., Glod, C., & Cole, J. O. (1990). Emergence of intense suicidal preoccupation during fluoxetine treatment. *American Journal of Psychiatry*, *147*, 207–210.

Van Putten, I. (1974). Why do schizophrenic patients refuse to take their drugs? *Archives of General Psychiatry*, *31*, 67–72.

V

THE PRACTICE
OF PSYCHOTHERAPY

Supervising Psychotherapy in the 1990s

ANNE ALONSO
ELIZABETH L. SHAPIRO

It has been almost 100 years since Freud first conceived of his "scientific experiment" in psychoanalysis. He did so both in the context of the German upper-class academic tradition at the turn of the 20th century, and the basic cultural assumptions that were syntonic with that place and time. These included, among others, an assumption of rigorous intellectual discipline informed by a strong immersion in art and music. He assumed an apprenticeship model of training as was common at that time, and still remains to some extent true for the contemporary European academic tradition.

Since that time, the field of psychotherapy has evolved in multiple dimensions. As is always true in the history of scientific thought, some of the changes in theory are due to more sophistication in the thinkers and practitioners, and some are responses to the realities and pressures of the times. In the field of psychodynamic psychotherapy, the decade of the 1990s carries into it a great many changes relating to theory, technique, training settings, and values. As is always the case, clinicians and their teachers and supervisors tend to look to their own needs belatedly, and this is especially true in the study of psychotherapy supervision. This chapter addresses some of these changes in the clinical field as they impinge on the supervisory process, examines the opportunities and limitations that the current zeitgeist imposes on the supervisory dyad, and offers some suggestions for improving the field of psychotherapy supervision.

This chapter will consider this evolution of the supervisory profession from a number of perspectives. We will consider those factors that are general and constant about supervising; we will also explore some of the ways in which the whole field of psychotherapy has evolved, and the impact of these changes on the supervision of our trainees. These changes relate to the evolution of theory, the structures of our training institutions, the position of the judiciary vis-à-vis work with patients, among others.

Some of the common understandings of supervision remain unchanged. Supervision is still perceived as the cornerstone for the training of novice clinicians in the craft of psychotherapy. It is assumed, as it always has been, that the clinician learns in an apprenticeship with senior members of the profession who guide, teach, critique, and set standards of safe and prudent practice. It is further assumed, as it always has been, that the supervisor establishes an attitude about the work, an approach to patients and to colleagues that is consistent with professional values and ethics, and that the supervisor is in a position to mentor the trainee either with the administration, or in the professional world-at-large. It stands to reason, then, that the supervisor is usually older and considerably more experienced than the trainee and that she or he exerts administrative and influential power over the student. There are exceptions, especially in the case of trainees who are coming to the field of psychotherapy from other fields, or who have interrupted their careers for a number of years due to family or other obligations. These exceptions present certain challenges that will be addressed later in this chapter.

The corollary of the power vested in the supervisor is the obligation to protect the student, to guide him or her up the professional ladder, and to maintain some level of professional loyalty and availability in the future should such be needed, as in writing letters of recommendation, etc. In addition to the obligations to the supervisee, the supervisor has a responsibility to the profession, such as participating in the continuing quality control of its practitioners from whatever direction of influence or control that he or she is called upon to exert.

CHANGES RELATING TO THEORETICAL EVOLUTION

If we date the origins of psychotherapy to Freud, we can then assume that the supervisory custom was consistent with the classical model of theory and treatment; supervision in that tradition was and remains a private dyadic relationship in which the supervisor and trainee establish a commitment to work over an extended period of time (often 1 year, but perhaps longer) to discuss the dyadic work of the student with the patient in long-term individual therapy or analysis. With the expansion of classical theory into object relations theory, ego psychological theory, and self psychology, the tradition of dyadic treatment and supervision remained foremost. Out of this tradition evolved the concept of parallel process in supervision, a concept that remains very important to clinical supervision at present. First described by Eckstein and Wallerstein (1963), parallel process has its origins in Klein's (1932/1959) theory of projective identification—a phenomenon by which the young therapist unconsciously merges with some of the patient's conflicts that are also unresolved for him or her. The therapist then brings both to the supervisor for healing and resolution. This process will be described in more detail later.

However, the development of newer interventions such as play therapy with small children, as originated by Anna Freud and Melanie Klein, brought other major players into the therapeutic field. It became necessary to work with the parents of the children, and the concurrent work with child and parents needed to be supervised. Also, since observation of little children was the primary method of intervention, films were made to record these children and these records of the work entered the supervisory arena. The "sacred dyad" was now subjected to modifications that included work with colleagues who were engaged in the same case, or learning from films in a group.

Still more drastic changes were to alter the face of supervision over the next decades. These shifts, with the movement from the classical intrapsychic to the interpersonal arena, and now to the systemic arena, signaled the origins of group theory and psychotherapy (Bion, 1959) and family theory and therapy (Bowen, 1971). Consequently, the supervisor, who is inevitably part of the system, began to move from an invisible role to one more central to the clinical field, and we began to see the phenomenon of a supervisor–student co-therapy team or even the observation of the live clinical work by a supervisor behind a one-way screen.

One of the most dramatic changes in modern supervision is a hugely expanded range of clinical options for treating mental illness. In addition to the original psychoanalytic method that relied on verbal dialogue over an extended period of months and years, short-term treatments, in-patient care, psychopharmacology, group treatment, family therapy, hypnotherapy, to name just a few, can dazzle and confuse the novice clinician and his or her supervisor as well. A new eclecticism has emerged, with multiple consequences. It is very useful to find treatments that offer new hope for previously intractable conditions and that stimulate intellectual dialogue and growth among a range of practitioners and theoreticians. However, eclecticism can become shaky terrain for the new clinician. It is one thing to make a shift in treatment modalities from an informed and experienced position. It may be quite another problem sorting out eclecticism from anxiety and countertransference resistance, especially at the beginning of a clinical career. To do this, the novice therapist must learn to internally integrate diversity. Until then, this tension will have an impact on the supervision of psychotherapy. Most training systems offer the novice a range of supervisors with varied theoretical and technical expertise. The trainee is then exposed to a profusion of theories and perspectives. At best, this confusion is creative and growth-producing, but it can also generate a certain cynicism and despair in which the novice falls back on an anti-theoretical pragmatism, or "splits" supervisors into good and bad polarities in order to relieve the tension of the ambiguity.

All changes, including these, bring some advantages and also some compromises into the supervisory field. Theoretical integrity is maintained by making clear that working more publicly and in collaboration with important others is valued not only for our patients but also for our training models. We probably manage to expose some of the more extreme vulnerabilities of the trainee in a way that allows us to intervene sooner and better. However, supervision may have lost its emphasis on the clinical development of the trainee by engaging the supervisor too immediately with the patient. Potentially, the student could be expected to become a "sorcerer's apprentice," technically emulating the mentor but without necessarily having to grapple with his or her internal conflicts and take the necessary risks of error that are integral to sophisticated professional learning.

LEGAL AND ETHICAL CONSIDERATIONS

The whole question of professional learning by "trial and error" raises vexing problems for all parties in the psychotherapeutic quadrangle — the patient, the novice clinician, the supervisor, and the administrators of the training program. But some major shifts have occurred here as well.

Psychoanalysis, in its inception, existed outside the established clinical settings, and the teaching and supervision took place in the dyadic privacy of the supervisor's consultation room. It was also assumed that each clinician was immersed in his or her own treatment that paralleled the treatment being offered his or her patient. Of course, legal and ethical liabilities were upheld in an unspoken "gentleman's agreement" in the profession, outside the province of the courts. In the late 1930s and early 1940s, many psychoanalysts emigrated to the U.S. and joined the medical establishments at that time, where psychotherapy was subject both to the rules governing medicine and to the consequences of malpractice. Now the supervisor served as a gatekeeper and a warrantor of quality, as well as an ombudsman for both the administration and the trainee. He or she was now duty bound to report to the administration about the trainee's progress, or lack of it, and straddled the sometimes uneasy path of dual loyalties. Still later, the administrative responsibility of observing governmental regulations entered the supervisory relationship. Legislation was introduced concerning patient's rights, duties to warn, confidentiality, etc. Both the clinician and supervisor now work within the mandates of the judiciary, and though these mandates are often contradictory both clinician and supervisor are potentially actionable in the case of a lawsuit ensuing from any violation of these mandates. The supervisor must now bear much of the anxiety of the conflict that arises between helping the student develop and use the self as an instrument, on the one hand, and the temptation to subtly control the treatment of the case. Of course, creativity flourishes at the intersect of these competing forces, but it is undeniable that the supervisory role is more complex and challenging than ever.

IDEAL SCENARIO

The ideal supervisory scenario is a successful synthesis of the needs and goals of the administration, trainee, and supervisor. In fact, the ideal scenario, or a close enough approximation, cannot exist without the cooperation and support of these three.

Supervisor as Teacher

Ideally, the supervisor operates within a theoretical model compatible with the supervisee — or exposes the supervisee to a new and intriguing model. Exposure to a new model or even to a more advanced technique within the same model demands an openness on the part of the student. No student likes to feel wholly inadequate and thus in the ideal scenario is encouraged to bring to the new situation skills and experiences that will facilitate learning. Sufficient respect and trust on the part of the supervisor enables the supervisee to withstand the narcissistic injury inherent in the regressive nature of deep learning.

The ideal supervisor is able to highlight the trainee's strengths and weaknesses in a balanced and empathic manner. This allows the two as a team to set forth and adapt learning goals for the duration of the relationship. Just as there is an ideal level of anxiety at which a therapist holds a patient, there is also an ideal level of anxiety a specific trainee can tolerate in the service of his or her professional growth and training. The distance cannot be too great between what the supervisee knows and what he or she is taught or he or she will not be able to make use of the information.

Supervisor as Role Model

The student looks to the supervisor not just as someone who teaches psychotherapy but as someone who practices psychotherapy. The student is anxious to have a supervisor who represents what he or she would like to become further down the road of his or her career. Thus, in addition to technical skills, that the supervisor brings to the supervisory relationship an ethical stance and a perspective on work, especially within the context of the rest of one's life. Thus, for instance, the enjoyment the supervisor actually receives from the work and the seriousness and openness with which he or she seeks continued learning throughout life complements the imparting of an especially accurate transference interpretation the supervisor may suggest offering to the patient. Oftentimes the former is not directly addressed in the supervisory hour, but it is nonetheless communicated in the supervisor's approach to the supervisee and the supervision, and constitutes a critical component of the ideal scenario.

Sometimes career development *is* specifically addressed in the supervisory hour, depending on the supervisee's particular developmental stage. For example, the supervision may take place in the second year of training when a psychiatric resident must decide which chief residency—psychopharmacology, psychotherapy, consultation-liaison—he or she will pursue for the following year. It is often the supervisor's job to enable the trainee to cope with the feelings of helplessness that may result in his or her making premature decisions to enter another subspecialty to feel more competent more quickly. The ideal supervisor models a capacity to tolerate the helplessness without denying a feeling of being overwhelmed by it, thereby enabling the novice therapist to use the helplessness as useful data to inform the treatment of a patient. Additionally, the supervisor's ability to find rewards as a psychotherapist, including in the possible adjuncts to direct work with patients — supervision notwithstanding — helps to highlight the many ways that the difficulties of this profession are offset. Sharing with a supervisor the joy that a patient has reached a more mature level of intimacy, or that a supervisee has had an "A-ha" experience are all important in supporting that trainee's professional development.

The Administration

The trickle-down effect is not unknown to the outpatient clinical setting. It is never a surprise when an agency or department that is not operating smoothly on an administrative level also does not satisfy the needs of the supervisor or the trainee. The supervisor needs the practice of supervision to be respected and promoted by the administration. Oftentimes the financial rewards of supervision are small or nil, so the value of supervision needs to be both overtly and implicitly communicated to all within the department. The supervisor also needs the support and overarching perspective of an administrator directly responsible for training. This person would ideally match trainees and supervisors, negotiate an impasse between trainee and supervisor, and monitor the overall training needs of the supervisee and the evaluation of his or her work. The trainee feels constantly judged by an excessively lax evaluation procedure that doesn't allow for learning to be assessed and problems in learning to be addressed.

The trainee needs the administration to provide patient availability in order to put what is learned to use. A sufficient number of patients are needed, as well as patients that span the diagnostic spectrum and provide demographic variability. Variety in supervision is also required so that trainees are exposed to supervisors who practice different forms of psychotherapy and whose supervisory styles also differ. The ideal administration must place importance on the value of psychotherapy vis-à-vis the other subspecialties so that the participants in the supervisory hour are not demoralized before they begin.

The Ideal Trainee

The ideal trainee is eager and open to the challenges of the supervisory relationship. He or she treats the supervisory hour as a gift and not as an obligation to be met in order to satisfy the requirements of a training program, recognizing that supervision of one's clinical work is at the heart of all professional training. The ideal trainee keeps resistances to learning, including unpreparedness, to a minimum. When resistances do occur, as are inevitable in any anxiety-provoking situation, the trainee has the requisite awareness and openness to working through the resistances—albeit often with the supervisor's support and skills in handling these difficult moments.

Each supervisor has a particular style of teaching and theoretical orientation. The ideal trainee has the capacity to learn from different types of supervisors, even if the particular supervisor does not perfectly match the learning style and theoretical orientation of the trainee.

Case Example

Dr. A, a 55-year-old psychiatrist with 10 years of supervisory experience, was assigned to supervise Ms. B, 40-years-old, who was entering the first year of a 2-year internship program. Ms. B had returned to school, a doctoral program in clinical psychology, after having practiced psychotherapy for several years with a master's degree in counseling.

In their first meeting, Dr. A and Ms. B agreed upon a regular time and place to meet for weekly supervision. The administrator of the Department of Psychiatry in their hospital assigned them an office for this purpose. The two of them traded information about their prior clinical experience, at which time Ms. B voiced both her eagerness and anxiety about learning psychoanalytic psychotherapy after years of practicing within a more educational and counseling mode. Dr. A commended Ms. B for the courage this took to learn a whole new perspective at a time when she was probably quite comfortable, competent, and respected within her initially chosen field. Dr. A also shared with Ms. B her own prior discomfort when she returned to her academic career after having suspended most of her clinical practice and her career advancement in order to raise four children. Together they flagged the likely effects of Ms. B's situation: a particular reluctance to enter the necessary but painful learning regression that accompanies new learning experiences, despite her already having endured such trials—at a much younger age—in her counseling career; a tendency to try to "solve" patients' problems for them, at least partially as a way to avoid sitting with her own and her patients' anxiety; and a desire to focus on learning about the transference and countertransference aspects of the therapeutic relationship, having already learned in her prior career with patients how to establish a good working alliance.

Dr. A also had Ms. B discuss her prior experiences in supervision, and was surprised to hear that Ms. B described all her past supervision in glowing terms. She pressed Ms. B on this, but to no avail. Dr. A then silently resolved to attune herself to anything in Ms. B's work that might shed light on this matter.

After some discussion, they agreed that Ms. B would present the case of a 28-year-old obsessional man, Mr. C, she would be seeing in twice-weekly psychotherapy. Ms. B stated a willingness to audiotape the sessions. At the mid-year and end points of the supervision they would hold a mutual evaluation session to assess the progress of the supervision.

The second supervision session yielded the first instance of resistance to learning on Ms. B's part: She came in and began to play the audiotape, at which point they discovered the tape was blank! The supervisor and trainee had a good laugh together about the pervasiveness of Ms. B's anxiety. Dr. A found herself tremendously relieved that Ms. B was so nondefensive about this effect of her anxiety, and decided that they were off to a good start. As it turned out, Mr. C had canceled his first scheduled meeting, so this was an opportunity for Dr. A to point out an example of parallel process: The patient was "blank" for his first session, much as Ms. B's tape was "blank" for her first supervision session. They used Ms. B's written notes on the session as a springboard for this day's supervision. Dr. A helped Ms. B look for opportunities to make empathic comments regarding Mr. C's anxiety about entering psychotherapy. Ms. B also asked for help in gathering information about Mr. C's object relations that would enable her to hypothesize possible transference dynamics.

Mr. C, a single white male working as a lawyer, came to therapy complaining of problems with procrastination in his work life and a dilemma of an affair he was conducting outside of his 3-year-long marriage. By his own description, Mr. C had two prior "failed" therapies, by which he meant that he had not gotten the help he was seeking for the same problems as he was presenting to Ms. B. According to Ms. B, the patient described a great deal of hope he held for this new therapy, and patient and therapist both seemed eager to work with each other.

Work proceeded fairly smoothly for the next several months, until the patient's negative transference began to emerge more clearly. He demanded more advice from his therapist, and Ms. B mistakenly conceded, without seeking to explore the transference. She began to come to her supervision sessions with the opening line, "Boy, I really need your help today." The patient decided he could no longer afford to come to therapy twice a week, and, again, Ms. B seemed willing to accept this without exploration. When Dr. A found herself feeling frustrated and critical of Ms. B's work at this juncture, she knew she needed to take a step back and look at what had happened. Upon reflection, Dr. A, with the help of a quarterly staff meeting designed to discuss issues of supervision, realized that she had recently gotten frustrated with Ms. B's eagerness to elicit input from her, but not using that input in her work with the patient. In responding to the patient's unanalyzed negative transference, the therapist had sought to squelch the negative affect with increased "helping behavior." It was likely that Dr. A was experiencing the anger and frustration that neither patient nor therapist was willing to own. Dr. A was reminded at this time that Ms. B had been reluctant to express any negative feelings about her prior experiences in supervision.

Dr. A decided to approach the problem through the work with the patient and not with the trainee directly, except where the trainee herself decided to do so. Having had a place to talk about her own feelings about the supervision, Dr. A was able to be less judgmental about Ms. B's falling into the trap of talking about content and not process. In the supervision, Dr. A began to focus exclusively on the patient's affect. She would intermittently stop Ms. B in her presentation of her process notes with the question, "What do you suppose the patient was feeling then?" thus completely sidestepping the content of the patient's associations. Ms. B found this helpful, and actually was quite accurate in her assessment of the patient's affects — once she turned her attention to them. She noticed herself that the patient frequently appeared to be angry without giving the anger direct expression. Dr. A and Ms. B began to look more clearly at the indirect ways Mr. C used to express his anger, including some ways that Ms. B recognized she had replicated in her supervision hour in parallel process fashion. Ms. B was able even to recognize her reluctance to express negative affect in her personal life; in fact, she reported to Dr. A that this had begun to arise in her own psychotherapy, and she was eager to examine its roots. The details of this remained in the arena of her personal therapy. Nonetheless, supervisor and therapist continued to remain alert to Ms. B's discomfort with negative affect and the need to pay attention to ways in which she tended to inhibit the patient's expression of his own already inhibited affect. Dr. A and Ms. B even became able to laugh in each instance that this issue reared its head.

As the work proceeded more smoothly in supervision, Ms. B and Mr. C deepened their work. As the patient began to more freely express negative affects, he began to acknowledge a false self he had created in childhood. This false self had squelched negative feelings but had more importantly prevented him from being rejected by a mother who seemed unable to tolerate strong feelings. A great deal of work was done through a focus on the transference, and how he had perceived Ms. B as similarly unable to tolerate strong feelings (rightly so, at least initially). Not surprisingly, Mr. C's hesitancy to become more committed to his girlfriend partially rested on his unconscious fear of not being accepted unless he was a "good boy." After testing out negative feelings with his therapist, it became safer to express them with his girlfriend, and he began to feel closer to her.

Although the preceding example of a supervisory experience was labeled as "ideal," it is apparent that it did not proceed without a hitch. It may be said that supervision without hitches (resistance) is as likely as therapy without resistance. Rather, success is measured by the capacity to confront the resistance and to work it through. The ideal nature of the above example arose from the secure foundation (working relationship) created by supervisor and trainee that allowed them to attend to the psychological growth of the patient, the professional growth of the trainee, and the mentoring rewards of the supervisor.

As is often the case in psychotherapy, it is the more difficult moments that can yield the greatest change. In the above example, Dr. A's forum at the hospital in which she was able to voice her experience of this difficult moment and obtain feedback from her colleagues allowed her to gain the necessary perspective to ultimately yield the change in both the supervisory and therapeutic relationship. Without that forum, it is possible that progress would have stalled. The administration of the hospital contributed to the success of this supervision. In practical terms, it provided a room for supervising purposes, but also the forum mentioned above for Dr. A to discuss her experiences. The administration also implicitly supported this supervision by providing a valued supervisor for Ms. B on a weekly basis.

IDENTIFYING THE IMPASSE

The supervisory experience, like the psychotherapy experience, is one that requires its participants to operate on a cognitive, emotional, and behavioral level. Addititionally, the supervisor is expected to be a teacher, a mentor, an administrator, a role model, a disciplinarian, and parental in regard to the supervisee. These many roles and levels of the relationship often produce paradoxical effects and can exert great pressure on the supervisor as well as on the therapist. In all hierarchical situations, the temptation is to blame the person further down the ladder when things go wrong. The problem with this solution, apart from its obvious inequity, is that it leaves the supervisor with little sense of what can be done to improve the situation.

This segment of our chapter is devoted to the exploration of supervisory impasse — its causes, its many forms, and its consequences. Some examples are offered of impasse and its resolution. It is far beyond the scope of this work to make definitive suggestions that can claim to be universally effective for the resolution of impasse; more research is needed to enable us to offer scientific guidelines for impasse resolution. Yet, there are some commonly occurring and observable phenomena that merit careful study and exploration. The examples herein are offered to stimulate the reader's imagination and memory. The problems described are samples of difficulties in the work. The examples are attempts to demystify the process so that the parties can disentangle from the confusion and allow for the supervision to proceed. In particular, we will focus on the supervisor's contribution to the impasse, with the understanding that this is hardly the only source of difficulty. There are, however, some other sources of problems.

Student's Contribution to Impasse

Students have trouble using supervision in a variety of ways. They most often have difficulty using supervision well because of "dumb spots" (Wallerstein, 1979), or simple lack of information, which is easily remedied by teaching facts of theory or of technique. Blind spots arise from areas of mutual conflict between patient and therapist that make it difficult for the therapist to accept a supervisor's efforts to explore aspects of the patient that the therapist is avoiding in him- or herself. Some patients develop a very intense transference toward the clinician, with demands that are hard to bear. An example of this is the dread that a student may experience in thinking about and reporting an hour with a severely devaluing patient. Whereas the more experienced clinician will recognize this response as normal, and a source of important data about the patient, the beginner is much more apt to be harshly judgmental of such responses in him- or herself, and to assume that the supervisor will also cast blame. Areas of chronic unresolved conflict in the student generate true countertransference reactions that will perennially interfere with learning to be a psychotherapist, until they are resolved in the student's personal therapy. Another student may have personal difficulties with learning that have to do with a personality style. For example, a very well organized, obsessive–compulsive student may feel too much anxiety to tolerate the amorphous affect that is inherent in the learning of psychotherapy. Unmanageable personality differences that disable the competence of both people in the supervisory dyad also occur from time to time.

Other sources of difficulty stemming from the student are an inherent lack of faith in the psychotherapeutic process, or great doubts about the validity of the theories that the supervisor is espousing. The student may have unusual difficulty with empathy and alliance formation due to personal limitation, cultural bias, or naivete.

> Dr. S had begun his residency after some prior training in a highly biological program, in which he was taught that only biological interventions made any sense in the treatment of psychosis. He chose an analyst as his supervisor in order to learn a new theory and technique, but he could not overcome his bias; he scorned the supervisor's input, and resisted any attempts to discuss the differences as a way of bridging the theoretical positions. The supervision ended badly, with both parties feeling anger and despair about their ability to be effective with the other party.

The administration may be contributing to supervisory impasse by undercutting the supervision, either directly or subtly. For example, a community mental health clinic made no pretense of valuing supervision except as a luxury to be indulged in if there were no patients waiting to be seen. They refused to allow supervision to be conducted in any of the clinical offices unless the supervisory dyad agreed to be interrupted at any time that the office was needed, by anyone needing to do clinical work with patients. Often supervision would be conducted in the clinic kitchen, or on the stairwell, with both parties feeling a little illicit for engaging in an activity that is perceived as frivolous.

At other times, too many people may get involved in the management of a patient, thus interfering with the work of the supervisor–therapist dyad.

These are just a few examples of supervisory difficulty that have their origins outside the supervisor. With this in mind, let us turn to the supervisor, and try to understand the difficulties that may lead him or her to bring the work to a stalemate. Supervision is a difficult word to hear clearly. It stimulates emotional responses laden with superego affects. The word implies superior status, and a measure of control exercised over another. Fantasies and realities of power coexist alongside the supervisor's need to be loved, admired, trusted, and remembered fondly. They may interfere with the supervisor's realistic responsibility to exercise authority and to provide appropriate limits.

Another source of potential conflict is generated by the supervisor's dual loyalties to both student and to administration. The supervisor must negotiate a sometimes awkward middle course between administration and supervisee, offering confidentiality and support for creative risktaking to the student, and quality and safety standards to the administration.

For example, a supervisor may feel that he or she is working with a too docile student, who may not be learning in any depth because of the student's tendency to negotiate a very conservative and safe course — one that is beyond reproach. The student may move to refer a difficult patient to a more senior clinician prematurely, or may employ several therapeutic modalities at once to cover all bases. There are arguments to be made for these approaches if they are decided upon thoughtfully, but the new clinician may be ill served if the choices lead to avoiding the anxiety of sorting out, thinking through, and learning to trust his or her own instincts. On the other side of the dilemma is the administration's need to avoid trouble in the form of repeated missed appointments by a difficult patient, vulnerability to litigation, or cost-effectiveness as defined and mandated by review boards. A similarly knotty problem surrounds the assignment of cases to a particular supervisee; the supervisor must participate in making a balanced choice between service to whatever patients need treatment on the one hand and the need to vary the clinician's case load for optimal learning.

These decisions take on a Solomon-like cast and may reach impasse proportions. Impasse here is defined as a stalemated conflict between supervisor and therapist or administration that resists resolution by logic or standard supervisory technique.

The Supervisor's Contribution to Impasse

Supervisors contribute to conflict in the supervisory relationship. The etiology of these difficulties is complex and has many aspects that are idiosyncratic for each supervisor. Still, there are some common sources of difficulty that can restrict the effectiveness of a supervisor. These are: (1) The need to be admired; (2) the need to rescue; (3) the need to be in control; (4) the need to compete; (5) the need to be loved; (6) the need to work through unresolved prior conflicts in the supervisor's own training experience; (7) spill over from stress in the personal or professional life that is overwhelming and contaminates all of his or her work, including the work of supervision; (8) tension between the supervisor and the administration; and (9) supervising across professional disciplines.

The following section will examine each of these categories in some detail, and give some illustrations drawn from the experience of supervisors from a number of disciplines, at differing levels of seniority and expertise.

The Need to be Admired

One factor that might lead people to a strong interest in psychology and psychiatry is an unconscious, sublimated identification with God (Jones, 1951). Charismatic leaders have a tendency to fall prey to fantasies of grandiosity that blind them to the reality of their situations, and to the people with whom they interact (Mehlman, 1974; Semrad, 1969; Searles, 1955). Supervisors of psychotherapy wear the mantle of benevolent superiority, even in their titles. One of the major problems is that authority figures may begin to believe in their own godliness, setting the stage for expectations that they will be adored and obeyed.

The supervisor caught in such a trap is prone to try a variety of maneuvers calculated to maintain the illusion of complete agreement and superior knowledge. In the work with the supervisee, he or she may avoid any criticism of the student's work, relying instead on unconditional support, and the fantasy that knowledge can be transmitted by a magical laying on of hands, or by keeping the student tied blindly to a certain theoretical position.

In another version of this problem, the supervisor assumes an entertaining posture, providing ever more brilliant and witty interventions and avoiding the tedious and more mundane aspects of the work. A student objected loudly to her training director that her supervisor was spending the time telling her off-color jokes that were sexist and embarrassing. The supervisor felt that his primary skill as a supervisor was his capacity to charm and excite the student's spontaneity so that the student would intuitively learn to be "as competent and confident as I am, by relaxing and playing intellectually as I do."

The supervisor may share in a rebellious misalliance with the student against the institution, or against other supervisors. In doing so, he or she may lose the opportunity to deal with the student's neurotic tendency to split off one authority in order to defy another.

An overwhelming need to be admired can sometimes be cloaked in an overly humble and self-effacing stance that protects the supervisor from being accused of ever having been wrong or imprecise.

The Need to Rescue

It is axiomatic among caretakers that many enter the field in order to do for others that which they wished had been done for them at an earlier time in their lives. Another major given is that the patient must be protected from being used to unduly gratify the clinician's wishes.

These same assumptions apply to supervisors with respect to their students. The affectional and collegial aspects of the supervisor–therapist relationship are some of the primary benefits for the supervisor, and a major motive for people to stay in the profession. A conscious acceptance of these impulses toward affiliation is needed to replace the somewhat guilty fantasies that interdependence continues to stimulate. The supervisor whose own needs to be protective and needed are excessive may distort the work with the supervisee.

Case Example

Dr. J was assigned to supervise Dr. Y in his work on an inpatient unit where the patients in his charge were in grave danger to themselves and to others. The supervisor insisted that the supervisee should call him each time any urgent situation arose, even if this should occur in the middle of the night. He insisted that the resident make no clinical decisions without consulting him first, and he would always offer to see the patient with the supervisee if necessary. The resident resented this greatly, feeling that the supervisor did not trust him sufficiently and was acting like an overprotective parent. Dr. J, in turn, felt that the student was greatly stressed by this case load, and should be supported every step of the way in order to survive this rotation.

Upon discussing the situation, Dr. J related that he had worked in a similar setting once, and been viciously attacked and physically scared by a patient. In his attempt to restore his own self-esteem after the assault, he tried to be very careful to meet the student's needs, but the press of his own unresolved anxiety interfered with his judgment of the student's neediness. In this case his own need to be needed was greater than the student's need to be dependent. In his overvigilance, he failed to see the student's mounting resentment and passivity. The student was waiting eagerly for the end of this rotation, so that he could breathe again.

Dr J's solicitousness may have given the impression that the student's other supervisors were unable to provide the same understanding or expertise. This undermining of other supervisors creates considerable tension for the student, and engenders a sense of disloyalty and suspicion in cases where the student is vulnerable enough to be pulled into an exclusive alliance of this sort.

The Need to Be in Control

The work of supervision adds another layer of distance to the clinical situation, and increases the ambiguity that the supervisor must learn to tolerate. The supervisor's real power and control over the clinical situation are less immediate. For some this decrease in control generates competition with the supervisee, or a need to be in charge in a maladaptive way that contributes to supervisory impasse.

For the novice supervisor, and for the more experienced one as well, issues of aggression, power, and competition are bound to surface and become a source of anxiety and gratification. On a conscious level, the supervisor has needs to feel in control, to be more competent than the supervisee, in order to be helpful and for his or her own sense of self-worth. If the supervisor experiences the supervisee as the validator of the former's sense of power and authority, there is a danger that the relationship will lapse into a struggle for dominance and control. Whether the supervisee is bright and very competent, or extraordinarily incompetent, the insecure supervisor is bound to feel threatened. Either he or she is about to be rendered useless, or the student is about to fail, and the rest of the world will hold the supervisor responsible. Such a dilemma, compounded by the less conscious issues of guilt and envy, leads the supervisor to respond to the student punitively or sadistically. Another form of impasse results when the supervisor, in an obsessive need to cover all the ground, launches a campaign to make the supervisee read massive quantities of relevant literature and consider all alternatives, thereby discouraging the supervisee's ability for affective and intuitive learning.

Case Example

Dr. W was known in the system as a superior clinician — and a difficult supervisor. She regularly demanded fully typed process notes on each session, to be presented 24 hours before the supervision, along with detailed rationales for each intervention made by the student. Dr. L, her student, was an energetic, spontaneous, charming young man who was gifted poetically, and who liked to take imaginary leaps that often led him to brilliant insights about a patient, but sometimes, of course, caused him to fail badly. Both situations generated a stern response in the supervisor, who was alternatively envious and punitively critical of her supervisee. The more she demanded structure and precise reasoning, the more he felt his autonomy at risk, and the less he revealed to her in the supervisory hours. Eventually, he found himself inventing data for the supervision, and asked another supervisor for help. This time, the student was able to use the advice of the trusted mentor who suggested that he go back to Dr. W and discuss the dilemma with her; together they worked out a reasonable compromise, and the year continued peacefully if not joyously.

The Supervisor's Problems with Competition

If a supervisor is naturally competitive and ambitious he or she may feel tempted to engage in activities that maintain clear superiority over the student. This might be accomplished in a variety of ways, such as overwhelming the trainee with data, rushing to solve the problem, dazzling with complicated and esoteric insights, or undercuting the student's creativity by ignoring or taking credit for it. Sometimes the supervisor may work with a student who is indeed much like a younger and somewhat idealized version of the self. The former may be so identified with the student, and so vicariously committed to this student's excelling, that the student's reality is compromised in favor of the supervisor's competitive instincts and dreams of glory.

Some of the more difficult competitive situations arise when a supervisor is supervising across disciplines, or across gender, race, or age barriers. These situations are extremely painful because the underlying issues are rarely addressed openly in training systems, and remain the source of shame and confusion in both parties to the supervision.

The Need to be Loved

The patient must be protected from being used for the gratification of the therapist. In the earlier sections, we considered the potential damage of the supervisor's need to be narcissistically gratified by the student's unquestioning adoration. This section examines the pull toward inappropriate intimacy and collegiality between supervisor and supervisee.

On the one hand, the affectional and collegial aspects of the supervisor–supervisee relationship are primary benefits for the supervisor. On the other hand, the potential for abuse of power and for interfering in the clinician's training are great and need to be carefully highlighted. To fail to do so is to risk damaging boundary violations such as sexual acting out or other illicit arrangements between the dyad. An example of the denial of this reality is expressed by Chessick (1971), who speaks with some embarrassment about the secondary gains for the supervisor, such as the need for company, for emotional relief from the deprivation of direct patient care and the stresses this produces on his or her personal life. The supervisor who is lonely, or angry, or depressed, and feels constrained from thinking that the work with the supervisees offers some appropriate relief is in danger of acting out these very needs in inappropirate ways. The supervisor who is aware of the need to be loved and gratified by the supervisee is in a position to keep careful check on the management of this object hunger, and to keep the affection in the relationship at levels consistent with the supervisory boundaries and goals.

The Need to Work Through Unresolved Prior Conflicts in the Supervisor's Own Training Experience

Another potential problem arises from the paucity of dialogue and training in the field of supervision. People enter with models from their own experience as supervisees, with little capacity to assess how much of what they've experienced was due to the failures or brilliance of their prior supervisors, and how much of their memory is tainted by the regressive transferences that occur in any normal supervision. There is no public arena for sorting out fantasy from reality and the distortions remain secret and charged with leftover feelings of distress or idealization. These same supervisors form the supervisory introjects for the beginning supervisor. To the extent that they experienced unresolved conflict with prior supervisors, they will run the risk of distorting their own professional development, in an unconscious variant of the repetition compulsion.

Case Example

Dr. S was supervising Dr. A, new to the field. Dr. S recalled that her first supervisor tended to criticize harshly and to demand unusual levels of competence; she resolved never to criticize a student for being inept in the first year of training. Whenever Dr. A presented his doubts about his performance in a particular situation, Dr. S would rush to reassure him that he was doing fine, and indeed was expecting too much of himself. This process continued and escalated, until Dr. S complained to her that he felt severely criticized for his wish to excell! The supervisor was horrified to find that she had replicated just what she had sought to avoid, and was able to make the necessary adjustment when she realized the source of her overdetermined "reassurance" of a student who didn't need or want this approach.

Spill Over from Stress in the Personal or Professional Life of the Supervisor (True Supervisory Countertransference)

If the supervisor is experiencing overwhelming distress in his or her own life, the chances are great that this will seep into the work of supervision. If the supervisor is conscious of it, even an acute problem rarely results in impasse. Impasse around this area results from unconscious intrusion into the work, from unresolved conflicts that are out of the supervisor's awareness.

Tension between the Supervisor and the Administration of the Institution

Where the supervisor feels unsupported, uncherished, or underpaid by the institution, there is serious potential for these conflicts to spill over into the supervisory hour. He or she may resist writing adequate supervisory reports for the training committee, bring resentment into the supervisory interchange, or somehow expect the student to make up for the sins of the system. In any event, the ombudsman function that the supervisor should provide for negotiating between the student and all other parties is virtually lost. In fact, the supervisor may unconsciously encourage acting out against the institution by ignoring the student, who may take on an insufficient work load, or adhere too casually to administrative policy, billing procedures, and so forth. Caught in a demoralizing bind, the student may withdraw in disillusion or seek more peaceful alternative areas of specialization for reasons other than his or her best interest or future career directions.

Supervising across Professional Disciplines

One of the enriching innovations in clinical centers is the increasing acceptability of supervisors from many professional disciplines. In part this is related to the increasing awareness that psychotherapy skills cut across professional disciplines. It is also true that with the larger range of treatment modalities, supervisors have tended to be identified as specialists rather than generalists. In addition, no therapist, even a generalist, can be fully expert in all current modalities. Therefore, it has become the practice in more sophisticated centers of training to utilize supervisors according to their expertise rather than their professional training. Psychologists, psychiatrists, social workers, and others all participate as supervisors in increasingly significant numbers. As supervisors gain more experience working with allied colleagues, new and unfamiliar variables enter the training situation. When a supervisor from one discipline supervises someone from another field, he or she is apt to encounter some attitudes, skills, and traits that are unfamiliar and potentially confusing to work with. Some specific responses have been reinforced in the training of psychiatrists that are unfamiliar to psychologists, and so forth. For example, medical students are trained to make spot judgments and action-oriented decisions. Psychologists, on the other hand, are often trained to contemplate all details surrounding an issue and to examine statistical probability before making a final judgment about a situation. Social workers and psychiatric nurses have often been trained to attend to the comfort of the patient and to move as quickly as possible to relieve distress emanating from external sources as a first treatment maneuver. These assumptions constitute the cultural mores that are agreed upon and practiced as a matter of course. A psychologist–supervisor, however, may be at a loss to understand the ready tendency of a young psychiatric resident to act in a way that the supervisor may judge to be rash and presumptive, when the resident is simply following the mores of medicine. Similarly, a social worker supervisor who is paired with a psychology intern may be distressed by the apparent passivity or callousness of the psychologist-in-training toward the patient's pain, whereas the trainee may feel that to move with insufficient data constitutes careless management of the situation and is potentially dangerous to the patient.

These professional assumptions are rarely conscious, and they are not often discussed in the supervision; when the work of supervision begins to falter, it would be very useful to step back and examine which of the differing perspectives are based in the professional culture of the supervisor and the student, and which represent a real failure in the training situation. Especially at the time of negotiating a supervisory contract, some attention to differing backgrounds of training can facilitate the capacity of each member of the supervisory dyad to see the world more empathically from the other's perspective. If the supervisor feels that the clinician needs to change his or her technique or perspective, at least both parties can be more sensitive to the enormity of the task.

Impasse sometimes occurs in ways that remain impossible to analyze and remedy. The common assumption is that the dyad is stimulating some powerful transferential and countertransferential reactions and the only real solution is to reassign the student, and to reassure the supervisor of his or her continued value to the institution.

MANAGING THE IMPASSE

Many of the difficulties and tensions between supervisor and trainee can be prevented with thoughtful ancitipation and respect for all participants. Regularly scheduled meetings of psychotherapy supervisors are a powerful resource for the resolution of impasse. These contacts encourage a dialogue among supervisors in which they can share supervisory tactics and experiences, and seek help from one another in difficult cases. They also model the supervisee role, reminding supervisors of the vulnerability of receiving help.

When both supervisor and supervisee value the supervision and their psychotherapeutic work with patients, and this value is shared by the administration, the most intractable of impasses often do not occur. Public recognition of this shared value of supervision is necessary. Presentations at grand rounds around the topic of supervision, or a presentation of a taped supervisory hour are ways in which the process is made public and less mysterious to both supervisees and trainees. Early in the training year, students should be instructed on how to use supervision optimally. Meetings with trainees can be used to discuss their experiences with supervisors. Further, there must be a consultant who can be available to the supervisor or the supervisee when they arrive at some stalemate. This could be the director of training, but ideally it would be a senior supervisor who is assigned this role in the department, and who can function as a troubleshooter and ombudsman in the supervisory system.

The administration should provide supervisors who represent a variety of perspectives — men and women of a broad enough age range to span all the developmental stages, who can interact with the supervisees from a richly heterogeneous set of assumptions and strengths.

The problem of impasse must be faced by the training committee in a way that deals realistically and compassionately with all concerned parties. Efforts must be made to reduce impasse situations by training young clinicians to supervise, and to develop fresh theory to inform the field of supervision in the future.

The supervisor and the student need to recognize the limits of the empathic capacity, and to make peace with some of these limitations.

An appropriate humility encourages an honest and realistic appraisal of the parties involved, and circumscribes the limits of any one person to enter another's experience, however much one may wish to do so. The supervisor's admission of his or her own struggles and limitations can encourage the student to explore his or her own boundaries with equal honesty.

In conclusion, this chapter has offered an overview of psychotherapy supervision, especially as practiced in an outpatient psychotherapy clinic such as the General Psychiatry Practice at the Massachusetts General Hospital. Our goal has been to elaborate some of the complexities of the process, to describe some of the roles, goals, boundaries, and limitations inherent in the supervisory work. We have sought to offer some suggestions for more effective supervision, and close with a fervent wish for a greater attention to this important aspect of a clinical career.

REFERENCES

Alonso, A. (1985). *The quiet profession: Supervisors of psychotherapy*. New York: Macmillan.

Bion, W. R. (1959). *Experiences in groups*. New York: Basic Books.

Bowen, M. (1971). Perspectives and techniques of multiple family therapy. In J. Bradt & C. Moynihan (Eds), *Systems therapy*. Washington, DC: Bradt & May.

Chessick, R. (1971). *Why psychotherapists fail*. New York: Science House.

Eckstein, R., & Wallerstein, R. S. (1963). *The teaching and learning of psychotherapy*. New York: Basic Books.

Jones, E. (1951). The God complex. In *Essays in applied psychoanalysis* (Vol. 2, p. 244). London: The Hogarth Press.

Mehlman, R. (1974). Becoming and being a psychotherapist: The problem of narcissism. *International Journal of Psychiatry, 3*, 125–141.

Searles, H. F. (1955). The informational value of the supervisor's emotional experience. *Psychiatry, 18*, 135– 146.

Semrad, E. (1969). *Teaching psychotherapy of psychotic patients*. New York: Grune/Stratton.

E·I·G·H·T·E·E·N

㵜

Terminating Psychotherapy: Calling it Quits

JAMES E. GROVES
A. EUGENE NEWMAN

There are times when, in spite of all attempts to deal with acting out, nothing changes. What does the therapist do when all tactics and therapeutic strategies seem ineffective? When, why, and how is it clinically appropriate for the *therapist* to terminate the treatment? Other chapters have dealt with other approaches to the self-destructive patient. This chapter deals with a distinct boundary—terminating treatment—not a group of interpretive strategies.

At the outset it is necessary to state the following thesis: Treatment is impossible when the patient utilizes the process (psychotherapy, management, or even pharmacotherapy) in order to stay sick, harm others, or achieve self-destructive ends.

Generally it is important to persevere in the treatment of resistant patients, especially those with personality disorders, but there are types of Axis II and some Axis I patients who develop "therapy impossible" situations. Some patients have an external situation that elicits or simulates character pathology, such as court-ordered treatment, disability or tort litigation and treatment paid by third parties—for example, Veterans Administration, the state, or a hated parent. Sometimes the transference itself becomes the stimulus for ending the therapy. This chapter presents an in-depth analysis of a particular case, a patient with borderline personality whose erotic transference psychosis destroyed the therapy. The patient developed an acute psychotic reaction to therapy—a specific subtype of psychotic transference known as eroticized transference. This psychotic–erotic transference will illustrate how the patient utilized the therapeutic process to stay sick. It also is an indication for the threat to terminate treatment, or, as psychoanalytic purists might call it, the interruption of treatment.

REVIEW OF THE LITERATURE

Franz Alexander (1971), in his work on the "corrective emotional experience," articulated the "principle of flexibility." Alexander specifically advocated the manipulation of frequency of sessions as a therapeutic technique. To diminish procrastination, contain acting out, or quell regression, he recommends decreasing the frequency of sessions. While he does not address therapeutic termination, he does note that interruptions in treatment can both gauge the patient's progress and avail one of extratherapeutic experience out in the real world. And even orthodox psychoanalysts have appreciated the necessity of using frame parameters to limit regression. Elizabeth Zetzel (1956) for years recommended utilizing only once-per-week therapy sessions to limit the borderline patient's regression and rage (sometimes iatrogenically induced). Friedman (1975) does not strictly limit the therapy to once-a-week, but he does frame treatment around the idea of reality limits on the patient's boundless demands. Zetzel would often point out to her sicker patients that she could not function well as a therapist by day if she had to be on the phone with them at night — a far cry from the blank analytic screen. A communication such as this takes place within her "therapeutic alliance," not in the transference.

Zetzel's idea that there is a rational part and irrational part to the treatment is one she drew partially from Freud and partially donated to Greenson's (1969) concept of the "working alliance." Greenson writes that failures in therapy occur when incorrect interpretations coincide with some failure in the "real relationship." And with primitive patients, he says, the framework of the treatment must be corrected before the incorrect interpretation is repaired.

Leston Havens is an analyst with Sullivanian and existential roots, who has written extensively on ways in which the therapist acts to diminish projection and enhance reality testing when necessary (1980). In a regressed patient, Havens feels the therapist should not use "empathic" communication (guessing how the patient feels, inferring affect, appearing to read the patient's mind). Instead of making the patient feel penetrated by therapeutic inspection, the therapist should use "counterprojective statements" — statements of the reality of how pain comes about. For instance, Havens says, if the regressed patient stubs his toe on an office chair, one does not say, "how painful" — reading the patient's mind and diminishing the boundaries. Instead one says, "that damn chair!" By so doing the therapist points out the realities of how the pain came about and focuses on external reality rather than on the patient's inner world. Sullivan learned to sit side-by-side with his very psychotic patients, as if to look out at the real world with them. When one says, "how painful," one penetrates; "that damn chair" is a statment made by someone sitting side-by-side.

Both Havens (1979) and Howard Corwin (1976) credit Robert Mehlman with the notion of the "narcissistic transference," in which deeply injured patients form transferences based on experiences pre-dating true object relations. Such a patient cedes to the analyst protective powers based on the child's magical perception of an omniscient, omnipotent mother. This helpful transference is protective for the patient but it is "irrational" and deserves balance with the "prosthetic alliance," a rational alliance in which the therapist creates structure by setting limits, supplementing the patient's lack of rational ego (Gutheil & Havens, 1979). The prosthetic alliance works like training wheels on a bicycle — stabilizing the patient until sufficient learning takes place and enables him or her to ride without them. By juxtaposing the patient's reality situation with his or her projections, the therapist helps the patient give up the projections. Havens's juxtaposition of the narcissistic alliance with the prosthetic alliance and Corwin's (1976) "heroic confrontation" are examples of this principle of bringing together and contrasting for the patient elements of rational (real relationship) with elements of the (irrational) transference.

Donald Winnicott's "holding environment" (1971, 1947, 1955) is a term clinicians use a lot and understand very little. It is often used as a catch phrase to connote the all-nurturing, all-accepting Rogerian therapist. But in Winnicott's terms, the "holding environment" also sets necessary limits that are equally important to providing nurture. Friedman (1975) points out the frequent misunderstanding of Winni-cott's (admittedly obscure) ideas as set forth in his paper "Use of an Object" (1971). There, Winnicott says that the patient internalizes the object–mother–analyst only after unsuccessfully trying to destroy it. Only then is the object perceived as external — and differentiated from other wishful hallucinations of the developing infant. But this is a gradual process, not to be accomplished in a single session in which the therapist heroically tolerates the patient's rage. It requires not only gratification of the patient's needs but also frustration of some of the patient's wishes. Differentiating frustration of the patient's wishes from fulfilling needs is an important property of the holding environment. In fact, in "Hate in the Countertransference" Winnicott describes

(1947/1975) how he tolerated a certain hateful child's behavior until he reached his limit and then he would routinely eject the child into the backyard. The child could come in when he was ready to behave — not exactly the unconditional positive regard some people intend when they use the phrase "holding environment." Winnicott is for, not against, limits on physical acting out; he says one cannot do therapy with a patient who carries a revolver.

Despite Otto Kernberg's (1987) belief in lavishing intensive, frequent, psychoanalytic treatment on borderlines, sometimes in long-term hospitalization, he states that it is crucial to set limits on borderlines. His mandate to persevere heroically with the primitive patient notwithstanding, Kernberg also acknowledges that therapeutic termination may be a necessary component of limits, a frontier of treatment. He and his colleagues (1987) write that the contract with borderline patients must be buttressed with a willingness to terminate treatment if the contract is not honored.

> It is important that the patient be instructed that the therapist has a range of responses which he can utilize when the patient violates or threatens to violate the treatment contract. These reactions run the gamut from simple confrontation and interpretation within the interview situation to suspending a particular session or enlisting the aid of others, to finally terminating the treatment. The therapist should exercise the least restrictive measure possible. (p. 928)

Therapeutically terminating treatment goes back at least to Freud. As early as 1895, when Freud and Breuer were discussing the treatment of Anna O.'s hysteria (1893/1955), they warned that a confounding element in such cases occurs when the therapy is disturbed by a personal estrangement, if the patient is overpowered by fear of becoming dependent on the therapist personally and enslaved to treatment, or if the patient is frightened by the discovery that distressing ideas are transferred onto the therapist. What they do not say in "Studies on Hysteria" is that Anna O. in fact developed a psychotic transference to Breuer. Sources other than Freud tell us she developed pseudocyesis, or hysterical pregnancy, with a delusion that Breuer was the father of the child. This precipitated Breuer's panicky termination of therapy, his family's flight from the town in which Anna O.'s family lived, and his abandonment of psychoanalysis as a career (Freeman, 1972).

Yet, in fact, true psychoanalysis, meaning also analysis of transference, was rooted in such disasters. In Janet Malcolm's (1984) view, "Freud stumbled on the concept of transference while desperately casting about for an antidote to the epidemic of iatrogenic lovesickness that had spread through his practice in the 1890s."

In 1914 and 1915, Freud explored two elements of transference-based therapies in his papers on technique, "Remembering, Repeating and Working-through" (1914/1959), and "Observations on Transference-Love" (1915/1959). In the first he speaks of a special class of very early childhood experiences for which no memory can be recovered. These are reproduced not as a memory but as an action. A repetition compulsion results when the patient acts out the past in order *not* to remember it. Transference is a piece of such repetitions. By giving the patient time and safe affective expression within therapy, the memory is recovered in the transference and the hidden events lose their power to cause compulsions.

In his paper "Observations on Transference-Love" Freud discussed the situation of a (female) patient declaring her love for the (male) doctor. When such a patient refuses the standard work of treatment because she seeks gratification, Freud suggests that a transfer to another analyst may be necessary, that the analyst may have to "acknowledge failure and withdraw." Such patients possess "an elemental passionateness" and are "children of nature who refuse to accept the psychical in place of the material" (p. 166). Such attachments are, he felt, resistance, not true love. The patient either must relinquish treatment or give up the satisfaction she demands. Such an infantile patient understands only the "logic of gruel" or the "argument of dumplings"—baby food in other words. As for the doctor, ethical considerations prevent reciprocating; it is more gratifying than receiving the patient's love to provide the opportunity for her health (1915/1959).

And, in 1937, we see Freud grappling with several themes in "Analysis Terminable and Interminable" (1937/1964). First, he surrendered some of his previous optimism that analysis not only solves neuroses but protects prophylactically against future conflicts. Second, he admitted the necessity for longer analyses owing to the refractory nature of some patients' problems, owing to constitutional weaknesses and the difficulty of perfect technique on the part of the analyst. Third, he explored the possibility of speeding up the analysis by fixing a time limit or setting a termination date; he felt this works, but only if one is able to hit on just the right time to announce it. His unaccustomed lack of total optimism about psychoanalysis is perhaps explained by the section of the paper in which he claimed the two main obstacles to the removal of resistances and hence, termination of treatment, are passive homosexual fears in the male and penis envy in the female, both based on bisexuality and oedipal issues. If we allow Freud's genius as a clinical observer and, with the accuracy of hindsight, substitute preoedipal dependency issues for Freud's theory about oedipal bisexuality, we can then say that he found that the biggest resistance to progress is certain patients' refusal (or, we would now say, incapacity) to give up the possibility of an actual love relationship with the therapist, one which, in fantasy, repairs a relationship with the preoedipal mother.

IMPOSSIBLE TREATMENTS

Treatment is impossible when the patient utilizes psychotherapy to regress unduly, to harm others, or for some self-destructive purpose. The ultimate proof of a treatment's impossibility lies in the patient's persistence in self-defeating, harmful, or antitherapeutic behaviors despite all the doctor's clarifications, interpretations, or confrontations.

In "Taking Care of the Hateful Patient," Groves (1978) repeatedly emphasized the therapist's using feelings about the patient as a kind of laboratory test as a way of preserving treatment. Dependency engenders a smothered feeling in the caregiver; entitlement a wish to counterattack; manipulation and help–rejecting a depressed feeling; and self-destructive denial a wish that the patient die and get it over with. By understanding these dynamics, the caregiver can avoid abandoning the patient. Of course, hateful patients tend to be diagnosed as borderlines. They are hateful — and full of hate. The Dependent Clinger is a way of talking about primitive, anaclitic depression; the Entitled Demander is a symbol of the devaluation of the therapist; the Manipulative Help-Rejecter illustrates both the approach–avoidance conflict of the borderline patient and the masochistic reluctance to get better lest he or she lose the caregiving system. And the Self-Destructive Denier is the suicidal borderline, whose hateful feelings need to be owned and not rejected. "It is crucial to recognize the limitations that such patients pose for even the most ideal caregivers and to work with diligence and compassion to preserve the denier as long as possible, just as one does with any other patient with a terminal illness" (p. 386).

There may appear to be a contradiction between those sentiments and this exploration of impossible therapies for which termination is recommended. But the contradiction should resolve as we go on to see that "calling it quits" is a therapeutic maneuver, helpful to the patient when it is used as leverage to enforce a contract or even when the therapist follows through and does at last call it quits. Patients learn from it. However, the self-destructive denier may be so far gone that he or she has nothing to learn from confrontations; calling it quits does not teach him or her anything new about human relationships.

With respect to patients with DSM-III-R personality disorders, let us scan some of the treatment-impossible situations that may develop. This is not an exhaustive list; the reader will also be able to think of examples.

Group I personality disorders may make therapy impossible by persistent withdrawal and paranoid attitudes short of psychotic transference or delusions. For instance, a colleague is wrestling with a paranoid personality disorder patient who specializes in litigiousness. Such patients can hamper therapeutic efforts by persistent threats to sue the caregiver. At present the patient is involved in a lawsuit against the minister who married him and his ex-wife, in order to prove it is not his fault the patient made a bad marriage. Although the patient's litigiousness is now directed elsewhere, it will probably soon turn toward the therapist as a concrete attack, a threat to sue. And the therapist will probably then have an impossible therapy.

Personality disorders in the second group can also render therapy impossible. Narcissistic personality disordered patients and some relatively mild antisocial personalities (those who will actually stay in treatment for a while) specialize in relationships and acts that are harmful to others — usually a spouse or a child, sometimes even an institution is the object. They are persistently destructive, hostile, and cruel. They inform the therapist that something illegal or immoral is going on, and refer to it intermittently without actually letting the therapist into the situation or get involved therapeutically. They then see the therapist's helplessness as passivity, passivity as assent, silent assent as collusion, so that the therapist eventually becomes an accomplice to their deeds, and therapy becomes as corrupt as they are. Borderline and histrionic patients develop psychotic transferences and erotized transferences; these will be discussed later.

Personality disorders in the third group are less prone to impossible treatment situations but can still achieve them. Passive and masochistic patients in particular get into situations in and out of therapy that are self-destructive and tie the caregiver's hands. Everyone has had experience with the patient who absolutely refuses to take the prescribed medication. Such individuals try every known medication or therapy except the ones likely to help, all the while supplicating the caregiver, berating the therapist for the lack of progress, and wreaking havoc in their family or social situation.

Axis I disorders also can make treatment impossible — schizophrenics who refuse neuroleptics, manics who refuse lithium, and so on. But the most troublesome category of patients here are substance abusers and victims of eating disorders (who can be viewed as addicts too — *thinness* addicts). Quite often we are referred a patient who has been billed "a borderline who occasionally acts out by drinking," or other substance abuse. We take the person into treatment and ride out the binges, again and again trying to understand the depression or anxiety that "underlies" the drinking behavior. And, again and again, nothing happens, no long-term growth. But finally we catch on: Such patients we now simply define as alcoholics and refuse to treat unless they attend Alcoholics Anonymous. Otherwise, we simply become another type of Enabler, taking the place of the masochistic spouse they drink *at* and then repent *to*. Severe eating disorders must have a weight limit below which they are to be hospitalized for life-saving reasons. But occasionally they will refuse hospitalization or create situations that preclude it. In these instances, the therapist becomes the collaborator in self-destructive behavior unless willing to confront the patient with a limit beyond which treatment will not continue.

And finally there are external situations that elicit or simulate character pathology. Generally they involve a triangle — the patient, the therapist, and a third party. In this paradigm, if the patient progresses or gets better, he or she gives in to the third party or loses something from the third party. It is for this reason, for example, we no longer undertake long-term psychotherapeutic treatment of patients with pending tort litigation. If they get better, they lose their case; we treat them short-term, pharmacologically, and for emergencies, but tell them to come back *after* the case is settled. For readers who work with service-connected disabled patients in the Veterans Administration, it is hard to know what to recommend: Many such patients are unable to get better because they then lose their pensions; yet since they are service-connected and entitled to treatment, it is difficult for the therapist, who works for the VA, to interrupt treatment even for sound therapeutic reasons.

We now turn to the extended case example of "treatment impossible" with a borderline patient.

Case Example

Mrs J, a 41-year-old grade school teacher and mother of a teenaged daughter and a younger son, complained of stagnation in her work and anorgasmia in her marriage. Two years of twice-weekly psychotherapy in her late 20s with an older woman analyst had helped resolve her ambivalence between two men, a dark-haired aristocrat overly tied to his mother, and the man she subsequently married, a kindly older blond man who, she had felt early on, was probably bisexual. At the end of this therapy, on the eve of her marriage, she was told that if she required further therapy, it ought to be psychoanalysis. Now in her

40s, she felt no particular desperation but a need for a re-evaluation in her life. Her favorite uncle recently died, leaving her a modest sum — and this, she felt, might be well spent on a year of psychotherapy.

As she presented herself at the initial interview, the patient was a tall, rawboned woman of great dignity and poise. She spoke with precision and a hint of fear. She appeared gifted, chic, vulnerable, and smart. Although orderly and attentive to detail she was not stubborn or devaluing. And though she had no real sense of humor or reflection, she was clever and terribly grateful.

The patient was the only daughter and the older of two children of an effete and disgruntled businessman and an angry, vibrant, head-strong mother who had given up her operatic career to become a parent. The patient was a Mayflower descendant, the "tail-end of a dribbled-out line." Her brother, she felt, would never amount to much — 10 years younger than herself, firmly in the grip of the parents, he was effeminate and probably a homosexual. Her earliest memories concerned being left at age three with her father and a nurse, as her mother braved the Second World War to go on a singing tour of England. The nurse hated her, "a real Nazi," she recalled, and her father probably also was angry at being left behind; she recalled being harshly dried after a bath he gave her, remembered her genitals being hurt by the towel as he dried her off.

At the second interview she promptly produced a dream of an old and beautiful house. She was about to fall from a dormer on its roof, as her son and her husband stood by, useless and unconcerned. Deep within the walls of the beautiful old house a hidden fire smoldered, a danger that threatened to find its way to the air and burst forth consuming the whole structure. An elongated carriage lamp protruded from a wall, sticking out and curving angrily upward, sparks flying dangerously off its tip, hissing "like some demented snake." Her associations were that it was an English country house and her interpretation was that it depicted herself, worried about hidden danger as her family stood by unable or unwilling to help. The therapist noticed but did not mention that the neglect came from males, and that the anger and danger concerned phallic symbols. He had the fleeting thought that she might be concocting this dream as some kind of joke or trick. It was so full of "good material" as to be almost a parody. Dismissing this thought, he wondered silently whether it depicted her mother's trip to England when she was 3, which abandoned her to a dangerous male.

Over the next several evaluation sessions the patient filled in details of her development and her current situation. After she agreed to work for a year or so, reviewing the relationship between her childhood and her present dissatisfactions, she brought two entirely new concerns to therapy: a fear that she was a lesbian, and a deep, powerful crush on a man she had met at work. These two things, she could logically see, contradicted each other but she did not *feel* the contradiction. Much of her work over the next half year involved this homosexual fear and her irresistible attachment to the man at work. She improved her work situation and got more distance on her marriage. She produced dreams freely and associated copiously. The therapist ignored the initial feeling of unease that the production of such material was abnormal — too much too soon, too good to be true. Given her psychological sophistication, he began to adopt a more probing style to clarify the material, a change that produced ever more copious amounts of dreams and associations leading ever deeper.

Nine months into the therapy and coincident with the therapist's return from a vacation (in England, as it happened) the patient began to experience increasing terror. She began to attack the therapist in the hours, thinking he disliked women and might be a homosexual like her husband, her brother, herself. She swore the therapist was experiencing erections during her therapy hours and badgered him with accusations, pointing to what she called "telltale folds" in his trousers, citing his seating postures as evidence. Again she did not see the contradiction inherent in the notion of a homosexual therapist hopelessly overstimulated by her, a female. She raged in the hours and would call between sessions to apologize. Or she would rage on the phone and then say in treatment she did not know how she could have said such awful things on the phone. She also began to split the people in her life into good and bad ones and to become dogmatic in her manner. She was losing sleep, waking from nightmares, and lost about 8 pounds in weight over a month. The patient's husband telephoned to say that she was drinking at night and throwing things at home. In therapy, she devalued anything male or masculine about the therapist. He suggested, in a transference interpretation, that these attacks on males outside the therapy might be the source of her problems with her husband and her male boss, and were perhaps displaced from feelings toward the therapist. She promptly went home and had an argument with her husband that ended in his striking her — the only time it ever occurred in their marriage.

The therapist felt trapped, felt that the transference was out of hand and that the alliance somehow needed to be strengthened, so that when the patient asked for a psychiatric textbook of his, he gave it to her. Also, at about this time his answering service accidentally enabled her to get his home phone number, but he rationalized that having his phone number would at least make him "realer" and less an object for the extremes of devaluation and idealization. When, after reading the book, she accused him of several countertransference blunders, he admitted to her that she appeared overstimulated and he was uncertain (which she correctly read as ambivalent) about whether to go deeper to get to the root of her disorganization or to terminate on schedule.

The next session the patient brought in a dream in which there was a mound of earth, a "telltale ridge" on a promontory overlooking the ocean. She felt sad and unbearably guilty, so guilty, she said, that she might have to cut herself with a razor just to see herself bleed. She refused to associate to the dream but insisted that the therapist was secretly in love with her. Alarmed, the therapist made another inter-pretation—he suggested the mound of earth in the dream was a grave, might be the grave of a male since she had used the same words describing it as she had in accusing him of erections. Perhaps, he said, the dream represented guilt about her wish to destroy the therapist's genitals. Suddenly the patient grew calm and said that it was not the therapist's grave, it was her uncle's grave, the beloved relative who left her money for treatment.

Then she brought in a flood of entirely new material. She said it was as if it had been conscious but walled off and inaccessible to words: This uncle had been one of the only warm, positive things about her childhood. She recalled how he would hold her in his lap and rub her when she was little. She believed that this uncle had systematically used her for masturbation from the time she was 4 until she went away to school at age 10. She recalled only positive things about him and looked at the therapist in disbelief when he suggested that she also might be enraged toward the uncle for using her sexually and then leaving her. At this moment in the therapy hour she suddenly experienced rage and a stabbing pain "like a razor" in her genitals. As the uncle became the villain of her childhood, the therapist suddenly became, she said, the only good thing in the whole world. At the end of the session she turned on the threshold and said to the dumbfounded and disbelieving therapist, "You are my mother, I know it now. Don't try to deny it." She said that she knew the therapist might try to hide it but she knew that he was going to divorce his wife as she would her husband, and inevitably, the two of them would be married. When the therapist contradicted this possibility, the patient said, "I know you want me to do this," walked into the office lavatory, and smashed the mirror.

Following the broken mirror incident, the therapist insisted on medicating the patient with a tricyclic antidepressant. This, plus conjoint couple's therapy, and an absolute ban on alcohol only partly arrested her deterioration. She slept, ate, worked better, and had some distance on her marriage and her life. Her uncle's legacy was almost exhausted, but she felt she had learned enough to go on — for instance, that she must eventually divorce her husband — and she suggested terminating treatment in 2 or 3 months. Relieved, the therapist agreed.

The patient began to work on termination. Yet behind the compliant facade she harbored the secret, conscious delusion that the therapist was her mother, loved her, would divorce his wife and marry her. Each time the therapist would confront this notion the patient would break something or hurt herself. She developed the unshakable belief that her anorgasmia would be cured if and only if she had an orgasm in his office. He wondered how he could possibly get rid of this therapy without her ruining his reputation.

Late on a Friday afternoon she appeared without an appointment after the last patient had left and pushed her way into the office. The therapist bodily ejected her from the office. He terminated with her by registered letter. She subsequently resumed therapy and did quite well, with an older woman therapist.

ACUTE PSYCHOTIC REACTIONS TO THERAPY

Before taking this therapist to task for a number of obvious errors, it is important to state what not to blame him for. The first thing is that her diagnosis, borderline personality disorder, was subtle and hard to make. She appeared well adjusted although neurotic, as many border- lines do at first, and she had had a previously successful therapy, without a psychotic regression, and a mandate to enter psychoanalysis if she needed treatment again. It was easy to miss the secret problem drinking, the intolerance to being alone, the subtle identity confusion. It was hard to spot the passionate quality of her relationships, vacillating from idealization to devaluation. She hid her impulsivity in her relationship with the idealized male at work, and neglected to mention her intense and hateful anger at her husband. She downplayed her unstable mood with its marked shifts and her chronic feelings of emptiness. And she showed no physical self-damage and had no history of brief psychotic episodes.

And it is hard to blame the therapist for being overstimulated by the patient. That was one of her survival mechanisms, she was good at it. And after all, he did not reciprocate her physical overtures, however ambivalent his attempts to distance her and introduce a reality relationship as with the loan of the textbook or allowing her to have his home telephone number.

The therapist failed by not creating a safe therapeutic frame for the patient, in Langs's parlance (1975). There should have been a more explicit treatment agreement, with the patient explicitly promised confidentiality and the therapist's obedience to Hippocratic principles, that is, talking, not touching—in exchange for the patient's truthfulness and keeping her therapy within the boundary of the treatment hour. Also, if the patient had funds for only a year of psychotherapy, the therapist should have worked more within the framework of the time-limited therapies—he should have worked more with the concrete realities of her life and less with the transference. When she presented herself shopping for a year of therapy, he should not have sold her the first of several years of deep analytic therapy. And when she got him to agree to time-limited treatment, he should have at least recognized that she had unconsciously gained control over one of the important boundaries of the treatment, the end point. Patients hire therapists to do that—therapists are to construct the frame, the beginning and the end the therapy hour and of the therapy itself. But he let her determine the end point and somehow subscribed to her notion that she should have 12 months of therapy, not more or less, and 12 months without interruption. Hence, he did not do what any therapist would usually do when a patient started breaking things in the office—he did not interrupt therapy, or, at least, get a consultation.

Another technical error, one understandable perhaps given his inexperience, was the therapist's failure to catch the message of the first dream, both in its timing and in its content. The dream content says that she is about to fall, that males do not help her, and that the penis is a danger to her. Though he understood this at first, he forgot to keep it in mind as the therapy progressed. The timing of the dream, presented before there was any agreement to work, may reflect the patient's wish to work outside the regular boundaries of treatment, perhaps even to break the boundaries. The therapist did not comment on the content of the dream, which may have been the correct thing, but he neglected to ask her gently what she thought of the dream's coming between the first and second evaluation sessions, a line of exploration that might have led to repair of the frame and establishment of workable treatment boundaries. Early, intensely charged dreams and dreams of fragmentation have previously been noted to foretell the danger of psychotic transference or severe regressive states (Rappaport, 1959; Shwartz, 1967), especially if the therapist is depicted as-is without symbolization in the dream. But in a patient with a history of a good previous therapy, such a dream is deceptive. And the therapist is to be pardoned for not knowing the literature on dreams in erotic transference.

But when deeply exploratory work takes place without a stable and

carefully maintained framework, accidents in treatment and therapeutic errors—both of which are bound to occur—get hugely magni-
fied. (Langs, 1975). He could not have known that she had been
molested as a child; she even gave a history of her father's disinterest in
her body, an unintentional red herring that lead the therapist away
from the idea. But although he did not know she had been systematically molested by the uncle until she was able to tell him, he ought to
have prepared a therapeutic framework that could tolerate the emergence of highly charged memories. Certainly by now, we should start
to suspect that almost any patient may bring in such material
(Swanson & Biaggio, 1985; Stechler, 1980; Yates, 1982). Recent
consciousness-raising about the prevalence of father–daughter incest
suggest it is far more common than previously thought—involving
perhaps 5–10% of female patients. We should know that we are going
to have to work with such material fairly often—and as a reality, not as
a product of the patient's wishful or fearful fantasies. (Miller, 1984).

So to recapitulate, a borderline patient who had a history of actual
incestuous molestation entered treatment that was overly intuitive and
probing in its interpretations of unconscious material within an
inadequate reality framework. By his stimulated probing, the therapist
collaborated in what the patient regarded and experienced as a
recapitulation of the earlier incest. And when she had an acute
psychotic reaction (in descriptive terms) or pushed the re-enactment of
the traumatic episodes in order to master them (in dynamic terms), he
panicked and rejected her in order not to get drawn into an actual
physical situation. He was paralyzed by sharing the patient's fantasy
that he could not terminate with her until the year was up, thinking that
a year was too little time as it was.

One of the hazards of doing interpretive psychotherapy with
borderline patients is the potential for the sudden eruption of psychotic
phenomena attached specifically and almost exclusively to the transference (Groves, 1981). There is alarming realization by the therapist
that there has been an abrupt loss of "observing ego" (Sterba, 1934) in
relation to the therapist so that the patient is now relating to the
therapist as the "significant other" (Sandler, Dare, & Holder, 1979;
Wallerstein, 1967; Nacht, 1958; Little, 1981; Frosch, 1967; Hammett,
1961; Blum, 1973; Rosenfeld, 1978; Rappaport, 1956; Hoedemaker,
1960). The "as if" quality of the relationship is lost. In knowing how to
treat such a "transference psychosis," it is critical for the therapist to
decide whether this is a necessary stage in the improvement of the
patient (Winnicott, 1955), or a threat to psychotherapy that must be
eliminated quickly (Frosch, 1967; Rappaport, 1956; Hoedemaker,
1960). If not handled properly, the therapy may be destroyed just at the

point of greatest benefit or carried to a point of very real danger in the form of self-injury or suicidal attempt by the patient or a maniacal attack upon the therapist. As Freud thought that the unconscious conflicts that constitute a neurosis become reborn within the analytic situation as a "transference neurosis," (1914/1958), several writers believe that an analogous "transference psychosis" can evolve in predisposed individuals (Rosenfeld, 1952, 1969; Searles, 1963).

The term "transference psychosis" is used generally to describe psychotic episodes that last from a few hours to several months in patients suffering from a severe neurosis with regressive features or from a borderline condition (Sandler et al., 1979). In such a situation, psychotic phenomena attach themselves only to the transference and interfere very little with the patient's life outside of therapy or analysis. Very common are reports of treatment of patients who develop a "delusional transference" in the course of which the patient ceases to know the therapist in a real way and *literally* mistakes him or her for a parent. In other words, the transference has become indistinguishable from the reality. Nacht (1958) describes the phenomenon thus,

> The neurotic reacts as if his father had been a bad father and as if his analyst serves as a substitute for the bad father, but if he has really had a monstrous father or an abominable mother, interpretations of this kind have no place. The patient unconsciously carried in him the presence of hateful and terrifying objects; the therapist is not likened to a bad object, he is for him a renewal of the bad object. (p. 272)

A neurotic patient can recognize the therapist as a real person who for the time being symbolizes his parents, as they actually were, or as he experienced them in childhood. The transference is delusional, according to Little (1957) when "there is no such 'stand-in' or 'as-if' quality about it. To such a patient the analyst is, in an absolute way, with the quality of 'authenticity,' both the idealized parents deified and diabolized" (p. 135).

Little says about treatment,

> It follows that the analysis depends upon breaking up the delusional transference. To do this reality must be presented undeniably and inescapably, so that contact with it cannot be refused, and in such ways that the patient does not have to use either inference or deductive thinking. It might be compared with the waking from a dream of a tiny child, but someone must be there to help the waking (p. 136).

Many authorities offer very specific advice on the subject (Rosenfeld, 1979):

"The analyst is encouraged to interpret only very little, and to listen very carefully to the patient's complaints which are often quite repetitive. It is particularly important to avoid interpretations of projection or projective identification in the transference, even if massive projective identification is evident in the patient's material. When the patient becomes provocative, it is essential for the analyst to avoid defensive behavior, because it is generally evidence for the patient of the analyst's weakness and inability to cope." (p. 492)

Frosch (1967), in his summary at the panel on "Severe Regressive States during Analysis," expressed the general consensus at that time for approaches to dealing with transference psychosis within the analytic setting,

"[some feel] the proper attitude could be achieved within the framework of classical psychoanalytic abstinence, and there is no need to resort to any supportive means such as sitting up, use of the telephone, etc. . . . However, [they are] in the minority, and even others who looked upon the severe reactions as unwelcome felt compelled to deal with many reality aspects of these regressive situations by permitting the patient to call on the telephone, sitting him up, and even hospitalizing him.

Certain guides for the therapy of such patients are suggested. Early in the treatment one should attempt to support the desperate struggle to maintain contact with reality and to preserve the object, the ego, and the self. Many [feel] that it [is] necessary to speak more often, answer questions more readily, and try to support reality contact, perhaps by the face-to-face position. . . . We may find it necessary to combat his fear of separation and objectless, in the event of real separation during analysis such as vacations, etc. This may be done by making available to the patient the means of preserving some contact with the analyst by telephone or letter, etc., or, if this is not possible, to make available the assistance of another psychotherapist" (pp. 618–619).

THE CONTRIBUTION OF INCEST

When there is actual molestation of the patient as a child, the sacred covenant against incest between parent and child is fractured. And, like a crystal with an invisible crack, the personality of the patient remains vulnerable ever after to events that line up along the axis of that fault. The ancient covenant of the doctor–patient relationship aligns with the same cultural axis as the incest taboo. Hence, even slight deviations in the traditional structure of the therapy relationship may appear to such a patient as a sign of impending taboo-breaking behavior, this time by the therapist. Major distortions in the perception of the patient's reality can ensue from minor deviations in therapist technique. Subtle perturbations in the treatment framework — that would not be so important to the neurotic patient or the nonsusceptible (i.e., nonincest-victimized) primitive patient — may be interpreted by the once-molested patient as actual intention on the part of the therapist to have a romantic or erotic relationship.

The psychotherapy situation closely recapitulates the incest situation in that it is *private*. Similarly, the child is captive, as to some extent the patient is. The therapist often even tells the patient not to discuss the treatment with anyone else — just what the incest victim is told.

Bringing in a third party, a consultant, is a simple but potent antidote to the patient's fantasy of a replay of the original incest. It demonstrates that the therapist, though perhaps embarrassed, is hiding no wrongdoing, no actual shame. As a result the therapist's anxiety or shame over the patient's implicit or explicit accusations becomes, under the light of social scrutiny, only embarrassing and mildly irritating. If the patient refuses a consultation or if it does not help, interruption or treatment is in order.

CALLING IT QUITS

About the termination itself, little remains to be said. Termination is not a defeat. It is an indicated procedure when the patient must have a corrective emotional experience to relinquish a delusion (gain "ego control") or assume responsibility for his or her own acts — "plug up superego lacunae." It is carried out in several logical steps, like other interventions in therapy.

After recognizing that an impasse exists for which therapeutic termination may be the only helpful solution for the patient, a detailed questioning is in order, in which the therapist calls attention to the patient's behaviors as they happen. A detailed history is also in order as well, and the therapist may need to call "time out" to go back and get one.

The next step — and a very critical one — is to interpret to the patient that there appears to be a fantasy of timelessness and limitlessness, that is, the patient appears to feel that the therapist is going to allow the behavior to continue indefinitely. The patient may even feel the therapist wants the impasse, or needs it. It is necessary to ask the patient, "How long do you think I am going to tolerate this situation — a session, a week, a month? How long?" The fantasy of timelessness is wishful and often comes from the patient's past experience. Finally, after the therapist gets the patient's fantasy and confronts the patient, a termination date (one to six or so sessions away) should be set if the patient's behavior does not change.

CONCLUSION

The tendency of borderline patients to develop full-blown psychotic transferences in psychotherapy has been examined with reference to the nature of the developmental flaw in borderline patients and its re-emergence during psychotherapy. We focused on the nature of the ego weakness in borderline patients that predisposes them to the formation of psychotic transferences. We also have tried to emphasize the nature of such focal delusional systems as a maladaptive attempt by the patient to force the therapist into the place of the original self-object or partner in trauma. Whether the therapist views the transference psychosis as a necessary event in the improvement of borderline patients or as a therapeutic catastrophe will determine how the therapist manages the treatment—whether there will be interruption of treatment and transfer of the patient to another therapist or whether the therapist will use confrontation, interpretation, and working through of the underlying dynamic of splitting that apparently emerges under the pressure of oral rage. Either approach appears capable of breaking the psychotic transference, with the threat to terminate to be used only as a last resort.

Acknowledgment

The authors here gratefully acknowledge the more than 20 years of exposure to the unique clinical genius of Dr. Anne W. Alonso.

REFERENCES

Alexander, F. (1971). The principle of flexibility. In H. H. Barten (Ed.), *Brief therapies* (pp. 28–41). New York: Behavioral Publications.

Blum, H. (1973). The concept of the erotized transference. *Journal of the American Psychoanalytic Association, 21,* 61–76.

Breuer, J. (1955). Fraulein Anna O: Studies on hysteria. In J. Strachey (Ed. and Trans.), *The standard edition of the complete psychological works of Sigmund Freud* (Vol. 2, pp. 21–48). London: Hogarth Press. (Original work published 1893–1895)

Corwin, H. (1976). Therapeutic confrontation from routine to heroic. In G. Adler & P. G. Myerson (Eds.), *Confrontation in psychotherapy* (pp. 67–95). New York: Science House.

Freeman, L. (1972). *The story of Anna O.* New York: Walker.

Freud, S. (1959). Observations on transference-love. In J. Strachey (Ed. and Trans.), *The standard edition of the complete psychological works of Sigmund Freud* (Vol. 12, pp. 157–171). London: Hogarth Press. (Original work published 1915)

Freud, S. (1959). Remembering, repeating and working through. In J. Strachey (Ed. and Trans.), *The standard edition of the complete psychological works of Sigmund Freud* (Vol. 12, pp. 145–156). London: Hogarth Press. (Original work published 1914)

Freud, S. (1964). Analysis terminable and interminable. In J. Strachey (Ed. and Trans.), *The standard edition of the complete psychological works of Sigmund Freud* (Vol. 23, pp. 209–254.) London: Hogarth Press. (Original work published 1937)

Friedman, H. J. (1975). Psychotherapy of borderline patients: The influence of theory on technique. *American Journal of Psychiatry, 132,* 1048–1052.

Frosch, J. (1967). Severe regressive states during analysis. *Journal of the American Psychoanalytic Association, 15,* 491–507, 606–625.

Greenson, R. R., & Wexler, M. (1969). The non-transference relationship in the psychoanalytic situation. *International Journal of Psychoanalysis, 50,* 27–39.

Groves, J. E. (1978). Taking care of the hateful patient. *New England Journal of Medicine, 298,* 883–887.

Groves, J. E. (1981). Borderline personality disorder. *New England Journal of Medicine, 305,* 259–262.

Gutheil, T. G., & Havens, L. L. (1979). The therapeutic alliance: Contemporary meanings and confusions. *International Review of Psychoanalysis, 6,* 467–481.

Hammett, V. B. O. (1961). Delusional transference. *American Journal of Psychotherapy, 15,* 574–581.

Havens, L. L. (1980). Explorations in the uses of language in psychotherapy: counterprojective statements. *Contemporary Psychoanalysis, 16,* 53–67.

Hoedemaker, E. (1960). Psycho-analytic technique and ego modifications. *International Journal of Psychoanalysis, 41,* 34–46.

Langs, R. J. (1975). Therapeutic misalliances. *International Journal of Psychoanalytic Psychotherapy, 4,* 77–105.

Little, M. I. (1981). *Transference neurosis and transference psychosis.* New York: Jason Aronson.

Little, M. I. (1957). On delusional transference (transference psychosis). *International Journal of Psychoanalysis, 39,* 134–138.

Malcolm, J. (1984, December 20). The patient is always right. [Review of M. M. Gill's *Analysis of transference*]. *New York Review of Books, 31*(20), pp. 13–18.

Miller, A. (1984). *Thou shalt not be aware, Society's betrayal of the child* (H. Harnum, Trans.). New York: Farrar, Straus, & Giroux.

Nacht, S. (1958). Causes and mechanisms of ego distortion. *International Journal of Psychoanalysis, 39,* 271–273.

Rappaport, E. A. (1956). The management of an erotized transference. *Psychoanalytic Quarterly, 25,* 515–529.

Rappaport, E. A. (1959). The first dream in an erotized transference. *International Journal of Psychoanalysis, 40,* 240–245.

Rosenfeld, H. A. (1952). Transference phenomena and transference-analysis in an acute catatonic schizophrenic patient. *International Journal of Psychoanalysis, 33,* 475–494.

Rosenfeld, H. A. (1969). On the treatment of psychotic states by psychoanalysis: An historical approach. *International Journal of Psychoanalysis, 50,* 615–631.

Rosenfeld, H. A. (1978). Notes on the psychopathology and psychoanalytic treatment of some borderline patients. *International Journal of Psychoanalysis, 59,* 215–221.

Rosenfeld, H. A. (1979). Transference psychosis in the borderline patient. In J. LeBoit & A. Capponi (Eds.), *Advances in psychotherapy of the borderline patient* (pp. 485–510). New York: Jason Aronson.

Sandler, J., Dare, C., & Holder A. (1979). Basic psychoanalytic concepts: VIII. Special forms of transference. *British Journal of Psychiatry, 117,* 561–568.

Searles, H. F. (1963). Transference psychosis in the psychotherapy of chronic schizophrenia. *International Journal of Psychoanalysis, 44,* 249–281.

Selzer, M. A., Koenigsberg, H. W., & Kernberg, O.F. (1987). The initial contract in the treatment of borderline patients. *American Journal of Psychiatry, 144,* 927–930.

Shwartz, J. (1967). The erotized transference and other transference problems. *Psychoanalytic Forum, 3,* 307–318.

Stechler, G. (1980). Facing the problem of the sexually abused child (editorial). *New England Journal of Medicine, 302,* 348–349.

Sterba, R. F. (1934). The fate of the ego in analytic therapy. *International Journal of Psychoanalysis, 15,* 117–126.

Swanson, L., & Biaggio, M. K. (1985). Therapeutic perspectives on father-daughter incest. *American Journal of Psychiatry, 142,* 667–674.

Wallerstein, R. (1967). Reconstruction and mastery in the transference psychosis. *Journal of the American Psychoanalytic Association, 15,* 551–583.

Winnicott, D. W. (1955). Metapsychological and clinical aspects of regression within the psycho-analytic set-up. *International Journal of Psychoanalysis, 36,* 16–26.

Winnicott, D. W. (1971). The use of an object. *International Journal of Psychoanalysis, 50,* 711–716.

Winnicott, D. W. (1975). Hate in the countertransference. In *Through pediatrics to psychoanalysis* (pp. 194–203). New York: Basic Books. (Original work published 1947)

Yates, A. (1982). Children eroticized by incest. *American Journal of Psychiatry, 139,* 482–484.

Zetzel, E. (1956). Current concepts of transference. *International Journal of Psychoanalysis, 37,* 369–376.

The Practice of Long-Term Psychotherapy in the 1990s

JOSEPH E. SCHWARTZ

The changes in the practice of long-term psychotherapy can be conceptualized as deriving from changes in nomenclature, changes in financial and social climate, and recent changes in theoretical climate in recent years. Although for purposes of discussion they will be addressed separately, all operate in interrelated ways, evoking shifts greater than the sum of the parts.

THE LANGUAGE

The Diagnostic and Statistical Manual most relevant to the practice of long-term psychotherapy was DSM-II. It was replaced by DSM-III, and then DSM-III-R, ostensibly for purposes of research, in an effort to eradicate theoretical orientations that might obscure newer conceptual models. It was an attempt to replace a "brainless" psychiatry with one which might include neurophysiological discoveries. On a political and economic plane it was also an attempt to find a niche for psychiatry distinct from disciplines of psychology and social work, by integrating areas of knowledge that reside closer to medical models of disease entities.

There are a number of implicit but definite effects upon the practice of long-term psychotherapy caused by this dramatic alteration in language, especially if one is mindful that the DSM is taught in residency training programs and that reimbursement for services is based upon this new language. Linguistic theorists (Martinich, 1990) of the 20th century tell us that without a word to attach to something, that thing does not fully exist. DSM-III-R does not simply widen the conceptualization of mental disturbance—it narrows it as well. It eliminates language for things taught to trainees in mental health in such a way as to eradicate psychological concepts of internal conflict, the bedrock of dynamic psychotherapy. The neo-Kraepelinian (1918) approach implied amounts to diagnosis by collection of superficially descriptive symptoms. The knowing is in the describing, and this obviates any requirement to understand. The data base is in the book, implying quite clearly that the data base of the patient's associations is irrelevant. In a sense, the data base most germane to dynamic psychotherapy, that is, associational flow, transference and counter-transference phenomena, have ceased to exist as legitimate, operational events of importance. The modern psychotherapist is lulled into believing that amassing lists of symptoms will suffice. The manual is quite successful at splitting the field into two groups, each using separate, almost exclusionary, languages. The mindful psychiatrist is now more lonely in his already lonely work in that he cannot communicate with his "brainful" colleagues.

There is another important linguistic twist to the new nomenclature. By ignoring important concepts of psychology—impulse and defense (Freud, 1926/1959)—the new manual focuses upon mental disturbances as disease entities. The resultant medical model implies that, like a flu syndrome, a psychic disturbance befell someone as an external event. The "ownership" of the experience is compromised. While this may alleviate superego pressure within a depressed person, it also fosters a state of expectant waiting for the external cure. The critical idea that the patient is an active agent in both the development of the problem and in the attempt at resolution is compromised in major ways. The optimistic core of psychotherapy, for example, the sense of active and productive collaboration, is easily lost. The shared sense that the therapist should be "doing something" can no longer be seen as a potential transference–countertransference distortion to be examined. Therapeutic understanding no longer suffices, for it has no niche in a disease entity defined by a collection of symptoms. When, therefore, the vectors press to some action in distinction to understanding, the press to action on the part of the therapist is yet another event lost to scrutiny as a potential transference and countertransference occurrence. What follows most often are the administration of medications, behavioral programs, and advice giving related to environmental manipulation. Although all of these actions have a place in the therapy repertoire, they are performed too automatically and regularly because of the therapeutic climate of the 1990s.

Another effect of the model of disease entities ("disorders") as opposed to neuroses or reactions is the implication of somatic supremacy. Many people can readily conceptualize, for example, that reduced central nervous system transmitters can cause depression; fewer people, however, are drawn to the idea that depressed affects due to psychological causes might reduce availability of central nervous system transmitters. Somatic supremacy is the notion that the body or brain leads the feelings or the mind. As a result both symptoms and character pathology are seen as somatically driven. Ideas of identification along with the need to understand such identifications are replaced by reliance on genetics. Discoveries in the field of genetics are piecemeal but there is the implied promise that further genetic research will answer those questions that remain. What eventuates from somatic supremacy are the ideas that a symptom should be treated somatically with medication, and that character pathology is simply complicated genetics about which we can not yet do anything constructive. We, therefore, should simply help the patient learn to live with it. There is little interest in the work of character pathology — the longstanding focus of long-term psychotherapy.

When one considers the nomenclatural climate and its implications, there would appear to be little impetus to do the personal, painful, and hard work of long-term psychotherapy. This kind of work is relegated to the patients' and therapists' masochism. It is clear why physicians who would likely have sought out psychiatry training programs in the past, are now training in family practice residencies. For those who undertake psychiatric training, however, there is ample social support for both the patients' and the therapists' resistances to internal scrutiny.

FINANCIAL CLIMATE

As medical costs in the United States have skyrocketed, involvement by insurance companies and health maintenance organizations has become mandatory. Health insurance coverage has long been an important part of each employee's compensation package. Medical benefits have become in most people's minds an entitlement program. This view has been increasingly shared by state and federal governments. When one considers the catastrophic financial consequences of a mere 2 week hospital stay the reasons become obvious.

The attitude of third-party payers toward mental health treatment has been varied and inconsistent. Some states have had to enact laws requiring mental health benefits. It is unclear what influences insurance companies to take the positions they do. At times it appears that the lack of precision in diagnosis and treatment plan evokes the suspicion that therapist and patient will unduly exploit the carrier. At times it appears that ignorance regarding mental function begets suspicion, as if unlimited benefits would lead people to be in psychotherapy in perpetuity. This gross misconception of how the mind works takes no account of fear, shame, and other common resistances. At times ignorance leads insurance carriers to the belief that therapy is no different from faith healing and, therefore, despite numerous studies demonstrating the efficacy of psychotherapy, must not be a medical treatment. Attempts to educate insurance carriers have been made primarily by somatic psychiatrists, with long-term psychotherapists remaining in their cottages. While such educational endeavors have been useful, they are also skewed in the direction of brief interventions. This leaves long-term therapy out in the cold. Whereas multiple approaches to medical treatment are hailed as advances, multiple long-term therapy treatment approaches is taken to mean that none of them are therapeutically worthwhile. Since insurance carriers and health maintenance organizations exist in a fiercely competitive world, it behooves them not to tell their subscribers that long-term treatment is a modality they cannot afford. Rather, it is in their best interests to inform the public that they provide all that is necessary and proven efficacious, and that long-term therapy is neither. The financial resources of these companies enable them to influence public opinion in major ways. When one considers a social climate in the United States that emphasizes the here-and-now, speed and action, the climate for long-term psychotherapy is not a good one.

There are other adverse conditions related to finance. The average citizen, debt-laden and tax-laden has fewer disposable dollars available for a product that is potentially painful, frightening, and poorly understood. In the past people who could not afford the cost of long-term psychotherapy could be, with confidence, referred to reduced fee clinics. These clinics were city or state government administered, hospital affiliated or attached to psychoanalytic institutes. For the most part, government subsidized units are understaffed, suffer from financial problems, and function primarily as mental health triage units or aftercare programs for the chronically psychotic. Chronic treatment is not the same as long-term psychotherapy. Whereas in the past hospital affiliated outpatient clinics would provide sliding scale fees related to patients' abilities to pay, this is no longer as available as it once was. Hospitals have become increasingly limited by laws and by contracts to be financially self-sustaining. They are less able to accept the financial losses incurred in providing long-term therapy at a reduced fee. They are more apt to make money in long-term group psychotherapy, not individual treatment. They are even more likely to retain any vestige of financial health by providing brief medication visits that are not all that frequent. In that way patients' insurance coverage goes further, out of pocket expenses after that may be affordable to the patients, and more patients can be serviced. Long-term psychotherapy for a hospital is a money loser. Relatively few patients are seen once a week and even fewer more frequently than that. With such retrenchment away from longer term work, one can only anticipate that disuse of long-term therapy skills will lead to atrophy on the part of hospital clinicians. When a clinician has not the time or encouragement to think about subtle communication the clinician will stop hearing such communication. Perhaps the only hope is the reduced fee clinics of psychoanalytic institutes. In recent years there have been abundant openings for people to see psychiatrists and psychologists who will treat in psychoanalysis people who are considered suitable for this modality. While a relatively small percentage of mental health patients are analyzable by traditional analysis, for those people who are, this treatment in financial terms is the biggest bargain in town. There are nonfinancial reasons for openings in these clinics. In recent years analysis has fallen into disfavor. It is long and difficult, and relies on introspection, a quality not currently in great favor. Psychoanalysis has suffered because of some of its antiquated, male-dominated sexual theories (Gilligan, 1982). While contemporary analysis has left behind many of those theories, and in fact is quite eclectic, it still suffers from its past reputation (Valenstein, 1980). As well, psychoanalysis requires referrals from other mental health workers and physicians. It is striking how infrequently these referrals are made.

The above conditions infiltrate into the fabric of long-term therapy in subtle ways. Although the recognition that financial resources for long-term therapy are finite may contribute favorably to both patient and therapist not "wasting time and money," it is doubtful that either party is so inclined. If anything, financial difficulties serve to reduce the number of available patients and, therefore, predispose to therapists' inappropriately keeping the patients they do have longer than is optimal.

The financial climate has other effects as well. Long-term therapy relies to some degree upon a sense of timelessness. The at "leisure approach" to exploration, to the methodical unfolding of unconscious process, fosters the sense of timelessness so necessary for the therapeutic regression called transference to make itself known. The experience of hurrying, practicing with a financial meter ticking in the background serves as a reality-based resistance to this unfolding. Reality-based resistances are the most difficult to address since the patient simply need invoke the reality that avoids examination of the parts of the resistance that are unconsciously determined. This is the same kind of difficulty as a government worker has in invoking doctrines of security clearance to avoid saying what comes to mind. It is in the same genre of resistance as a person who was traumatized in the past and who can now see all of his fears as "realistic" since there once was a real danger. The fabric of patient and neutral attention is threatened when one feels the need to "hurry up."

The therapist also is vulnerable to the patient's message to hurry up. As well, the therapist is less supported in his work by his psychiatric and medical colleagues. This predisposes to shifting to more short-term goals, or perhaps worse, premature interpretation of material. In this financial climate it is harder for a therapist to do what is essential for this kind of work. That is, sit, perhaps for hours at a time, in a sea of unknowns as he tries to understand. It is harder to do in a climate of "hurry up, time's a wasting."

The fact that long-term therapy has been practiced as a "cottage industry" is in part responsible for its decline in a time when health-care delivery systems have become more corporate in nature. It is axiomatic that long-term psychotherapists are more comfortable in private, small settings. They are more at home in a cottage industry. But it is also true that this setting contributes to the beneficial aspects of the work. When community psychiatry advocates suggested alliances with local police forces and political power structures, individual long-term therapists reacted against this idea, since they felt that alliances with one person, the patient, were complicated and difficult enough. If one needed to hospitalize a person who might be annoying to the local gentry in an effort to retain an alliance with the community, one would risk the alliance with the patient in his struggle against his problems. Today, since insurance carriers foot the bill, it behooves the mental health practitioner and the patient to retain a good relationship with third-party payers. The alliance and in some cases the transference is split. While at first glance it would appear that all players could live in harmony, this is often not the case. Depending upon how the new "golden rule" ("He who has the gold rules") is interpreted, many problems can arise.

The most obvious problem is the issue of confidentiality. For reasons of epidemiological study and the need to know diagnoses in an effort to work out insurance cost structures, every third-party carrier insists on knowing the patient's diagnosis. As stated earlier, diagnosis of character pathology is not best achieved using DSM-III-R as a guide. In addition to this difficulty, it is in the best interests of getting the insurance carrier to pay for the therapist to include all diagnoses. The idea is that the "sicker" the patient is reported to be, the more likely the insurance carrier will be to pay the bill. For example, should a patient carry the diagnosis of narcissistic character disorder, there is a certain likelihood he may also suffer from an addiction and/or a perversion. How important is it to reveal such details? How damaging can such revelation be to the therapy? Take a shame-ridden character who uses denial and put him in such a situation. The patient agrees to have the therapist report to the insurance carrier, but he denies his shame and of course his rage at exposure. He may quickly go from "don't get sad, get mad," and "don't get mad but get even," and simply flee therapy with an excuse that seems unrelated to the insurance reporting events. As is often the case, we get into trouble largely from what we do not know about, not what we do know about.

The issue of reportage to the insurance carrier has become so commonplace that therapist and patient fail to discuss it, look at it, and explore it. It is likely that forms are filed and that this fact is split off from the fabric of the therapy as simply a necessary financial task. How often does the therapist discuss with the patient what he will report? How often does the patient have a chance to say what he thinks he suffers from? How often are feelings about the act discussed? The temptation is for patient and therapist to deny the angry helplessness that emerges because there seems to be no other way around it. It is important to note that this dilemma usually surfaces very early in the therapeutic encounter, at a time when trust and alliance have not yet been established, when verbalization is not nearly as free as it will be later in the work. The vectors are all in the direction of not integrating this act into the fabric of the therapy.

In addition to denial of these issues, further defensive maneuvers may occur. Once the shared helplessness with regard to the intrusion of insurance carriers is driven into the unconscious, it has the potential to return to the therapy insidiously. For example, patient and therapist may tacitly join in an unexamined alliance against the big bad behemoth, and this agreed-upon bad object can serve as a misalliance for the two parties. The insurance carrier can then contain psychic elements for both parties, and this can serve to siphon off dysphoric affects. The misalliance then can go on to further change the transference and countertransference elements residing in the therapeutic relationship. Countertransference anger, despair, hopelessness, and helplessness can be felt as deriving from the limits of the insurance coverage or the intrusive practices of the insurance carrier, and the informative aspects of countertransference, that is, the therapist's use of his affects to inform him of unconscious process within the patient are readily lost. Transference reactions act similarly. Transference elements to intrusive or impotent parents are easily attributed transmuted to the good therapist who is just doing his best against the corporate giant, the insurance carrier. Although it is true that the need for diagnosis, the need for the patient and therapist to periodically assess cost benefit issues within a therapy, can be facilitated by the over-the-shoulder presence of the insurance carrier, it is more likely that insurance carriers intrude themselves into the very frame of the therapy and that this very "real" and ubiquitous presence promotes the deleterious effects described.

Should the therapist be employed by the insurance carrier in more direct ways, further trouble may ensue. If the therapy occurs in the framework of a health maintenance organization the therapist is aware that oftentimes bonuses and/or promotions are based at least in part upon the therapist being a "team player." Since the viability of these organizations depends upon each patient's not taking too much time and expense, the therapist's success in his system relies on not doing too much long-term psychotherapy. In this situation the therapist and patient are directly pitted against one another. As with other chronic, on-going issues where the fundamental therapeutic frame is skewed, the affects will be driven underground. The therapist dare not be too angry with the organization that pays his salary and this inner tension must go somewhere. The same applies to his sense of helplessness. When the patient complains of the nasty receptionist, over time the therapist will think less of the transference communication that this complaint may imply and more in terms of "So what. I have to live with it too and I can't bear to have my patient confront me with it." Where the therapist functions in a prepaid professional provider group (PPO), similar events take place. As well, repetitive requirements for reports to the PPO wear down the therapist. He never knows if his report will be accepted as grounds for the continuation of treatment or whether his last few sessions will go unpaid, whether he may have to suddenly discontinue the therapy with the patient who cannot afford it without the support of the PPO. In addition to the issues of confidentiality previously described, the patient and therapist are in the position of trying to get into the in-depth relationship of long-term therapy while never knowing if it will suddenly end. This is simply not possible. In fact issues of loss, trust, abandonment are all too real to ever be interpretable as intrapsychic experiences from which the patient might learn.

THEORETICAL CLIMATE

The changes in theoretical climate in recent years represent both greater complexity and difficulty for the practice of long-term psychotherapy as well as an exciting challenge. In the past psychotherapists had their own versions of cookbook categories, much like the DSM of today. Theory was largely dominated by classical Freudian theory in the United States. The benefit of this monolithic theory is and was the ability of the therapist to contrast the classical evolution of alliance and transference with what was in fact occurring in the treatment. When you color within the lines you can readily see when the crayon goes outside of the lines. These were certain safely held tenets that served to help the therapist with anxiety about his work. As with all ideas, these served both growth and the perpetuation of ignorance. Theory can serve the function of a good mother for the therapist, providing an internal good object, a holding environment during anxiety-or depression-inducing times. Theory can also lead to a clinician's tendency to "make the pieces fit" the theory, whether or not in fact they do.

In the past clinicians used certain theoretical models that led readily to belief systems. For example, the model of repression being pathogenic led to the belief that remembering childhood events was curative (Freud, 1914/1959). In this model remembering led to ego mastery, whereas concepts of affect tolerance, or, for that matter, a theory of affects in general, was relegated to a secondary position. With more recent emphasis on object relations theory, which posits that ego growth occurs through affective experience within the context of an object relationship, repression is not necessarily pathogenic nor is remembering per se curative (Buckley, 1986). What is more to the point is the affective experience with the therapist in both the alliance and transference, and the distortion of the ego that derives from the distorted relationship. The emphasis then is shifted more to experiencing and mastering affects than to remembering, although it is obvious that in truth they go together. This theoretical shift, however, is merely one, but it has far-reaching ramifications. In this newer context the old therapist as blank screen (an idea which was likely never really practiced as much as purported) is no longer tenable. The idea of therapist as thinker wanes as the idea of therapist as co-experiencer grows. The idea of countertransference as the therapist's aspects of unanalyzed personality in reaction to the patient's transference, countertransference as interference to be analyzed away so as not to interfere with the work, falls away more. What takes its place is the therapist who analyzes his countertransference not only as his infantile issues but who uses it more to understand that the patient is communicating to him in this way. There is greater emphasis on the therapist's emotional experience as well. The older idea that words are the only tools has been supplanted by the idea that words are one tool among many others with which to communicate.

Due to a widening of the therapeutic scope, as exemplified by the shift from ego psychology to more object relations approaches, more than simply neurotic psychopathologies are being treated today with long-term psychotherapy. Since preverbal pathology communicates more commonly through the projective identification described above, therapists have found renewed interest in early life pathology (Sandler, 1976). In the past, when early pathology was treated with "supportive psychotherapy," this term was often used to simply denote that the patient was not in analysis. That is, the therapist was being "nice" to the patient, not analyzing defenses as much as shoring them up. Often the word "support" was used ambiguously so that no one knew what it was that was being supported. Often "support" was a euphemism for giving up on the real treatment of analyzing. Since the renewed interest in early life pathology and since the integration of object relations theory into ego psychology, the old distinction between exploratory and supportive treatments has become blurred. Another major therapeutic theory, self psychology, has compounded this blurring even further. This school suggests that the self is the supraordinate psychic structure that grows in successive interactions between the self and the object. Ideals and ambitions are the currency of this growth, that occurs in an optimal environment of mirroring (Kohut, 1977). Again, there is the idea that this kind of "support" is the growth-promoting agent. Again, support and exploration, psychic holding environments, and growth are not clearly distinct. In fact, old distinctions of being object-related or nonobject-related fall by the wayside through the self-psychological model of self-objects. To make matters even less clear, one can see in self psychology not only object relations theory, but the old notion of Rogerian therapy (Rogers, 1951). Emphasis on affective experience in recent years also touches on older notions of the corrective emotional experience. Just when one thinks certain theories have given up the ghost, they return in different forms.

There is another distinction that seems to have become seriously frayed. Years ago, when one thought of employing psychotropic medications it raised the eyebrows of many a long-term psychotherapist. It was argued that this was an "action" taken by the therapist and patient, that it represented an "acting in" of the transference, and as such prevented certain areas of the transference from being analyzed. It was argued that the transference was now split between the therapist and the therapeutic pull, and that it violated the frame of the treatment. In fact, these statements were often true. There probably have not been viable counterarguments except for the following: Medications that work to relieve suffering are worth using. Additionally, it has been noted that when medications work the patient often becomes more available to talking therapeutic intervention than before the use of medications. The advances in psychopharmacology in recent years are many and it is almost impossible to find any psychotherapists who categorically object to the use of medication anymore. Older distinctions between "endogenous" and "exogenous" have become unclear.

It is obvious from the above that the theoretical climate of the 1990s can leave no one theory in the cat bird seat. No theoretician can remain sanguine, and no sacred cows are left to rely upon blindly. The 1990s are bridging psyche and soma, development and genetics, presenting us all with an exciting and confusing time in which to work.

It would appear that although the theoretical integration described would provide people with better therapeutic experiences, the financial, linguistic and political climates represent major limiting forces against the acceptance of long-term psychotherapy into the mainstream in the 1990s. Long-term therapy has been seen in the past as the province of the wealthy and select, and current trends indicate that hopes for broader inroads into the population will likely not occur in the near future. The always uneasy truce between long-term psychotherapy and the medical profession is unravelling. It may simply be that long-term psychotherapy can only exist on a relatively small scale, as a cottage industry. It may be that growth in size may be antithetical to growth in depth. It may be that its original position as gadfly to the established medical community as it was in the 19th century is the locus from which it can do the most good, and that it is from this position that it will thrive.

REFERENCES

Buckley, P. (Ed.). (1986). *Essential papers on object relations.* New York: New York University Press.

American Psychiatric Association. *Diagnostic and statistical manual of mental disorders* (2nd ed.). Washington, DC: Author.

American Psychiatric Association. (1980). *Diagnostic and statistical manual of mental disorders* (3rd ed.). Washington, DC: Author.

American Psychiatric Association. (1987). *Diagnostic and statistical manual of mental disorders* (3rd ed., rev.). Washington, DC: Author.

Freud, S. (1956). Inhibitions, symptoms and anxiety. In J. Strachey (Ed. and

Trans.), *The standard edition of the complete psychological works of Sigmund Freud* (Vol. 20). London: Hogarth Press. (Original work published 1926).

Freud, S. (1958). Remembering repeating and working through. In J. Strachey (Ed. and Trans.), *The standard edition of the complete psychological works of Sigmund Freud* (Vol. 12). London: Hogarth Press. (Original work published in 1914).

Gilligan, C. (1982). New maps in development: New visions of maturity, *American Journal of Orthopsychiatry, 52,* 199–212.

Kohut, H. (1977). *The restoration of the self.* New York: International Universities Press.

Kraeplin, E. (1918). Dementia praecox. London: Livingstone.

Martinich, A. (Ed.). (1990). *Philosophy of language.* New York: Oxford University Press.

Rogers, C. (1951). *Client-centered therapy.* New York: Houghton Mifflin.

Sandler, J. (1976). Countertransference and role responsiveness. *International Review of Psychoanalysis, 3,* 43–47.

Valenstein, A. (1980). The concept of classical psychoanalysis. In H. Blum (Ed.), *Psychoanalytic explorations of technique.* New York: International Universities Press.

Index